University and Society

Essays on the Social Role of Research
and Higher Education

Higher Education Policy Series 12

University and Society

Essays on the Social Role of Research and Higher Education

Edited by Martin Trow and Thorsten Nybom

Jessica Kingsley Publishers
London

First published in the United Kingdom in 1991 by
Jessica Kingsley Publishers Ltd
118 Pentonville Road
London N1 9JN

Copyright © 1991 the contributors and the publisher

British Library Cataloguing in Publication Data
University and society: Essays on the social role
of research and higher education.
 - (Higher education policy series)
 I. Trow, Martin A. II. Nybom, Thorsten
 III. Series
 378

 ISBN 1-85302-525-9
 ISSN 0954-3716

 Printed and bound in Great Britain by
Biddles Ltd, Guildford and King's Lynn

Contents

I. KNOWLEDGE AND SOCIETY

II. RESEARCH AND HIGHER EDUCATION

Foreword

This collection of essays had its origins in a conference held in Stockholm in May 1989 on the occasion of the retirement of Dr Eskil Björklund from his position as Director of the Research on Higher Education Program at the Swedish National Board of Universities and Colleges. Half of the essays have been revised and adapted from papers read at that conference. They have been supplemented by others which deal with issues of importance that were not reflected in the conference itself. Apart from their common interest in the study of higher education and research, all the authors of the volume have been associated with the Program in some way.

The aim of covering a wide range of topics does not only reflect the traditional universalistic spirit and dimensions of higher education and research, but also grew out of the conviction that the intention of honoring an admired friend and colleague was best achieved by a volume that in itself reflected the breadth of interests and topics that Eskil Björklund himself held and served.

Even though the volume primarily is a Swedish initiative from *The Council for Studies of Higher Education* at the NBUC, it nevertheless tries to raise and discuss issues far beyond the Swedish setting. This is shown in part by the inclusion in the list of authors of three internationally renowned and distinguished American scholars, all eminent experts in the field of comparative higher education. Beyond that, *all* the essays in this volume address problems of a broad and general nature.

At the center of the volume is the crucial question of the role of research and higher education in society - both today and in historical perspective. Three essays discuss from different aspects the intellectual impact, moral responsibility and social role of German higher learning from the mid-19th century to the present days of reunification (Nybom; Runeby; Wittrock). One is a fresh historical interpretation of the *other* great model for higher education and research - the American research university (Geiger).

Another group of essays discuss some of the perennial problems of higher education from different points of view: the relations between different forms of knowledge, on the one hand, and teaching and learning, on the other (S. Björklund; Bergendal); the precarious and delicate interdependence, interaction and competition between teaching, study and research in modern/future higher education and research (Clark); the role and impact of professional knowledge in modern society (Torstendahl).

The essays discussing the American system of higher education (Trow) and the critical analysis of the role of the OECD in higher education and research (Gustavsson) are both comparative and international in scope and conclusions. And finally, the contributions devoted to Swedish problems and conditions are also relevant to problems which face all systems of higher education in advanced industrial societies. Two essays deal with the issue of external influences and interventions in higher education and research (Odén; Ruin). A third discusses the impact and role of scientific competence and knowledge in the realm of social planning and policy making in the Swedish context (Premfors).

Berkeley and Stockholm, February 1991
Martin Trow - Thorsten Nybom

Introduction

Martin Trow

I am honoured to have this opportunity to recognise the accomplishments of Dr Eskil Björklund and 'his' Research Program at the National Board of Colleges and Universities (NBUC) in Stockholm. My observations will very much reflect my own deep respect for the man and his accomplishments; but I am also speaking for all the scholars in every field in many countries outside of Scandinavia who are in some way indebted to Eskil and the Research Program, and who have been encouraged to contribute to it through their attendance at international conferences, through papers and publications and above all by being drawn into the intellectual community that has been created around this Program.

I will not specifically refer to Eskil Björklund's recent retirement even if that may be how the Swedish Civil Service sees the event in May 1989. Instead, I have reason to hope that Eskil will spend the next year or so writing the history of the Program that he has developed and led; that he in a sense is under a certain moral obligation - to the Program and to higher education in general - to write a history that only he could write. The short account he gives in this volume seems to be a very promising start and makes me even more eager to read the full story. This story, I suspect, will not only illuminate an aspect of modern Swedish social policy but also contribute in various ways to our understanding of the interplay of knowledge and power, of the relations of the world of learning and the world of policy. It may also teach us something about creativity in public administration, and how public agencies can best support the life of the mind, a life which is ultimately beyond programming and shows its genius precisely in its spontaneity and unpredictability. These are all things that Eskil Björklund will be called upon to engage in on his 'retirement'.

There are surely many people who know of Eskil Björklund's years at the NBUC much more intimately than I do, but as always there may be some value in a comparative perspective. As an interested, and admiring observer of Eskil and his work over some fifteen years, my sense is that his accomplishment can be seen as the sum of four or five distinct accomplishments, distinct at least to a fairly remote observer.

I would see those accomplishments in this way: First, Eskil completely recast the mission of the Program, and thus its central contribution to public policy and to the world of higher education. It seems to me that the Program's initial mission was to define and sponsor research, largely on a kind of contract basis, that would contribute to the definition and implementation of immediate or short-term policies affecting Swedish higher education. I think that Eskil Björklund's vision from the very beginning was that the Program must have a larger and different set of missions. One part of his vision was to create a Program that did not just sponsor research on the basis of which good advice could be given to decision-makers in the Government. Rather, he envisioned a Program that would initiate and support a body of research that would more broadly *illuminate* the world of higher education in ways that would enable decision-makers in government and in higher education itself to understand more deeply the processes and the institutions of learning whose fates they were shaping through local and national policy. Eskil himself has charted some of these shifts in character and direction in his own periodic summary reports. As he observed in 1982:

> At the beginning of the 1970s studies of the effects of higher education typically dealt with certain outer measures of efficiency and productivity, while a few years later the concept formation of the students is the focus of interest . . . Questions of organisation which were studied in the initial shape of the Program's existence were concerned with outer circumstances such as localisation, organisation of studies, administrative processes, etc, while the organisational research today instead is concentrated on the inner life of higher education as expressed for instance . . . through the knowledge traditions of various study programmes, etc.

And he continued,

> This deeper penetration of higher education issues has gradually broadened the purpose and extended the interest groups of the Program. In the beginning, the Program was seen as a part of the central decision-making organisation of higher education, its tasks being to increase the knowledge of the outer frames of the higher education activities, which should and could be planned and controlled from the political level. This was probably a reasonable ambition for that period, but it is no longer adequate in the decentralised system introduced in 1977, where decisions about direction, content and forms of activities are now taken in various higher education institutions. It is, therefore, now necessary that the research Program serve all higher education interests more openly and independently, by contributing towards more coherent and, at the same time, deeper knowledge concerning the tasks of higher education, its internal life and its function in society.

> Given this more general purpose, it is also natural that the research Program should work in a multi-disciplinary way. The Program should give a multitude of perspectives. The types of study to be included, and the disciplines to take part, are just as important a consideration as the questions and fields to be studied. Research must illuminate higher education from all sides, so that it can be understood and treated not only as an educational or a research system, but also, for example, as a political system - and not least important - as a cultural phenomenon, and in a historical perspective. Such research on the realities of Swedish higher education should also increasingly rely on international comparisons.[1]

And in 1988, Eskil defined the Program's mission in these terms:

> By undertaking studies of high quality according to the criteria of their different disciplines the research groups (of academics) should enhance self-understanding within the universities and colleges. The Program should be 'higher education's own research into the foundations of its own activities'.[2]

So part of Eskil's achievement was to redefine the concept of policy related research in the area of higher education to bring it over time closer to what we think of as basic studies of learning and of the institutions in which learning takes place.

During the nearly two decades that Eskil Björklund directed his Program, higher education in the Western world underwent significant change, not so much of sheer expansion as of increasing diversity and complexity. And these changes in the character of higher education, arising out of its growing significance for economic and social development, inevitably have affected its relations to central government everywhere. The tendency, of course with national variations, has been toward the recognition by governments that universities must be able to recognise and respond to rapid changes in the map of learning, and to every society's needs for useful knowledge and competent people. And this means more autonomy in the institution. Not the autonomy of the old elite universities, preparing a handful of people for the old professions and government service, but the autonomy of mass institutions, preparing a broad range of qualified people for a world changing so rapidly that it defeats all efforts at detailed forecasting and manpower planning. Governments everywhere reluctantly surrender the dream of manpower planning and the accompanying close management of universities as training facilities, and slowly come to see that diversity is higher education's central resource for responding to unforeseen change. And diversity and institutional autonomy go hand in hand.

In Sweden, the so-called U68-reform and its implementation in the 1970s marked the furthest advance of central state planning and direction of higher education. The trajectory of higher education planning in Sweden has been charted and analyzed more carefully than that in perhaps any other country, and there is nothing for me to add on this subject. But the evolution of the Research on Higher Education Program coincided, and surely contributed to, the slowly changing relationship between the state and higher education in Sweden. This change had two distinct components:

1. A revival of support for 'basic' research and scholarship, based on a growing recognition of the intellectual autonomy of the academic disciplines, and the legitimacy of problems defined by the inner logic and development of those disciplines.

2. A parallel tendency to restore autonomy and initiative to the institutions of higher education which are the home of those disciplines, and of their research communities.

Along with these two broad trends in Swedish educational policy we have seen the tendency - documented by Eskil Björklund's annual summaries of the work of the Program - to shift some of its support from the disciplines that are most useful to central state planning, like economics and educational studies, toward subjects like philosophy, history and the 'soft' social sciences which are the vehicles for illuminative rather than prescriptive research.[3] This, I believe, was the Program's response to the two broad trends in higher education policy which were rooted in even broader political, economic and intellectual currents which are crudely captured in the concept of 'liberalism'. But the Program's response certainly reflected and encouraged those trends; its success, in conjunction with Eskil Björklund's own unique leadership qualities, undoubtedly was made possible by the fit, the congruence, between the work of the Program and these currents of thought in higher education, in Sweden and in the Western world.

But over and above this redefinition of the Program's mission, Eskil was equally sensitive to the importance of creating an infrastructure for this newly expanded research agenda - an infrastructure that took the form of a broad and growing intellectual community, first among scholars and social scientists in Sweden itself, and then extending that community to connect with the invisible college of students of higher education all over the world. This it seems to me was a very important insight and a significant achievement - to recognise that good and illuminating research, whether applied or basic, must rest on a body of people who are equipped, trained, and motivated to work on those problems. But beyond that he recognised that this must be not just an aggregate, but a *community* of people in touch with one another and with one another's work, and bound together by ties of professional association and friendship. The achievement here is an extraordinary one and I must repeat its key elements: first, a redefinition of the intellectual mission of the Program; second, the recognition that this intellectual programme must rest on the work of a body of competent and motivated scholars - a body of scholars who must be found and then nurtured; and third, the recognition that those scholars must be not just an aggregate of people situated here and there, but would have to be brought together as members of a community engaged in an ongoing and continuing discussion among themselves as well as with the National Board, among others.

It would have been a very considerable achievement to have seen the possibilities of moving in the direction I have just sketched. It was quite another achievement to have actually accomplished it. And here I must stress the importance of Eskil Björklund's own personal qualities. He was able to bring people together in ways that allowed their own talents and relationships to develop and flourish. Moreover, he understood the basic principle that activities generate interactions, that from those interactions arise new attitudes, norms and values, and that ultimately it is on these values and attitudes that a body of significant professional work rests. In this effort Eskil's own personal support was always present if often concealed. His letters and phone calls went all over the world, the radial lines in a spider's web that linked all of the members of this invisible college, this intellectual community, to one another and to the Research Program in Stockholm.

Moreover, Eskil Björklund not only initiated new lines of work, new studies and projects, but he continually put much of himself and his time into the support of existing projects through the encouragement of researchers, people on the whole of large if tender egos, needing criticism and resenting it, and yet taking it from Eskil! And that is perhaps because it was clear to everyone that he was totally impartial, without special loyalty to any discipline or university.

Finally among his several achievements is one that I find most astonishing and, for a foreigner, least understandable - the considerable achievement of detaching a bit of Swedish civil service from its ordinary functions and activities, and giving it a quite different character and mission. Perhaps the greatest of Eskil Björklund's achievements was this transformation of a unit within a part of the Swedish civil service into something else - an institution, at least semi-autonomous, which served a number of different constituencies in addition to the state through the enlightenment rising out of a body of scholarly work, rather than directly in the form of applied research underpinning specific policy recommendations. Let us think a bit of what this consisted.

The Program under its original name of *R&D for Higher Education* had, like other parts of the Swedish civil service, a primary responsibility to central government - to advise the government, to help it shape plans and policies, and even help to implement them. But Eskil Björklund did something more radical than anything I have hinted at so far: under his direction the Program became increasingly the servant of the intellectual community that it was creating, rather than exclusively or even primarily the creature and agent of central government to which it nominally belonged. Looked at in another way, 'Eskil's Program' accepted its responsibility to serve the State, but eventually did so by creating and then serving an intellectual community that stood outside the state, and did so on the grounds that ultimately that Program and the community it created would better serve national interests than would an R&D unit more directly harnessed to short-term government policy.

But to do this required that the Program gain a large measure of autonomy from the NBUC, and from its own administrative hierarchy, and thus from the boundaries and definitions of the unit seen as an ordinary part of the Board's regular structure and mission. Eskil Björklund fought for and won that autonomy, an achievement on which all his other substantive achievements rested. A knowledgeable Swedish observer said to me recently that, 'at the NBUC nobody told Eskil what to do', and that doesn't quite fit the model of the ideal-typical Weberian state bureaucracy. How he accomplished that is to me a really crucial part of his story. One or two key factors were apparent even to an outsider like myself. For one thing, Eskil, for all his gentleness and modesty, was with respect to his beloved Program and its autonomy a tough and stubborn fighter. I would not like to have been a Chancellor trying to cut it back or trammel its freedom; indeed it is a testimony to the wisdom of several Chancellors who have headed the NBUC that on the whole, and with only one or two exceptional years, they did not trim its budget, but broadly supported the Program and its autonomy.

All of that testifies to Eskil Björklund's devotion to the Program and to his bureaucratic skills and toughness. It testifies also to the wisdom of the Chancellors who accepted the Program's special status. But even that would not be enough to explain this aspect of the history of the Program: two other elements I believe were involved in the Program's autonomy and its freedom to change its character and mission in the way that it has over the past fifteen years.

One of these is the authority that gradually accrued to Eskil Björklund by virtue of his devotion to the Program rather than to his own bureaucratic career. Even a stranger could see that the directorship of this small unit in the NBUC was not one of the pinnacles of the Swedish civil service. In purely bureaucratic terms it is a kind of middle level position. And no one can tell me that someone of Eskil Björklund's experience, intelligence, energy and imagination would not have gone much higher in the Swedish civil service if that had been his normal and honorable ambition. But the fact is that he didn't do that, but refused to leave his beloved Program, and the rather modest administrative rank that its director could command on the organisational charts. It is easy to recognise the phenomenon that people gain a considerable measure of personal authority when they visibly sacrifice careers and higher status to make a special commitment to an institution or a cause. When such a person becomes very closely identified with an organisational unit or Program, at some point he no longer merely occupies an administrative office, but in a sense *becomes* the Program, becomes himself the institution. There is in this transformation into institution a kind of organisational trade-off: a gain in that person's moral authority based on the recognition by others of his personal qualities and institutional dedication, which is paid for by the surrender of power and influence elsewhere in the organisation that would accompany higher administrative rank and position. The moral authority that Eskil Björklund gained over the years was I believe a central element in the practical business of gaining the autonomy that he needed to reshape and redirect the Program.

But at the same time as Eskil Björklund was helping to create and sustain an intellectual community focused around the study of higher education, the community that he was creating was becoming a central supportive constituency for the Program, a constituency outside of government which nevertheless government and the civil service both had to take into account. Thus, when the University of Stockholm awarded him an honorary doctoral degree it was first and foremost the academic world's acknowledgement of Eskil Björklund's services to scholarship, but it did also help to strengthen the standing and the autonomy of the Program.

So ultimately the autonomy that Eskil Björklund needed to carry out his vision of what this Program should be like rested, I believe, on three elements: first, the personal moral authority that Eskil gained through a widespread recognition of his character and commitment to the Program, a commitment that led him to sacrifice an ordinary career in the Swedish civil service; second, the support of the academic community, which saw in him a civil servant after their own heart; and third and not least, wise politicians and Chancellors who came to recognise that his Program, even if somewhat out of the ordinary in its searching examination of the assumptions of Swedish policy and practice, might in fact provide what Eskil Björklund hoped it *would* provide, a deeper and fuller understanding of the nature of higher education, on the basis of which better policies might be made in response to long range developments in the worlds of learning, research and scholarship. I think all three of these legs of the stool had to be present for Eskil's very substantive achievement to have been fulfilled.

So far I have been discussing what in Eskil Björklund's accomplishments was special and unique. But there are characteristics of his work and vision which he shares with other thoughtful academics, administrators and politicians. Indeed it may be that one secret of his success was to create a unique instrument in the service of consensual values. However bold and original the Program was in linking Government and learning, policy and scholarship, the ultimate values served by the Program are really consensual values in a society that to a high degree rests on consensual values, and on the search for their expression and implementation. One of these root values in the area of higher education is a concern for the 'internationalisation of higher education', to which I want to turn briefly.

The concept 'international education' is becoming fashionable and trendy, and for this reason if no other it may be useful to unpack the idea and to see what substance it may have. Of course, at the core of the term there is an implicit educational policy - the policy of linking one's national system of education to worldwide currents of thought, scholarship and research. And Sweden, for various and obvious reasons, is firmly committed to remaining part of the international community of discourse in science and scholarship. And it does this in a variety of ways, indeed, through the six meanings of the term 'internationalisation of higher education'.

First, of course, is the movement of students across national boundaries, and from university to university. Students have been doing this since the founding of universities in the Western world in the 12th century. The idea and indeed the practice of student migrations has never died, but was constrained in modern times by the rise of the nation-state, its concern for national power and prestige and a distinctive national culture rooted in language, art, literature and scholarship. But one aspect of the current internationalisation of learning is the effort to transcend the more parochial aspects of nationalism in scholarship and emphasise once again the relevance of learning across national boundaries. The movement of students between countries increases every year, partly in response to the emergence of a global economy, but partly also to the weakening of tribal aspects of national identity.

Second, with the emergence of European institutions, the strengthening of the EEC and hopefully also the reunification of the two parts of Europe, the internationalisation of higher education takes legal and organisational form through the creation of internationally accepted academic standards, qualifications and degrees; the ERASMUS Program is a case in point.

A third dimension of internationalisation is the movement of ideas about higher education - for example, about its organisational arrangements, about the right balance of institutional autonomy and accountability, about regionalism and non-traditional forms of higher education - ideas, models, and the lessons of experience which cross national boundaries and influence national systems.

Fourth, there is the movement more generally of science and scholarship across national boundaries. All modern scientific and scholarly disciplines have this international character but in varying degrees. I have suggested elsewhere that there are national characteristics that mark the work of any national scholarly community, but these bear much the same relation to a discipline as it exists internationally as a regional dialect bears to the common language of a nation. But these regional or national dialects are stronger in some fields than in others - for example stronger in studies of law, business administration, social welfare or education than in physics, chemistry or mathematics.

Fifth, there is the direct introduction of study material into the curriculum specifically aiming at the broadening of our understanding, and our students' understanding, of foreign cultures, and the parallel support of scholarship and research centres devoted to the study of foreign cultures, social, economic, and political systems. These centres of research and study are sometimes related to national interests in foreign policy and foreign trade. But the study of other cultures and societies is also a part of the internationalisation of higher education in that it enables us to appreciate more fully and more sympathetically the contributions to civilisation of other nations, and of their artists, scholars and scientists, and even their occasional statesman.

Sixth, the internationalisation of higher learning takes the form of the physical movement of scientists and scholars across national boundaries for longer or shorter periods - anywhere from a flying visit to read a paper, to the permanent settlement of expatriates and refugees. On the latter score we in the US know well how immeasurably enriched our society and its universities were by the refugees from Nazi persecution who came to us in the 1930s. Their impact on mathematics and the sciences in the US is well known, but they also transformed our way of thinking about man and society as well. And Sweden, with its similarly generous laws of political sanctuary, has also benefited from accepting into its universities scholars fleeing from political oppression. But shorter term visitors from abroad also have a large influence on national and domestic intellectual life of a somewhat different kind.

The Research on Higher Education Program that Eskil Björklund developed and led was devoted, and properly so, to strengthening Swedish higher education and through it, Swedish society. He has done this in part by encouraging the comparative study of higher learning, and by involving foreign scholars in his Program: to point to only the most obvious of these connections - of the 232 written contributions to the Program's conferences held between 1971 and 1987 (itself an impressive figure), fully 67 or 27 per cent, were contributed by non-Swedish scholars; indeed, for the most recent period 1980-87, the figure is 54 out of 142 papers - or 38 per cent.[4] What those figures do not show are the connections made or strengthened by the Program between the communities of higher educational studies in Sweden and its counterparts overseas in Germany, Britain, the US and elsewhere - not to speak of other Scandinavian countries.

The Swedish Research on Higher Education Program has contributed to at least three of these dimensions of the internationalisation of Swedish higher education:

1. It promoted the movement between nations of information and ideas about universities and higher education systems.

2. It stimulated the exchange and development of knowledge and theory in the cultural sciences generally.

3. It created opportunities for the movement of researchers and scholars of higher education across national boundaries, and especially across Sweden's boundaries.

The third dimension had probably unplanned dividends which took the form of professional and personal relationships that also developed between Germans, Brazilians, Dutchmen, Englishmen, Americans and everybody else. All these were relationships that began at Eskil Björklund's conferences. And I speak here very much as one who has profited from the Program's outreach to foreign scholars. Over the years I, along with foreign colleagues, have had a number of opportunities to attend the Program's conferences, and to learn at first hand how Swedish society sees its educational problems and opportunities and how it has gone about addressing them. In the course of these visits I have made many friends and learned much from the impressive contributions to the international conversations on these matters made by Swedish scholars. And we in Berkeley - and most certainly so at the Center for Studies in Higher Education - at the far end of one strand of Eskil Björklund's web, have been able to take advantage of these connections to invite members of the Swedish scholarly community (including Eskil himself) to the Center. Berkeley has profited greatly from the contributions of Swedish scholars to the intellectual life of the University of California; that is not only my own judgement but that of everyone at Berkeley who is in any way knowledgeable about these matters. I am especially gratified that the fruitful connections between Sweden and California will be maintained in the future under Eskil Björklund's successor, Thorsten Nybom.

One last thought on Eskil Björklund and his Program: There is I believe rooted in Swedish culture and national character a peculiar pair of attitudes towards individual distinction existing side by side. On the one hand there is the attitude that Australians speak of in their own culture as an inclination to cut off the heads of the tall poppies. Alongside that attitude, happily, Swedes show a quite contradictory readiness to acknowledge, to celebrate, to honour genuine distinction, a distinction based on accomplishment and not merely on status or reputation. It was that readiness to honour extraordinary achievement that gave rise to this volume.

Part I

Knowledge and Society

Chapter 1

Vagabonds, Specialists or the Voice of the People

Scandinavian Students and the Rise of the Modern Research University in the 19th Century

Nils Runeby

In June 1869 the students of Scandinavia gathered in the Norwegian capital in order to celebrate a general student meeting. The initiative came from the student union in Kristiania (Oslo) and the invitation had been accepted. Representative delegations from Copenhagen and from the Swedish universities in Uppsala and in Lund were selected and they travelled to Kristiania with official pomp and circumstance. Discussions, banquets, receptions and excursions succeeded each other along the route, and during the meeting, according to the academic rituals of the time, lectures, speeches, addresses, concerts and recitals created the right atmosphere, both dignified and cordial.

It was far from obvious before the event, however, that such a meeting could be organised. Student meetings had for several reasons become a much disputed matter, as had student unions in general. Unions and meetings were closely connected with the turbulent 1840s and with the so-called Scandinavist movement, proclaiming a close co-operation between the Scandinavian states and a common activist foreign policy both in the east and in the south. The students were deeply involved, and the Scandinavist activities had created an organised and politicised student body that had not existed in this way before. The political endeavour turned out to be a failure, however, and the defeat was most clearly and devastatingly demonstrated in the Danish-German war of 1864, when Sweden left Denmark alone. The Swedish government refused to become involved in the Scandinavian aspirations. A student meeting planned in 1867 had to be cancelled. The Scandinavist activism that had been the political programme for the mobilisation of the students had proved to be a very fragile and inadequate platform, and through this failure all student activity was put into question. The crisis not only affected the Scandinavist movement but even, on another level, ideas about the mission of the students in society in general.

The first half of the 19th century in Europe and in Sweden had witnessed the rise of political student movements connected in different ways with various revolutionary currents. The ideological basis for these movements was a concept, most clearly articulated in German classicism and idealism, of a truth-seeking research university responsible for true progress and for the moral health of society. A cosmopolitan brotherhood of learned men, acting in full freedom according to their mission, was supposed to pursue truth without looking for personal gain or serving separate interests.

Renegades, who deceived about their mission, were harshly judged. The learned brotherhood also had the task of introducing the gifted student into the community. The student could, however, claim his own rights against the intentions of his academic fathers in part because he was young. Participating in the process of *Bildung*, he was also the man of the future. He could demand the right to formulate his own goals and to act by himself. From the Napoleonic wars to the February revolution, from the *Burschenschaft* movement to the Progress students the programme changed, but the aspirations remained, often resulting in violent conflicts.[1]

The student emancipation movement contains a further complication. In the Romantic tradition a close connection exists between the learned man and the creative genius who follows his own path and fights for higher ideals. There are a number of variations on this theme, but some basic ideas are common. Among them is the idea of self-realisation. The most important thing in life, according to one commentator, is to express oneself 'through creative work and to realise fully one's individuality'. The creative genius has the right to disregard everyday conventions and rules that stand in his way. The genius is a gift from nature, and he represents the higher values of civilisation.

If a person looks upon himself as related to the genius, the conclusion is inevitable. He is far above the everyday world, and those who oppose him are Philistines, 'whose main interests are material gratification and the enjoyment of the cruder forms of power'. The existing society is seen as banal or inhuman 'regardless of the technological complexity or institutional efficiency which may accompany it'.[2] Well-known symbolic figures - the eternal wanderer, the rebel, the outcast - are chosen to illustrate the development of self-consciousness towards insight and self-understanding. As it has been pointed out, one can find here 'intellectual rebels like Faust, moral outcasts or wanderers like Cain or Ahasverus' or 'rebels against society and even against God himself, like Prometheus or Lucifer'.[3] The 19th century is abundant in Faustian men and Promethean rebels.[4] If now the men of learning and their adepts are related to the rebels and the outcasts, a conflict between their rejection of society and their assumed responsibility for it is evident. In both cases their aspirations, especially those of the students, can be looked upon with suspicion.

When the Scandinavian students gathered in Kristiania at the end of the 1860s, they still had to discuss their position in relation to the ambiguous heritage of the 1840s, and to consider the task that could 'truly' be assigned to them. It is the purpose of this paper to analyse - with the help of the discussions at the Kristiania meeting - the character of their rethinking. It is thereby necessary, in order to make the arguments more clear, to recapitulate some earlier Swedish positions and even to give a few references to European themes. I want to argue that the reformulated platform came to imply a 'turn' to the 'people', on one hand, and on the other to academic specialisation and research, which had great importance for the further development of both society and the university. As a background it is necessary to specify somewhat the character of the assumed student mistakes.

The Vagabond

At the beginning of the 1840s Israel Hwasser, the well-known and controversial idealist Professor of Medicine at Uppsala, considered it vital to analyse the young people of his time, and tried to divide them into categories according to their behaviour. Hwasser's publication gives a good summary of his hopes and anxieties, and his opinions were not his alone. Even later they were considered to be of importance. Hwasser starts his analysis with a long quotation from another of his shorter works, dealing with matrimony, and this starting-point is very illuminating.[5] Matrimony, he says, and its necessary moral and Christian foundations have nowadays been attacked both in France and in Germany. The assaults that can be seen in the manners and morals as well as the literature of the French, 'especially those living in Paris', depend upon 'an anti-religious sophistry, that considers feeling, emancipated from the power of religion, as the highest human spiritual force . . . '.

This idea, Hwasser writes, comes originally from Rousseau, but it has 'in a more crude form' been advocated by later writers such as Saint-Simon and Fourier. They have in their turn inspired 'a number of sects with fanatical followers, conspiring against state and society', and they attack not only religion and matrimony but also the right of property. The consequences of such licentious feelings were clearly seen during the French revolution, during the Terror. As a professor of medicine Hwasser finds it necessary also to warn against 'the desires of somatic propagation instincts', which are 'degrading and demoralising' and ruining the physical health of those who give way to them. Against the disintegrating tendencies Hwasser wishes to put 'the fundamental knowledge/*vetenskap/*' which will make 'true reason master of the false rationalism, that for such a long time has usurped its name'. The moral decay can also be found in Germany, and the threat is here easily summarised: *Das junge Deutschland*. The writers belonging to this group advocate a gross sensuality and the demands of the flesh, an *Evangelium des Fleisches*. They maintain that 'the spirit has to be subdued . . . in order to liberate the flesh'. Hwasser's worries on this point were not unfounded. In Sweden, too, young writers were inspired by 'The Young Germans'.[6]

Hwasser reacted especially to one particular epithet that these and related writers used to characterise themselves. 'They all call themselves young. They decorate themselves with the name of youth . . .'. In our time 'the youthful' is given 'a much greater importance than before', and the destructive ideas of youth are put forward in an aggressive way. '*Wir haben lang genug geliebt/Wir wollen endlich hassen*' (We have loved for too long/Now it is high time for hating), Hwasser quotes from the revolutionary poet Georg Herwegh. Through the 'exaggerated vigor of the young' the disease has rapidly increased animosity between the classes and 'demoralisation' of the lower ones. 'The youthfulness', Hwasser emphasises, 'that the destructive forces of our time claim for themselves, is only a usurped title'. The aspiration to be young - 'a thoroughly false doctrine and a real lie' - result in 'sensuality' and 'false freedom', and can have effects both 'inwards' and 'outwards'. The outward aspirations cause a 'violent and hateful struggle' against 'existing circumstances' and against society. The inward aspirations cause 'lust for emancipation from the traditional conceptions of the sacred and the spiritual'. In an unhappy way the young 'lust for freedom' has 'been excessively praised and above all it has loudly and intensely praised itself'. Hwasser has also noted with concern that the period when someone is considered 'young' has become longer. The young men, he writes, postpone 'far too long their choice of a profession'. Hwasser seems to imply that 'the young' are especially unreliable when they still are in a socially 'floating' or 'outside' position, when they are not yet settled. The older generation is also responsible, however, for this unhappy development. 'The spiritual foundations of traditional culture' have been taught to the young people in an abstract way and with certain reservations. Some of the older have even adopted 'the seemingly positive and important title of leaders of youth and men of the future'.[7]

When Hwasser thus looks upon the past fifty years and tries to discover what has shaken Europe to its foundations, he finds a doctrine that has combined an idea of freedom with a dangerous idea of the legitimate emancipation of the younger generation. It is further evident, according to Hwasser, that some of the older generation have betrayed their mission to transfer the true heritage to the young, and have even sanctioned the improper spirit of revolt. The situation is, however, not completely desperate. There is, Hwasser says, a group of young people, a small minority, 'that faithfully maintains the holy demands of truth and justice'. They also devote themselves to 'the altruistic truth-seeking that is the true life of scientific research'. Among these young men there still exists 'veneration for the Higher Ideals' and through them Hwasser has caught a glimpse of 'the rising sun of the future'.[8]

The sun did not rise immediately, however. The insolent young groups (and their followers) that Hwasser had observed, the heralds of sensuality and the evangelists of the flesh, the big city morality, in Paris for example, the attacks on Christianity and common decency, the class antagonism, the contempt for true scientific research, all this did not disappear during the 1840s. On the contrary, the situation only got worse. Max Stirner, one of the real outcasts and member of the circle around the ex-theologian Bruno Bauer in Hippel's *Weinstube*, in the big city of Berlin, summarised in the concept 'vagabonds' all individuals, 'who appear to the bourgeois suspicious, hostile and dangerous'. 'Every vagabondish way of living displeases' the bourgeois, Stirner says. There are also 'intellectual vagabonds', who find the cultural heritage

> too cramped and oppressive . . . ; instead of keeping within the limits of a temperate style of thinking and taking as inviolable truth that furnishes comfort and tranquillity to thousands, they overleap all bounds of the traditional and run wild with their impudent criticism and untamed mania for doubt, these extravagating vagabonds. They form the class of the unstable, restless, changeable, of the proletariat, and, if they give voice to their unsettled nature, are called 'unruly fellows'.

The bourgeois finds 'his quiet enjoyment clouded by *innovating* and *discontented* poverty, by those poor who no longer behave quietly and endure, but begin to *run wild* and become restless'. The bourgeois sees only one solution to the problem: 'Lock up the vagabond, thrust the breeder of unrest into the darkest dungeon! He wants to "arouse dissatisfaction and incite people against existing institutions" in the State "stone him, stone him!"'[9] It has been pointed out that it is during this period that the concept 'radical' comes into general use, and it gets by and by a pejorative meaning.[10]

After the revolutions Wilhelm Heinrich Riehl, university professor, author, social theorist and a prominent figure in the history of German ethnology, launches his theory of the so-called 'fourth estate'.[11] In Riehl's analysis, which is very relevant in this context, Hwasser's premonitions seem to come true, and it can also be said that he tries to characterise and give a social background to the vagabonds. Hostility to the big cities is a main theme in Riehl's work. He looks with deep distrust upon the 'new' bourgeois society and with concern upon the transformation of the old estates.

There are, according to Riehl, four estates, and he divides them into two groups, '*die Mächte des Beharrens*' (powers of stability), ie farmers and aristocracy, and '*die Mächte der Bewegung*' (powers of change), ie the bourgeoisie and the remarkable fourth estate. The last one consists partly of a 'proletarian aristocracy', partly of '*die Proletarier der materiellen Arbeit*' and partly - which is of special interest here - of '*die Proletarier der Geistesarbeit*', that can be compared with Hwasser's insolent youth or Stirner's vagabonds.[12] The last mentioned group is 'the fighting church' of the fourth estate, which 'openly and self-consciously has broken with the existing social organisation of society. '*Die geistige Proletariat*' wants to tear down the old social order 'practically and theoretically'. The group is a very mixed one, and Riehl makes a long, expressive enumeration: 'proletarian civil servants, proletarian school-teachers, 'vagabondish' priest-candidates, starving academic *Privatdozenten*, literati, journalists and artists of all kind, from travelling virtuosi to wandering comedians, organ-grinders and street singers (*Bänkelsänger*)'. Among these there are, as can be seen, no professors, but *Privatdozenten* and organ-grinders.

The intellectual proletariat is the result of an overproduction of academic people and shows that something is wrong in '*der gesamten Nationalarbeit*'. This proletariat is '*überstudiert*'; it mixes up its real task with an imagined one and has extremely exaggerated ideas of its own importance. The revolution in 1848 is an example of what they can bring about. One can '*kein bei*βenderes Epigramm auf unsere öffentliche Erziehung schreiben, als wenn man die Durchschittsziffer der verdorbenen Literaten ermittelte, welche alljährlich durch unsere gelehrten Staatsschulen zum Kriege gegen die Gesellschaft eingeschult werden' (write no more biting Epigram over our public education system, than by telling the number of depraved *Literati*, who every year are trained in waging war against society through our state school system). This is a completely new group, a product of new cultural movements, without historical traditions and recruited from all estates. One finds here '*verdorbene Schneider*' (depraved tailors) as Wilhelm Weitling and '*verdorbene Grafen*' (depraved counts) as Saint-Simon, and they want all to take revenge on the state. The ideal type of a fourth estate member in Riehl's analysis is the Jewish intellectual proletarian. Even if he well knows that there also are '*unbeschnittene* (uncircumcised) *Literaten*', he finds that they are '*beschnitten im Geist* (spiritually circumcised), *wie der Apostel sagt*' (according to the apostle). When they give vent to their personal destructive antipathies in the press, they also show their hunger for power.

The only way to neutralise the damaging influence of these literati is to raise the standard of living of the workers and thereby prevent a coalition between the two groups. It is necessary, Riehl writes, to promote industrial education and natural sciences. '*Das Gedeihen der materiellen Arbeit ist der Todesstoss für das eigentliche Literatenwesen*' (The encouragement of practical labour is a death-blow to the 'Literati system'). Then no one will believe in their social '*Schwindeleien*' and their '*Evangelium des Sozialismus und Kommunismus*'. The radical intellectual proletarians have never shown any interest in the 'practical disciplines' which lead to prosperity. Instead they have studied theology, aesthetics, natural law, '*philosophische Staatswirtschaftslehre und Sozialtheorie*'. They proclaim the modern illusions that art can be created through aesthetics, '*ein öffentliches Leben*' through natural law, and they put philosophy of religion in place of the church. The characteristic feature of the fourth estate is '*die verneinende Bedeutung für die Gesellschaft*' (the turning-away from society). The true man of literature has to be a '*Bürger*' as everybody else and not an agitator. The influence of the rebelling literate can in times of unrest (1848!) be disastrous, but in times of peace not many will fall into his traps. Moreover they are dependent on the economic laws of the market.[13]

Riehl's analysis of the fourth estate is remarkable from several points of view. His description shows very instructively the complicated and problematic relations between the 'free' (literati, artists) and the 'educated' and the 'learned' (*Gebildeten, Gelehrten*). His analysis leads him to a harsh criticism of the existing university system and a deep distrust of a free and uncontrolled production of 'learned men'. There exists an optimum that is not to be exceeded, because over-production is dangerous. There also exists an optimum of 'true' knowledge, and society does not need people that are '*überstudiert*' (over-educated); that can also be fatal. Riehl can combine in a remarkable way, on one hand, a deep contempt for the new 'proletariat' and, on the other, a concern for their dangerous influence. They devote themselves to illusions and wishful thinking, lack contact with reality and exaggerate the importance of theories. Their members are marginal, and - at least during peacetime - in a way harmless, because their distorted thinking is then evident to everybody and they become an easy prey to the market. Riehl's approval of what has been called 'the policies of diversion' is also very remarkable. 'Practical' education (technology, natural sciences) is not supposed to attract presumptive members of the fourth estate, and it is therefore appropriate actively to recruit students to these useful and socially well-integrated subjects. It is a way to prevent the rise of a learned proletariat.[14] It was earlier mentioned that Hwasser very much disliked young people's late choice of profession.

Even if the ideas of the learned proletariat are obviously absurd, and they have a wrong conception of reality, they nevertheless are a disturbing element in society. The reason is the overestimation of their own importance due to their false knowledge. They mix the private and public, and, when their aspirations are not fulfilled, will try to get revenge. Then they will go into politics, become revolutionaries and subversives. This is also due to the fact that they do not belong to any of the traditional and organically grown classes, estates or corporations. They have no natural home, they are 'Jews', 'cosmopolitans'. Riehl saw an alternative to making these uprooted into technicians and scientists. He believed in organic growth and for this reason saw the farmers, the representatives of the close and harmonious contact between man and nature, as the main counterweight to the dangerous cities and their unreliable inhabitants. Riehl, who has been called one of the last great spokesmen of the old Europe, saw it as an important task to initiate serious research into the life of the 'people'.[15]

References to an alternative similar to Riehl's can also be found in the Swedish context. Through a strange coincidence Israel Hwasser was succeeded in the Swedish Academy by the poet, orator and ex-student leader Carl Strandberg, the most prominent spokesman of the rebellious students and of the Young Germans in the 1840s. Strandberg did not believe any longer in engaged political poetry. In his presidential address in 1863 he talks about the true mission of the writer. It has happened too often, Strandberg says, 'that the muse, instead of visiting the beds of sickness of the times, comforting, encouraging, healing, giving strength as a devoted harbinger of eternity, comes as a cursory and mawkish visitor. With an indecent obtrusiveness she tears off the bandages from the bleeding wounds that she has no competence to handle, no authority to treat and no power to heal. Poetical talents, working in this way, do not enrich our times'.

Instead of devoting themselves to 'the eternal and fundamental' the writers get caught up 'in things temporal', which leads to 'exaltation', 'confusion', 'darkness'. 'They fill the moment of the day with their boisterous uproar, and they rapidly collapse into nothing. They must endure the ungratefulness of the world'. A possible way out of the dilemma is to turn to history. If the contemporary epoch is too 'shapeless, confused and unmanageable', the world of the past lies there, 'already put into order, visible and available for the poet'. Another way is to go to the people. The people have from their infancy been 'brought up with song and legend' and they receive 'with eagerness' 'the gifts of the muse, if they are of greater worth than the products of the day'. If the songs reflect 'the inherited, native spirit of the people' and is performed 'with deep and humble sincerity', 'straightforward truth', 'the convincing tone of a deeply felt simplicity and manliness', then the people will be listening.[16] Strandberg's wish in his maturity is to be a mouth-piece for the spirit of the people, transparent and well-ordered, as manifested in history. The debates at the student meeting in Kristiania have now to be seen in the light of an analysis of the young like Hwasser's, of an attempt at social analysis like Riehl's, and of an account of a failure like Strandberg's.

To Kristiania!

The invitation to a Nordic student meeting in Kristiania was greeted with pleasure in Uppsala and in Lund, and committees were organised in both cities to handle the necessary preparations. Even the students of Copenhagen accepted the invitation although there were different opinions about the renewed attempt to bring the Scandinavian students together. At both the Swedish universities historians became spokesmen of the delegations, Dr E. W. Montan in Uppsala and in Lund the university lecturer Martin Weibull. It became later the task of the Lund students to collect material from the meeting and from the participants and publish the official report.[17] There were reasons for the Lund delegation getting this assignment. It is especially important to stress the contribution of Martin Weibull. It is highly probable that he had a decisive influence on the content of the report. Weibull was deeply involved in Scandinavian matters. It must also be remembered that the committees were very 'official' ones, and they contained not only students but also representatives of the university teachers. Per Hedenius, professor of medicine and a well-known academic orator, acted as honorary chairman in Uppsala and from Copenhagen came Carl Ploug, a veteran in Scandinavian affairs. The large delegations did not travel to Kristiania in secrecy. Their departure from the university cities was accompanied by all traditional festivity and along the route they were greeted by the local *honoratiores*. Addresses, speeches, songs, poems and receptions are thoroughly and reverently described in the report. In Gothenburg the delegates had the opportunity to pay their respects to His Majesty the King.

The Lund report uses an unmistakably 'revisionist' style to describe these activities, and is very anxious that no false impressions will be given about the ambitions of the delegates. At the earlier meetings, it says in the report, the Nordic students had 'under the influence of their youthful exuberance and vision of the future', 'organised themselves on their own responsibility as a Scandinavian "union parliament"'. They talked 'about the future of Scandinavia as if it depended only on them'. Now they have been forced to realise that the expectations 'had not been very well founded; the *people* had not kept to what the *students* had promised'. Even if the student meetings evidently had contributed to the promotion of the Scandinavian idea, some have argued - understandably enough - that the era of student meetings 'now for ever is gone' and the role of students finished. The idea of a new student meeting had been criticised in Copenhagen. It is necessary, however, the report says, to realise that even if student meetings can no longer claim the political importance that they once did, they nevertheless have other important tasks. They can bring together 'the noblest youth of Scandinavia', supply knowledge and promote a feeling for 'sincere friendship' among the Scandinavian people. 'Even if the students have not been able to play the role of commander and leader of the people, that they saw as their duty', they can anyhow be 'the standard-bearer' of the people and raise high the banner of idealism for the masses as well as for their real leaders'. The characterisation has a certain similarity to Hwasser's description of the truly idealistic youth. Even during the students' route to Kristiania speakers touched on the subject. In Gothenburg the well-known liberal publisher and journalist S. A. Hedlund harangued the students. It is not the task of the universities, Hedlund said, only to accumulate heaps of knowledge', but to develop 'as institutions of *Bildung*' 'a noble mind, that is the foundation of all *Bildung*'. This leads to a sense of duty, patriotism 'and a sincere devotion to all true human interests'. It is possible to compare Hedlund's statement with Per Hedenius' address at the arrival in Kristiania. The student, Hedenius says, must not forget 'the moderation that is a sign of real inner quality'.

Only once during the student meeting were ideas of a different kind expressed, even if they are formulated with great care. It is only natural, the report says, that at a Scandinavian student meeting Scandinavism is mentioned, but this was done on the clear understanding that the meeting 'from the beginning had renounced all pretentions of playing a direct political role'. The episode had, however, some overtones. A rumour had been spread that Carl Rosenberg, the Danish literary historian and journalist, was going to make a speech on political Scandinavism. The chairman of the session was eager to deny this rumour. It was a misunderstanding. Rosenberg's subject is instead, he says, the recent development of Scandinavian thought in Denmark, and the efforts to make the people conscious of Scandinavian solidarity. When Rosenberg spoke, however, he allowed himself some notable remarks. He talked about the political necessity of Nordic cooperation, about the threatening danger from abroad, about Poland as a warning lesson. One can argue, Rosenberg says, that with his speech he is addressing the wrong forum, that young people shall not mix in political affairs. It is true that mistakes about the importance of student meetings have been made in the past, when 'students got the idea that they were a kind of representative of the people and their feelings an expression of the people's will'. This mistake has now caused 'an almost hysterical fear' at the eventuality of a student political meeting. It would be unnatural, however, Rosenberg says, if the students completely refrained from talking about political matters. The Scandinavian idea was originally a student one, the student meetings have in fact had a political importance, and this shall not be denied.

No one commented on Rosenberg's remarks, no discussion followed his speech. At several occasions during the meeting, however, the problem was touched upon, but then the speakers expressed themselves in a different way. Anxiously they emphasised the subordinate and serving role of the students. 'We are the avant garde of ideas', Carl Ploug says at a reception, 'we are the light troops of the people, but only the light troops, not the real army that alone can win the battle'. Moreover, from another point of view, the students cannot be said to represent the people. Most of the students become civil servants, but the majority of the people are farmers and burghers. A Norwegian student reminded the participants at the concluding festivities of 'the spirit of closeness to the people' that had characterised the Kristiania meeting, and a Danish student emphasised that the students have to fulfill 'their holy mission in the service of the people'. They should not imagine that this mission is comparable to 'the brilliant and honorable task of the statesman, no, it is a humble work in the low cottage of the common man'. Martin Weibull paid a warm tribute to the University of Kristiania, 'that has become powerful and influential because it has seen itself as a spokesman of the people's soul, to which it has given a true expression'. He also praised the impressions that he had formed of Norway that 'form the anchorage for all uniting ideas' when 'kept deep in the sentiment of the peoples'. 'In the loving care of this conviction lies the task of youth'. The Danish author and priest Christian Hostrup addressed, he said, not the 'critical' youth, but the 'caring youth', and he especially stressed that the students now have got a wider sphere of action when they have realised 'that it is their mission only to be the avant garde, that can do nothing without the people'.

This humble attitude - the guardians of the ideological heritage and the (non-political) mouthpiece of the *Volksgeist* - became, however, somewhat complicated when a specially problematic part of the people was taken into consideration: the workers. The workers and the 'social question' were a topic of discussion at the meeting, and in this context the students could be given a more active role. The main speaker here was a Danish publisher, C.V. Rimestad, heralded as 'the most active man in Denmark for the cause of the workers'. Rimestad had, he says, for a long time eagerly wanted to talk to students, 'because through them goes the road to regeneration'. Rimestad is worried about the social question and most notably about the workers in the cities. The social order of the state is in danger if they are left alone. As their standard of living now has increased, their demands have also become more pretentious. It is important that they are taught self-help. 'Help from the state means communism, help from the local authorities is simply poor-relief and help by Christian charity means to support idleness'. The upper classes can spread 'information and true *Bildung*' not only through books and lectures but also through personal influence. The educated shall bow so low, that he 'can reach the hand of the worker; then both shall rise together'. The university student can learn from the worker 'resignation, perseverance, diligence and hard work'.

A prominent participant in the student meeting, Eilert Sundt, who has been called 'a founding father of the social sciences in Norway', replies that the people are not to be underestimated. The people have studied in the school of life, and the great, the true and the good that can be found in the heart of the people, has to be trusted.[18] Rimestad does not deny this and points out that his special concern is the urban workers. The most famous of all participants in Kristiania, the world-famous Norwegian writer Björnstjerne Björnson, asks if the workers are taking part in the voluntary rifle associations (which were considered to be educational). Ploug wants to make sure that it is 'the mature young men', that are supposed to be 'teachers of the workers' and not those 'who still have not an enlightened mind'. Rimestad answers that in his opinion, the students should first of all talk with the workers, visit them as equals, 'sit down at their side, take part in their troubles and delights and in this way contribute to their improvement'. These activities have evidently nothing to do with 'politics'.

The difference in the conception of the 'people' (the true and the sound) and the urban workers is evident. The workers are unreliable and they have growing pretensions. City-life makes them especially unreliable. These are the people to whom the students shall bring reason by giving them higher views, if, that is, the students have reached a mature judgement and a clear insight into the order of things. Ploug's concern about 'immature' youth is obvious. The combination of urban workers and 'immature' students was ominous. Riehl (and Stirner!) had come to the same conclusion. It was desirable, Riehl said, to prevent this cooperation through an improvement of the worker's standard. Rimestad talked about self-help and mature students. The students could then themselves learn diligence and industry.

The students (the 'concerned' but not the 'critical') should moreover cultivate what is sound in the people, be their servants and not mix too much in the 'temporal' (to paraphrase Strandberg). This implies, however, knowledge about the people. Eilert Sundt had a dream of how this knowledge could be acquired. He hopes that the time will come, 'when universities and academies will regard the simple conditions of the people as worthy an object of scientific research as the study of birds and fishes'. This seems to be congruent with Riehl's ambitions. The study of the people was an important task and should be given academic status.

The Swedish art historian Bo Grandien in an interesting essay has pointed out the remarkable growth of interest in outdoor life during the nineteenth century and especially in walking-tours.[19] Walking by foot is given a specific ideological significance. In his essay Grandien compares Riehl's theories of city and country with similar Scandinavian ideas. In Scandinavia they are combined with the search for a Nordic identity founded both on the Nordic nature and the old Norse past. Walking by foot is supposed to bring about a special contact with nature and people, and give opportunities for folkloristic research. When the present is in 'disorder', Strandberg wrote, the poet can find help in 'the settled world of the past'. Grandien points out that during the 1860s and 1870s there existed a romantic image of Norway, inspired for example by the works of Björnstjerne Björnson. There is no difficulty in finding this image of Norway in the report from the student meeting. At an art exhibition in Gothenburg the delegates admire Norwegian artists (Gude, Tideman, Eckersberg): 'In our fantasy we then entered Norway', the report says, 'the country we longed for. We travelled over reflecting fjords, between steep, abruptly sloping fields and in the shadows of deep forests. There live people, vigorous, honest and God-fearing'. An Uppsala delegate talks about 'the serene, deep and powerful' in the Norwegian people, 'a reflection of the nature that has nurtured you, of your high mountains, your deep valleys and violent currents'. A song with words by Björnson was seen as especially suited for the occasion. 'When we stay here', it says, 'we are falling in love with the wide countryside where the farmers still embrace the loyalty that is our honour and a heritage from powerful forefathers, whose glory was our sunrise'. With this understanding of the people the students were supposed to enlighten the workers of the cities.

The question about the position and mission of the universities was of course of great importance for the platform; that can be seen in the discussions, declarations and rhetoric during the meeting. Due to the special situation in Kristiania these debates also took on a special character. Different opinions were more openly demonstrated here than was the case on the other issues. Martin Weibull tried in an extensive statement to specify a number of reforms in order to make possible a closer cooperation between the Scandinavian universities. A comparative survey of courses, examinations, research and student organisations ought to be made and a Nordic university and student calendar be published. He argued for Nordic scholarships, exchange of teachers and continuous student meetings. He also proposed to make examinations valid throughout Scandinavia, and eventually to organise a kind of specialisation among the universities in order to raise the professional standard. Weibull's suggestions were far-reaching, and meant among other things a specification and publication of academic requirements, a controversial issue that could be seen as an infringement upon the liberties of the teachers - *Lehrfreiheit*.[20]

Weibull's contribution was opposed from a somewhat unexpected quarter, when Björnson attacked it in an apparently temperamental way. Weibull's suggestions were meaningless, he said, if the students did not first come out of their 'student context' and enter into 'the people's context'. The universities should be opened up for everybody who wanted to study, and all education ought to be given the same goal as the voluntary folk high schools, that is 'to *found*, to *build up* a true human being and not to pile heaps of knowledge'. 'The student way must go, the people's way must come'. Björnson's attack was immediately and strongly contradicted. The Hegelian philosopher Marcus Jacob Monrad, Björnson's compatriot, so disliked his ideas that he did not even want to take them into serious consideration. Instead he turned against Weibull. He feared a standardisation of the universities which would contradict 'the character of our Germanic peoples. We do not want to form huge, compact masses as the Latin people do. We have too strong a feeling for individualism to consider such a thing'. Monrad could accept cooperation, and research 'is everywhere the same and not bound to nationality', but should not be moulded in the same form.

Carl Ploug came up with another suggestion. The universities should not be tied to an official examination system. Today the subjects for lectures have to be chosen with regard to the examinations, and universities must submit their ambitions to national requirements. Instead they ought to be 'centres of human *Bildung*'. Free and unlimited research should not be sacrificed to a memorising of standard courses. The universities should liberate themselves from the state, and that would make a freer cooperation possible. Germany is the model. Ploug rejects Björnson's ideas and stresses emphatically the difference between a university and a folk high school. The folk high school is completely dependent on the university for the dispersion of *Bildung*. 'It is quite another thing that is now more and more recognised, that the mission of all *Bildung* is to teach and improve the people'. Björnson replies that he does not want to close the universities, only to liberate them from the examination system and allow free admission, so that the students 'not will look upon themselves as a special corps'. The school also ought to be reformed, so that it promotes faith, Christian faith, patriotism, creates whole personalities and 'teaches for real life, not for *examen artium*'. Björnson's ideas were met 'partly with disapproval, partly with consent'.

The opposition between Björnson and the university professionals gives another aspect to the complicated relations between the educated and the people. Björnson seems to have a sceptical attitude to university people, a distrust of their theorising and accumulating of facts. These activities lead to a distorted opinion about the character of true knowledge, and promote a false idea of corporate exclusiveness. Contact with real life is lost in the examination system and the routine compiling of dead knowledge. The boundaries between institutions have to be torn down. As mentioned above academic people can also oppose the examination system, but they do it in the name of free research and scientific standards. Free research is the specific task of the universities and no boundaries shall be torn down. For Ploug, for example, it is quite obvious that the prerequisite for all true *Bildung* is the free research of the universities, and that this *Bildung* is spread from 'above', ie from the universities and out into society. The concern for scientific specialisation, guaranteed through 'the liberty' of the universities, stands against the demands for socialisation in the state and society, founded on the sound legacy of the people and true to the strivings of idealism. In both cases the aim was to counteract the extravagance of the threatening fourth estate.

The difficulties in combining these two perspectives were not easily overcome. The author of the Lund report draws, however, some very definite conclusions from the student meeting. There is no room for ambiguities he says, in what the students must realise. The student meeting has started a new epoch, because the young delegates have understood that politically they must hold 'a modest and unobtrusive position', and find the way through which they 'just as students can work for the future of Scandinavia'. They have also realised that they shall not 'isolate themselves from the people, the workers, the common man, in whose hands in the end the future lies'. Even if the men of the university have a more profound *Bildung* and greater knowledge, 'they do not possess the right, as they once thought, to talk *on behalf of* the people, but the much greater obligation to talk *to* them'. And the author quotes Björnson: 'When the vernal wind of the people is blowing through glens and forests and awakes thousands, then comes the hour of reunion'.

Student, Civil Servant or Man of Learning

The programme recommended in the Kristiania report, the critique of the past, the necessary work in the service of the people, was - as mentioned - not accepted altogether and by everybody without reservations. The words of Carl Rosenberg, that the meeting showed a 'hysterical fear' for 'the political', are clear enough. Even later references to the period can express a disappointment at the development. An example is Viktor Rydberg, poet, novelist, essayist, idealist philosopher and one of the prominent figures in Swedish intellectual life in the latter half of the nineteenth century. When he looks back at the situation after 1848 and its influence on the Swedish university milieu, he makes some remarkable statements. He talks about the 'discouragement' all over Europe that came after 'too high hopes', and this was also felt, he says, in 'the small university city' of Lund. The 'servants' of the university limited themselves - in accordance with a general 'lack of energy' - to the 'restricted duties of a discipline'. 'We felt as if it was forbidden to look out over these borders'. Rydberg makes this retrospective reflection in a very special context. It was earlier mentioned that Carl Strandberg in the Swedish Academy talked to the memory of Israel Hwasser. It became the duty of Rydberg to honour the memory of Strandberg, and Rydberg now tries to defend him also against himself. Rydberg remembers that Strandberg and his comrades 'took literature, for long banned from everyday life, out into the battlefield of contemporary ideas', and they were looked upon by the young men as 'a generation of heroes'. Rydberg also refers to Strandberg's self-criticism quoted above, but he is not willing to agree with him. When Strandberg formulates his criticism and thereby uses 'the rigour of his mature judgment', it is evidently 'the academician looking reproachfully back on the poetry of the student'.

Rydberg is now anxious to stress Strandberg's noble motives, his idealism. He wishes to place him in the right 'group', 'among those young men, whose character once was described by his profound predecessor in this chair (ie in the Swedish Academy): Israel Hwasser'. As expected, Rydberg counts Strandberg in the small group that puts 'the eternal and its demands', the good and the true, in the first place. It is obvious that Rydberg wants to 'save' Strandberg, but he also adds some more ambiguous attributes to Hwasser's chivalry of the rising sun: 'They are not always friends of the existing situation. As citizens of two worlds they are inclined to protest against reality when reality is in flagrant opposition to the world of ideals, and they are not afraid of sacrificing their worldly future in favour of the dream of an ideal one that they see as the true legacy of mankind'.[21]

If you want to keep the banner of high ideals flying, you unavoidably - according to Rydberg - get into a conflict. Rydberg was definitely not a vagabond, but he came from the ranks of the unstable literati, and he was familiar with Prometheus and Faust. He could judge *Herr Doktor* Wagner, who continuously dwells in the shadow of Faust, very harshly. Wagner, Rydberg says, tries as a university professor 'to create an *homunculus*, a *mixtum compositum*, a new man, that is to say: in the learned way with crucibles and retorts. This is a difficult undertaking, even if our school system in a way has solved the problem. I do not know Doktor Wagner's later fortunes: a folk-tale says that the devil got him. My guess is that he ended up as a minister of education, which is not to say that the folk-tale is completely untrue'. Wagner has all the virtues that can give him 'some well paid position in the service of the state and the church'. He will never be persecuted as a heretic, he will never be burnt at the stake, but will 'as a reliable man come to good income and honours'. He is the 'preserving element in research and in society', 'the necessary counter-weight to the fervour of truth-seeking and to that sense of justice that strives for a distant ideal'.[22]

Rydberg's hard words about the uniformed civil servants of academies and universities, who not only have yielded to power but sold themselves to it, and upon the homunculus they get out of their educational retorts, are almost an echo of Schiller's anathema upon *'Die Brodgelehrten'* a century earlier.[23] In Rydberg's time these *Brodgelehrten* still can be found in Germany in new versions, violently attacked as *'Kopfverderber'* by Schopenhauer and *'Bildungsphilister'* by Nietzsche. They have given up (and now look down upon) the search for truth, they have chosen the easy way, hustling and meddling, 'as if research was a factory work'.[24]

But - as mentioned above - all enemies of the university system cannot be lumped together. Neither Ploug nor Björnson had any high opinions of the existing academic system and its artificial products, but they could not agree on a positive alternative, and there existed definite limits to the independence of young people. For Nietzsche, who contrasted life and history, the liberation of youth has to be its own task. No help can be obtained from God or men. Youth has to liberate itself. Then life, that has only been hidden, chained, but not withered or dead, will also be liberated. Through his conception of youth, a commentator writes, *'mythisiert Nietzsche das noch nicht entfremdete Leben. Deshalb scheint ihm die Jugend berufen, aus der Kulturkrise herauszufinden'* (Nietzsche views the still unalienated life in a mythical light, this is why he believes that it is the call of youth to break away from the general 'Cultural Crisis'). This apotheosis of the youthful liberation does not, however, lead back into society, but out of it and definitely not to the people. The creative individual does not 'engage' himself. He strikes mankind as a bolt of lightning.[25]

Such a vision requires the destruction of the old society and the disintegration of its organisations, guilds, ranks and parties. Bruno Bauer saw the coming of an 'empire', a conformist, absolute state, that rises against the isolated individual. He talks about his contemporaries as *'nackte, in sich haltlose Individuen'* (naked and empty persons). The individual has been transformed into an atom. He has lost the identity that he earlier had as a member of a guild or a party. In a remarkable way Bauer's analysis, his 'critical nihilism', is comparable to Riehl's, even if the moral is quite the opposite. The universities are in complete decay, Bauer says, the number of students is decreasing, and would be still lower if the group was not enlarged by engineers and technicians, who study natural sciences and want to get *'einer Anflug von allgemeiner Bildung'* (a touch of general education). *'Die Völker'* feel that they do not need the universities any more, that they only need the engineer, the founder of industrial enterprises. The engineer, Bauer says, *'das ist der Mann, dem die Völker in ihrem praktischen Kampf mit Raum Zeit ihr Vertrauen schenken'* (this is a man to whom the people give their trust in their daily toil). Not even governments need the universities. Their universities are the armies, which will teach the subjects law and order in a modern way. The old universities are only tolerated *'wie man eine alte Ruine neben einem neuen Etablissement duldet, so lange das dringende Bedürfnis noch nicht ihren Abbruch verlangt'* (just as one tolerates an old ruin beside a new establishment as long as it does not get in the way).[26]

Riehl talks about the decaying university that produces decaying literates and recommends policies of diversion. Bauer talks about the decaying university (and the end of philosophy) and looks upon the engineer as the man of the day. Schopenhauer dreamt of a free philosopher, who as '*die Alpenrose und die Flurenblume*' can only grow '*in freier Bergluft*',[27] and so did Nietzsche. The universities were, however, not pulled down. Their development took another course. An attempt was made, it is said in a summary of the Prussian university policy, to transform '*die "Vorlesungsuniversität" zur modernen, durch Seminare ergänzten Arbeitsuniversität*' (convert the lecturing university through seminars to a working university) in order to accommodate '*den geistigen Anforderungen an das Bildungssystem*' (the spiritual demands on the education system). The result was what has been called a '*Grossbetrieb der Wissenschaft*' (industrialised scientific work) close cooperation with private capital and industry '*durch Einrichtung von Instituten und Forschungslaboratorien an den Technischen Hochschulen und Universitäten*' (through the establishment of research institutes and laboratories at the Technical and ordinary universities). The ideal of a '*Menschenbildung*' in the Humboldt system was replaced by a '*schichtenspezifisches Ausbildungs- und Anpassungssystem*' (a socially diversified education and socialisation system).[28] The student organisations experienced - according to Konrad Jarausch - a '*Tendenzwende*' and stood during the empire '*fest und treu hinter dem neuen Staat*' (solidly behind the new state).[29]

The Swedish development is not the same as in Germany, but some tendencies of a similar nature have to be pointed out. Almost half a century after his Uppsala years Sigfrid Wieselgren, now a prominent civil servant, looks back at the 1860s, and he finds little to report about idealistic engagement or about service to the people or the workers. Instead he remembers the non-commitment of the students.[30] 'The social question looked much the same as it had always done, and did not bother us very much'. Another type of activity, however, attracted the student's attention. Paradoxically enough this is a period of active student organisation. A student union was formed and its importance recognised during the 1860s, Wieselgren says. 'We realised better and better that such a union could more effectively form a uniting bond among the students'. Even other organisations became attractive. 'The scientific interest was rapidly growing and specialised studies were pursued more and more intensely'. This could be seen in the organisation of specialised societies and clubs within the different subjects and faculties. 'In these societies a devoted work was done, that influenced the members in a positive way and also inspired and encouraged people outside the societies'. The activities in these associations, where older and younger members of the academic community could meet, were, however, not accepted by everybody. 'There were some who argued against this kind of studies and regarded them as a harmful specialisation'. These opponents, Wieselgren says ironically, 'were of the opinion that *Bildung* meant a "little of everything", a hybrid of bits and pieces taken from all scientific subjects. Against this opinion it was emphasised that university studies ought to be more specialised, and that specialisation was a necessary condition for true *Bildung*'.

Wieselgren's emphasis on both specialisation and on new forms of scientific training is very remarkable. Reforms were also undertaken in order to promote greater efficiency, and both in Germany and in Sweden the organisation of seminars was supposed to raise the scientific standard of the university.[31] The content of the *Bildung* concept changes towards specialisation and methodology. It must also be remembered that by this time - as Riehl and Bauer observed - technical studies were given university status. All this can be seen as an answer to the critical vagabonds. Of course this 'turn' to research and professional training could, as has already been pointed out, be combined with an idea of the educated as servants of the people, as long as political aspirations were kept in check.

You Shall Not Rule Until Your Youth Is Gone

At the beginning of the 1880s the historian and political scientist Wilhelm Erik Svedelius retired after a long university career in Lund and in Uppsala (Martin Weibull considered himself his pupil). He bade farewell to his students in a publication in which he described his experiences and formulated some fatherly admonitions. Svedelius follows an easily identifiable model. He continues the tradition from a man, Svedelius says, that he came to know when he was a young man, and to love as a most sincere friend of young people. 'It was Israel Hwasser.' The Hwasser model has also very clearly influenced Svedelius' own work, and at the same time he tries to draw some conclusions from the forty years that have passed since Hwasser's time. Hwasser's different types of youth, even the degenerate ones, can be found in Svedelius' analysis. He mentions the 'admirers of the flesh' who 'revel in the pleasure of false research and low literature' and hate 'all disciplinary order'. 'These are inaccessible for true research and noble literature'. Among the 'guardians of the spirit' there are also some who are unstable, uncertain and lack character.[32]

There is also, according to Svedelius, a 'desperate' youth that 'has no light to guide its thinking and no firm ground for its faith'. In their desperation these young people can turn 'with an inextinguishable hatred against all established order, which they only feel as a coercive oppression'. They attack the 'sanctity of property', become 'prophets of false doctrines' and believe that they 'act in the name of truth'. They advocate licentiousness, which they call 'liberty and human rights'. They can preach 'antisocial and immoral theories', 'an earth without heaven and a time without eternity', and believe that these 'will regenerate mankind'. Such 'mendacious apostles' are perhaps not outright criminals, but definitely comparable to 'bandits in the dungeons'. They call 'vice and crime' 'the rights of man', and 'the offsprings of deceit' are called 'moral principles'.

Youth, Svedelius goes on to say, has immature judgement, little experience, a superficial and unstable disposition, makes pretentious demands and becomes easily a prey to false prophets. In order to prove his statement he makes a summary of 'malicious deeds of political fanaticism' since the beginning of the nineteenth century. He reminds his readers of the student Carl Ludwig Sand, who during the days of the *Burschenschaft* movement killed the *Hofrat* von Kotzebue, and makes a reference to later 'presumptive regicides. The year of 1848 with all the destruction that then haunted Europe, is especially instructive'. All this wickedness can be studied in 'the curriculum that is called the gospel of the flesh, in the insolent contempt that communism has for social order and property rights, and in the savage and inhuman movements that we have seen in Russia, and that have got a special name: nihilism and nihilists'.

In Svedelius' catalogue one can without difficulty find that gospel of the flesh that Hwasser attributed to the Young Germans, and among those who believed in an earth without heaven he could have counted Bauer and his companions. Svedelius also mentions among the vagabonds such people who devote themselves to 'scandals of a dissipated life'. One can find them, he says, 'in the annals of cultural history, even in the annals of poetry'. They have, however, never developed into full maturity. 'The fruit never became more than half-ripe, it was eaten by the worms'.[33]

It is a recurring theme in Svedelius' exhortations to the students, that youth talks too much about imaginary rights and too little about duties. He must realise, Svedelius says, 'that he is only young, and that he can not demand more than what really belongs to his age'. He has to 'restrain his desires to take possession of his realm prematurely' and consider his true virtues, modesty and self-control. He will certainly come to power in the future, but he will not rule 'unless his youth is gone'. From abroad 'the echo of a young arrogance' is sometimes heard. It 'thinks, that it is capable of making the world new, if it is given the lightning of world control. But this is only foolishness and stupid obstinacy, and the arrogant ones will break their necks'. All this ought to be, according to Svedelius, a serious warning even to Sweden.[34]

The continuity between Hwasser and Svedelius is beyond doubt and needs no further comments. Svedelius has only added some more degenerates to the list beside Hwasser's Young Germans. The development from the early German student movement to Russian nihilism is for Svedelius quite logical, and so also is the connection (as for Riehl) between presumptuous students and worm-eaten literates. Svedelius rejects as much as Hwasser (and Ploug) the youthful claims to rights (only in the name of youthfulness), when modesty and self-restraint would be more suitable. In spite of the humble attitude of the Kristiania meeting (and the movement towards the people and nature), Strandberg's rethinking and retreat to history, and in spite of the hopeful signs that Wieselgren found in the new research orientation, the urge was still strong to warn against false apostles, communists, nihilists, revolutionaries, immorals, Riehl's proletariat. Svedelius had even sharpened the tone. It is also part of the picture, however, that Svedelius was very much interested at an early stage in the organisation of the students. It was not organisation as such that was wrong. Organisation could be very useful in order to promote cooperation, a true student identity and educational innovations. Even the Vice Chancellor of Uppsala University, the idealist philosopher Carl Yngve Sahlin, was involved in the new experiments.[35]

It must further be mentioned that Svedelius, like Martin Weibull, in his historical work adopted a rather 'modern' outlook. Already in his earlier publications, according to Rolf Torstendahl, he combined idealism 'with a deliberately empirical research orientation' and a critical attitude towards the source material. This line was later pursued by Weibull.[36] Hwasser's profound and Svedelius' true research were most certainly based on different assumptions. The new outlook did not mean, however, that the historian should refrain from moral judgments. They belonged on the contrary to his duties, and the interests of the state should be the guiding moral principle of his work. Björnson's argument against specialisation in the name of 'life' and in this context the people could not have much weight. He had mixed up the different levels of *Bildung*. The outsiders could then *ad libitum* make ironic remarks on Wagner's achievements as a minister of education or sulkingly retire to the Alps in the name of their genius and meditate over the dangerous utopia of the young, liberating himself. The era of the Kristiania meeting, the period from Hwasser to Svedelius, is important in the history of Swedish education. Schools, institutes and universities were organised in a coherent system with clearly defined and socially adapted goals for the different institutions, where everybody had his right place. Over this system the students of the universities were supposed to keep the banner of high ideals flying and thereby fulfill their mission in the service of the people.

Chapter 2

Knowledge and Power

Constraints and Expansion of Professional Influence
in Western Capitalist Society

Rolf Torstendahl

Differences Between Professionals

It is striking, when looking at the professions, that one can see less of a common pattern
than one would expect from the literature on these occupational groups. The professions
changed fundamentally over the period from the beginning of the 19th century to the
1980s, but they are also different in different contemporary social settings. This latter
fact means, for example, that there are considerable - some would say basic - differences
between the professions in Britain and in France at the same time. The importance of
the social setting means also, however, that there are considerable - indeed fundamental
- differences between professions at the same time and in the same country. This, in
turn, may be explained by saying that some professions are more professional than
others. It is quite justifiable to make the concept one of degree, but if the scaling variables
are not precise, this will remove the core of the concept. This concept, however vague,
has as its sole justification the ability to crystallise something that some occupations
have in common, which may be explained as a phenomenon of a common character.
Looking for an explanation of professionalisation, however, turns out very much to be
a search for an explanation of its variations.

In this essay,[1] we will concentrate on the differences between professions in some
European countries. By 'professions' I understand, on one hand occupational groups
that enjoy a limitation of competition in their labour market and make their theoretical
knowledge the basis for their claims on their labour market. Second, I understand by
'professions' a group that aspires to the standing of a profession and tries to make a
particular body of theoretical knowledge its strategic base. Professional groups are thus
taken to be knowledge-based groups.[2]

Semantics and the Concepts of 'Professions' and 'Elites'

What has already been said above means that professional groups have not all enjoyed
the same conditions of work and that they have not all aimed for the same goals. It is
even questionable by which criteria we shall decide which groups are professional.
Because the semantics are very complicated and empirical semantics regarding the
concept of professional are possible only for the English language, it is hardly fruitful

to make conceptual history the essence of the distinctive marks of the professional groups. In other European languages the concept is transferred as a sociological and technical term having no sense beside this usage or, eventually, quite another sense in a domestic tradition.[3]

The concept of 'elite' has almost exactly the opposite characteristics as the concept of 'professionals'. The problem with the concept 'elite' is partly that it is broad and with no definite and exact empirical content in any specific social context. This means that the concept, when it has been used in everyday language, has been left vague and ambiguous. Thus, there is no hope of bringing clarity to the concept by historical and sociological empirical investigations. Another related part of the problem of using the concept of elite is that it is a relative concept in many contexts. Where he will look for the elite depends very much on which step of the social ladder the respondent stands. Few people seem to count themselves immediately as part of 'the elite'. In the rich literature on elites the concept often remains vague. Giddens, in his contribution to this topic, has made it a virtue to leave different interpretations open, though he has clarified the alternative interpretations in terms of recruitment, structure and power.[4]

Elite is a concept loaded with evaluation, and consequently, with a political ring in many contexts. It is, however, also used by social scientists in order to identify the strata in which political and economic power are concentrated in societies. Often the boundaries have been left vague, and theoretically the concept has not been a forceful tool.

Different Patterns

Same knowledge-base - different levels - different professions

Strategy is fundamental to professionalism. It is not, however, the sole foundation of the allocation of status that is connected with professionalism. Some groups have had, for a long period, a strategic aim that is evidently professional in the second sense, but all the same have not succeeded in acquiring the caste mark of the professionals. Nurses constitute the best example of this kind that I know of. In many countries they have made a certain amount of medical knowledge a prerequisite for the occupation. Specialist schools give the necessary education. They have formed associations to keep track of their members, and they have cut themselves clear from the wider community of nursing personnel. However, they are not looked upon, and have certainly not been remunerated, as 'real' professionals.[5] They don't share the wide recognition of the doctors. One may ask: why not?

Doctors and nurses share, to an extent, the same theoretical base of knowledge for their occupational activities, though nurses are seldom trained for the same period and seldom in the same theoretical depth as doctors. On the other hand, doctors have not covered all parts of the training of the nurses, especially the parts which refer to general nursing care.

Same knowledge-base - different levels - same profession

It is interesting to compare this difference between doctors and nurses with the apparent similarities between engineers of different levels of educational achievement in some social contexts. It is here necessary to note differences between countries. France is not at all like Britain in this respect. Sweden is rather like Germany (after World War Two I refer only to the FRG) but there are some peculiar dissimilarities. However, in all these countries there are sections of the engineers' labour market open to competition between engineers with different schooling; only after a long-standing struggle was the title of engineer protected in some countries in order to exclude competition from the non-schooled.[6] Exclusion was thus a weak strategy among engineers in general. This, in its turn, has given rise to specific high-level organisations and titles reserved for those with high-level education. The *VDDI* in Germany is an example of the former, with *Diplomingenieur* in Germany and *civilingenjör* in Sweden being examples of the latter phenomenon. In spite of these efforts in Germany and Sweden to create a stratification, according to levels of education, among engineers, this has had no effect in the labour market. In these cases differences in schooling signifies clear differences in level of schooling. This means that what applies to nurses and doctors does not apply to engineers, at least not generally: there are no real boundaries between the levels of schooling.

Same knowledge-base - same level - different professions

Another peculiarity becomes obvious when one also takes also lawyers, in the American sense, into consideration. Lawyers, ie the '*Juristen*' in German, are not a homogeneous profession in most European countries. They are divided into judges, public prosecutors, barristers, solicitors, etc. The categories vary somewhat in different European countries, but they share the same basic theoretical knowledge. The 'law school diploma' which in many European countries is a diploma from a university law faculty often qualifies one for several of the legal professions, even though the candidate may have concentrated in his/her studies on the subjects which are regarded as most relevant for the specific legal profession that he or she is aiming for. If these aims are not fulfilled, because of superior competition or a simple change of heart, other paths may still be open.[7]

Conclusion

Of course, the characterisation of the different types of lawyers as different professions and the different types of doctors as one profession, is only a question of degree. There are striking similarities as well as some differences between these two cases. It is important, however, that while the single theoretical knowledge-base of lawyers may give rise to a split in professions, the shared knowledge-base of doctors and nurses gives rise to different professions by virtue of the level of schooling, and the same type of shared knowledge-base that is taught at different levels does not give rise to any clear division between professions among engineers, even if there are speciality-groups among them.

State Interests

The state - conceived as a network of certain formal structures[8] - was given new interests in the formation of professional strata in the 18th century. These interests were kept and developed later. State interest in the field of professionalism, according to the state concept that was current on the European continent, was to maintain competence in certain fields. There were two basic models for securing this competence. One was to establish a corps or craft, where the skills and knowledge were transmitted from master to apprentice. The other was to promote education through open educational institutions. Both models were practised early in Europe, and the first model dominated in England (and later Britain). From medieval times the state, alongside the church, had taken an interest in education, and universities were often sponsored by the state. Through universities competence in theology, medicine, law and teaching was guaranteed. The guarantee lay in the diplomas for the degrees given.

In the 19th and 20th centuries the state took on a more varied responsibility for competence in divers fields. This became evident in three different ways. First, the state created specific professions. It did so long ago, when it appointed the judges in courts and created judiciary systems of different sophistication. In the 19th century states were especially active in creating professional positions in the health care systems - hospitals, asylums, etc - with regionally distributed doctors, and also a veterinary system based on the same principles. Later, technical inspectors and controllers, and in the 20th century different kinds of social workers, were also created by state action. Significantly, the state did not always employ the professionals. It just created the preconditions for the profession.

When the state had created a profession it also had an interest in providing the education necessary for the practice of the profession. Educational institutions of different kinds in medicine, veterinary medicine, accountancy, engineering, social work, etc were created through the state. It was also sometimes regarded as a state interest to provide education for socially necessary professions even if these were not related to state action. Many engineering schools were created as a stimulus for industry and business in general and not because of a state need. In this respect there is a difference between Britain and the Continent on the one hand, and between France and the rest of the Continent on the other. In Britain, the limited attention given to technical education by the state had to do with the non-institutional forms of technical education that were favoured in Britain,[9] while in France a strict division between state purposes and private purposes regarding technical education was upheld until, in 1856, the *Ecole centrale* was made a state institution. In Germany and Scandinavia the aim of the state was primarily to stimulate industrialisation through education.[10]

A third type of state responsibility was to provide rules for the profession. Lawyers were probably the first to attract the attention from the state in this way, but in the 19th century the activities of doctors were more or less regulated because of their importance for life and death. Around the turn of the century state regulations were extended to different fields of a technical character. Even in countries where railways were not regarded as a state prerogative it became normal to legislate about the security problems attached to railway systems. Ship security, lifts and other technical systems where injuries might be inflicted on people, were other objects of state regulation. These fields had a direct relation to professional activity.

In all West European countries the state took an interest in matters concerned with professionalism. Sometimes this interest was manifested in activities that affected the conditions for professionalism both directly and indirectly, but in some countries the state played a more constrained role, and acted only indirectly in the fields of interest of professionals up to the 20th century. By then, it seems that the boundaries of state interests in professionalism had become much wider, especially after World War II.

Interests of Capital and Capitalists

In much the same way as the state, capital has had interests in professionalism which have manifested themselves in different ways. These interests have been mainly indirect. They have been directed primarily towards the consequences of professionalism, the products that can be marketed and which are outcomes of professional activity, and to some extent the services that are provided by professionals and can be marketed. Marketable products are closely connected with engineering and engineers and their services were an object of interest to capitalism almost as soon as the profession had arisen. The services of doctors only slowly and to a small extent came to be regarded in a capitalist light, and doctors only recently - through the development of hospital equipment - became interesting to capital because of their relation to products.

Engineers and doctors may be regarded as examples of the interest relations that have existed between professionals and capital. Only a few of the professionals provide services that are useful for collectivities. Engineers do so, but doctors mostly do not. Engineers are also directly related to the production processes for marketable goods, while doctors are not. Managers and lawyers are interesting to capital mainly because of their marketable services, i.e. services that are useful for collectivities. A physician of high reputation and in fashion among the higher strata of society may earn a lot of money through his connection with the capitalists, but to capital, he is exchangeable and can easily be replaced by another physician, as demand is not by capital but by individual capitalists, and the supply of able doctors far exceeds the needs of capitalists.

The main thing that has changed in the history of professions during the era of industrial capitalism is that demand for the services of professionals has changed in nature. This holds true for the old and long established professions, because only they have existed long enough to have experienced the change. The new ones have only seen the conditions created in the later phases of industrial capitalism. The change in demand means that personal, individual demand for service has become less important compared to demand by collectivities, either private or public. This change is a most important one, as the position of the professional is quite different in relation to big organisations or the state than in relation to private persons. The family doctor, who comes to see his patients or whose patients visit his clinic is in quite a different position in relation to his patients from that of the hospital doctor. Still more different is the position of the industrial company doctor whose loyalty can always be suspected - rightly or wrongly - of being as strong to the company as to the patients or to the profession as such. The professional who has sold his labour is no longer in the same position and has got other interests than the one who sells only his services.[11] The change in demand from individuals to collectivities has entailed this change in supply, from service-supply to labour-supply. It means that professionals have become more like other groups in the labour market. There are still private practitioners in most groups of professionals, but their importance and strength in the profession has declined in many cases. As regards engineers this was already evident early in the 20th century; as regards doctors it became evident during the first half of the 20th century, and regarding lawyers it has gradually become more visible.

In the new professions, such as social work, there has never been a period of private practitioner dominance. They are seldom in the market even as consultants. Thus they have never been able to fall back on the main supports of the older professions, claims to status and remuneration. To quite another degree, the new professions have been the victims of their creators. When in demand they have been amply remunerated, as in the case of computer programmers or of social workers, the numbers of which consequently multiplied. However, these professions lost their appeal when the winds of collective demand changed. And these winds have changed. Among the victims have been the newly created professions, especially those created by the state, who rarely have means for their self-assertion. Some professionals have thus become part of a lower professional stratum, while others have risen to heights as professional elites.

The Relation Between Status, Resources and Influence of Professionals

Institutions and the formation of professional elites

Elites are only elites in relation to an institutional setting. If we regard professionals as only non-bureaucratised groups, they cannot form part of elites in the most commonly used sense of this concept.

Consequently, we may note, professionals are not mentioned at all in most of the contributions to the volume *Elites and Power in British Society*. They may be mentioned as fathers of men of property,[12] but the only connection in which they occur in their own capacity is in politics, where they are mentioned (like the working class) as the point of social origin of some MPs.[13] Not even in the chapter on university education is professional schooling a subject matter. The key question is which universities people have attended. The content of education is hardly discussed.[14]

It is necessary to make this clear, because differences between social settings are great in this respect. If we turn our attention to France, it is education at certain schools that is relevant for the elite. The elite is discussed mainly in terms of schooling, and the schools in question are such that give professional schooling, according to English terminology. The *ENA*, the *Polytechnique*, the *Ecole Normale*, the *Ecole Centrale* and the rest of the *grandes écoles* are those that are discussed when one wants to define membership in French elites after 1789. For a long period a training in the prestigious *Polytechnique* was intended to prepare people for posts in the civil service. As transfers to the private sector grew in number, a process known as '*pantouflage*', it became accepted that some students went directly into the private sector, but the rule has remained that the highest prestige is connected with going to the 'application schools' attached to the *Polytechnique*, especially the *Ecole de mines*, leading into public bureaucracy. However, pantouflage has not disappeared, which means that there is much movement from the public to elite positions in the private sector. In the private sector these people have become leading industrialists or leaders of commercial firms, nowadays usually in a position as *president-directeur général (PDG)*.[15]

It is significant that people with an education in a technical professional school, like the *Polytechnique*, a teachers training institute, like the *Ecole Normale*, or an institute dominated by professional management, like the *ENA*, should belong to the public administrative elite and to the political elite of France. Of course, it is partly misleading to call these institutions professional schools. They are elite schools, where special training is presupposed and a very special competition takes place before anyone is admitted. Only very few students are accepted in these schools each year - a tiny number compared to the numbers studying at the universities.[16] However, as regards the content of education, these schools are professional schools, and it is noteworthy that this elite professionalism more or less automatically leads into the economic and political elites of society.

The German system represents another model. While the curriculum in the elite institutions of Oxford and Cambridge may have caused the studying of Greek and Latin to become associated with the British elite, *Bildung* was emphasised in 19th century Germany in a broad sense which clearly included the professions. Professionalism was regarded as one of the important links between property and culture. However, professionals were not immediately recognised as belonging to the elite - and are still not so - even though they were regarded as being in the same bourgeois stratum as the wealthy.[17] Some engineers might climb into that elite, but then they had to use the means that capital set at their disposal rather than the mere professional education provided by the state. This latter type of ascendancy is and has been still more evident in Sweden, where there existed no real *Bildungsbürgertum* in the 19th century that corresponded to the German cultural elite. In fact, professionals were never really part of the cultural elite after the middle of the 19th century, but a cleavage seems to have arisen between academics and professionally active people, with only university professors of medicine being classed in both categories. Engineers, especially the *civilingenjörer* with a diploma from one of the top engineering institutes, had a very high standing in general but, as in Germany, they had to use the capitalist organisations in order to become members of a real elite.

The three systems for integrating professionals in society - the British, the French and the German-Swedish - corresponded to different means of identification for the professionals. Siegrist has shown that there is no clear-cut model that has been dominant in the long history of professions,[18] but gradually the three models became more dominant.

In Britain, with its tradition of the master-apprentice relationship, professions were more guild-like than they became on the Continent and in Scandinavia in the 19th century, and it became natural to cede professional status to the membership of a professional body which had an official authorisation or an informal social approbation.[19]

In France the establishment of the *grandes écoles* in the 19th century meant a new phase in professionalism in the fields affected by these schools. The students of each school were closely knit together. Their allegiance was with the school and its students, and their main working loyalties were with other *anciens élèves* of their school. Professional associations were formed but, at least in some cases, were weak instruments for policy formation.[20]

The third model was developed in Germany and Sweden and probably in other countries as well. There, professionals initially attached their standing as professionals to their education within a state-sponsored system of education which gradually gave more and more place to the education of professionals at specific types of schools, or specific courses at universities. It is important that professionalism was attached to the type of school rather than to the specific school attended. Professional associations were formed as instruments for lobbying, but membership in these associations was not the source for a professional status.[21]

In this way professionalism was transformed according to the social conditions given in each country. As has been emphasised recently in several contexts,[22] there was more than one model for professionalisation and there was no single professional standing in society. Among professionals some groups got a high-ranking elite position in their society, while others did not come very far up the social ladder. The social constraints, evoked through state and capital, affected different groups in different ways.

Changes in Tools and Arenas

Thus, on the whole, professionals are not members of elites in their societies. Occasionally, professionals may become members of the elite, and more often so in France than in the other countries mentioned here, but professionals normally belong to a stratum in society below the elite. Depending on the definitions mentioned above - if professionalism is merely the result of a strategy or if a successful strategy is regarded as part of the preconditions for professionalism - we may even find that some of the professions are not even clearly in a stratum that is far above white-collar workers in its most general sense. The relevant term in French is *employés*, which language has a more developed terminology in this area than English.

In spite of this fact, i.e. the non-elite status of typical professionals, it is important to note that this does not mean that the influence of professionals in society has stagnated or diminished. Rather, many people seem to think that the influence of professionals in society has been growing for a long time and that it is still increasing. This may be due to several factors. I will not discuss two of the obvious ones, but they have to be mentioned. First, an increasing influence may depend on growing numbers in the professions, which may make their penetration of society more effective. There seem to be reasons for this expectation in many professions in Western Europe. Second, an increasing influence may depend on the creation of new professions, which may be the outcome of successful exclusionary strategies in specific groups. But it may also be related to state policies, specifically regarding education and industrial policies. Obviously, these two reasons for an increasing professional influence are not mutually exclusive, and it seems most probable that the professionals, as an aggregate, and the professions, as collectivities, may have had an increasing influence in society during the last two hundred years. However, what is specifically interesting here is not this general trend, but rather the differential developments in respect to the influence of professional groups, as collectivities that may be discerned and the reasons for such differences.

In order to discuss further this development and the influences from the surrounding world which have influenced professions, I will introduce the two concepts 'arenas' and 'tools'. By 'arena' I understand the social setting in which professionals communicate their crafts to clients, other professionals and other groups. 'Tools' is used to denote the instruments of divers kinds which are used by professionals, which may be necessary for the practice of a specific profession and may play an important role in the communication between professional and client, between professionals or between professionals and other groups.

Lawyers seem to have had the most stable development of all the professions. Their standing in society has been constant. They have enjoyed a high prestige in all countries discussed here, and this prestige seems not to have changed much over the last two hundred years. The tools for the practice of their professional activities have not changed much. No new technology has substantially changed the conditions for either barristers, public attorneys, judges or solicitors. Computerisation has meant an increase in productivity for helpers in the offices, but has not really affected the productivity of the lawyers themselves, who have remained dependent on their knowledge of laws and rules and the application of society's normative basis in specific cases. Further, their arenas have continued to be the same. They negotiate on a person-to-person level on one hand, and have access, in different capacities, to the courtroom on the other. More specialised courts have developed, but fundamentally the same media persist for the professional activities of the lawyers.

Engineers have, to an extent, subdivided into specialities but seem content, not necessarily individually, but collectively, to compete on a broader basis for their employment. There is a wide variety of social standing ascribed to engineers. It is different between societies: it is high in France, Germany and Sweden, and in all those countries where a high priority is given to education and relatively low in Britain. It has also changed considerably over the past two hundred years. Engineers were not recognised professionally until around 1880,[23] when they started to become necessary for industrial performance and became attached in large numbers to the industrial firms as salaried employees. Before that, they were regarded either as proprietors and capitalists rather than as engineers, or as machine-producing craftsmen and engine operators, as they have tended to remain in Britain. Note for instance the name 'Amalgamated Engineers' for a trade union of such workers.[24] From the turn of the century the prestige of engineers has tended to stabilise, over a rather broad spectrum in all countries, but still a difference has persisted between Britain and the rest.

As already mentioned, in France, the prestige of professionals and primarily of engineers was connected with certain institutes of education rather than with the level of education, and certainly not with its connection to research. In Germany - and following in its train, in Sweden - engineers have been subdivided less by specific institute than by level of education. This distinction was already established in the first half of the 19th century in Germany,[25] and in Sweden a plan to this effect was formally decided upon in 1851, and has been in effect since then even though slightly altered a couple of decades later.[26] In both these cases a connection between engineering and science became important, and the equality of engineering institutes with universities, including their right to confer doctoral degrees, was deemed crucial. The elevation of the German polytechnics to *Technische Hochschulen* in the 1870s was one step (followed in Sweden by the *Tekniska högskolan* in 1877), and the *Akademisierung* was gradually upgraded by the right to confer doctoral degrees, first bestowed by the Kaiser on the Berlin *Technische Hochschule* in 1899. In Sweden this happened in 1927.

The tools used by engineers were developed considerably during this period. Gradual improvement in the instruments for design were created during the 19th and early 20th centuries. The technology of calculation also gradually improved, though fundamental changes were not at hand before World War II. The post-war period, especially since 1960, has seen a revolution in the means available for engineers. Both design and calculation have leapt forward through micro-electronics and a new integration of industrial production with other potential applications, even though CAD-CAM computing was not even imagined two decades ago. The improvement in the quality of tools has been of benefit throughout Western Europe.

The arenas of engineers have also changed considerably. Industrial enterprise is a broad type of organisation, in which many engineers have worked, but the nature of industrial enterprise has changed - as have the other kinds of organisations in which engineers have become involved. The size of firms has changed. The departmental organisation has developed, and in some cases become superseded by an organisation by divisions. Furthermore, the shop floor, where many engineers have had their actual place of work, has changed in shape and content, and staffs have been modernised and then again been fragmented and recreated in new forms. Hierarchies in firms have changed in rigour, size and internationality.

In short, the arenas of engineers have developed in many ways. Their tools have changed fundamentally during the last decades but previously they had already been the object of continuous improvement, and their prestige has varied immensely between societies and periods. It is, however, clear that the institutional differences have been the only one of these three factors to vary between societies, and it should therefore be possible to explain a good portion of the variation on a societal level.

As regards doctors and nurses it is significant that educational institutions for doctors have changed little during this period, as has their prestige. There was a difference, both in training and in standing, between surgeons and physicians in the 17th and 18th centuries. The main source of this distinction, that surgeons were not looked upon as real doctors and had their origin in the despised occupations of barber and military barber-surgeon, had almost disappeared in the early 19th century. The two groups, surgeons and physicians, tended to expand together, and both were trained in a university faculty of medicine in the West European system of education.[27] Nurses, however, were a late creation; they originated from the need of assistance by doctors in late 19th century hospitals. They soon made efforts to cut the bonds with other nursing assistants by emphasising their education, knowledge and special personal attributes, and were rewarded with some prestige. They were not given a university level education until the 1960s, but had their own training schools of a different quality.

The tools with which doctors have practised their profession have developed enormously during the last two hundred years. From a rather simple set of tools the doctor's kit has become a real emporium of diverse instruments. Since the beginning of the 20th century only hospitals have been able to afford all of the equipment that has become needed. X-ray apparatuses, laboratory aids, a variety of surgical instruments etc, have been developed as well as a wide variety of drugs and pharmaceuticals to be used according to indications.

This enormous development of the tools for the doctor's profession has not had a real counterpart in the tools for nurses. They have had the use of some traditional tools, and have been allowed to assist doctors in the use of several new instruments and drugs without being allowed to use these themselves. Their standing has been more dependent on their position in the nursing hierarchy (with assistant nurses and nursing assistants and sometimes also other personnel to manage) than on the application of their knowledge-base in an independent way. Some nurses have had this function, (for instance district nurses) but they have never been allowed to use the whole range of new tools and apparatuses that were at the disposal of doctors.

The arenas for both doctors and nurses have been fairly constant. Doctors have worked as private practitioners, state-sponsored provincial private practitioners, in some countries at least, and as hospital doctors in different hierarchical positions. They have met their patients in slightly different settings, but the relation between doctor and patient has always been the core thing. This relation is by definition an individual one. Nurses have less often than doctors been able to work on their own as private practitioners or district nurses, but have mostly been dependent on employing doctors or employing hospitals, where they have been subordinated to doctors or organised in a system in which doctors have been their superiors. However they have also met patients in an individual relationship, and have been able to support their claim to professionalism by being widely acquainted with patients.

In sum, doctors have gained an enormous wealth of new tools for their profession during the last two hundred years, while they have been practising in much the same kind of arena situation. Their clients/patients have been, mainly, individuals. The same applies to nurses, except that they have not gained use of a substantial part of the new facilities that have been developed in the medical sector.

State, Capital, Tools and Arenas

The scattered instances given here show, in spite of their non-scientific randomness, that institutions, tools and arenas have varied considerably for professions and professionals during the last two hundred years. State and capital have played important roles in the formation of the conditions and the environment of professions. The systematic pattern, however, is not immediately clear.

While the state has created important educational institutions for professions in most countries, capital has been a prime mover as far as arenas is concerned. This conclusion, however, does not take the welfare professions in the post-World War II era into consideration. In this period the state created the main arena for the new professions of social workers (of different kinds). There is, however, one important difference between this period and the professions created then, and the arena creations of capitalism at the beginning of the century. Capitalism did not create its professions from nothing; they already existed in a different form. The state, however, started out from virtually nothing. Some of the earlier state creations may even be seen just as precursors of the same invention. This may be turned to say that while capital has been content with manipulating an existing market, the state has been able and willing to create new markets for professionals out of nothing.

On the other hand, with regard to professions capital has been more profoundly interested in tools than in the professions themselves. Tools, instruments and apparatuses have been marketable, and the professions have been the market, or - in the case of employed professionals - have decided the need in the market where organisations have been the purchasers. This is how doctors finally came to the interest of capital. Their activity, their patient-centred relations with their clients as individuals were nothing that could create markets.

Conclusion: Constraints for Autonomy in Environments

Professions have not been constants but the objects of historical pressures for change and the subjects of development. There are several different variables. Society, represented by formal structures in the state network and capitalistic firms, has created arenas where professionals could perform their arts. But some of these arenas, such as the civil service or private industrial enterprise, have been under continuous change while others have been rather constant like the court. The professionals have had to orient themselves in new worlds all the time, not only as private citizens but also when practising their professions. Professional content has not been exactly the same from period to period during these circumstances.

The individual-related professions, such as doctors and nurses, have a more constant content in one sense than the professions which may have individuals or collectivities as their clients, where clients may as well be employers. Collectivities have tended to be dominant as employers and, in the professions that are suited to being collectivity-oriented, they have become the dominating clients, buying the services or the labour of the professionals.

In this development professionals have not only had one strategy to employ, the strategy of exclusionary closure. They have applied it with success in some cases, but the application by nurses achieved no great gain. Only when combining it with trade union strategies and aiming at specific advantages available for other groups - usurpation in Frank Parkin's terminology - they have succeeded in getting more payment. It is questionable, however, if their professional standing has improved or not by this change of strategy. The trade union strategy is, however, a common instrument among professions, at least since World War II. Doctors apply it, engineers apply it, but all tend to play the professional first and not show off that they are also trade unions.

The focus of interest that capitalism has thrown on some professions rather than others should not deceive. In many cases it has more to do with the means they use than with their services. The market for instruments may be important, but professions are important to others primarily for their services. If their spell over their clients vanishes, professionals can use neither one nor the other of their strategies.

This may serve as a last uncontrollable variable. Knowledge seems to be of use. That is the foundation of the power of the professions. It is probably also the reason for the weak influence of the social workers. Their clients do not see that social workers have a special knowledge or skill that is of value to them. It is just the employers - the state or local community - that wants to find an applied value in these professionals. By contrast, doctors, engineers, nurses, lawyers have, all of them, a wide recognition by clients. Their work is respected, rightly or wrongly.

Only the strategy of exclusion applied in specific societies such as those of mid-19th century Western Europe will produce strong, autonomous professions. Society has changed. Professions have been forced into new situations by capital as well as by the state. Professions have applied new strategies and professionals have been tempted to apply strategies of their own. This is the lesson that history teaches about professions: that changing social environments have brought different constraints to the autonomy of professions.

Chapter 3

'Bending with the Breeze'

Political Preferences and Institutional Reforms in the Modern University
System - A Case Study

Olof Ruin

During the past quarter-century, Sweden's universities and colleges, like the higher
education systems of most other western countries, have been engulfed by a great variety
of reforms and reforming ideas. The spirit of the age has varied. The academic world
has proved sensitive to trends, while at the same time constituting in itself a highly
distinctive organisation and sector of society. The development of universities and
colleges, as a result, has come to reflect general developmental tendencies in society.
These tendencies have been capable of operating both concurrently and consecutively.
Some of them have actually resembled swings of the pendulum.

My own experience of these tendencies has varied somewhat, due to my point of
vantage in the Swedish university system. During the past quarter-century I have come
to be active at various levels of a many-tiered Swedish university system. But my
starting and finishing points are the chairmanship of one university department: the
Department of Political Science at Stockholm University. My first chairmanship came
in 1966 and now, at the beginning of the 1990s, I am back again in an appointment
which I have held on several different occasions during the intervening quarter of a
century. This makes it natural for me, when discussing the reforms and reforming ideas
which have swept through the Swedish university community in past decades, to focus
on a particular university department, my own. The division of Swedish universities
into separate basic units, corresponding to American departments, appeared relatively
late, but it was fully developed by the mid-1960s.

In this essay I will confine myself to six developmental tendencies in society during
the past quarter-century. These are:

(1) Planning

(2) Democratisation

(3) Corporativisation

(4) Decentralisation

(5) Re-professionalisation

(6) Marketisation

How, then, have these trends, characterising both society as a whole and universities and colleges as a sector in their own right, been experienced and observed in what remains the shop floor of the universities, the individual department?

Planning

Planning in the mid-1960s was quite obviously one of the catchwords of social debate in Sweden. Social reform accelerated during what have retrospectively come to be known as 'the record years' of post-war Swedish history. It became common to refer to programmes of different kinds, to express oneself in terms of goals and means, to call for more long-term perspectives and coordination in public activities. A succession of institutional changes were made for the encouragement of this planning work. Government departments - ministries - were reorganised from the inside.[1] A series of new national authorities, separate from the ministries, were set up. The ambits of these authorities were enlarged. In this connection, universities and colleges also acquired a central planning and coordinating authority, when the ancient office of the Chancellor of the Universities of Sweden was developed into a regular national administrative board, known for short as *UKÄ*.

The 'planning' of an individual university department in Sweden in the mid-1960s was still determined by a completely unregulated intake of students. Intake was high everywhere in the country, but in the Department of Political Science in Stockholm it amounted almost to an explosion. Political science as a subject had become popular and well-known, partly as a result of a successful radio course. First-time enrolments for one term's studies were 508 in the autumn of 1964, 721 in the autumn of 1965, no less than 825 in the autumn of 1966, and so it went on. For some years the department was the second largest of all university departments in Sweden, regardless of faculty and locality. Large premises had to be rented in town for lectures and examinations. The main hall of the *Norra Latin* high school in down-town Stockholm was barely sufficient for welcoming newly enrolled students. The newcomers crowded along the walls and in the doorway. New money for recruiting extra teachers chinked forth as the number of new enrollees went on rising. Teachers for courses whose intake was frequently doubled at the very last minute almost had to be hunted down in the highways and byways. It was remarkable - and in a way impressive - that this department, like many others in the university community, was still able to cope with such an uncontrolled onslaught. Sometimes, though, the mass production seemed unsatisfactory and frightening.

Towards the end of the 1960s it became clear that all the talk in the community at large about the importance of more active planning was also going to leave its mark on the higher education system. The newly established UKÄ began playing the part envisaged for it from the very outset. An official at the Office had been entrusted with the task of investigating the question of centrally-regulated combinations of subjects in social sciences, as well as in humanities and natural sciences. This resulted in the first of the so-called *UKAS* proposals. And the Chancellor of the Universities became one of the three directors-general who, together with the Under-Secretary of State at the Ministry of Education, formed an inner circle in a Government Commission called *U68*, set up to investigate all aspects - research excepted - of Swedish higher education. The recruitment of that Commission, with its emphasis on officialdom, seemed to deviate from what had been the regular practice in Sweden's extensive fabric of official inquiries. In itself, though, it was an eloquent expression of the technocratic planning mentality of the 1960s.[2]

During the early 1970s, while the work of the U68 Commission was progressing at national level, a change took place in the concrete planning situation of individual university departments such as the Department of Political Science in Stockholm. The tremendous influx of students in the previous decade gave way to a shortage of first-time enrollees. For one thing, the size of the student population generally declined somewhat in the country as a whole, while above all, political science came to be less popular, relatively speaking, because it had not been made the first subject in any of the combinations of studies recommended under the - somewhat emasculated - UKAS system. This brought a quick change of attitude. A department which, only a few years earlier, had been virtually inundated by students, now had to learn new habits and begin actively marketing itself and promoting its distinctive subject interests.

A regular, classically political contest developed on the 'shop floor' of the universities between different subject departments in preparation for the anticipated national policy decisions on intake restrictions and the creation of closely integrated study programmes. Efforts were made by each department to secure representation within different study groups and committees and to secure territory for one's own subject in the multidisciplinary courses or integrated study programmes which were being discussed. People both formed coalitions and tried to checkmate each other. Departments given responsibility for large parts of study programmes and courses inspired both admiration and envy. In these aspirations, the Department of Political Science behaved no differently from other departments, even though its representatives, with their experience of analysing conflicts of interest in the community at large, could give a smile of recognition at the look of things in their own immediate surroundings.

During the 1980s the planning situation for a single subject department became stabilised insofar as undergraduate studies were divided into programmes and single-subject courses between which, admission capacity permitting, students could choose freely. To begin with, though, there was a good deal of concern lest a department like the Department of Political Science, based above all on single-subject courses, would not be able to survive as a vigorous entity. Perhaps the places allocated under the system of intake restrictions would not be taken up; perhaps potential students would tend more and more to opt for closely integrated study programmes.

This has not happened. For one thing, one finds the individual students still choosing single subject studies, even at the price of submitting to an absurd system of admissions: when a course is over-subscribed, selections are made by the drawing of lots. Then again, the existence of many study programmes made up of different pieces joined together has been found to pose problems. One such programme was Government Administration, for which a special programme institution, known as the Government Administration College, was established in Stockholm during the 1980s. At the end of the 1980s the board of the Stockholm University decided to dissolve this multidisciplinary department and transfer the hosting of the study programme to the Department of Political Science. That decision could be termed symbolic of the survival capacity of subject departments in spite of all attempts at dividing up university activities on different bases.

Today, in the early 1990s, planning is seldom a buzzword in social debate. If anything, the accepted practice is to stress the uncertainty of different forms of planning. In contrast to the mood of the late 1960s, people often tend to be ironic about the possibilities of setting programmes for different sectors of society. What is more, they challenge the possibilities of unequivocally selecting means conducive to the realisation of certain predefined aims, and they often doubt whether anything defined centrally will ever be realised locally. With the prevailing restriction of student intake, however, the planning situation of an individual university department today is simpler than it was 20 years ago. Our knowledge of future needs is far more reliable today than it used to be.

Democratisation

Demands for greater influence, more democracy, flared up in different sectors of society during the late 1960s, in organisations and companies, at artistic establishments and in hospitals, in prisons and in army units and so on. Nowhere, however, were those demands so audible and palpable as in the university community. A wave of student unrest swept through the world, reaching Sweden in May 1968.[3]

In fact it all began in the Department of Political Science in Stockholm. A group of students, angered by a drastic statement of one of the teachers in the department, delivered a harsh verbal attack on teaching and required reading. Mass meetings were organised, the students asked for studies to be differently organised, and above all they demanded more say in the running of the department. For a few days we received intensive media coverage, and the Ministry of Education responded. But the revolt soon went elsewhere. The Student Union building in Holländargatan, Stockholm, was occupied and after the occupation was over a procession of shouting students made its way down towards Gustav Adolfs Torg - and the Opera House - following the 'revolutionary agenda' set by the Sorbonne students in Paris a couple of weeks earlier. Among those mounting the rostrum in the Student Union building and flocking through the town we recognised a rather impressive number of political science students. The unrest in Stockholm quickly spread to other universities and colleges in Sweden.

When this unrest suddenly engulfed the university community, the decision-making machinery operating in Swedish university departments was only a couple of years old. All formal decision-making powers were still vested in a head of department, but at the same time he had to consult a departmental advisory board. This in turn included all teachers affiliated to a department, as well as two student representatives. I recall these gatherings as large and unwieldy, with a feeling of uncertainty about the apportionment of authority between the chairman and other participants. The head of department had to both listen and reconcile differing opinions but at the same time assume sole responsibility.

In June 1968, fairly quickly after the disturbances in Stockholm, the Office of the Chancellor of the Swedish Universities sent the Government a letter concerning powers, under the current Universities Statute, to experiment with new decision-making procedures. In other words, the central authority, with its current ambitions of planning and coordinating, took upon itself the task, in the spirit of 1968, of stage-managing experiments in wider democracy.[4] Various decision-making models were constructed for use in the field.

The Department of Political Science in Stockholm University received special treatment. We were given permission to follow a special constitution which we ourselves had set about framing fairly soon after the disturbances in May 1968. One distinctive feature of that constitution was the insertion of an organisational tier between an executive committee and the employees and students. We were suffused with the principles of representative democracy. Policy-making mass meetings were anathema. Instead we took sidelong glances at the construction of other units in the community - a municipality, an interest organisation and so on. This intermediate tier, peculiar to ourselves and dubbed the departmental council, acquired the character of a representative assembly, a miniature parliament. It consisted of student representatives, elected with courses and seminar groups as constituencies, and all members of the departmental staff. Individual proposals were put forward in the form of motions on which the executive committee elected by the council had to make pronouncements. The various proposals from the executive committee, in their turn, were drafted by different committees on which teachers and students were equally represented, and so on. To accommodate all of us, the rooms in which we met had to be fairly large, especially as the student representatives initially demanded gallery accommodation for fellow-students who were not on the council.

Learning to live with this new decision-making procedure took time. Discussions in the departmental council were protracted and frequently got bogged down on points of order or else on highly concrete problems. One frequently recurring problem of this kind was the suitability of individual publications in the reading lists put forward for approval. I remember, for example, that a lot of energy was devoted to a book like Seymour Martin Lipset's *Political Man*. Demands were constantly being made for a guillotine and a final list of speakers; meetings kept having to be adjourned because of insufficient attendance. We were sticklers for form. Teachers brought up in an old-fashioned public-servant tradition sometimes felt rather out of place in a decision-making climate where various coalitions, many of them unholy, were formed, while others - myself among them - with previous personal experience of student politics felt more at home and recalled various dodges from the student union debates and meetings of their youth.

This 'democratisation' in the spirit of the day naturally incorporated various conflicts of principle. On the one hand, teachers and researchers were expected, as public employees, to comply with central directives, while on the other hand they were also expected to comply with decisions made by the shop-floor collective of which they formed part. There were cases of these local decisions conflicting with the centrally issued directives. Furthermore, many teachers and researchers, by virtue of their education and long experience, possessed unchallengeable expert knowledge on matters which had to be decided, yet their hands could be tied by decisions directly contradicting that knowledge. On the one hand, teachers and researchers were assumed, for decision-making purposes, to be on a level with representatives of students and young researchers at the beginning of their career, while on the other hand the latter were really quite dependent on the former. On the one hand, all members of the community, through their taxes, financed the activities of the universities and for this reason surely ought to be entitled to influence these activities, while on the other teachers and researchers, as producers, and students, as consumers, were allotted especially powerful influence, and so on. These and other contradictions of principle, however, were seldom referred to by name. For the most part people just grumbled and got on with the job, in the best pragmatic Swedish tradition of trying to make the whole thing work by means of compromises and various symbolic posturings.

The distinctive model of the Department of Political Science at Stockholm University could not be sustained in the long run. The time-consuming departmental council was abolished during the 1970s, and essentially the same decision-making model came to apply with us as in most other Swedish university departments. Then again, the demands put forward by students within this simpler constitution varied from year to year. Now they wanted more teaching, now they wanted less, one year they wanted more theoretical reading, another year more factual, this time they wanted different parts of a course to be taken in a certain sequence, next time they wanted a different sequence, and so on. Those teachers who have become old hands frequently remark on these fluctuations and readily recall the time when the actual demands for democracy were originally presented. They themselves feel that 1968 was only the other day, while their young listeners, courteously uninterested, feel it is pre-history.

But present-day students are not the only ones who may feel that the late 1960s are long since over and done with. There has also been a reversal of the general climate of society. In the Sweden of the early 1990s, there is less talk of grass roots and participation and more of decision-making efficiency.

Corporativisation

Corporativisation as a name for tendencies in the relations between interest organisations and the State became fashionable once again during the 1970s in political and social-science debate in the western world. The rediscovery of this concept came particularly early in the Swedish debate. Sweden has had a tradition of very strong organisations, organisations which further strengthened their position during this very decade, the 1970s. What was true of the country as a whole was perhaps even more true of its higher education system.[5]

At the end of the 1960s, fairly soon after students had presented demands for more influence in the running of the universities, similar demands were pressed by local personnel organisations on behalf of employees. The right of co-determination was looked on as a prime union issue. *UKÄ* reacted quickly and favourably. The personnel organisations not only came to organise elections of representatives of previously unrepresented employees to different bodies within the university world, they also came in their own right to be an integral part of the decision-making machinery. Thus places intended for employees *qua* employees came to be divided between the local branches of Sweden's three trade union organisations:

- *LO* (the Swedish Trade Union Confederation), basically representing manual workers

- *SACO-SR*, representing graduates and professionals

- *TCO* (the Swedish Confederation of Salaried Employees), representing salaried staff.

Another side of the growing corporativisation of the 1970s was an increasing willingness on the part of the central interest organisations to take stands on different social issues and to assume vicarious social responsibilities. Higher education policy was looked on as an important field to keep under observation and concern oneself with. Originally only SACO and the national organisation of students, *SFS*, had felt this commitment, but during the 1960s both LO and TCO as well as the employers' interest organisation, *SAF*, had come to feel increasingly involved. This involvement accelerated during the 1970s. It became regular practice for the central organisations of the labour market not only to have firm opinions on different aspects of higher education policy but also to step into decision-making functions at the various levels of higher education.

However, at the basic level of university life, the individual departments, it was not until the end of the 1970s that the corporativising tendencies of the decade became directly perceptible. Thus at the beginning of the decade, the local personnel organisations had not come to be involved in the election of employees to departmental governing bodies; teachers and administrative staff continued to elect their representatives without any union interference. But the TCO representative on a central organising committee charged with elaborating the 1975 *Riksdag* decision of principle concerning the future of the universities had, in a separate statement, advocated giving the personnel organisations within the individual departments the task of appointing employee representatives, as was customary elsewhere in the labour market. That proposal had not met with approval.

Nevertheless, the entry into force of a new law, the Co-determination Act (*MBL*), in 1977 necessitated a direct meeting between individual university departments, such as the Department of Political Science in Stockholm, and the personnel organisations. Thus, under the MBL system the departments also came to negotiate with and inform the local union organisations. Those organisations in turn appoint delegates among the employees who have the task of keeping themselves informed of what is going on within their own department. Within the Department of Political Science, direct negotiations have been held with union representatives, for example, on matters of principle concerning the allocation of duties and facilities.

In the 1960s and early 1970s, the Stockholm Department of Political Science, as the first subject department to incur demands for more democracy, had above all equated those demands with 'student democracy'. During the 1970s and 1980s this department, like all others in the country, came to be characterised by what may be termed 'corporate democracy'.

Decentralisation

Decentralisation developed during the 1970s into a central reforming strategy for the public sectors of several welfare states. This development was rooted both in a desire to bring different types of decision-making closer to the people directly affected, and also in the notion that central institutions were staggering under an excessive workload. In both scientific analysis and social debate generally, it became a commonplace that the central institutions of welfare states were suffering from overload, with all this implied in terms of inefficiency. In Sweden too, the higher education sector came to be very much affected by this conscious bid for decentralisation.

It began with the central administrative board, renamed *UHÄ* (the National Board of Universities and Colleges). In future, the Board was expected to interfere less with the detailed regulation of the 'private lives' of different universities and colleges than, for example, had been the case with the centrally directed experiment in new decision-making procedures at the end of the 1960s. Instead the emphasis was to be on such tasks as investigation, evaluation, follow-up, information, service and so on, all of which were duties of a kind which eventually would also come to dominate the everyday lives of several other national agencies.[6]

Earlier, when the central authority was known as UKÄ, it had, from the vantage point of a single university department, appeared as a very palpable power in the land.

The Chancellor of the Universities, viewed in this light, had had almost the status of an omnipotent deity, and his associates that of demigods when, from time to time, they descended from their Olympian heights to visit 'the field'. Individual university departments, therefore, had for their part been very intent on maintaining their contacts with UKÄ so as to keep themselves informed of events and be more able to influence the handling of specific questions. A change occurred at the end of the 1970s. The central authority, with its new and different tasks, seemed to vanish into the mist from the vantage point of individual departments. Contacts with UHÄ began to seem rather pointless. The Board's own personnel, for their part, began to feel bewildered and uncertain, isolated as they had come to be from 'the field' over which they had once had so much influence through the implementation of laws, the allocation of funds and the scrutiny of different programmes.

A lot of the things formerly decided by UKÄ on a day-to-day basis now became the responsibilities of individual universities and colleges. As a result, their central governing bodies, as well as their central administration, should also have begun - once again, from the viewpoint of an individual university department - to seem increasingly worth cultivating. Something of the kind did happen, but to less of an extent than had been expected.

One reason for this was that the bid for decentralisation resulting in the transfer of decision-making powers from central, national authorities to various higher education establishments came in turn to be repeated within those establishments. Just as the central administrative authority might formerly have seemed overburdened with duties, it has also been possible to discern overload on the part of individual universities and their various governing bodies. In this atmosphere, any number of matters have, quite simply, been left to individual university departments to decide. To a great extent, then, the departments are expected to run their own affairs. This also applies to the hard core of an organisation's activities: decisions concerning the funds at the organisation's disposal. Under the principles of programme budgeting applied since the end of the 1970s, individual departments have acquired quite extensive liberty in this respect in relation to the governing bodies of their university or college. True, there are pre-defined aims to which funds must be applied; but just as there have often been cases where the central leadership of universities, when lacking funds for what are considered indispensable purposes, has felt obliged to distribute allocated funds on a different basis from that envisaged in nationally defined objectives, similar shifts of emphasis have been possible in the deployment by individual departments of the funds allotted to them by the funding authority of their own university. Financial administration in Swedish higher education today has in fact acquired a baffling complexity.

Another reason why the individual university department today perhaps has less day-to-day contact than one might expect with superior levels within its own university is the structure of those levels. They are inchoate. In principle, the 1977 reform did not leave a coherent intermediate level at Swedish universities. Various committees - the study programme committee and the board of faculty respectively - were expected to take charge of undergraduate studies and graduate studies/research. But in many parts of the Swedish university sector in recent years, there have been moves to amalgamate these entities, even though this has not yet happened within the Social Science Faculty of Stockholm University. As a result of this division into different agencies, nobody at the intermediate level of the university feels really responsible for individual departments as a whole. True, there exists an integrated top level for the university in the form of a University board chaired by the Vice-Chancellor. But the university board as such often plays no more than a symbolic role; it is heterogeneously composed and any amount of its business is delegated to the Office of the Vice-Chancellor. The latter in turn is divided into two parts: a Vice-Chancellor recruited from the university teaching staff and appointed for a fixed term, and a senior official who heads the administration. This office, of course, is not capable, should it even aspire to doing so, of maintaining a continuous dialogue with all the basic units of a large university. In deciding its standpoints it, just like study programme committees and faculty boards is greatly dependent on the reports presented by various full-time administrators. And so it is primarily to these persons that an individual department will turn whenever it wishes to make contact with superior levels in its own immediate surroundings.

As a result of the conscious bid for decentralisation in recent years, then, an individual Swedish university department today leads a much more independent life than did its predecessors a quarter of a century ago. It has extensive control over cash flows, it makes its own assessments of the new posts which need to be created, it has more to say than it used to concerning the content and focus of its study programmes, and so on. The inevitable price paid for this independence is that more time now has to be devoted to administrative duties on the 'ground floor' of the universities. This is borne out by the Department of Political Science at Stockholm University - a department with a budget of just over 10 million SEK and a staff of about 50. This, moreover, is a subject department, but at the same time today it also hosts a study programme. The technical and administrative staff today has about ten members. In addition, more than five teachers have quite a considerable administrative workload over and above their teaching and research duties.

In recent decades it has been widely asserted that the university world is getting more bureaucratic. As a rule, this ambiguous term has denoted three things: growing complexity of the actual rules of decision-making, an increasing amount of time devoted to administrative duties, and a growth of influence wielded by full-time administrators. Many of these allegations of increasing bureaucracy have implied a vertical dimension, the idea being that the tendencies deplored are mostly operating at levels superior to the basic one where the critics themselves live and have their being. But the greater independence of the university departments and the concomitant duty on their part of diversifying their business also calls for a different perspective on what is referred to as bureaucratisation. Even at the basic level, the rules of decision-making have grown more complicated and more time is now having to be devoted to administrative duties. This has meant more influence being wielded by those who at this level devote themselves entirely - or extensively - to administrative duties.

Reprofessionalisation

Reprofessionalisation is the term I choose to apply to a social trend which in itself is more vague and elusive than those previously dealt with. This trend is assumed to include emphasis on such values as knowledge and competence. The trend began to make itself felt during the second half of the 1970s as a reaction against the mood of the 1960s, with its emphasis on equality as a central, overriding value. It is natural that this revival of interest in knowledge and competence, occurring as part of the general social debate, should elicit a response in the university world - a world in which the production of knowledge is a prime concern, and where the issue of competence is central.

This trend helped to bring about a shift in the attention which during the 1980s came to be devoted to undergraduate studies and graduate studies/research respectively. Two decades ago, under the impact of the tremendous influx of new students during the 1960s, undergraduate studies quite clearly occupied the focal point of interest in the university world, while research and research training attracted less attention, even though important decisions affecting postgraduate studies had been taken in 1969. The U68 Commission too operated entirely in the perspective of undergraduate studies. A decade later the situation had changed. At the same time as social debaters once more began referring to the necessity of competence and expertise, there was a decline of interest in undergraduate studies and a growth of interest in research and graduate education. Several official inquiries at the national level, mostly employing a research and postgraduate perspective, suggested improvements. [7]

Another change of attitude in the university world, also coinciding with a general social trend, was the additional emphasis put on high quality, in undergraduate studies as well as in graduate education and research. Previously, again under the impact of the heavy influx of new students during the 1960s, quantity had been the prime concern, the aim being to show that the doors of Swedish universities were wide open to all seekers after knowledge. Just over a decade later, more attention began to be paid to the necessity of the education offered and the research undertaken being of a good international standard. Quality became a buzzword. Symposia were organised and books written concerning the nature of quality in academic life and how it was to be achieved. The courses offered were condemned as being excessively brief; advanced programmes of different kinds were called for and it was said that higher standards must be set for various degree theses; and so on. There were even cases of people actually commending themselves on having centres of excellence within the integrated Swedish higher education system, which until then had made universal equality of standards one of its characteristics. An individual university department like the Department of Political Science was not unaffected by this new frame of mind. When recruiting temporary teaching staff we tried, harder than before, to ensure good formal competence. We became more willing than previously to include 'difficult' books in our teaching. In testing the eligibility of applicants for graduate studies we tried to arrive at a substantial assessment of their capability of completing a graduate programme. We laid down procedures for the coordinated scrutiny of all theses in manuscript before disputation, and so on. Attempts have also been made to bridge the unfortunate gap, typical of Swedish universities, between two categories of teacher: those serving at undergraduate level and those teaching graduates and being themselves engaged in research.

Perhaps another symptomatic expression of a spirit of the age encouraging the promotion of excellence is that many university departments today, including the Stockholm Department of Political Science, publish an annual account of their achievements during the previous year. These accounts include not only statistics concerning new enrolments, graduations, staff, teaching items etc but also data to indicate that the department is in good health and is maintaining a high standard of quality. Thus we are told about all the foreign researchers who have visited the department, the international conferences to which members of the department have been invited, the books and articles which the staff have found time to publish, the assignments they have held, and so on. With today's emphasis on good quality and competence, then, modesty is only admissible in moderation.

Marketisation

Marketisation, finally, is a trend which has also left a profound impact on the 1980s and the early 1990s. Capitalism, pronounced dead by many in the previous decades, has flourished. The principles and attitudes characteristic of private enterprise have in many respects been cited as examples to public activity. And, in delight at these workings of private enterprise, demands have been made for the direct privatisation of parts of the public sector. This characteristic trend of the past decade, like trends of earlier decades, has also affected the university sector. In a variety of ways, the presence of the market has been more strongly felt than before. One manifestation of this is all the talk, in the higher education environment as elsewhere, of the importance of leadership. True, that talk is not only characterised by developments in private enterprise but is affected by the general growth of interest during the past decade in individual leadership. That interest in turn is rooted in things like a reaction against far-reaching democratisation experiments, a sense of the paralysing complexity of organisations and a born-again belief in the ability of individuals to put things back on course. Many arguments concerning the importance of leadership in the internal life of higher education, however, are derived from private enterprise. Universities are spoken of as 'conglomerates' and university vice-chancellors are compared with 'group presidents'. Individual university departments are compared with small businesses, and heads of departments with small entrepreneurs, and so on. The leading position of a Swedish head of department has been very conspicuously strengthened in recent years.

But the most striking manifestation in Sweden of the way in which the values and attitudes of private enterprise are also to be applied to the higher education community is the principle of pay according to achievement. Rates of pay used to be basically identical for all teachers in the same category and age group. Today vice-chancellors' offices are expected to propose pay rises for individual professors who are particularly sought after in the market or are contemplating leaving Sweden, who are credited with special achievements on behalf of their higher education establishment or who are considered outstandingly skilful. The heads of department, for their part, have been requested, within certain intervals, to propose salary upgradings for departmental staff according to a judgement of their competence. The system of rewards in higher education used to be of a different and more subtle variety: election to academies and advisory committees, quotation by colleagues, students' appreciation, invitation to take part in debates, and so on. In the world of the 1980s and early 1990s, by contrast, it is felt that competence should be rewarded and encouraged with something as unambiguous and at the same time four-square as money. This is a disturbing development and one which has already engendered a variety of tensions.

Another expression of the growing proximity of the market to the higher education system is corporate 'sponsoring' of services within higher education and the sale by universities of their services to the community at large at market prices. Within the Department of Political Science too, we have had 'commissioned studies' since 1984. Courses are sold to national and local authorities, and sometimes also to companies, in subject fields where the department feels it has a good level of competence. It should be stressed, though, that these activities have deliberately been kept within fairly close bounds, so as not to jeopardise the quality of regular teaching.

Marketisation today stands out as the latest of the social tendencies which have swept through the university community during the past quarter of a century. I will not deny that, personally, I am very sceptical of the possibility of reconciling this tendency with the ideals and attitudes which have characterised university life up until now.

Summing Up

Many of the social tendencies referred to above have both indicated a reaction and created counter-reactions. Belief in the value of long-range planning has given way to scepticism of such activities; an effort to enable the individual, by various means, to take part in decision-making has been superseded by emphasis on the importance of leadership; a notion of the value of central authority and decision-making competence has been followed by tendencies towards decentralisation; a determination to promote equality has had to give way to something approaching élitism; belief in the distinctive character of public activity has been replaced by a bid for this activity to be dominated by forms of behaviour derived from private enterprise, and so on. To some extent all these tendencies have left their marks on the activities of an individual university department. One can speak of a departmental terrain littered with clearly discernible relics of the social tendencies of different decades.

The big difference between heading a university department at the beginning of the 1990s and the 1960s is connected with the radical change which has occurred in the status of these basic units. Their liberty of movement has been greatly expanded, assuming that everything develops satisfactorily and they themselves are not very small. Sometimes indeed one may feel that, despite its division into many different levels, the Swedish university world really consists above all of a host of basic units in the form of departments and an apex in the form of a Ministry of Education. Everything in between - study programme committees and faculty boards, university boards, UHÄ - fades into insignificance.

This change in the status of basic university units presents both advantages and disadvantages. One disadvantage is that these fairly strong units are very liable to become self-contained. The incentive for horizontal and interdisciplinary contacts presented by the old faculty meetings, in which all members of the permanent teaching staff of several related departments were required to attend, no longer exists either. Swedish universities, or at least the University of Stockholm, have in fact made a bad job of creating mechanisms of a kind possessed by many American universities, mechanisms promoting multidisciplinarity parallel to strong university departments. As a result, Swedish university departments are in danger of becoming self-centred. Another disadvantage of the greater independence of departments today may be that alarm signals are not transmitted fast enough when the departments mismanage themselves or are suffering from internal tensions. These basic units in themselves are still very brittle organisations. On the other hand, the great advantage of the increased liberty of movement enjoyed by individual university departments today lies in the incentives with which they are thus provided for assuming responsibility and using their own initiative. For this reason, heading such a department has come to be more fun today than it was a quarter of a century ago.

Chapter 4

Humanities as a Mirror of Society:

The 'Battle of the Historians' in the Federal Republic of Germany
in the late 1980s

Thorsten Nybom

One of the constitutive elements of German culture and intellectual life seems to be a
constant need to discuss 'fundamental principles' and 'existential dimensions' of
scholarly *wissenschafliche* activities. Usually, these intellectual disputes have had the
tendency to spill over the boundaries of traditional scholarly debate and become general
discussions of society, politics and *Kultur*. To an outsider the actual background and
frontlines of these intense struggles usually seem to be an opaque mixture of professional, theoretical and moral preferences which escapes any one-dimensional and
simple interpretation. This is one of the reasons why they are not seldom removed from
the agenda of the international scholarly debate, either as being too 'Teutonic and
speculative' to be understandable for an outsider, or as being too deeply rooted in the
particular history and political reality of 20th century Germany to be of general interest.

The fierce and drawn-out dispute over contemporary German history and historiography - the so-called '*Historikerstreit*' (Battle of the Historians) - initiated by the
Frankfurt philosopher Jürgen Habermas in the summer of 1986, was no exception to
this general rule.[1] The aggressive argument almost instantly developed into a general
discussion of future German politics, and of the moral and political implications and
responsibilities of historical research in the German setting. These particular dimensions, but also the fact that the debate soon engaged almost the entire community of
German scholars - within and outside the Federal Republic - are good enough reasons
to discuss the background, impact, significance and possible outcome of this still
continuing intellectual battle.

The need and obligation to contemplate, and indeed even try to analyse, the
developments in German intellectual life has certainly not become less imperative for
professional historians anywhere, in light of the more or less cataclysmic changes in
the political and economic geography of the European continent in recent times. But
apart from these political and human dimensions there are a number of scholarly and
professional reasons for an outsider to discuss and evaluate the '*Historikerstreit*'.

First, there is an imperative obligation for each and every historian, regardless of
his/her speciality or professional interest, to be reasonably well informed about the
ominous period 1933-45 in German and European history.

Secondly, in the '*Historikerstreit*' fundamental theoretical and ideological questions of modern cultural and social research which deeply concern all cultural scientists were brought to the fore.[2]

Thirdly, from a purely professional point of view there are obvious reasons to keep oneself informed of general developments in present-day German historical research, as one of the more expansive and interesting branches of contemporary social and cultural research. Furthermore, there has been a remarkable revival of the prestige of 'History' and historical research in German political and scholarly debate during the last decade. Once again history or the 'historical dimension' seems to have become a necessary prerequisite for the understanding and organisation of society.[3] Even if this revival must please every professional historian there is nevertheless an urgent need to contemplate the various implications of this development both in regard to the present situation and to the role played by historical research in German history.

As I have already indicated, the fundamental and principal importance of the *Historikerstreit* was not exclusively or even primarily connected with the empirical questions of the 'uniqueness' or ultimate genesis of the Holocaust, even if this and other issues of the Nazi era initially triggered off the debate and guaranteed its particular moral and emotional intensity.

It would also be incorrect to reduce the intellectual turmoil to a traditional academic struggle of power within *Die Zunft* (the guild).[4] Nor would it be adequate to analyse and understand it in purely political terms, even if deliberate and blatant political manifestations, no doubt, inspired Habermas' initial attack. In his first two articles in the prestigious weekly *Die Zeit* Habermas accused four prominent West German historians - Ernst Nolte, Andreas Hillgruber, Michael Stürmer and Klaus Hildebrand - of deliberately and persistently trying to revise or 'normalise' modern German history. He saw this as a more or less integrated part of a combined political, institutional and intellectual campaign which under the label of '*Tendenzwende*' ('turning of the intellectual tide') had been instigated in the late 1970s and was intensified in the early 1980s by people in politics and intellectual life closely affiliated with the rising 'New Conservatism' in Europe and the US.[5]

Initially this political and scholarly offensive was met by rather weak opposition. The reluctance of German scholars to react is understandable in view of the fact that it was not only supported but partly also initiated and defined by a powerful phalanx within the dominating conservative parties CDU/CSU, under the active leadership of the Chancellor himself, Doctor Helmut Kohl.[6]

The peak (or at least the most spectacular official manifestation) of this campaign was perhaps the joint appearance of Kohl and President Reagan at the military/SS cemetery at Bitburg in May 1985. The combination of naiveté and cold calculation of the Bitburg incident might seem to have been rather harmless. But this tragi-comic ceremony in remembrance of *all* the fighting men of World War II, and the following reaction, became something of a watershed in the German debate.[7] After Bitburg it seemed obvious to both German and foreign observers what Kohl and others, who like him had had the 'blessing of being born late enough',[8] actually meant by the catchword '*Tendenzwende*'. Not least important was the reaction by prominent members of the American scholarly and intellectual community.[9]

It is also important to mention that the main political target of this intellectual offensive was probably not primarily the German Social Democrats, SPD or even the rather small groups of left-wing radicals in Germany. It was rather aimed at the particular kind of enlightened liberalism and deep moral concern, that the President (and nominal fellow party member of Kohl) Richard von Weizsäcker has represented so eminently and persistently.[10] In their deep contempt of this 'obsolete' ideology which they quite correctly saw as the main obstacle to any real political and intellectual 'renewal', the Pre- and Post-Modernists were united.[11] These fundamental affinities also became apparent in the 'Historikerstreit'.

History and Politics

The following is not primarily an analysis of West German domestic politics or a detailed account of the arguments and counter-arguments of the *'Historikerstreit'* on particular historical issues partly because several excellent studies of these kinds are already to be had,[12] and also because, in my opinion, it is more important to regard the central dimension of the battle as a dispute of principle concerning the ideal nature of politics and social debate, and their epistemological values. In such a discussion it is not peculiar but perfectly natural for the focus of attention to be on the ideological and theoretical foundations of social science, and more especially those of its parent, historical research. This, then, is not peculiar to the Federal Republic with its purportedly powerful 'interference' between politics and historical research, but is something which probably is, and should be, of general validity.

It would seem fair to say that relations and the interaction between politics and historical research are far closer in the Federal Republic than they are and have been in many other Western countries. However, if one compares the Federal Republic with its predecessors on German soil in the past hundred years, this statement not only appears uncertain but downright mistaken.[13]

Thus, whereas historical research elsewhere in Western Europe at the end of the 19th century, under such banners as those of positivism and critical analysis, took a decisive step in its emancipation from everyday politics and national considerations, the neo-Rankean generation of German historians in the ascendant at that time if anything formed common front *'gegen das seichte Aufklärungsdenken und den Positivismus'* (against the shallow thinking of the Enlightenment and against Positivism!), placing historical research directly in the service of the expansionist German nation state.[14]

This intellectual *'Sonderentwicklung'* (Unique development) came to have prolonged and harmful consequences for German historical research. This goes a long way towards explaining the none too honourable part played by the discipline during both the inter-war years and after 1933. There are, admittedly, only a few Martin Heideggers to be found in academic historical research, but even so, no difficulties whatsoever were experienced by living in supreme harmony with the new order.[15]

Then, from the early 1960s, in the Federal Republic, there began a gradual transformation of German historical research into a 'normal' western discipline, and in this process it is fair to say that the great 'Fischer Controversy' over German policy before and during World War I, for all its vindictiveness and political overtones, constituted a species of research ideological 'matriculation' and a disciplinary milestone. Thenceforth, pluralism in the theory and ideology of science, as well as intra-disciplinary criticism, came to be acknowledged as a necessary and natural component of a humanities discipline in which, although political implications and preferences are always more or less inevitable, there should be no political obligations.[16]

'Paradigmatically', i.e. in terms of conventions and overtones for societal and scientific discourse, therefore, there is no longer any essential difference between the

Federal Republic and other liberal western democracies. But the Federal Republic does differ from most other western countries in that its latter-day history necessarily requires a constant and active defence and recodifying of these epistemological and emancipatory advances. Thus the somewhat delayed but vehement reaction against the different but co-varying revision attempts by Ernst Nolte, Michael Stürmer and others in the late 1970s and early 1980s was not primarily an expression of exaggerated 'concern for popular education' or an attempt to establish a politically conditioned, morally motivated 'question ban' in latter-day German historical research. If anything it should be taken to express a genuine fear that an existing consensus on the theory and ideology of science was breaking up when *'Vergangenheitsbewältigung'* (over-coming of the past), *'Identitätssuche'* (search for identity) and *'Sinnstiftung'* (creation of meaning), as from the end of the 1970s, once more looked like being promoted to the prime tasks of historical research, both in scientific theory and practice and in day-to-day politics.

Pre- and Post-Modernism as 'Zeitgeist' and Background

In order for the background and values of the German *'Historikerstreit'* to be properly understood and appreciated, it may be useful to relate the shift or redefinition of the purpose and tasks of social research, as formulated by Michael Stürmer in theory and ideology and as introduced and defended in research practice by Nolte and others in a different, more socio-intellectual context than that of pure everyday politics. One's intention in doing so would in no way be to deny or even tone down its obvious political significance, but to put the discussion in a context where the epistemological and research ideological dimension could conceivably become accessible in a completely different manner.

Thus it is highly relevant to analyse and discuss the 'revisionist' tendencies of the *'Historikerstreit'* as expressions of a general research ideological process. We are concerned here with a politically and intellectually heterogeneous tendency which, referring to social and 'mentalitarian' changes, considers itself entitled not only to violate but also to reformulate the existing rules and the overriding objectives of man's search for, and use of, knowledge in the social sciences and humanities.[17]

Thus what the 'revisionists' of the *'Historikerstreit'* reflect according to these various neo-conservative and post-modern critics of civilisation is nothing more or less than the acute need to redress the intellectual disorganisation and mental 'loss of direction' following in the train of the allegedly obvious bankruptcy of the 200 years project of enlightenment and modernisation.[18] This epochal breakdown is taken to have involved not only the utter discrediting of communism but also, and perhaps not least, the economic, moral and political collapse of the social democratic/social liberal welfare project.

This post-modern 'truth' of 'history being at an end' and the non-existence of an objective reality (Baudrillard) must, according to its proponents, necessarily also imply that an array of intellectual, epistemological and moral conventions surrounding the search for knowledge, based on the philosophy of the Enlightenment, can be considered more or less obsolete. At all events, they have lost their status of over-riding regulatory principles with regard to methods, epistemology and scientific interest. Thus we are concerned here not only with the normal and trivial fact of the humanities or social sciences self-evidently redefining their topics of inquiry, problem definitions and disciplinary focus, according to the demands of the age. Instead what is suggested is that thoroughgoing social changes now also demand a fundamental transformation of the overtones, focus and main tasks of the study of history.[19]

One central aspect of the '*Historikerstreit*', which in itself can be said to reflect these problems, concerns the relations between collective identity and historical research. If, like Stürmer on the one hand and the so-called '*Alltagshistoriker*' (everyday historians) on the other,[20] one interprets 'identity' as referring mainly to a consensus-promoting, stabilising sense of community serving primarily to contribute towards the enhancement of self-awareness, self-understanding and collective capacity for action both within complete social formations and within individual groups and corporations, then histori- cal research acquires an immediate, instrumental task which it neither should nor can accomplish.[21] In this kind of 'historicising' it goes without saying that 'progressive' and critical historical and social research, which among other things has employed systematic analysis, detached understanding and systematic theory as its epistemologi- cal correctives, no longer appears to be satisfying the needs of the general reader or to be relevant for scholarly purposes. And so it was perfectly natural that this kind of social research should occupy the focus of attention at a time and in a controversy when 'conquest of the past, evolution of meaning, identity creation, immediate understanding, intuitive empathy, direct recreation, active partisanship etc' are again being presented by both neo-conservative revisionists and postmodern populists, with various motives and shades of meaning, as the obvious demands of the new age.[22]

This is because critical historical research has, on epistemological grounds, queried and even denied the possibility of intuitive or immediate understanding of either past or present. The assimilation of reality and attempts at explanation in historical research, then, can only be mediate. For historical research, therefore, the articulation of vanished realities and horizons of opinion through analytical categories, and not through recrea- tion or empathy, is the only possible and relevant approach. Yet at the same time as one acknowledges this essential limitation of historical research, one maintains the basic postulate of the philosophers of the Enlightenment that history is a unitary, indivisible secular process. Man's collective endeavour must be viewed neither as an impenetrable mass of individual and disparate 'histories' nor as part of an unfathomable divine plan. With this point of departure the past becomes, in principle, possible to understand and explore in terms of actors and structures, motives and actions, as well as causes and consequences. Together with the gradual introduction of imperative methodological and epistemological norms, professional historical research has thus come to be ascribed by the critical historians a specific and limited but not necessarily higher cognitive value than other endeavours to understand and explain the past.[23]

Furthermore, the 'progressive' definition of science has also entailed the rejection, on research ideological grounds, of active partisanship. This, of course, has not meant viewing practical activity as essentially detached from ethics and politics. On the contrary, explicit reference has frequently been made to general, overriding values and principles such as liberty, democracy, justice and so on. What has been rejected is direct and programmatical instrumentalisation and the possibility of research findings being adapted or subordinated to various external preferences and loyalties.[24]

The Actors, Significance and Scope of the '*Historikerstreit*'

I realise that what I have said above is in danger of proving to be an excessively grandiose and perhaps even pathetic background to a controversy among historians, in which the main conflicts of opinion can primarily be said to have concerned the question of the 'uniqueness' of Auschwitz and the scope and implications of the *Gulag*, and also to some extent the relations of German historical research with the Nazi epoch. Even so, this broadening of the perspective is necessary in order to understand the focus, lines of argument, scope and short-term results of the *'Historikerstreit'*. Perhaps, not least, it can help to explain why certain 'green/left' post-modern groups in the discipline of history have either shunned or as a matter of principle condemned the interchange of opinion as such.[25]

Thus, to begin with the last mentioned point, many observers have noted with surprise or approval that a large proportion of the so-called everyday historians, mentality historians, 'text interpreters' and post-modern critics of civilisation have kept silent or remained on the defensive throughout the interchange of opinion. But in view of the societal overtones, the political consequences and the actual epistemological implications of the debate, I do not find this very surprising.[26]

Stürmer's conservative programme of identity and *'Sinnstiftung'* and the programme of intuitive understanding or introspective text interpretation were asserted by certain everyday historians and other group-specific historians as well as critics of civilisation. Similarly, whereas Stürmer concentrates on the nation and national consensus, there is an equally distinct element of active partisanship in the 'history from below and within' which justifies its choice of perspective primarily with reference, not to benefits in terms of scientific practice and epistemology, but to the 'correct' moral, psychological and political implications.[27]

Even more significant, it seems, are the humanists who wish primarily to allot historical research a therapeutic or aesthetic task. In the post-modernist epoch, these interpreters tell us, the illusion of history as a science can no longer be sustained.[28] The idea of the past as a uniform, comprehensible process, as well as faith in rational argument and rational or causal explanation, has proved to be *'ein bildungsbürgerliches Phantasma'* (an illusion of the educated middle classes).[29] Instead the task of the historian is identical with that of the fiction writer, namely to recall and re-create past realities, myths and dimensions which the process of modernisation has suppressed or defined out of existence. Relevance and importance, then, hinge on the power of depiction and empathy, not on the theoretical and practical conventions of scientific discourse or the tenability and explanatory power of provisional concepts of truth.

In that 'post modernist' perspective it becomes possible not only to regard every epoch in history as unique, or to use Leopold von Ranke's famous expression: *'unmittelbar zu Gott'* (immediate to God) but also, and more important in this particular connection, either to dismiss the *'Historikerstreit'* as a contest between two intellectual dinosaurs, involving fundamentally obsolete contradictions of fact and scientific ideology.[30] Or, it could be described as part of a universal process whereby, in principle, the activities of the 'revisionists' merely fulfil - or at least remind us of - the new, historically determined tasks, beyond morality and politics, which from now onwards will also be incumbent on historical research.[31] In these terms it is also possible to describe and 'understand' the resistance and indignation of Habermas and other 'progressivist' as, primarily, a manifestation of the obsolete intellectual project's fear of losing its old institutional, epistemological, ideological and political hegemony.[32]

From a 'revisionist' viewpoint, one can at least try to describe the vehement reaction of the allegedly retreating 'progressive camp' against Ernst Nolte and other 'revisionists', not primarily as empirical and theoretical objections concerning central problems of recent German history, and especially the valuation and determination of the period between 1933 and 1945. Instead, it could be presented as a kind of vicarious contest in which the 'progressive' scholars in their apologies for modernisation try to define out of existence those 'alternative' research perspectives, interpretations and topics of inquiry which might impede or even preclude the further use of the Nazi epoch as the obvious,'conclusive' argument in favour of the projects of social reform, rationalism and liberalism cherished by themselves.[33]

The epistemological, or rather research ideological, dimension outlined above can also help to explain why the *'Historikerstreit'*, instead of being confined to a dispute between the existing 'progressive' and neo-conservative groups in German historical research, also came to involve independent and even conservative researchers on the 'progressive' side. To a great extent the attacks on Ernst Nolte, Michael Stürmer and others also took on the character of a massive reaction by traditional historical research against what several of its exponents looked on as a deliberate attempt by a number of eminent historians, supported by the *'Zeitgeist'*, to change and perhaps annihilate in certain respects the epistemological and practical scientific advances of German historical and social research in recent decades. When, moreover, Habermas argued - rightly or wrongly - that the long-term, essential aim of the 'revisionists'' activities was to break down the liberal-democratic consensus on which the whole political and intellectual self-understanding of the Federal Republic was founded, the interchange of opinion had taken on dimensions extending far beyond shades of fact concerning the character and genesis of Auschwitz.[34]

Questions of Fact and Principles

From the very outset it should be made clear that Habermas' attack, contrary to what has been alleged by a number of his opponents, did not represent an attempt on his part to introduce any politically or morally motivated 'blanket' on research into recent German history, nor were his observations combined with any demand for censorship on grounds of 'popular education'.[35]

What he and others did demand was that Ernst Nolte, Andreas Hillgruber, Klaus Hildebrand, Michael Stürmer, Joachim Fest and other 'revisionists' should also take the moral, political and epistemological consequences of their own publicly declared 'explanatory attempts', convictions and recommendations for action. In other words, these historians too should fulfil what Theodor Mommsen has already looked on as the inalienable social, moral and intellectual duty of every social researcher, namely *'die Pflicht der politischer Pädagogik'* (the duty of political education).[36] Therefore I firmly maintain that anybody justifying his defence, above all, of Nolte's 're-interpretation' of the Holocaust and European Jewry, by saying that all it is really meant to accomplish is the safeguarding of 'scientific liberty of communication', the defence of methodological and epistemological pluralism as an indispensable asset to the humanities, must entirely lack credibility.[37] Instead there is good cause for suspecting that he has other political and intellectual investments to safeguard. This is perfectly legitimate but, according to Habermas and others, it should be done openly and in direct confrontation.

Turning to the case of Ernst Nolte,[38] then, whatever has been maintained to the contrary, the most devastating objections to him and to others have not been political or moral.[39] Instead their foundations have been purely intra-disciplinary, including both theoretical and empirical elements. Thus nobody has contested Nolte's entitlement to compare Auschwitz with practically anything whatsoever. But here as in all comparative historical research, the quality and relevance of the results are immediately connected with the choice of entities for comparison and the criteria stated for that choice. If the entities are manifestly incommensurable and the criteria irrelevant or bizarre (Kampuchea - Nazi Germany), the comparison is patently and utterly worthless.[40] This being so, then as a rule it can be quietly dismissed.

But, for various reasons, it may sometimes be interesting and necessary to ask why an eminent, qualified historical specialist at a particular point in time presents and persists with theses which, right from the outset - and still more so afterwards - are devoid of any visible intra-disciplinary relevance. This is exactly what Habermas and others have done.

The same applies to Nolte's thesis of the *Gulag* and the Bolshevik *Kulak* persecutions being 'more original' than Auschwitz, and of the exterminations of the Jews deserving to be looked on as a reaction to - or even a species of defensive precaution against - 'coming Asiatic Bolshevik outrages'. The concept of this causal nexus between the *Gulag* and Auschwitz can be treated as a normal and relatively simple historical explanatory theory which can be tested and possibly rejected. And indeed it is after this kind of testing that Nolte's project has foundered completely.[41] Thus the thesis has not been rejected because of its admittedly obvious political explosive power but on account of its equally obvious lack of both empirical foundation and theoretical consistency. If in this situation the author still persists and the 'theory', moreover, has lacked these foundations from the very outset according to unanimous research, then it is not only plausible but also perfectly natural and logical to ascribe to its originator and defenders other serious motives than those of an intra-disciplinary nature, in which case there is good cause to suspect that those motives are purely political. It is this very intellectual respect which has been shown to Ernst Nolte by his critics.

Furthermore, Michael Stürmer's and Hagen Schulze's re-vamped '*Mittellage*' (middle position) concept,[42] whereby geography has ultimately determined and can 'explain' the 'tragedy' of the past 200 years of German history, has not been dismissed on account of its documented political connotations in terms of genesis and use. It is above all being called into question because there is good reason for denying it all but the most trivial explanatory power. For the central position is a perfectly arbitrary concept which, in principle, can be applied to virtually *all* existing geographical entities and, therefore, has no specific epistemological importance.[43] Thus if anything it was France which was to occupy this 'centre', at least until 1870 or perhaps even until 1905! Then again, the adherents of the '*Mittellage*' are distinctly unwilling to declare their many epistemological and scientific precursors, thereby also violating one of the most fundamental conventions of scientific discourse. It may be understandable that this reluctance to discuss one's sources of inspiration is primarily due to the possibility of the persons concerned evoking unpleasant political associations, but this has no bearing on the question of principle.[44]

Finally, as regards Andreas Hillgruber,[45] objections have not been concerned with his raising one of the topics still taboo in German historical research, namely the fate of the German civilian population in the East. What has above all been attacked is the programmatical absence of perspective and the lack of detachment. When Hillgruber comes to analyse the last phase of the war, he automatically does so through the eyes of the German army fighting on the eastern front, referring expressly to the theoretical and practical scientific programme of the everyday historians. This does not only affect matters of selection and perspective. It also tends to resurrect the old myth of Germany's war as the struggle for European civilisation, so that Germany's defeat becomes that of the whole world and victims and assailants are liable to get mixed up, which indeed the title of the book confirms.[46] The stipulation that a historical process be elucidated from as many - past and present - perspectives as possible and that the author maintain a necessary detachment from his research field and his material is not only a matter of plain justice. If an investigation with the objective and overtone declared by Hillgruber himself does not confine itself to elucidating the specific, momentary self-perception of the soldiers at the front and the author, like Hillgruber, feels at liberty to draw conclusions and determine consequences extending far beyond those immediately apparent from the declared explanatory level and the material, then a fundamental rule of method has been broken. Criticism of Hillgruber has emanated from this fact.[47]

Research Ideology

As already indicated, the explosive power of Habermas' attack was due to his not confining it to the virtually bizarre allegations of fact made by the philosophical maverick Ernst Nolte concerning the 'origin' of Auschwitz and 'the war guilt of the Jews'. For these were things which, if they proved to be a mistaken speculation in popular opinion, could easily have been disavowed by 'revisionists' as 'exaggerated, unprofessional speculations', having no real connection with or relevance to 'serious historical research'.[48] That could have been the end of the matter, with no harm done and nobody compromised. In a word, 'order' could have been restored and a more favourable opportunity awaited.[49] But Habermas also included the 'ordinary historians': Andreas Hillgruber, Klaus Hildebrand and (last but not least) Michael Stürmer,[50] with the result that, from the very outset, the conflict acquired a research ideological, epistemological dimension which made it both general and unavoidable.

In this way the respected Chancellor's intellectual adviser Michael Stürmer had, in a manner of speaking, become the principal character of the controversy and not Nolte, 'the one-man paradigm', as certain people, for various tactical reasons, persistently maintain.[51] Thus the conflict came to concern the focus, responsibility and societal role of the humanities - above all of historical research - and not solely or even primarily issues of fact concerning the Nazi era, even though that epoch remained the specific historical litmus paper from which scientific ideology and political preferences could be read off most easily.

All at once it became possible and necessary to ask oneself what the historian (Stürmer) really means by elevating 'formation of opinion' and 'creation of identity' to the first and last duty of the historian and at the same time 'rediscovering' and advocating 'the ideas of 1914' concerning Germany's encirclement. This allegedly intolerable, fateful '*Mittelage*', according to Stürmer, constantly been 'forcing' a tormented nation into 'special solutions' of domestic politics and no mean degree of recurrent external aggressiveness.[52] This question has not become less acute after the political events of 1990.

It becomes still more acute if the same eminent historian also argues, in a Western European parliamentary democracy, that 'Pluralism in terms of values and conflicting interests in a society . . . eventually leads to such conflicts as to endanger the general social interest'.[53] Or if the historians maintaining that 'empathetic understanding' and relativising comparison must be the scientific and moral regulatory principles of humanistic and social research, argue at the same time in their research practice that Dresden, in its meaning, consequences and implications, was comparable to Hiroshima and that Idi Amin's Uganda and Pol Pot's Kampuchea are eligible for comparison with one of the cultural states of western civilisation.[54] Or, finally, they hint that the defeat of the German army on the eastern front was as great a historical and human disaster for Germany and Europe as the extermination of European Jewry.[55]

To arrive at a proper understanding of the intra-disciplinary context, it is necessary to briefly sum up what has happened in German historical science over the past 30 years. What happened, starting in the mid-1960s, was that German historical research underwent an epistemological and disciplinary revival which not only transformed the West German humanities but also recovered for them a certain measure of world reputation, by virtue of their scientific quality, their innovative power and their disciplinary diversity.[56]

It should be pointed out right from the beginning that this 'progressive' breakthrough did not entail any kind of a concerted 'view of history' - that is, in the manner of traditional Marxism, a total conception of the meaning and aims of history, or a desire to claim primacy for a particular line of research - (for example, social history). Instead, we find an articulated view of science emanating, in terms of research ideology and epistemology, above all from the manifold works of Max Weber.[57] The basic premise of this 'critical' or 'emancipatory' social history' can primarily be described as a conviction that the necessary cognitive connection between past and present can only be established through a historical science relating questions of change and continuity to structural and societal levels. It can do this only if it is developed into a science permeated by theory. Its explanatory power, social relevance and justification as an independent academic discipline, in other words, are derived from its scientific cognitive interest, not from its '*Sinnstiftungskapazität*'. It is only this kind of historical research, guaranteeing equitable, de-mythologising re-interpretations of the past, which is the necessary basis of all possible thoughts of 'identity creation' and a viable 'national consensus'.[58]

The Revisionists and Modern Historical Research

As stated above, this 'progressive' programme has been the target of the most concentrated attacks, from both '*Sinnstifter*', neo-historicists on the one hand and certain everyday historians and postmodern 'deconstructionalists' on the other. Through their emphasis on criticism, emancipation, structure and theory, the social historians are alleged to have neglected 'the most fundamental tasks of historical research' - national and group specific identity creation - and also to have promoted dissolution and historical homelessness through their refusal to 'understand' and their systematic' denigration' of the past.[59]

What Stürmer and other '*Sinnstifters*' are asserting, then, is not the truism that historical research is also a part of the creation of national identity and collective self-understanding or that its results - whether we like it or not - have political implications and can be put to direct and arbitrary use in the hurly-burly of politics. Instead he expressly insists that the professional historian not only realises and accepts the political dimension of his work but also places his research at the disposal of certain political persuasions. Thus the value of research findings would seem primarily to be commensurate with their instrumental political usefulness, but above all in the service of nation-building.[60] And so, instead of referring to a never challenged right to freely 'theorise' and problematise, there is if anything good reason to begin discussing the research ideological and political consequences of the fact that Heinrich von Treitsch-ke's programme is once more apparently hovering in the ambit of German historical research.[61] Undeniably, interpretations of Germany's recent history - and especially of the Nazi era - can be said to a great extent to reflect both the general political climate and the balance of research ideological power in German and western historical research. The standpoints taken, or the different points of departure in the '*Historiker-streit*', therefore have a considerable amount of political and moral implications. Hence, it is not only a scholarly but also a political and moral statement, if one denies the conclusion by Habermas and others that 're-interpretations' by Nolte et al should primarily be characterised as a deliberate attempt to revise the criminal record of the Nazi era, at least with regard to frames of interpretation and premises. This is also the case if one refuses to interpret Stürmer's research ideological programme as a dedicated bid to re-establish a conservative sense of history in the Federal Republic.[62] It is equally interesting not only from a scholarly point of view if instead, like the neo-conservatives, post-modernists and others we dismiss the '*Historikerstreit*' as a non-event, either as being obsolete and therefore fundamentally uninteresting or downright harmful shadow boxing to one side of the real 'cutting-edge of research'.[63] Or if we call it a more or less desperate political and institutional defensive battle by a progressive camp which has lost a good deal of its former hegemony and credibility, not only with regard to specific assumptions of historical theory and epistemology but also as regards its 'emancipatory' hopes and moral priority of interpretation.[64] All these statements are good enough reasons for taking a closer look at the way in which 'revisionists' interpret, describe and use the practical results generated by the increasingly intensive and, in disciplinary terms, expansive research of recent decades.

There are, as I see it, two consistent traits in the efforts made by the 'revisionists' to 'empirically' substantiate their theses of the lost 'hegemony' of the 'progressives' or when they are presenting 'the ideas of the future'. Firstly, they very seldom refer to original research findings or independent research strategies of their own, articulated on the basis of their own declared or latent scientific ideology. Instead they have to a great extent concentrated on re-interpreting pre-existing and long-discussed research findings.[65] Rainer Zitelmann and his book '*Hitler, Selbstverständnis eines Revolution-ärs*' (1987) could serve as an illustrated example in this respect. Thus, according to different kinds of revisionist reviewers, Zitelmann has presented a 'new view' of Hitler and National Socialism by pointing out the anti-bourgeois ethos of the movement, its modernisation plans, its revolutionary character and so on, and, by arguing that the leader was by no means a hysterical carpet-biter but, above all, a coldly calculating, rational politician. What has clearly most endeared Zitelmann to the 'revisionists', however, is not primarily his results but rather his tendency to integrate Nazism with modern social development as rooted above all in the rationalism of the Enlightenment and in modernisation. But, without wishing to belittle the value of Zitelmann's debatable book, I would maintain that even very limited familiarity with the research of the past few decades is enough to establish that none of these particular observations in itself adds up to a directly sensational or exclusively 'post-modern' re-interpretation of Hitler or National Socialism. The 'progressives' appear - as usual, one is tempted to say - to have got there about 20 years earlier![66] The crucial difference appears to be that previous researchers have not attached the same type of political (!) hopes and expectations to these analyses and empirical studies of theirs as Zitelmann et al appear disposed to do.

Bearing this in mind, it is hardly surprising that pre- and post-modern 'revisionists' of immensely differing hues have primarily come to attach their greatest hopes for the future to the attacks delivered at regular intervals against the so-called '*Sonderweg*'-thesis, because for various reasons, and to some extent rightly, this thesis has been allotted a paradigmatic key position, in terms of both general ideology and epistemology, in 'progressive' German historical research.[67]

Firstly, it should be said that the concept of some form of German 'deviation' has partly acquired a general symbolic function, insofar as it has also been looked on as an indirect West German admission of special political responsibility and moral guilt.

Secondly, in terms purely of definition, the '*Sonderweg*'-thesis has obstructed all possible attempts at 'normalising' German development or integrating it with general Western European history. And so by designating something as '*sonder*' (special), one has also allotted it such qualities that it can only be treated and perhaps, integrated on its own terms.

Thirdly, and perhaps more important, this explanatory attempt on the plain of historical theory emanates explicitly from theories attached to notions of the western world as being enclosed in a general process of modernisation which has not only involved a specific form of economic and industrial development but whose implications have also been determined by an ongoing political, intellectual and cultural emancipation. At the present point in time it is not least this latter point which has caused a possible abolition of the '*Sonderweg*'-thesis to acquire a particularly ominous implication and also, therefore, its eventual dismissal, an unusually high 'future quality' in 'revisionist' circles.[68]

The different exponents of the '*Sonderweg*'-thesis claim for German history a continuity which might help to explain the clearly perceptible deviations from developments elsewhere in North Western Europe.[69] Sometimes the structural inflexibilities have been roughly summarised as 'incomplete modernisation', in the sense of politics, culture, mentality, institutional forms, social integration etc not co-varying with a rapid or at least 'normal' Western European economic and military renewal process and expansion of power. Having said this, however, one has not only or even primarily claimed that the Nazi 'solution', through 'feudal structures and residual atavisms', has been more or less programmed into Germany's history at least since 1871. Instead an attempt has been made to assert that structural and cultural inflexibilities and restrictions in the past have prevented the emergence of the measure of socio-political know-how which was absolutely needed in order to overcome the combined military, political, economic and intellectual collapse which the First World War implied. The consequences to Germany of this constitutional deficiency were especially acute in a period when politics appeared to remain the only possible and legitimate way to social re-organisation.[70]

The importance and explanatory power of the '*Sonderweg*'-thesis among the 'progressives' themselves have always been greatly divergent and the thesis has been the subject of such an intensive 'internal' debate that one is barely entitled to speak of an existing consensus concerning its range and status.[73]

The '*Sonderweg*' explanations have traditionally been challenged and opposed by conservative neo-historicists on the one hand and orthodox Marxist-Leninists on the other.[74] The differences with regard to points of departure, lines of argument and general explanatory models, however, have been so great that these attacks have not been regarded as coordinated or even as mutually complementary. Interestingly enough, a certain change in this respect seems to have occurred during the 1980s, in that the anti-*Sonderweg* persuasions nowadays refer to one another. The neo-conservatives, not least, have made very eager use of the 'new left criticism' in their unceasing attempts to get at the thesis.[75] Perhaps, though, this should not be regarded exclusively as an expression of bare-faced opportunism. Instead we have cause to refer once again to the partly convergent attempts to regard and analyse the origins and character of German fascism mainly in terms of one of a succession of failed modernisation projects, albeit perhaps the most grotesque of them all.[76]

An illustration of the renewed debate on the '*Sonderweg*'-thesis is the widely noticed critical contribution made by the British left-wing historians David Blackbourn and Geoff Eley. What they presented, together with Richard Evans and others, at the end of the 1970s can be described as a kind of sophisticated 'Dimitrov'-thesis,[77] purporting to show that the German bourgeoisie had acquired at least the same degree of influence and strength as its French and British counterparts. The arguments put forward by Blackbourn/Eley are fundamentally the traditional ones, relating to similarity of productive conditions and ownership structure.[78] Similarly, according to Blackbourn/Eley, Wilhelmine Germany was possessed of an impressive potential for modernisation. Finally, Blackbourn/Eley consider it improper and mistaken to speak in terms of a common Western European 'normal' development, in the sense of a normative model, from which Germany has significantly deviated.

To my knowledge, these assertions have not been rebutted by any qualified '*Sonderweg*'-proponent, and least of all by the principal adversary, Hans-Ulrich Wehler. What he and others have said, on the other hand, is that this influence came about within a specific social structure with uniquely German overtones and conditions.[79] As regards potential for modernisation, this did not come to embrace society as a whole but was limited to certain sectors of German society and therefore helped to create a fundamental societal imbalance. One incontrovertible piece of evidence on this point, which Blackbourn et al, significantly enough, almost entirely avoid discussing, is the position and development of political and cultural liberalism in a comparative perspective.

Thus, whereas liberalism in practically all other European states achieved its historical apogee between 1870 and 1914, in Germany it was reduced to a social and political nullity.[80] Besides, even if Western Europe cannot be used as an ideal or abstract norm, we still have its value and significance as a historical/empirical corrective. Unlike its Northern and Western European neighbours, Germany, as is well known, became fascist and totalitarian. This is and remains the essence of any discussion of the *Sonderweg*-thesis. It is 1933 which makes it virtually inevitable and gives it its relevance. This, in practice, also means that every thorough-going revision and normalisation of National Socialism must be preceded by a coming to terms with the different variants of Sonderweg theories.[81]

Another widely noticed example of neo-conservative research utilisation or re-interpretation concerns Henry A. Turner and his 20-year research project on relations between German big industry and National Socialism during the 1920s and 1930s.[82] In this connection he has fairly convincingly shown that German high finance before 1933 did not by any means look on National Socialism as its natural political ally. Similarly big industry - with just a few significant exceptions - also refrained from giving the National Socialist movement any material support before its advent to power in 1933, even if it did adapt very rapidly to new political realities after the take-over. The criticism levelled at Turner has to a great extent been concerned with his unilateral acquittal of German high finance. Other researchers have instead focused attention on the profound and, on the whole, harmonious cooperation which was very quickly established between the two spheres of power, and on the incontrovertible fact that big industry does not appear to have developed any form of active or passive resistance.[83]

Turner's research, laudable in many respects, is and remains a systematic attempt at falsifying the Marxist-Leninist 'agent theory' (first developed by Georgihu Dimitrov, the Comintern secretary in the 1930s) of fascism as the spearhead of monopoly capitalism and therefore, on the surface could seem to be highly 'anti-progressive', with its value and usefulness in the *Sonderweg* discussion appearing more than a little dubious. But the very attempts at explanation which have been based on, or have developed, this old Comintern analysis, are those which, over the years, have most consistently opposed and challenged the *Sonderweg* explanation. Thus, instead of ascribing any special position to German development, the dogma of fascism as an in-built, natural consequence of the capitalist system has, with different variations, been insistently propounded. In this analysis of structural coercion and 'the same fascists here as there', Germany represented something deviant only in the sense of possibly being the most extreme instance of a universally active process.[84]

Similarly, it is above all the representatives of these agent theories who have most conscientiously and vigorously cultivated the myth of the untarnished fighting German working class.[85] And accordingly, the 'revisionists' have also argued that the membership and voting surveys undertaken by Jürgen Falter, Richard Hamilton, Konrad Jarausch, Michael Kater and others since the early and mid-1970s have demolished a fundamental precondition of the 'progressive' analysis.[86] The 'Dimitrov analysis' which according to the provisionists is thus correctly 'anti-progressive' regarding the Sonderweg-thesis, is presented here - as in the case of Turner - as the nucleus of the 'progressive' view of National Socialism.

This, however, is not only questionable in terms of the logical consistency of the argument but, in terms of fact, is essentially wrong. For in reality these 'progressive' electoral analyses have discussed and revised something quite different. Thus they have above all shown that the thesis, launched by the American political scientist Seymour Martin Lipset in his famous book *Political Man*,[60] of Nazism as mainly a movement of the lower bourgeoisie needs to be revised or at least heavily nuanced.[87] The thesis of Nazism as a traditional, homogeneous *'Mittenextremismus'* or a revolutionary avant-garde is, quite simply, not correct. These findings ought further to reinforce the thesis of the genuinely German character of National Socialism and thus rather provide support to the *'Sonderweg'*-thesis![88]

In these surveys, in which the statistical material has often been broken down to regional or district level or in which interest has been made to focus on individual occupational groups and corporations, the picture emerges of National Socialism as a genuine people's party, with adherents in practically all social and demographic groups. Thus, according to Falter et al, the proportion of working-class voters, not least, was significant, even though relatively speaking they remained under-represented in proportion to their share of the electorate. It is true that a certain over-representation can be observed among the lower-middle-class strata and also among the farmers, but most remarkable in this respect is the upper-middle class, and not only as represented by certain professional groups such as doctors and lawyers.[89]

More important for our purposes, however, these surveys, like Turner's works and Knut Borchardt's studies from the end of the 1970s and the early 1980s concerning the relative movement of costs and wages during the last years of the Weimar Republic, do not touch on or discuss the *Sonderweg* problem.[90] If a real attempt were to be made to discuss these essentially different studies in Sonderweg terms, then it seems likely to me that their main results would if anything further reinforce the hypothesis of a German *Sonderweg*! Thus, whereas it is arguable that virtually all dictatorships since 1793 have been imposed on the population either through external intervention or through direct action by well-organised, strategic minority groups, German fascism was installed through the medium of an impressively broad-based popular support and in due constitutional order. It is not least this particular fact that makes the German case so special, and which has made the question of guilt and responsibility such a burning and unavoidable one in both German historical research and politics.[91]

There is, however, one feature common to the examples given here of new and fruitful approaches in recent research into National Socialist Germany, apart from all of them having been quoted as evidence of the crisis of 'progressive' historical research. None of them, with the possible exception of the works of Knut Borchardt, can in any reasonable sense be attributed to any new, 'anti-progressive' school of research. Instead, these very contributions can to a great extent be looked on as direct results of the disciplinary expansion and active problematisation which the 'progressive' break-through at the end of the 1960s de facto implied.[92] Thus the studies quoted here ought primarily to be regarded as direct responses of practical research to the appeals for a conscious 'historisation', for example, a critical takeover of the inter-war years and Nazi epoch which were already voiced in the 1960s in 'progressive' quarters and have since been re-formulated and refined by scholars such as: Hans Mommsen, Martin Broszat, Heinrich August Winkler and others.[93]

This critical 'historisation', however, rested on a basic research ideological conviction which, in terms of cognitive interest, research focus, theoretical stringency and scientific responsibility is in many ways quite contrary to the type of 'historisation' which, from various vantage points and on various grounds, has been proposed by different kinds of 'revisionists'.[94] Thus the new and varying 'demands for historisation' should not to be understood as an attempt to remedy some constitutional deficiency of German historical research or to eliminate a politically prompted research 'moratorium' on certain subjects and problems. Instead the aim is essentially for different kinds of 'historicisation' from those which have actually been occurring and have been gradually reinforced ever since the mid-1960s. There are good grounds for suspecting that what one is hoping for is a kind of 'historisation' in which the critical takeover and structural explanations have been replaced by understanding', 'empathy' and 'comparative normalisation'.

In a perspective of historiography and principle, one can look on this heterogeneous 'historisation offensive' - emanating from both the 'black' and the 'green' camp - as the third serious attempt since the end of the war to normalise or defuse the period between 1933 and 1945 both in modern German history and in latter-day German politics.[95]

The first, propounded immediately after the war, could best be termed 'the strategy of defining out of existence': the period between 1933 and 1945 was presented as a historical anomaly, with a fundamentally healthy German nation falling victim in the first instance to political terrorism or to a natural disaster of mass psychology. A variant of this explanatory attempt is the so-called '*Hitlerismus*'-thesis, whereby Nazism is thought of almost exclusively as a consequence and emanation of Adolf Hitler's personality and mental energy.

The second attempt is represented by the totalitarianism theory of the 1950s, in which, by reference to formal congruences between different modern authoritarian power systems, an attempt was made to integrate and normalise German fascism too as part of a universal pattern.

With some simplification I would designate the third variant of the '*Historikerstreit*' the modernisation/normalisation thesis. This time German fascism is presented and explained mainly as one consequence of a universal western modernisation project, in which the utopian resort to the future, security and the good life has made possible and promoted a rootless collectivism and instrumentalisation. This being so, National Socialist Germany, including its barbarism, could best be understood and assessed in relation to other, rival modernisation projects and certainly not only communism. In this perspective the New Deal and German Fascism represent basically the same thing.

Summary

The implications and observable consequences of the *Historikerstreit* have confirmed the ancient truth that epistemological premises, explanatory models and topics of inquiry in social and humanist research are never chosen in a social vacuum. Declarations and preferences, which formally speaking express only research ideological and epistemological basic principles, may thus also be an expression of more or less specifically political and moral preferences.

Secondly, this has not only been a contest between two articulated schools of historical research - the 'progressive' and the 'neo-conservative'. Instead a large part of the German historical community has been involved in several of the weightiest 'anti-revisionist' contributions - in terms of both fact and research ideology. They have thus come from independent and outstanding scholars whom only the most ignorant and unscrupulous could conceivably refer to or lump together in some kind of 'progressive' camp: Martin Broszat, Eberhard Jäckel, Richard Löwenthal, Christian Meier, Wolfgang J. Mommsen, Kurt Sontheimer, Heinrich August Winkler etc.[96] A greater and more representative sample could hardly ever or anywhere else have taken part in a public 'historical debate', with the possible exception of the German's own 'Lamprecht Controversy' round about the turn of the century![97]

As I have already claimed, there were two main reasons for this massive involvement and for its not being subject to the traditional right-left constraint. Firstly, the latter-day contributions by Stürmer and Nolte above all came to be regarded, not least against the background of the prevailing intellectual climate and research ideological propositions, as a more or less overt calling into question of the epistemological and practical scientific advances of the past quarter-century. Secondly, it then became clear that there existed among West German historians a relatively widespread consensus on the social role and status of historical research. In a word, people were unwilling to accept the idea of a social research beyond politics and morality.

And so, what has happened - at least in the short term - is that neo-revisionists of different hues and persuasions in the German humanities have suffered a crushing political and ideological defeat, because to their own unconcealed astonishment, it has become apparent that a considerable majority of German historians, whatever school they may belong to and whatever their epistemological premises, were more or less 'progressive', as the current terminology has it.[98] Whether this will still be the case after 3 October 1990 remains to be seen.

Thirdly, it seems as though the discipline of history has returned to the central position which it has traditionally occupied in German social debate, with all the moral and epistemological problems this may come to involve. As a professional historian, one might perhaps be excused for spontaneously rejoicing at this development, but one should not hide the complications and perils which growing power to attract the media and politics implies for the autonomy, scientific expansion and intellectual integrity of a humanist discipline. The dangers of too close a political connection has been amply illustrated in German historiography during the last century![99]

Fourthly, the *Historikerstreit* confirms that theoretically aware, actively problem-oriented, historical research in the Federal Republic is not confined to a negligible group on the margin of things. Thus the closing years of the 1980s, at least where historical research is concerned, are not a companion piece to the expulsion during the closing years of the 1920s of virtually all forms of problem-oriented social research. In this respect the *Historikerstreit* also differs from the Fischer controversy of the 1960s in which an overwhelming majority of traditionally-minded, conservative 'politico-historians' made more or less common cause against Fritz Fischer and his young students. It has, moreover, illustrated the special position still occupied by Jürgen Habermas in German intellectual life and in the humanities. Some commentators have maintained that 'In the ultimate analysis the *"Historikerstreit"* is concerned with a struggle to prevent the reconstruction of a conservative view of history in the Federal Republic'.[100] Even though, in the light of what has now been said, this standpoint may appear somewhat over-simplified, there is still quite a lot in it. For it seems safe to say that efforts to 'normalise' the recent history of the German nation through comparative trivialisation or amoral 'normalisation', and similarly to convert the discipline of history into some kind of secular substitute for religion and to subordinate it to political and vaguely 'national' considerations have, on this occasion at least, borne an unmistakably conservative imprint, even though one ought to point out that it is not only wrong but above all pointless in this connection to make use of such designations as 'Nazi apologetics' and such like.[101] Instead it might perhaps be appropriate, by way of summing up, to quote the assessment by Charles S. Maier, the American specialist in recent European history, of the direction in which the various 'revisionist' propositions could lead, be they concerned with Stürmerian 'search for identity', Noltean 'explanatory theories' or post-modern 'anti-rationalism':

> 'it could lead to some form of ugly politics, some infringement of dissent or attack on diversity: the political fantasies of the *Bild-Zeitung* rationalised in the language of '*Existenz-philosophie*'. Even if no practical consequences followed from the revisionist view, if West Germany remained as robust a democracy as it has been, its civic culture would be degraded by the distortions of historical memory involved.'[102]

As I see it, these observations are not only a keen appraisal of the West German situation and debate but also an illustration of the admittedly indirect but still unambiguous social dimension and responsibility of the humanities. Whether the propositions discussed here can conceivably return with similar or completely different political and research ideological implications in a re-united Germany or elsewhere is hard to prophesy. The implication and course of the *Historikerstreit*, however, ought perhaps to provide some food for thought in this respect, within the historical discipline everywhere.

Chapter 5

Cultural Identity and Nationhood
The Reconstitution of Germany - Or the Open Answer
to an Almost Closed Question

Björn Wittrock

The modern world is premised on sets of cultural practices which make this world
intelligible and which help to locate human beings and their institutions in a social
universe which emerges as meaningful beyond the multiplicity of ceaseless interactions
and movements. The institutions of higher education are key vehicles for the continuing
existence of those cultural practices which are characterised by a high degree of
reasoned discourse and which require long periods of apprenticeship and training for
their mastery - and their transformation. In the late 19th and early 20th century there is
a close interaction between the cultural practices of emerging social science and the
search for solutions to both 'the social question' of industrial civilisation and the
question of cultural and national identity in the post-traditional and post-Napoleonic
epoch.

Similarly, the two institutional projects of creating and reforming modern nation
states and of creating the modern research-oriented university are coterminous in the
latter half of the 19th century. In almost no country is this more evident than in Germany,
and German solutions to both the social question and to the institutional and intellectual
problems of organising modern science and humanistic scholarship as well as modern
universities came to serve as international models.[1] In no country, however, were those
solutions more fundamentally questioned and challenged in recent times, and in no other
European country has the problem of constituting a cultural and national identity led to
such disasters and remained an open question for so long. The recent reunification, of
course, may well be seen as a long-delayed solution to the problem of finally linking
cultural identity and polity to each other in a viable way in the German context. This
may well be so in pragmatic terms. However, in discursive terms, reunification just as
much as separation is in need of being made intelligible, more precisely in terms which
make compatible the predominant universalistic political self-understanding of the
Federal Republic with the inevitably culturally non-universalistic rationale behind the
very process of reunification.

The Quest for Nationhood

Starting roughly 4000 years ago, a vast conglomerate of Germanic-speaking peoples spread out over most of the European peninsula and the British and Nordic isles off its coast, speaking the shifting tongues of their tracts, exhibiting more or less kinship to those of other dialects, merging with others, succumbing to superimposed standards or disappearing into non-Germanic local dialects and national tongues. And parts of those peoples have sometimes been taken to speak something which they or at least their educated visiting linguistic brethren have termed German.[2] Some of these latter have sometimes in recent history claimed to constitute a nation and a state and indeed a nation state, a Germany. But even at the peak of power of the greatest of great German realms, millions of German speakers have dwelt outside the borders of that realm - some more than willingly, as in the Swiss confederacy, some, like those in Russia, without the issue of choice ever being made a question. Thus any polity claiming to constitute Germany, whether united, reunited or united anew, will be premised on some type of appropriate relationship between cultural-linguistic identity and political organisation.

To 19th century national liberalism these types of answers were equally obvious and unproblematic. Political freedom and national liberation were but two sides of the same coin, and blocking the road to the realisation of freedom were the rulers of an antiquated multiplicity of minor principalities. The events of the century after the defeat of the mid-19th century liberal-radical revolutions in Germany have, if anything, thoroughly dispelled any notions that these types of answers could ever be obvious or simple. Furthermore, they have made disreputable answers which were long seen as quite acceptable and fairly non-problematic in other Germanic-speaking countries, answers emphasising the bond between cultural identity and notions of spatial organisation. In the German context, the Nazi experience meant that large shares of quite common bourgeois conceptions of nationhood and all sorts of rural-nostalgic views of the peasant life of the past had become so inextricably linked up to the genocidal version of early 20th century racism, as to make them utterly impossible in any cultural context whatsoever.

It has, however, been noted that whereas the German scene saw the total Nazi appropriation of notions of the *Volk*, in Scandinavia the Social Democrats were equally successful in doing much the same in the same historical period. The real alternative to the *Volksgemeinschaft* of the fascist warfare state may have been neither Soviet-style communism, nor British-style aristocratically-tinged parliamentarianism, but Scandi-navian-style *völkische Demokratie* and its version of a pursuit of the common good of the people; not in a terror-ridden Nazi *Volksgemeinschaft* but in a half-participatory, half-paternalistic *folkhem* (People's home).[3] It is ironic to note that both the term 'People's home' - later to be picked up by Swedish Social Democracy - and the term 'National Socialism' (in its Swedish-German one-word linguistic garb) may well have been coined by one and the same person in 1912 and 1916 respectively, namely by the ultra-conservative and anti-democratic theoretician of geo-politics, Rudolf Kjellén. Kjellén was Professor of Government at Uppsala after the turn of the century until his death in 1923, leaving no disciples behind in the academia of newly democratised Sweden but with eager German adherents, such as Karl Haushofer, to follow his lead.

Thus the demise of Nazi rule did not just mean that Germans had to come to terms - or choose not to come to terms - with the legacy of a regime and its numerous servants guilty of atrocities beyond comprehension. It also meant that, in the of semi-starvation under a liberation brought about through occupation, the Germans were faced with a radical disinheritance of large parts of traditional popular culture. Both American-style constitutionalism and Soviet-style socialism were ideally suited to fill this ideological gap since both of them - in contrast to the political cultures of pre-Nazi Germany, of Scandinavia or, to take an example from another cultural context, Japan - were premised on an entirely non-spatial, a-territorial conception of political-cultural identity.

The two post-Nazi Germanies could thus be construed to represent almost ideal-typical versions of these two universalistically-oriented types of polity. One Germany was based on a constitution - or rather a proto-constitution basic law - drawn up in the expectancy of the final coming of a real constitution. The other Germany resting on the universalistic tenets of a universalistic ideology - one which, although having been brought to Germany by an occupying liberator had nonetheless been originally conceived by exiled representatives of 19th-century German radicalism - an ideology which came to be the never-to-be doubted, always to be cherished and honored touchstone of statehood, decency and identity.

In the early part of the post-World War II era, the Germans themselves, apart from the enormous activity involved in sheer physical reconstruction of the country, were involved in endless discussions on 'the German question' and on the problems of 'coming to terms with the past' (*'Die Bewältigung der Vergangenheit'*). Much of the rest of Europe had had quite enough of Germans and German questions in their own recent past to bother too much about these discussions, as long as the Germans stayed busy reconstructing their divided and unarmed country. There was also every indication that there was little or no need for men and women of good common sense to do anything else. After all, who except Germans, professors of German studies and hopelessly Germanistically-enmeshed theoreticians would like to waste their time on a 'question' which was not a question at all. The division of Germany into two clearly distinct, not to say diametrically opposed, states had given this 'question' an answer which everyone was quite happy to live with for the foreseeable future. Everyone, that is, except maybe the Germans.

But then again, anyone with good common sense and knowledge of the actual political situation in Germany in the 1950s could tell that a reunification of Germany was about as realistic as putting a man on the moon - or maybe even a woman. The Soviets, of course, would be all for it as long as it took place within the framework of an expanding Soviet-style socialist world system. The creation of NATO, though, did not make that a very likely scenario. The West German Social Democrats in the early 1950s had been fighting a losing battle against rearmament and close links with the Western military alliance and in favour of neutrality, some kind of socialism and, possibly, eventual reunification.

That battle, however, had been irreversibly lost and with the 1959 Bad Godesberg programme West German Social Democracy re-entered the world of West European political realism acquiring a concomitant rock-bottom commitment to the Western alliance with capitalism seen as reformed and socially palatable. Also, the Christian Democrats under Konrad Adenauer were consistently following a version of the French saying from the late 19th century when it came to reunification; 'always talk about it, but don't risk achieving it too soon'. Small wonder then that in the 1960s, 1970s and 1980s, young Germans grew increasingly bored and irritated when constantly confronted by interested foreigners asking them what they thought about their German identity and about 'the German question'. Their answers tended to be variations on a common theme of 'not much'.

The more conservative of the West German youth became virtual epitomes of young American executives, indistinguishable apart from the Teutonic twang in their accent.

Also, the more radically inclined were not only part of the more general European youth rebellion but did everything to look and act as the very epitomes of anti-authoritarianism. Any suggestion to these young Germans that all of this was but a thin veneer of civilisation covering, in one case, capital and cash and, in the other, alternative lifestyles, and that they all secretly nourished the dream that their united Fatherland would rise to take its just place as the dominant nation of a New Europe, would at best have been perceived as the expression of a particularly stupid and insensitive outsider visiting Germany for the very first time.[4]

The Unexpected Answer to 'the German Question'

Yet German reunification did happen. And when it did, it was the most natural thing in the world. An East German population bereft of what West Germans for years had taken to be the necessities of life was suddenly faced with the possibility of sharing in the wealth of the West while reuniting personal and family bonds and simultaneously getting rid of a regime lacking legitimacy. Although to the Federal Republic, reunification might have entailed some short-term drain on financial resources, these were not more than could be conveniently encompassed within its giant economy. There were also some very realistic prospects of major future returns from these expenditures.

Perhaps the most stunning feature of this rapid reunification was the ease and calm of it all both inside and outside Germany. The opening of the Wall in the night between November 9 and 10, 1989 did not lead to chauvinistic celebrations but to hundreds of thousands, having done their window shopping, taking a leisurely stroll down the posh shopping-street Kurfürstendamm on a late Friday night with little drama but much wonder and amazement. And likewise, without exception Germany's neighbours received the news of the momentous transformation with the utmost equanimity, much like some very interesting football result in the first division of a nearby country; certainly an object worthy of attention and maybe comment, but nothing to really get all worked up over. This lack of high drama might have been highly natural in a country characterised by extreme continuity in statehood and national identity, like Britain or Sweden. But Germany? There could hardly be a country in Europe with a more cataclysmic passage from the early modern age up to the mid-20th century.[5]

Thus when the rest of Europe abandoned medieval universalism and built the early modern territorial state, the German lands clung on to an outdated quasi-universalistic political order, which only made them an easier prey for the military might of their more powerful neighbours. And when the Germans had learnt to master the modernities of enlightened absolutism and the state of persistent but limited warfare, systemic rules were again transformed in fundamental ways, and the vast scale of post-revolutionary warfare swept away even the best trained military machines of the German lands and reduced them once again to subjugation and occupation.

Finally, in the late 19th century, Germany and Britain, the young, the old and international lead nations saw their curves of economic success, one rising, the other declining, intersect. But both countries, partly intentionally, partly inadvertently, contributed to a new balance of power in Europe and beyond, one nation ruling the waves, the other the land, and both being willing to trade with each other and the world. Once this balance was toppled, competition was no longer that of giant corporations and trade but of territory, colonial expansion and giant military machines. In the decades leading up to World War I, German politicians were either unable or unwilling to reinstate such a fragile balance effectively. Nor were they able to find a formula whereby the late 19th century version of a unified Germany could assert all its scientific-technological and industrial-organisational achievements without increasingly risking the undermining of their very foundations in the wake of deep-seated transformations of an international system of states drifting towards war.[6]

Given all this, not to mention the unspeakable atrocities of the Nazi period, how could a major realignment in the centre of the European continent be received by most observers with as little interest as a new long-term weather forecast? Basically because at the time it was largely perceived as both unavoidable and innocuous. Who except hopelessly suspicious and malevolent observers could seriously fear a reunited Germany? In the decades past, not even the most suspicious outsider could deny that on almost any count - economy, social policy, environmental concerns, attention to education, science and culture, immigration policy, industrial democracy, foreign aid - the Federal Republic equalled or, often enough, surpassed its neighbours and allies. A generous economic super-power in the midst of Europe, deeply committed to liberal democracy, social welfare and the protection of the environment - who could be vehemently opposed to that? In any case, nobody really was, with the equally inevitable and insignificant exception of the perennial left-wing fringe groups in the larger German cities, themselves a testimony of the very vitality of the liberal democracy they were protesting against.

In this perspective, it is not surprising that analysing and reanalysing this new version of a German unification, which would inevitably leave millions of German-speakers outside the new German state, was to be reflected upon in an endless series of more or less celebratory, more or less critical articles and books. However, the relative importance of a medium-size European power in the late 20th century could, of course, in no way be compared to that of a European great power a century earlier. In terms both of sheer numbers and of access to knowledge, technology and social organisation, neither Europe in general nor Germany in particular, had anything like the semi-hegemonic, not to say quasi-monopolistic position in the world it had occupied a century earlier.

Thus the new unification put the Germans in a double bind. They were offered, and willingly accepted, the role of economic locomotive for much of Central and Eastern Europe, thereby in a sense both repeating their own achievement of the first part of the post-war period and resurrecting a traditional German position in Eastern Europe which had been lost already in the wake of defeat in World War I.[7] All of this would sap energies and resources in purely economic-physical terms. More importantly, it would force Germans to temporarily close in on themselves in a gigantic effort to firstly raise the former GDR and then much of the rest of Middle Eastern Europe to West European standards of living and spending. All of this carried a substantial risk of limiting the German span of attention to the national and the near in a period when this might be tantamount to repeating as farce a Euro-centric, or even Germano-centric, parochialism that had been the tragedy of the German Mandarins in the period of Wilhelminian and Weimar Germany.[8]

But then again, the word 'farce' carries highly misleading connotations; the new German unification might in one sense have been so much less cataclysmic than various other events in German history that celebrations and analyses of it might have appeared as little but the fulfillment of some equally unnecessary and unavoidable obligation. However, at the core of this process, there was a fundamental and very real dilemma which was forced onto the Germans by reunification, a dilemma that in essence was also facing the rest of Europe and the developed parts of the world. The dilemma revived by unification was posed by the dual history of a Germany caught between modernity and enlightenment, on the one hand and romantic nationalism on the other. It was symbolised from the late 18th century onwards by the draft outline of a constitution of Germany by the youthful and rebellious Hegel and by the romantic, classicistic, nationalistic, revolutionary poetry of his friend Friedrich Hölderlin.

Writing in what was in those times sometimes desperately called *Das Jahr Null* (The Year Zero), amid the ruins of the Third Reich, the old historian Friedrich Meinecke tried to decipher the disastrous course of that project in a little book *Die Deutsche Katastrophe* (The German catastrophe).[9] Clearly, in Meinecke's perspective, the rule of robber barons and ruthless adventurers under the veil of a 'third' *Reich* marked but the last disastrous steps on a path where the demise of intellectual stature coincided with a growing worship of power and force. In the Year Zero, in the ruins of the wrecked *Reich*, it was no longer possible to conventionally invoke an intellectual heritage which had been invoked too often for too dubious a purpose; it is difficult not to recall the short stories of Wolfgang Borchert, the author of the lost German generation, with their lines about young men being sent off to the winter war in the East with the thin consolation of the poetry of Hölderlin, the most romantic and most classicistic of the German poets of the revolutionary generation, in their pockets.

All through German literature in these post-war years the conceptual rupture and spatio-temporal co-existence of traditions of enlightenment and the realities of atrocities were being explored, reconstructed and deconstructed, whether in the novels of Herman Hesse and Ernst Jünger or in the social philosophy of Theodor Adorno and Max Horkheimer or, for that matter, Karl Popper.[10] And yet post-war Germany had to be reconstructed on the basis of this unresolved dilemma, relinquishing as much as had to be relinquished of Nazi-permeated cultural memory traces, yet retaining as much as could be retained of a general classicistic cultural heritage without too much of an exercise in double-think.[11] Time and again these unresolved tensions surfaced in post-war Germany, whether in a leftist version, as in the student rebellion of the late 1960s and early 1970s, or in a rightist one, as in the efforts of revisionist historians to restore 'normality' to German historical consciousness.[12]

Reunification and the Ambiguities of Nationhood

Reunification once again raised the fundamental questions of the relationship between language, cultural identity and state formation. Obviously, some kind of linguistic commonality had always formed a necessary condition for the constitution of a national cultural identity in the German case. However, it had certainly never been a sufficient condition. The controversial lines in the national anthem (omitted after World War II) of a Germany from the river Maas to the river Memel and from the river Etsch to the Danish Belt, i.e. the more or less continuously German-speaking, broadly interpreted and generously delineated area which to 19th-century national liberals had appeared as the natural fatherland, referred to an area which had certainly never been even roughly incorporated within any single political entity. In the post-World War II era *none* of these waters was part of any state called Germany. However, the 'smaller' German solution to the national question as it emerged in the imperial state was for all practical purposes a modern nation state, albeit with some Slavic-speaking minorities within its boundaries. In the words of Meinecke before the First World War, this 'state nation' had as its basic rationale the mission of promoting and strengthening the German 'cultural nation', a concept which over and above linguistic commonalities carried connotations of a common cultural identity.[13]

In the dominant discourse of the times - echoed also in many statements by Max Weber - this mission was seen to entail a willingness to risk upsetting the established European balance of power in an effort to develop a 'world policy' and, eventually (to quote the title of Fritz Fischer's provocative volume from the early 1960s on German policies in this period) an effort at reaching out for world power - or at the very least European hegemony. A Germany which would not be ready to upset this European balance would, in Max Weber's view, be doomed to the status of either a junior partner of the Anglo-American world or that of a subordinated province of a despotic Russian realm - a description not too far from the realities of the two Germanies for a long period in the post-World War II era. The risk-averse option would, again in Weber's view, be for the Germans never to embark on the quest for a nation state in the first place but to have been content with remaining citizens of a multiplicity of smaller principalities bereft of any real influence on the course of European events and subject to the whims of other and greater powers.[14]

In the post-World War II era there is a strange ambivalence in the political rhetoric of the two Germanies. In the late 1940s and early 1950s the East German regime consistently portrayed itself as the true guardian of the German fatherland, deploring the fact that the Western provinces had been lured away from the heartlands of the nation by foreign powers and had thus seceded from the core of the nation. Time and again in these years, East German leaders pledged their solemn allegiance to the national obligation of restoring national unity.[15] In the Western part, on the other hand, it is clear that the dominant Adenauer policy from the very beginnings of the post-war period was premised on an unwavering allegiance to an alliance with Western powers. All through the following decades the consistent policy being pursued was that of trying to achieve the distant objective of reunification via the long route of giving up parts of the newly regained national independence - though not full sovereignty - in favour of a deepening Western cooperation.

From this point of view, the events of 1989-90 was the long awaited, but hardly expected or envisaged, triumph of this basic policy. Ironically, the Federal Republic - by far the most successful German polity in modern times - was premised on a severely circumscribed view of its own legitimacy and viability with a provisional constitution, awaiting a seemingly never coming new national unity. How many leading West German politicians had not, in the latter part of the 1980s, declared that reunification was not a viable option in this century? Conversely, as noted by many observers it was really only with the eventual achievement of this unlikely objective that the citizens of this polity came to fully realise that they had an identity as different from that of East Germany as from, say, that of Austria or, for that matter, the German-speaking province of Alsatia.[16]

Many a great German social theorist has been groping for a description of this evasive cultural identity, much like an old picture, which when finally recovered from darkness and oblivion almost immediately starts to fade away. Theorists who had quarreled for decades about the systemic and hermeneutic properties of modern civilisation, suddenly had surprisingly similar analyses of this cultural identity, some-how only too often coming up with economic performance as a lowest common denominator to describe the key features of the West German national experience, the stable, but potentially fragile, source of its legitimacy and claims to loyalty.[17]

In the traditional European pattern, rural popular culture had tended to be pictured as localised and relatively stable. In the course of the 19th century this stability was increasingly disrupted and shattered in the wake of the cultural upheavals of the revolutionary and Napoleonic wars on the one hand and industrial and economic transformation on the other. Simultaneously the cultures of educated practices underwent a gradual shift in the course of the 19th century from transnationalism, if not universalism, towards nationally contained forms of high culture closely tied to a range of emerging national cultural and scientific institutions.[18] In this period the modern nation state emerged as both a solution in administrative terms to the problems of managing the transition to modernity and as a cultural container for closer links between popular and high culture. This was partly a natural but also a largely socially and politically constructed solution to the problem of cultural identity. In the late 20th century both popular and educated cultural practices shifted towards transnationalism and away from the cultural containers of the old nation states, searching for, though not yet finding institutional vehicles for the mobilisation of resources and rules to help underpin the new cultural practices.

The German reunification tended to be interpreted as entailing either a continuation of the post-war policy of the Federal Republic, i.e. a promotion of German interests however delineated only by way of retaining deep links to the West, or else as marking, certainly still within a Western alliance, the possibility of asserting some kind of German position with slightly more self-confidence. Liberal and pro-Western articles calling for an end to the self-enforced foreign policy abstinence of the Federal Republic were expression of this tendency. However, in some ways this new situation was reminiscent of earlier epochs when the cultural identity of the Germanic-speaking peoples had been much less tied to the particular features of a particular polity.

Once again, it was possible at least in principle, to formulate questions - no matter how unlikely their realisation might be - about a type of cultural identity which might encompass the particularistic and the perennial in the human condition beyond the constraints of a narrow nation state or a power-permeated Mandarin culture. Maybe the Faustian bargain of modernity in the late 20th-century promised no more - as Horkheimer and Adorno had suggested already in the 1940s - than a growing technocratic knowledge turning inward towards the potential destruction of the very basis of human life. However, this also might be a time for breaking the bond of the traditional German quest for political predominance and a nationally circumscribed cultural identity in a world which promised mingling currents of culture rather than the high cultural aquaria of 19th-century style nation states.[19] In Meinecke's terms of 1946, the birth of German patriotism during the anti-Napoleonic wars, long before the creation of a modern German nation state, entailed that, there occurred a change in 'the essence of German human beings', involving, as observed eg by Wilhelm von Humboldt, maybe more down-to-earth realism but also a certain curtailment of intellectual imagination. Nothing could be further from the ethos of the post-reunification young Germans than to invoke the high-flying rhetoric of German universalistic philosophy of the early 19th century. Yet that period was the period of the birth of modernity and the parting of roads which were to lead in the most disastrously diverging directions.

But then again, maybe German reunification should just be seen as heralding the beginning of the end of the whole project of the nation state and the return to a much more familiar situation in Europe where the boundaries of polities did not, except by chance, coincide with those of any single ethnic group. Thus a political order might well be based on a linguistically dominant group but neither the rulers nor the ruled would pay overly much attention to this fact, and people would move across frontiers without carrying passports - as Europeans did up until the First World War - and without being overly concerned about something called nationality when they sought and found work and entered and left the political arenas in various regions. The old states would still be there and their names would still be the same, but they would not be - to use Gellner's term - 'aquaria' but rather world villages with locals, visitors and travelers. And in the really long run their relevance might gently fade away and be seen as a fond memory of an antiquated political structure much as Europeans now regard the quaint multiplicity of overlapping polities which covered the political map of the continent at the advent of the early modern state.

Cultural Identity and Political Order

The constitution of identity has tended to be interpreted in terms of two major dimensions. One pertains to the basis of political entitlement and the delineation of the set of legitimate members of a political order - a problem sometimes captured in terms of a distinction between *ethnos* and *demos* - to use the categories of Emmerich Francis and M. Rainer Lepsius; i.e. between a culturally, linguistically constituted ethnic community versus the politically constituted citizenry of a given polity with its inherent rights and obligations.

In this context I shall distinguish between three types of such bases of political entitlement, namely a communal-encompassing one, a political-institutional one (where the category of 'citizen' is the crucial one in the modern state just as that of 'subject' is the archetypical one in a traditional or absolutist state), and finally a cultural-ethnic one (where in modern times the category of 'compatriot' is a key one). The other dimension deals with the particularism versus universalism of the political order in its self-definition and in its willingness to include individuals as members of that order and to bestow on them the rights and obligations inherent in the given political order. In the simplest form this yields six basic types of political order.

The first two pertain to a communal-encompassing basis of commitment and played a truly significant role in European history only in the era before the emergence of the early modern state. In a particularistic version, the communal characteristics of a group of people basically defined in terms of kinship serve to delimit the relevant range of the socio-political order. One important type of such an order with a particular longevity has been that of the clan, another one that of the 'folk-tribe'. (Incidentally, the term 'folk-tribe' was for long part of normal German political rhetoric and used to describe the various component parts of the German people. Thus the constitution of the Weimar Republic opens with the words: 'The German people, united in its tribes *(einig in seinen Stämmen)* . . . has given itself this constitution'.)

Whereas the various types of kinship-based orders are inherently particularistic, the ancient and the medieval Church explicitly embraced a universalistic conception of membership in an encompassing community and universal societal order. This feature of the Church's self-understanding also had far-reaching implications in the early modern era. Not least did it mean that the Church was in principle eager and willing to include the inhabitants of the newly conquered territories of the early colonial empires beyond the seas. Many authors, and maybe most eloquently so Octavio Paz, have highlighted the deep-seated difference in this respect between 16th century New Spain and 17th century New England.[20]

In the European states of the early modern and the absolutist era, the object of political allegiance was constituted by a polity, more or less governed through a mode of personalised rule, and with little or no consideration for the linguistic and ethnic peculiarities of its subjects. Thus a localised identity was linked to a traditional state based on loyalty to the person of the ruler, whether king or emperor or just the prince of a minor area. Only by chance did the territorial boundaries of such a polity encompass one and only one linguistic-ethnic group. Even in the case of the precursors of modern nation states, a multiplicity of linguistic and ethnic groups were included within the borders of the realm. Even in a country on the northern periphery of Europe such as 17th century Sweden, at least three languages - Swedish, Finnish and German - were used all the time in official interactions, and half a dozen others (such as Estonian, Lappish, Latvian, Ingrian, Polish and Russian) in the daily life of its inhabitants. Thus a political-institutional basis of delineating the political order tended to be linked to a particularistic conception of the nature of that order.

The birth of modernity in the latter half of the 18th century was concomitant with the emergence of revolutionary political orders, in France and in North America, which propounded a universalistic conception of political-institutional allegiance. No longer were the members of the political order just the subjects of some ruler but rather the creators and upholders of that order, the free citizens of a free republic. The basis of the order was conceived in political-institutional terms but not in the particularistic terms of an absolutist state. Instead the political order came to epitomise, in its own self-understanding, fundamentally universalistic features and explicitly recognised the universal validity of basic political and human rights.

However, the new polities not only represented the universal strivings of mankind. For all practical purposes they also happened to be circumscribed in relatively clearcut cultural-linguistic terms. In Europe the ensuing revolutionary and Napoleonic wars came to both shake the foundations of traditional states and forms of order and to highlight a new need to reconstitute political order in terms of linguistically and culturally continuous entities, nations. And for all its indebtedness to a common heritage of the period of revolutionary upheaval, the 18th-century project of the nation state, meant that the basic delineation of the polity shifted its basis from a political-institutional one to a cultural-linguistic one and from a universalistic to a particularistic one.

Thus it was only really with the emergence of the idea of a nation state in the early 19th century that nationhood and ethnicity rather than just the state of being the subject of some ruler came to serve as a basis for the definition of cultural and political identity, an identity, however, which was particularistic precisely in its exclusive focus on a given culturally delimited nationality. The century of violent efforts to force ethnicity and political organisation to coincide in territorial terms is coterminous with the evolution of the project of the modern nation state.[21] Fascism is in a sense a strange fallback from this project into that of prior ideas of loyalty to the person of the ruler. The key formula of National Socialism - *'Ein Volk, ein Reich, ein Führer'* (one people, one realm, one leader) - captures this merger of the idea of the nation state with that of personal allegiance of an earlier epoch.

Inherent in the project of the nation state was a deep-seated tension. On the one hand, the very emergence of nation states meant that a traditional situation of a conglomerate of different ethnicities within a given polity suddenly became problematic in the sense that the state would tend to embody no more than one - or at best a few - of the high cultural needs of the various ethnic groups. Thus ethnic and linguistic identity without the explicit support of a polity no longer appeared as a viable option in an era of increasingly high-culture-permeated practices whether in the field of education, or in scientific and industrial institutions. On the other hand, a nation state set up to promote the linguistic or cultural development of one particular ethnicity could not but offend the rights of other ethnicities, especially if it made ethnic belonging itself a defining characteristic of citizenship.

The only way of overcoming this dilemma seemed to be to make the constitutional rights themselves the touchstone of nationality and to leave all ethnic considerations to the side. This type of constitutional community, this - to use a German term - *Staatsbürgernation*, would signal a way out of the particularistic dead-end of the traditional, more or less (and, even if ever so tacitly so) *völkisch*-oriented, nation state.

German polities in the course of the 19th and 20th centuries had represented extreme forms of a lingering multi-national state, the Habsburgian empire, and of a modern nation state in its most assertive appearance, the united Germany in its second and third realm incarnations. Thus it was hardly surprising that leading German social theorists in the late post-war Federal Republic came to advocate a strongly argued version of a constitutional, republican state as the only viable solution to the 'national question'. In this sense, the Federal Republic would be a universalistically-oriented constitutional polity as would be, say, France or the United States. And this would have been the most natural note to end on if it were not for one small problem.

This problem concerns the fact that the theory of the universalistic constitutional polity can make little or no sense of the very process of reunification. True enough, why should the Germans of all people be denied the right to self-determination, which was so widely acclaimed and practiced all across the world? But then again, why should a universalistic polity care for any territorial alterations whatsoever? And if it, or rather its citizens, did, could the rationale be explained in any other terms but those of a particular cultural and national heritage and identity?

Faced with this dilemma, the social theorists might still provide an escape from the route heading towards an embarrassing return to notions of ethnic particularism, namely a reinterpretation of national culture in universalistic and non-spatial, non-territorial terms. So a given cultural heritage and identity would only take on real meaning and would derive its final merits not from its particular nature *per se* but rather from the fact that it reflected through a particular prism of experience concerns and quests in some sense shared by all of womankind and mankind. Thus the fact that Königsberg and East Prussia are no longer part of Germany - or for that matter Greifswald and Pomerania part of no Swedish realm - do not make Immanuel Kant - or Thomas Thorild, the Swedish intellectual of the same generation - any less part of German and Swedish culture respectively.

This type of answer undoubtedly helps save consistent cultural universalism. However, it does not help explain the societal process of citizens actually bringing reunification about any better. Nor for that matter does its three-penny-opera version in terms of materialist universalism explaining reunification solely in terms of narrowly materialistic East Germans desperately longing for the goods and goodies of the West. So did a lot of other people who neither wanted to join the Federal Republic, nor would have been welcome had they tried. More important, however, is the fact that if cultural universalism is accepted, then the whole rationale of the nation state in the first place seems to erode.

Why should a nationally confined state, no matter how universalistically and constitutionally conceived, be the ultimate point of departure in the first place, if this polity has no unique role in upholding a particular cultural and linguistic legacy? And if it has - which I believe it is difficult to deny in purely descriptive, not normative, terms in the case of any of the traditional European nation states - how can universalism really be upheld? The Swedish solution of granting each and every member of a minority certain basic cultural and linguistic rights might be described as a cumbersome way of seeking a way out of this dilemma - but laudable though these policies might be, they cannot but transpose the problem of cultural rights and societal organisation to a yet more aggregated level.

But then again, maybe the solution to the problem of cultural identity and socio-political organisation will indeed be found in terms of the complex intermingling of cultures in the processes of forming individual identities in the inevitably multi-cultural communities which already exist all across Germany and Europe and where there are few or no indications that the newly reunited nation will try to replace the fallen frontier with a multiplicity of new ones. Yet such a cultural conception of the basis of the political order has not been elaborated in its universalistic version. And though it may actually in some sense already exist in contemporary Europe, it is by no means discursively underpinned in anything like the same way as the lingering but eroding project of the modern nation state has now been for the past century and a half. It is hard to believe that the historical and social sciences will remain permanently incapacitated to enter into a dialogue about the constitution of such a trans-cultural political order.

Chapter 6

'Scientific Bureaucracy'?
Research Implementation and Swedish Civil Servants

Rune Premfors

Introduction

In an often quoted statement Thomas Anton argued some twenty years ago that:

> Swedish policy making is extraordinarily *deliberative*, involving long periods of time during which more or less constant attention is given to some problem by well trained specialists. It is *rationalistic* in that great efforts are made to develop the fullest possible information about any given issue, including a thorough review of historical experiences as well as the range of alternatives suggested by scholars in and out of Sweden. It is open in the sense that interested parties are consulted before a decision is finally made. And it is *consensual*, in that decisions are seldom made without the agreement of virtually all parties to them.[1]

Anton, as well as many others, observes in addition that the contents of public policy in Sweden have been relatively radical, and that this may largely be attributed to the long reign of the Social Democrats and their almost symbiotic relationship with a reform-minded administrative elite.[2]

This interpretation of Swedish policy-making has been quite severely criticised since the late 1970s. The traditional 'Swedish model' has increasingly been portrayed as fundamentally technocratic, as a manifestation of '*Zweckrationalität*' - rather than '*Wertrationalität*' and its basic function has been to preserve the power of Social Democrats and their allied administrative elites within the Swedish state. A specific feature of this general critique has concerned the narrow instrumentalism of Swedish higher education and research policy. Policy-makers have been too eager, critics argue, to design the academic research system so as to fit the goals of public policy-making in various sectors of government. In particular, Swedish researchers have been coopted into government through their participation in the work of governmental commissions and through the growing importance of so-called sectorial R&D. In addition, many new research positions within higher education institutions have been designed so as to fit the logic of public policy-making. All in all, critics argue, this government policy has undermined both the quality and the autonomy of academic research.[3]

Interestingly, both critics and supporters of 'the Swedish model' of knowledge use in government have largely accepted the premise that this 'instrumentalist' policy has worked effectively. In this essay some evidence is presented which, in my view, supports the argument that both critics and supporters may be quite wrong. More specifically, I will show that while top bureaucrats in Swedish government extensively use research knowledge as an input in policy-making, they seem to do it in a different fashion from what both critics and supporters of the instrumentalist view would expect.

Research Knowledge and the Swedish Administrative Elite

I will now present the main findings from a study of the use of research knowledge by the administrative elite in Sweden. This study is primarily based on a questionnaire which was distributed to a representative sample of top bureaucrats in central government.[4] As defined in the study, the population consisted of about 1200 administrative leaders and specialists in virtually all sectors of central government including and above the level of heads of bureaus (*byråchefer*). Excluded were officers of the courts and the State church. The sample drawn was 200.[5]

The response rate was eventually 150, or three-quarters of the sample. An analysis of non-respondents points to a certain, but not very dramatic, bias in the (expected) direction i.e. those not responding may be less involved with and less interested in the use of research. All in all, however, I have deemed it reasonable to use the responses to the questionnaire as representative of top bureaucrats in Swedish central government. The response rate as well as the possible bias caused by differences among respondents and non-respondents necessitate, however, considerable caution with respect to small differences in frequency distributions and - in my view - preclude the use of more advanced statistical techniques.

The questionnaire consisted of three parts. The first part included questions on the nature of the respondents' work tasks, and on their educational background and personal experiences of research activities. The second section contained questions of the respondents' use of research knowledge in their own work.

The third part of the questionnaire, finally, asked for their views on some general issues of research use in government, especially concerning obstacles to effective use. This part of the questionnaire was also distributed to a different set of respondents: heads of sectorial R&D programmes in central government. These 'R&D managers', as they will be called below, were responsible for running the approximately 60 sectorial R&D programmes which have in recent decades been created in Sweden in order to support and develop public sector activities. Four-fifths (50) among the R&D managers returned the questionnaire and their responses will be compared with those of the top bureaucrats.

Education and Research Experience

We may reasonably expect our top bureaucrats to be highly qualified in terms of their formal training. This is confirmed in Table 1.

In comparison with their political masters, top bureaucrats in Sweden have significantly more formal education. While virtually all among the latter have basic university degrees, this is only true of about a third of the members of the Swedish parliament, the '*Riksdag*'. Cabinet Ministers score on average higher than MPs, while 'Junior Ministers' (*statssekreterare*) are at least as highly trained as our sample of top bureaucrats.[6]

Nearly one-fifth among the administrative elite have at least a Master's Degree (*licentiat*) which implies (in Sweden) that they have performed independent research

Table 1. Formal Education of Swedish Top Bureaucrats

Educational level	Absolute No.	Percentage
High school	10	6.7
Basic higher ed degree	94	62.7
Research degree	27	18.0
Other (esp. military)	19	12.7
	150	100.1%

in an academic discipline. But they were also asked directly if they had personal experience of doing research work. The responses are presented in Table 2.

Table 2. Top Bureaucrats' Experience of Research

Type of Experience	Absolute No.	Percentage
Research degree	27	18.9
Other experience	29	20.3
No experience	87	60.8
	143	100.0%

From Table 2 we learn that about four out of ten top-level bureaucrats in Sweden report personal experience of research work. The responses to a follow-up question explains why the proportion with such self-reported experiences is considerably greater than the proportion with formal research degrees. The difference is mainly due to two factors: first, quite a few have interrupted their master's or doctoral work and, second, many (especially among engineers) have done extensive research work without aiming at a formal research degree.

Finally, respondents were asked about the disciplinary orientation of their formal education. The results are shown in Table 3.

Table 3. Top Bureaucrats' Educational Orientation

Educational orientation	Absolute No.	Percentage
Science and technology	25	16.8
Social sciences (incl economics)	56	37.6
Law	36	24.2
Humanities	6	4.0
Military	16	10.7
No higher ed	10	6.7
	149	100.0%

Those having a social science background (including economics) make up the largest group, followed by those trained in law. Earlier studies show that the situation was the reverse not very long ago. Traditionally, bureaucrats with law degrees have dominated the higher administrative echelons of central government in Sweden.[7] We may also note from Table 3 that those having a degree in the humanities are quite few, even fewer than those among the top-level bureaucrats who have an advanced military training.

Self-Reported Use of Research Knowledge

Since our respondents, with a few rather insignificant exceptions, cover the entire scope of Swedish central government, their work tasks are extremely varied. Their high positions of course imply that many of them are administrative leaders. But their answers to a direct question on this topic show that many are in fact specialists rather than generalist leaders.

To what extent does this rather heterogeneous set of bureaucrats use research knowledge as an input in their own work? Table 4 contains their judgments about the importance of such knowledge.

Table 4. Importance of Research Knowledge to Top Bureaucrats' own Work

Importance stated	Absolute No.	Percentage
Very great	34	22.7
Great	61	40.7
Quite little	39	26.0
Very little or none	16	10.7
	150	100.1%

Nearly two-thirds of the top bureaucrats in Swedish central government state that research knowledge is of great or very great importance for the accomplishment of their own work tasks. Only one out of ten reports that such knowledge is of little or no importance to them. My preliminary conclusion from this is that the appreciation of research knowledge is very high among the Swedish administrative elite, probably even higher than that reported in studies of other national contexts.[8]

Some simple cross-tabulations may illustrate systematic variations in self-reported research use. Table 5 shows variations according to the educational level of respondents, illustrating the somewhat expected correlation between educational level and research use. Still it is worth pointing out that among top bureaucrats with a research degree more than nine out of ten report that research knowledge is of great or very great importance to them in performing their own work tasks. If we correlate self-reported research experience with research use we, again somewhat as expected, find a somewhat lower appreciation of research knowledge - but it is still considerably higher than that of bureaucrats without any research experience at all.[9]

Table 6 shows variations in self-reported research use according to the disciplinary orientation of respondents. It should be noted that some cells of Table 6 are very small; this is particularly true of those containing respondents with a background in the humanities and those without a higher education degree. Among the rest we find the following ranking order with respect to research use: first, those with a military training;

Table 5. Top Bureaucrats' Research Use and Education. Percentages.

Formal education	Importance of Research Knowledge			
	Very great	Great	little	Very little or none
High school	10.0	50.0	30.0	10.0
Basic higher ed degree	13.8	37.2	35.1	13.8
Research degree	48.1	44.4	7.4	-
Other ed	36.8	47.4	5.3	10.5

Table 6. Top Bureaucrats' Research Use and Educational Orientation. Percentages.

Educational background	Importance of Research Knowledge			
	Very great	Great	Quite little	Very little or none
Science and technology	40.0	40.0	16.0	4.0
Social sciences (incl economics)	23.2	37.5	33.9	5.4
Law	5.6	38.9	33.9	22.2
Humanities	16.7	33.3	33.3	16.7
Military	37.5	56.3	-	6.3
No higher ed	10.0	50.0	20.0	20.0

second, respondents trained in natural sciences and technology; third, social scientists (including economists); and, finally and quite far behind, lawyers. To me this ranking order is quite expected. Is not the top position of the military surprising? Hardly. In the armed forces the input of technical R&D knowledge is very important, especially among the central military staffs and agencies included in this study.

What about variations in terms of different substantive areas of government activity? The data do not permit an analysis according to individual government agencies. All we can accomplish is a cross-tabulation of 'ministerial areas of responsibility',[10] and self-reported research use. Table 7 shows the result in the form of a ranking order among the 'ministerial areas' according to the proportion of respondents who stated that the use of research knowledge was of great or very great importance to their work.

Each 'ministerial area' encompasses agencies and work units of very different kinds. This implies that few generalisable observations can be made about the 'research intensity' of different substantive areas of government activity. In addition, the numbers are small in some cases. Still, the general pattern of responses seems valid and also a rather expected one. This is true, for example, of the position at the top of Defense and Agriculture as well as the low position of Commerce, Foreign Affairs and the Treasury.

Table 7. Top Bureaucrats' Research Use and 'Ministerial Area'.
Rank Order. Percentages.

Ministerial Area	Very Great/Great Importance of Research Knowledge
1. Defense	89.3
2. Agriculture	87.5
3. Social Affairs	80.0
4. Industry	78.8
5. Justice	75.0
6. Education	75.0
7. Home Affairs	66.6
8. Commerce	60.0
9. Communications	57.1
10. Foreign Affairs	50.0
11. Housing	50.0
12. Treasury	44.5
13. Labour	33.3

A bit surprising is perhaps the high ranking of Social Affairs - but one should recall in this instance that this 'ministerial area' encompasses health care as well as personal social services and social insurance. I am also a bit puzzled by the low position of Housing and Labour.

In response to a follow-up question, nearly two-thirds of the top-level bureaucrats gave specific examples of their use of knowledge. The answers illustrate the extreme variety of research and substantive issues involved, and they cannot be reported in a systematic fashion here. Altogether, however, they confirm the picture of a very high degree of research use at the central government level in Sweden.

Another question asked *where* the research activities are performed which top bureaucrats find useful in their work. The answers vary greatly here as well - from specific projects at specific institutions to entire research fields or disciplines of rather indeterminate institutional location. Still, a rather unexpected finding is that only about one-sixth of the sites/institutions mentioned are among the sixty-odd 'sectorial R&D bodies' mentioned briefly above. The average top bureaucrat seems to a surprising extent to be oriented toward traditional university departments and university disciplines. More than three-fourths among them mention research performed in such institutional settings as most relevant and important for their own work tasks.

Finally, the respondents were asked about the importance of various channels of research information. Table 8 shows how the Swedish administrative elite rank-ordered ten possible channels. The findings largely support results of earlier studies of research communication in public policy-making. This is true, for example, with respect to the importance of direct, informal and oral communication between decision-makers and experts. We may also note the position near the top of professional journals. A follow-up

Table 8. Importance of Different Channels of Research Information to Top Bureaucrats.
Rank Order. Percentages.

Type of Channel	Very Great/Great Importance
1. Discussions with outside experts	70.4
2. Discussions with own experts	59.5
3. Professional journals	59.3
4. Government reports containing research findings	55.3
5. Research monographs	44.1
6. Research reports	43.3
7. Conferences	39.1
8. Courses	35.3
9. Daily newspapers	28.6
10. Radio/TV	14.4

question asked respondents to mention what specific journals they found to be of particular relevance. Again, to a surprising degree many show a 'search profile' quite similar to the average academic teacher/researcher.

Research Use in Government: The Views of Top Bureaucrats and R&D Managers

What general views do top-level bureaucrats hold on the role of research knowledge in governmental policy-making? And how do their views compare with those who are directly responsible for financing and communicating 'usable research' i.e. R&D managers?

In one question respondents were asked to react to the statement:

'It is sometimes argued that research results aimed at being utilised in government activities are in fact rarely used. Do you think that this is . . .'

Table 9 shows the four alternative answers that respondents could choose from and the distribution of their choices. Among top bureaucrats a large majority, or 70 per cent, agreed at least partly with the statement. Very few seem to think that the problem of under- or non-utilisation does not exist. R&D managers were, perhaps quite expectedly, more optimistic. About half of them agree partly with the statement, while one-fifth disagree completely.

Here respondents were also asked to provide concrete examples of effective uses of research knowledge. Again, these illustrations are extremely varied in character and cannot be meaningfully summarised. However, particularly frequent instances of research use concern macroeconomic policy, health care, energy, the environment, defense, communications and education. Many respondents refrained from answering the question, noting that utilisation may be observed 'everywhere'.

Table 9. Top Bureaucrats' and R&D Managers'
Views of Non-Utilization. Percentages.

'Research results are in fact rarely used'	Top Bureaucrats	R&D Managers
Disagree entirely	4.0	18.0
Disagree partly	16.7	32.0
Agree partly	56.7	46.0
Agree entirely	14.0	4.0

What, according to top bureaucrats and R&D managers, are the problems associated with the effective use of research knowledge in public policy-making? The following simple model was shown as an introduction to a question of this topic.

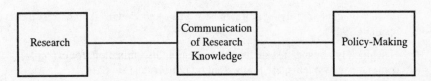

Figure 1. Research Utilization: A Simple Model.

Respondents were then asked to rank-order these three 'sub-systems' according to the extent to which they constitute obstacles to effective utilisation. A simplified account of the responses is shown in Table 10.

Table 10. Top Bureaucrats' and R&D Managers' Views of Where to Locate Obstacles to Effective Utilization. Percentages.

Located in:	Top Bureaucrats	R&D Managers
Research	12.0	10.6
Communication	36.8	23.4
Policy-making	51.2	66.0

As may be seen from Table 10, slightly more than half among the top bureaucrats and two-thirds of the R&D managers argued that obstacles to effective research utilisation are primarily located within the subsystem of decision-making, while only about one out of ten in both groups primarily blame the research subsystem. One-third of the bureaucrats and less than one-fourth of the R&D managers state that such hindrances are mostly located in the subsystem of linkages between research and policy-making. In sum, then, if we are to believe these well-placed observers in Swedish central government we ought not to look for the chief obstacles to effective research utilisation among researchers or the way in which research activities are organised. Problems - and potential improvements - are instead to be found primarily among decision-makers and their way of going about their business, and, secondarily, in the practices designed to provide linkages between research and public policy.

Another question consisted of no fewer than 35 statements containing arguments about obstacles to effective knowledge utilisation. Virtually all of these statements were formulated on the basis of Carol Weiss' admirable inventory of studies on the non-utilisation of research knowledge.[11] Virtually every statement has, then, been advanced - as a hypothesis and/or a finding - in this growing literature. Still, however, the question did not work very well. Many respondents refrained from answering a question containing so many bold generalisations - or, as one respondent put it, such a long list of prejudices - without being allowed to make nuanced judgments about each. Below, only a few summary observations will be made about the responses to this question.

Respondents were asked to register their views on a scale ranging from 1 (agree) to 4 (disagree). The following six statements elicited the greatest *support* on average - including both top bureaucrats and R&D managers:

- 'Research results are found in information channels, for example, academic journals, which are rarely used by policy-makers' (1.939).

- 'Policy-makers are relying more on "everyday knowledge" than on research results'(1.967).

- 'Technically advanced systems of information dissemination, for example, computerised systems, are rarely used by policy-makers' (2.034).

- 'The dissemination function is normally underdeveloped' (2.040).

- 'The distribution of influence in policy-making rarely fits with the implications of research findings' (2.089).

- 'The language of researchers is not well understood by policy-makers' (2.120).

And the following six statements provoked the largest number of disagreements on average:

- 'Research methods are not relevant and well developed' (3.119).

- 'Research results concern obsolete conditions' (3.040).

- 'Researchers allow ideological convictions to affect results and recommendations' (2.994).

- 'Researchers lack theories or "laws" of general application' (2.942).

- 'Research results are trivial' (2.941).

- 'The turnover among policy-makers is too great for effective research utilisation' (2.939).

It seems reasonable to argue that the responses to this complex question support the patterns established by the simple question on obstacles to effective research use. Researchers are much less to blame than are policy-makers.

Were there any significant differences in responses to the complex question between top bureaucrats and R&D managers? Very few and small. And the differences that did occur are not easy to explain. The greatest difference (0.435) concerned the statement:

- 'Policy-makers rarely act on the basis of factual evidence, but according to what is politically "rational".'

Perhaps somewhat surprisingly, top bureaucrats found this statement much more reasonable than did R&D managers. Maybe this should be interpreted as an expression of professional optimism on part of the R&D managers? Their role as 'middlemen' or 'brokers' may explain their propensity to paint a somewhat rosier picture of the behavior of policy-makers than the latter themselves do. Alternatively, the bureaucrats being closer to politicians than are R&D managers, may simply be more realistic about how politicians behave, and less judgemental.

A Summary of Findings

Top bureaucrats in Swedish central government are highly educated. Virtually all have a basic university degree; almost one out of five has a research degree; and four out of ten report personal experiences of doing research. Two-thirds state that research knowledge is of great or very great importance in performing their work tasks; this is true of nine out of ten of those having a research degree. The heaviest users are found in the policy areas of defense, agriculture, social and health care, and industrial development.

Research knowledge is communicated to these top bureaucrats primarily through their discussions with experts from both within and without their own organisations, but professional journals also make up an important channel. Special conferences and courses as well as the mass media are judged to be of much less importance.

This overwhelmingly positive view of the usefulness of research knowledge among Swedish bureaucrats does not mean that they judge the effective utilisation of research knowledge in public policy-making as being without problems. A majority agree that under- or non-utilisation is an important problem. Only one out of ten top bureaucrats state that no such problems exist. R&D managers in Swedish central government are, perhaps not surprisingly, a little more optimistic; one out of five see no problems with respect to effective research utilisation.

As for obstacles to effective utilisation, both top bureaucrats and R&D managers locate them primarily among policy-makers and the policy-making process. Fewer find fault with the communication linkages between research and policy-making. And only one out of ten puts the blame for ineffective utilisation on research and researchers.

Caveats

The picture that has emerged from the analysis of the responses to the questionnaire is, then, quite unequivocal. However, at least three caveats are worth mentioning.

First, and probably most important, our analysis has concerned *self-reported* use of research knowledge. There are good reasons to believe that a high level of use is *per se* positively valued among a majority of the administrative elite in Sweden. It is an essential part of their political and corporate culture. Consequently our respondents may well have exaggerated their own level of research utilisation. A confirmation of sorts of this propensity may be found in the fact that while they report very high levels of use in their own work, most top-level bureaucrats are at the same time willing to agree that the effective use of research knowledge is a considerable problem in other parts of central government.

A *second*, and related, caveat stems from the fact that what respondents report on starts from a *self-defined* concept of research. We cannot be entirely sure that the high levels of research use found in the study are not due to an overly generous definition of the basic concept of research knowledge on part of many respondents. The problem is real and does of course apply as well to other key concepts such as 'use' or 'utilisation'. Unfortunately, the problem is also largely intractable when we use simple question-naires as instruments of investigation.

Third, and finally, the rate of response was, as mentioned above, only 75 per cent. To some extent this has probably created a certain bias in the direction of high levels of research use and favorable attitudes toward research as a basis for public policy-making in Swedish government.

Discussion

These caveats in mind, I still think that this study provides yet another body of evidence about the importance of research knowledge to policy-making in Swedish government. More interestingly, however - and, admittedly, in a more speculative vein - it also points to the inadequacy of a strictly instrumentalist view on how research knowledge feeds into policy-making. To put it somewhat provocatively: the Swedish administrative elite does not consist of 'innocent generalists' who are force-fed highly specific bits of knowledge, preferably produced, packaged and disseminated within the context of sectorial R&D programmes. Instead they are very often sophisticated specialists, having a formal research degree or at least with personal experience of doing research. They try to learn from research through direct discussions with researchers and other experts or by reading professional journals. Their 'search profile' is surprisingly similar to that of academic researchers within the same field. When pondering about problems of non-utilisation Swedish top bureaucrats primarily find fault with policy-makers - including, presumably, themselves - and policy-making, rather than putting the blame on researchers or the way in which research is carried out.

If my argument about the inadequacy of the instrumentalist view on research utilisation in Swedish government is reasonably correct, a host of policy implications follow. I suggest, however, that we begin by doing more extensive and careful research along the lines suggested here. If I am right, Swedish policy-makers will eventually learn from such research.

Part II

Research and Higher Education

Chapter 7

The Fragmentation of Research, Teaching, and Study

An Explorative Essay

Burton R. Clark

The German university reform in the early decades of the nineteenth century, to which we attach the name of Wilhelm von Humboldt, established as an enduring principle the encompassing idea of a unity of research, teaching, and study. While variously defined in actual practice, and much altered over time, this academic ideology has possessed several core imperatives. Those who teach at the most advanced levels of the educational system should be deeply involved in research. The research-centred professor should not only train students for research but should involve them in research. In the seminars and laboratories of the university, the students should become investigators as they seek answers to research problems that professors specify or that the students set for themselves. Ideally, professors and students become research colleagues, joining hands in a common search for the truth in the form of new knowledge. With research the foundation, the role of the university professor unites research and teaching, while the role of the student integrates research and study. Primary in the orientation of both professors and students, research folds teaching and study into a seamless web of commitment to the elaboration of knowledge.

This breath-taking principle has been deeply influential in the nineteenth and twentieth century development of higher education around the world, especially in the most advanced nations, serving as a central and even dominating concept in the German, British, and American modes of higher education and in the many adaptations in other countries of elements from these international centres of learning.[1] It is expressed in the basic university forms known as the seminar and the laboratory. We find it institutionalised in budgetary allocations for the support of teaching staff that presuppose they will spend a third or a half of their time in research. It is reflected in many countries in the definition of advanced students as 'research students' who will be invested in a research-based thesis from the day they enter upon graduate work. Higher education 'teachers', we may also note, are prepared largely by training in the theories and research methods of particular disciplines. The unity principle may be formally denied in such central international models as the French and the Soviet in which much research is concentrated in academies or research institutes and thereby separated from university teaching. But even in these cases many professors engage in research, base their teaching on their research specialty, and involve advanced students in research projects. The principle is so widespread that its cogency and its application are simply assumed by traditional academics in societies that define themselves as advanced, or at least semi-advanced, in their devotion to the scientific enterprise.

At the same time, those who believe in this principle, firmly convinced of its wisdom, have had much cause to worry in recent decades about the actual unity of research, teaching, and study. It is one thing to uphold the view that research and teaching are best done in each other's company, to assert that preparation to do research is best done by involvement in research, to maintain that even students destined for professional careers should be immersed in research practice and technique as well as told what recent research reveals. But it is another thing to observe the substantial development of research in non-teaching settings, in industry, government ministries, and non-university research institutes; *and* to note, in systems deeply invested in mass higher education, the substantial development of teaching in non-research settings. Modern forces that undermine the unity principle seemingly run strong.

To explore the fate of this relationship near the end of the twentieth century, after its long run since the days of Humboldt, a three-year study of the research foundations of 'graduate education' (in some countries, 'postgraduate education' or 'advanced education') was initiated in 1987 in five major countries of the Western world: the Federal Republic of Germany, Great Britain, France, United States, and Japan.[2] During the 1987-88 academic year, colleagues in each of these countries investigated the 'macro' structures of research and higher education.[3] During the following year, they pursued the 'micro' interaction of university faculty and students in three or four disciplines: in common, physics, economics, and history; separately in several cases, a commanding field such as engineering in Japan and biological sciences in the United States. The results of these intensive country studies will appear in ten papers authored by the country experts in an edited volume tentatively entitled *The Research Foundations of Graduate Education: Germany, Britain, France, United States, and Japan.* Cross-national comparison will be extended in a second volume, tentatively entitled *Places of Inquiry: Graduate Education and Research in Modern Society.*

Early comparative analysis of the disparate results of this study suggests many developments specific to the individual countries that on the one side fragment the research-teaching-study relationship and, on the other, serve to maintain its unity. Given different national histories and traditions, and different contemporary academic and societal structures (especially governmental ones), the isolation of country uniquenesses is a necessary part of any complex analysis. The 'specialness' of France, the 'exceptionalism' of the United States, must be given its due. But amid the welter of national structures and processes we can also discern generic forces that everywhere act to fragment the historic relationship, thereby attenuating the unity principle. We can also identify generic counterforces that stubbornly undergird the connection of research to both teaching and study, thereby maintaining the Humboldtian ideal in a modern form. This exploratory essay presents an overview of the generic forces that promote a separation, trends evident in the broad structures of research and higher education that, if unopposed by countervailing elements, place research in certain settings and teaching and study in others.

The Intensification and Diversification of Research

Internationally and nationally, higher education continually experiences 'substantive growth'; growth in academic tribes that follows from the proliferation of academic territories.[4] In a self-amplifying cycle of effects, research and scholarship steadily fashion more cognitive domains - disciplines, specialisms, interdisciplinary subjects - whose respective devotees then push on with new specialised categories of research. Each major discipline, each major cluster of academic fields, and the research enterprise at large simultaneously intensifies and diversifies. The 'high knowledge' components of higher education systems, spurred by the drive for new knowledge, steadily become more esoteric.[5] Intense, diverse, and esoteric, these components exist as *substantive* concentrations that require concentration in research resources, research infrastructure, and research-related personnel. It becomes difficult, if not impossible, to develop and maintain these necessary concentrations in the traditional locales of teaching and study.

The modern-day inner logic of the research imperative may thus be seen as containing a divisive tendency. This imperative can now often be best served by research-devoted groups that do not have teaching programmes and student needs on their minds. Thus, the very dynamics and core needs of modern research promote a drift of research from normal university teaching locales to organised research units that do not have teaching responsibilities and which in part are operated by full and part-time research staff serving as non-teaching academic personnel. Where research, fully and completely, comes first, science education and even research training take a back seat. These concerns fall into someone else's domain; they are not intrinsically the responsibility of those who, in a concentrated fashion, are directly engaged in research activities.

The drift of research toward non-teaching concentrations does not stop of course at the boundaries of universities. As research groups form around cognitive domains in other sectors of society, we must speak of substantive growth as a societal phenomenon, not just as one occurring in higher education. Research becomes a common activity in industry, civilian government agencies, the military establishment, and the non-profit sector, all structurally divorced from the university. In the last half of the twentieth century, research has undergone a certain 'massification.' In its many esoteric clusters, it can still be properly viewed as an elite function. But in its great multiplication and diffusion, it has become an activity in which many non-university institutions are involved and in which hordes of knowledge workers can claim a role. From medicine to fashion design, every profession or would-be profession develops a research wing. Off as well as on the grounds of universities, research finds homes where little or no teaching goes on and where few if any students are found.

In short; the intensification and diversification of research at the hands of the research imperative itself creates, and will create evermore, research settings that leave teaching and study behind. In a sense, restless research moves out in many directions to new frontiers, while its consolidation in the knowledge of teaching and study lags behind.

The Differentiation of Mass Higher Education

Substantive growth, centred on knowledge itself, acts most directly on the research component of the historic connection. In contrast, there are two major forces involved in 'reactive growth' that act most directly on the teaching-and-study components to encourage a divorce from research. Reactive growth is growth in institutions and staff that follow as a reaction to student growth and to labour force demands.[6] There is on the one side - the input side - mass access demand; on the other - the output side - ever broadening labour market demand. Most advanced industrial nations have moved to mass secondary education, well away from the elite pattern of five to ten per cent age group participation, and on into mass access to 'post-secondary' education. Simultaneously, an increasing number of professions and occupations insist upon some education beyond the secondary level. Clark Kerr has cogently argued that in the labour market of an advanced industrial nation at least 25 per cent of all employees are now in the categories of professional, technical, and administrative personnel for which post-secondary training is appropriate. Adding in the equity pressures from the access side, and allowing for dropouts, suggests systems that accommodate 30 per cent or more of the upcoming age groups; the 30 per cent figure is already surpassed in Japan, USSR, the United States, Canada, and Sweden.[7]

In these twin input and output forms, reactive growth exerts tremendous pressure for greater internal differentiation of higher education. Differentiation is the master structural trend in modern systems. In its bearing on the unity of research, teaching, and study, we can distinguish three types: differentiation among institutions and major types thereof; differentiation within the university, the main research-centred type; and differentiation within graduate education, the most advanced level within which research has been most comfortably located.

Widely observable in modern systems of post-secondary education is a differentiation of types of institutions in which pure teaching institutions are set apart from ones that are research-centred. The use of 'post-secondary' as a substitute for 'higher,' or as a way to refer to a more encompassing set of institutions, is a good marker for this trend. The pretense that all students, advanced as well as pre-advanced, will be trained either for research or in research is surrendered, even if academics do so with much reluctance and resistance and officials let their rhetoric trail the reality of change by a decade or two. New forms of higher education are created that stress little or no involvement in research. Among existing institutions, different research-teaching-training linkages are delineated, explicitly or implicitly, by type of institution. The historic principle of close unity is then expected to apply in one type of institution, the university, but not in other types, the 'non-U.' colleges and the short-cycle colleges. Even among the universities substantial differentiation occurs as various ones are officially designated, or evolve in an unplanned fashion, to be a full research university, or one only partially invested in research, or one without a research base and given over entirely to teaching.

Beyond the differentiation among institutions that pulls research out of many teaching settings is the ongoing internal vertical stretching of universities by levels of curricula and degrees. The student-input demands of mass higher education greatly increase the burdens of introductory teaching in a first cycle of pre-advanced education. No longer do all students come from selective academic secondary schools and from families sophisticated in matters of the mind. More preparatory work is then needed, beyond that provided in secondary education, to bring students up to the first stages of specialised study that is increasingly demanding. The students may come to higher education to enter a specialty, the pattern that remains dominant around the world; or to first immerse themselves in a 'general education' that was not completed at the secondary level, as in the United States. But in either case a first tier of instruction of a relatively introductory kind becomes necessary. Entering students are not at a level of sophistication in a given knowledge domain whereby immersion in research, or direct training for research, is seen as appropriate. Instead, a first introductory cycle is established as prerequisite to a second level, which then finally leads on to a third cycle or a true postgraduate level. The American version takes the form of lower division undergraduate, upper division uppergraduate, and graduate school. Most teaching within the modern university takes place at the first two levels; research-based teaching is overwhelmingly reserved for the highest tier. The multiplication of vertical university tiers moves much teaching away from research settings - and much research from the predominant teaching settings. This key form of internal differentiation of universities is now operationalised in many countries in the growth of 'university lecturer' positions defined as full-time teaching with no research involvement. The university thereby creates two classes of faculty, only one of which - the 'professors,' as traditionally understood - is expected to do research and is granted appropriate conditions of time and resources. The newer class are 'teachers,' even if given the same titles as those in the first career line. Because of its noticeable similarity to teaching roles in secondary schools, the creation of this second class of instructors is sometimes viewed by staff and students as a convergence on the practices and ethos of secondary education. At the least, it is a clear and definite structural adjustment to the huge instructional needs of mass higher education.

The inclination within universities to have teaching programmes with little or no foundation in research does not stop with greater differentiation of beginning, inter-mediate and advanced levels. It is also found within the most advanced or postgraduate level. Graduate programmes with little or no base in research steadily grow in import-ance. They take two forms: terminal master's degree or sub-doctoral programmes in the arts and sciences - the so-called basic disciplines - that are explicitly designed for non-research students; and professional degree programmes in an expanding array of practice-oriented fields. Both types reflect the growing amount of specialised knowl-edge that the labour market demands as thresholds of recognisable competence in a large number of occupations.

The American system of higher education is well-known as an enormous producer of doctorates: at the end of the 1980s, the output stood at over 34,000 a year. But the system is many times over an even larger source of master's degrees (nearly 300,000) and 'first professional' degrees, (approximately 75,000), the latter all separate from the nearly one million bachelor's degrees. The central output of the Japanese graduate school is engineers at the master's level. British higher education is steadily investing in 'taught master's' programmes that will grant a terminal degree and lead straightaway to the job market. Other countries are similarly widening the base of the post-bachelor's (or advanced) level of the university. Thus, we can now even speak of a growing massification of advanced education. Driven by expansion in enrolment, knowledge, and professional preparation, the advanced level is increasingly something more than just a place for the research student and the awarding of the research-based Ph.D. It is numerically evermore a home for non-doctoral programmes, non-research students, and the attainment of non-research degrees.

The Impulses of Government

Interacting closely with these 'natural' forces of substantive and reactive growth are the impulses of governments. Acting as *the* patron of modern systems of higher education, the government in every country has some concerns that push hard against the unity of research, teaching, and study. Three concerns are commonly operative: to limit costs; to concentrate research; and to effect change on a political timetable.

The Concern to Limit Costs

Near the end of the twentieth century the Humboldtian principle is an increasingly expensive ideal. In a day of ever-expanding knowledge, particularly in the scientific fields, research-based programmes have insatiable appetites for enhanced budgetary support. The cost of attempting to give all advanced teaching and study a sturdy research foundation, let alone teaching and study at the much larger pre-advanced stages, presents a bill that governments are unwilling to pay. With expenditures in mind, they are prone to advocate and support the non-research, full-teaching sectors that are everywhere less costly. In addition, they find the costs of undergraduate instruction more to their liking than the outlays for hugely expensive graduate programmes. Cost is a primary motive among financial backers for the inclination noted earlier to distinguish several types of universities that are funded differentially by extent of research commitment. Cost containment is also reason to differentiate fellowship and other financial aid for advanced students so that only a few students obtain full support while others must take loans, engage in outside work, and otherwise support themselves.

Especially looming large at the beginning of the 1990s is the tendency for governments to question sharply the budgeting of universities by means of a main 'institutional line' of funding that leaves the support for teaching and the support for research so blended that their respective costs are indistinguishable. Despite the protests of academics and their institutions that such funding is the most appropriate way to support activities that are in fact blended in the daily work of professors and the operation of the base units, economisers in funding circles are sorely tempted to try to fund teaching and research separately. Mature universities naturally contain much slack that is buried in lump-sum budgeting. Critics also steadily point out that much academic research is 'useless,' especially in the intensification of purportedly research activity throughout the humanities, the social sciences, the professional schools, and even the arts. A common drift in thought then is to take support for research, including subsidised time for research, wholly or partly out of the institutional line and to put it into a 'research council' line where funds will be awarded on a competitive basis by peer review of the merits of submitted proposals. Governmental actions in Britain and France and Japan during the late 1980s are prominent examples of this general tendency. In the American system, the separate support of research has long been institutionalised as a basic line of involvement on the part of the national government. The federal investment in research takes place on top of the general institutional line of support for teaching and research that is built into the funds the fifty states give their main university campuses - *and* on top of the support provided by institutional funds, for example, from tuition, endowment, annual gift-giving, that private universities raise and have at their disposal. When the funding of research is separated, then some academic fields can be favoured, others given little or no support. Even in the fields in favour, only some academics obtain support for their research, while others, perhaps even a majority, receive nothing. And from the medical school to the classics department, those who do not obtain grants to support research and scholarship thereby find they are expected to do more teaching.

By such means, the budgetary constraints exacted by governments in their support of higher education systems tend to cut deeply into the research underpinnings of teaching and student learning. The government formula becomes: economy and efficiency equals less research across the board and more teaching where research is deemed less important.

The Concern to Concentrate Research

Governments have numerous reasons to concentrate research by removing it from the base units of universities that are invested in teaching and study. Some parts of important scientific fields are now so expensive that their work must be concentrated in a few laboratories or institutes too large to be placed under department management. Involved scientists often agree that concentration should triumph over scatteration: champions of 'best science' are rarely to be found on the side of wide distribution of equitable shares. The desired research concentrations, large or small, may be located on university grounds, even formally listed as research units of the universities. But they are formally and spatially set apart from the teaching units. Some graduate students may find their way to these concentrations, brought over by professors serving in a dual capacity as research directors or taken on as employed research staff, part-time or full-time. But not all advanced students in the relevant disciplines, usually the majority, are so admitted.

The research concentrations may also be placed outside the university framework altogether. Ostensibly, they can be better managed if placed on their own and allowed to concentrate on their research tasks. Off campus they escape the traditional encrusted bureaucratic and professional practices of the universities. Research accountability is clarified; assessment of research productivity can be less clouded when research performance is separated from teaching and training activities. Governments find such reasoning especially tempting when cost containment is high on their agendas. They also push in this direction when they distrust the political climate of the universities, even heartily dislike a steady diet of anti-regime faculty and student activism. Why give 'them' more money? Why pour more good money down 'that bottomless pit,' even 'that rat hole'? Reform frequently means a bypass of traditional institutions, and top-down reform of scientific research offers the opportunity to move research out of 'the university mess' and into scientifically safer as well as more concentrated locales.

The Concern for Short-Run Action

Academics may sturdily maintain that there is nothing so useful as a good idea, and that basic ideas are best produced by unfettered research supported by stable, dependable funding oriented to the long-run. And, at the same time, for the future capability of the scientific community, that teaching and training must be supported and integrated with the on-going flow of unguided research. But both elected and unelected government officials may well maintain that in the long run we will all be dead and that reform and improvement need somewhat shorter deadlines. There are so many economic and social problems plaguing each nation on which academic research can seemingly help that the need to move faster looms large in regimes that are reasonably awake. And the self-interests of politicians and bureaucrats dictate deadlines of a few years that parallel re-election campaigns on which political careers depend and the reviews of accomplishment in administrative posts on which bureaucratic careers are built.

The short term-long term difference in the thinking of politicians and academics is systemic, a matter not of personality characteristics but of the institutional chariots to which motivation is attached. And it bears significantly on the willingness of governments to leave research in the unguided, 'soft' settings of university teaching departments. The need for responsible government actors to get things done in a definable time span strongly supports the concern to concentrate research in what appear to be immediately productive settings. It exercises a bias for specialised institutions over comprehensive ones, for research units that can be funded and evaluated on a five-year cycle in comparison to university departments whose blend of research, teaching, and training is fixed in budget categories established in days past that seemingly will go on forever. National planning will nearly always have a relatively short-term horizon - one year, three years, five years - that necessitates at least the promise if not the production of results in the definable here and now. To leave research to the ways of academic staff committed to the long-term and enmeshed in the slow processes of education then appears as a risk best not taken. In the urgencies of political agendas and executive action governments find additional potent reasons to seek to steer research and support it in concentrated centres.

The Interests of Industry

The term 'R and D' has become so commonplace that we are likely to overlook its basic meanings: that research should lead to useful application; that in turn technological and other 'developments' spring from research. The R&D idea exerts a different pull on research than the ideas of research and teaching ('R and T') and research and study ('R and S'). The R&D conception of reality ties research particularly to the economic sphere and to how research is understood by industrial and commercial firms. Industry has preconceived goals; its bottom line is monetary profit. Its activities are under the constant pressure of commercial necessity. Some large firms, in the interest of generating new knowledge that can in turn lead on to new processes and products, do indeed support basic research within their large R&D laboratories. But even in these cases the firms are not basically in the business of expanding the frontiers of science. Even more they are not fundamentally in the business of training the future generations of scientific investigators. As a general institutional sector, industry is not positioned to operate as if it were a set of research-centred universities. In the economic context, research is the handmaiden of the development of the individual firm and of the competitive progress of whole sectors of industry and commerce.

Thus, industry develops its own research capability for purposes of practical application and not for reasons of teaching and study. Industry also increasingly develops direct connections to universities in order to gain access to new ideas, to encourage industry-relevant research, and to promote the transfer of knowledge and technology from the university laboratory to settings that are more development minded. Some of these connections can be made with university departments. But increasingly they involve the elaboration of a sub-set of institutes and laboratories that stand half-way between higher education and industry or exist on the margin of the traditional core. Such collaborative centres exist to do research, not to teach; they typically employ non-teaching staff; they may have a few graduate students as part-time research assistants but most of the graduate students in the related departments will be outside their interest and their reach. Despite some impressive cases to the contrary, the interests of industry shape research in a way that divorces it from the university settings in which the steady stream of teaching and study goes on.

The Internationalisation of Science and Higher Education

The last half of the twentieth century has witnessed a steady internationalisation of disciplines, especially in the physical and biological sciences, and of universities, especially ones that have a strong research foundation. As scholarship has intensified and diversified, and the means of communication have dramatically improved, highly specialised academic researchers have been all the more driven by the intrinsic and extrinsic rewards of their work to reach out to others of their kind no matter where located in the world. In the academic world, it is a far better thing to be a 'cosmopolitan' than a 'local.' For both training and permanent employment, the most eager researchers are particularly attracted to universities known to be strong in their own discipline or specialty. Such willing mobility expands the international trade of talent - brain influx and brain drain - in which some countries are winners and others are losers. National and institutional pursuit of scientific and technological progress turns this mobility and trade into an international competition for 'best science.' A host of personal, departmental, institutional, and system interests thus push for the development of internationally-recognised centres of excellence, intellectual magnets that attract talent from the world-wide pool of researchers, professors, and students.

The growing international mobility and competition leads to an international ranking of universities and departments, a hierarchy of prestige based largely on perceived research capability. Through science citation analysis, quantitative comparisons of research output are also now readily available, by institution and by country, for various disciplines and research specialties.[8] This procedure places easily understood numbers on the very complicated phenomena of quantity and quality of scientific research that is lodged in a general way in the awareness that scientists have of related work and of where the best conditions for research are found. Such summary numbers can be factored readily into political thought and administrative logic and thereby used to goad institutional reactions and stimulate national effort. In short, the global competition in which science and technology are linked to the economic if not the military strength of nations is likely to increase rather than relent. This form of internationalisation is in itself a major force in the intensification of research, and the related concern to concentrate research, that, as noted earlier, tends to pull research work out of the university base units that are responsible for teaching and student training, particularly at the introductory and intermediate levels of instruction and then finally even at the most advanced level.

The universities that have substantial international reputations, and thereby attract many foreign students, also generally face a training dilemma. The students from abroad arrive equipped with an educational preparation that does not parallel in style and content that found in the host country. They have language problems. They often cannot stay for more than one or two years. Such limitations encourage universities to develop short-term programmes deemed appropriate for them. They are judged to need pre-sessional courses. Another common response is to offer them tailor-made short programmes that lead to a postgraduate diploma or a one or two-year master's degree. In notable contrast to PhD work, such programmes typically do not have firm research components. Time and resources are limited and students are judged not to need an international gold-standard level of expertise but one appropriate to the conditions of research and training found currently in their home countries. Adaptation to this type of student in the international university extends the numerical predominance of advanced-level programmes based largely on instruction that offers little involvement in research.

Disciplinary Variation in the Nature of Research, Teaching, and Study

We may observe that in its very nature modern research has some tendency to wander away from teaching. Since teaching involves systematic, orderly presentation of materials, it becomes organised in classes, courses, and curricula. It has an integrative bent, one that is worked out with students' learning in mind. In contrast, research is ambiguously open, given to zigs and zags, even to hunting for a needle in a haystack. It attempts to move into uncodified terrain, and it is increasingly esoteric in the sense of distance between it and what non-experts and students know. As a result, where professors are intellectually positioned in their research is often quite a different matter than the cognition categories used in the classroom. In the normal course of change in modern academic work, we should expect much drifting of university research work off to cognitive corners of its own making.

The nature and extent of such research drift is, of course, markedly affected by the nature of research in the various disciplines and specialties. Here, many distinctions can be made: for example, hard-soft, pure-applied, convergent-divergent.[9] A rudimentary example can be offered in a simplified contrast between physics and history. In physics, advanced students are commonly assigned topics by mentors; in history, such students freely select their own topic. In physics, the graduate students involved in research, even at the level of the doctoral dissertation, work on a piece of a large project; in history, students work on their own holistic project. In physics, young scholars-to-be publish articles, often jointly authored; in history, they attempt to write books. The one is interested in scientific objectivity; the other in the power of individual interpretation.

In general, research-centred professors need graduate students. But that need is much more compelling in science and engineering where laboratories and projects have to be staffed with several levels of expert personnel. Advanced students are needed and are utilised as research assistants. This need to bring the student to the bench is an important force for the integration of research with teaching and study. In contrast, professors of history are likely to work on their own studies while their graduate students quite separately and individually work on theirs, with perhaps some coming together in a seminar or two and in personal interaction of dissertation supervision. But in one society after another, advanced students in the humanities and the more qualitative social sciences report that they are generally detached from the on-going scholarship of their professors. The chief counterforce here, with a host of special problems of its own, is the highly integrated patron-student clusters that become schools of thought within a specialty, ones that rival and compete with other schools of thought.[10]

Interaction of the Factors of Fragmentation

The factors of fragmentation here identified are so intertwined and interactive that it is difficult to isolate one from another. Notably, the forces involved in the diversification of research and the differentiation of mass higher education promote each other so intensely that they seem at times to be simply two parts of the same phenomenon. In turn, the concerns of government to limit costs and to concentrate research, and to otherwise improve efficiency and effectiveness, both react to and act upon the ongoing flows of research specialisation and institutional differentiation. The linking of research to development in the economy and to the behavior of industrial and commercial firms adds further force. And international competition intensifies everywhere the tendency to develop research centres of excellence without regard to their educational effectiveness. As they interact, these factors of fragmentation diminish greatly the play of the classic Humboldtian ideal.

In many modern systems of higher education, as a result, it is widely understood that not all higher education teachers will be researchers. As a counterpart, in and out of the academy, full-time research becomes a career in its own right, without a commitment to teaching and training. And it is increasingly utopian to expect each university student, even at the most advanced level, to be invited to work 'at the bench' with a research-renowned mentor or even to be given a place in the advanced seminars that serve in the humanities and the social sciences as the equivalent of laboratories.

Thus the Humboldtian idea is not in command across modern systems of higher education and related systems of research. For large sub-sets of educational and research enterprises, research and teaching, and research and study, proceed on different pathways. But the old ideal is not dead. Against the forces of fragmentation reviewed here there are counterforces of integration that uphold in modern form the blending of research, teaching, and study. The ideal itself, as a widely held belief, has much continuing force; research remains central in faculty reward systems; university scholars need and use graduate students as research assistants; and the simple idea that the best researchers should be involved in the training of future generations of researchers is hard to deny. The interplay of the generic forces of fragmentation and integration therefore does not rule out the modern application of this now age-old ideal. Instead it is limited to certain settings where it may be more intense than ever. Only under certain supporting conditions does the Humboldtian image truthfully dominate. The analytical task remains to identify those conditions in various national systems of higher education and research organisation. Only then can a balanced picture be presented of how, and how much, modern research serves a foundation for the most advanced teaching and training.

Chapter 8

The University: *Bildung* or *Ausbildung*

Scientific Dominance in Modern Higher Education

Gunnar Bergendal

Some time ago I got a letter from a friend in mid-Sweden. He enclosed 'a contribution from the great world worth consideration', taken from James Boyd White's *Heracle's Bow: Essays on the Rhetorics and Poetics of the Law*.[1] It reads as follows:

> This bureaucratic language is very deep in our ordinary culture as well: think of a conversation at a curriculum committee meeting where someone says: 'Let us first state our educational goals and then determine how we can arrive at them.' That is a dreadful way to talk about teaching, yet it is dominant in our world, and once the conversation has begun on those terms it is almost impossible to deflect it to address any true educational concerns.

We often speak of educational goals, and White is warning us not to be trapped in this bureaucratic language, this dreadful way to talk about teaching. Certainly all of us, who have for some years or decades been in Swedish teacher training or educational planning, can recall our belief that what it was all about was first to decide on the goals, and then to find the way to reach them. We can also recall our belief that both these things were possible.

Surely, it is both reasonable and necessary to state that pre-school teachers are educated here and priests or nurses there. Or more generally: that we reflect on the future in connection with this or that type of education. But what should be indications of direction, giving perspective to education, too easily become allegedly exact formulations which we believe can be broken down into subgoals in order to derive detailed educational plans. We often speak of goals as if they were attainable, and as if once they were reached all would be well. There is an over-confidence in educational goals. This may be connected with our strong belief in planning, although planning has its limits. At the core is probably - and this is what the quotation is about - our bureaucratic culture; once goals have been formulated and confirmed, our efforts no longer concern the thing itself, but the stated goals. We have set a trap and got caught in it. We have believed that the production goals of the automobile industry could have their counterpart in school and in higher education. So far, it seems that child care and nursery schools have been spared.

The English word 'education' is translated into Swedish simplistically by the word *utbildning* (training). But our school dictionary gives *fostran/bildning* as first alternative. *Fostran* means 'up-bringing'. And the Swedish *bildning* - like the German *Bildung* - is not first and foremost to be a cultivated person (*bildad människa*) but rather to be a human being in formation, in maturing. Therefore, Hans-Georg Gadamer says in his

Truth and Method that we should be suspicious of educational goals, both of the word and of that which it stands for.[2] Educational goals can be neither exactly stated nor attained. The motive force of education is within ourselves, in what concerns us. When J. B. White says that it is dreadful to talk about educational goals, this may be what he is aiming at: that educational goals are impossible, that the word is self-contradictory. He prefers to speak about educational *concerns*.

What then *are* our educational concerns? During my fifteen years as a mathematics teacher at the university and - for a shorter period of time - in high school, my concern was to present my subject in such a clear fashion that all students could understand it. The contents were given by the position laid down by the science of mathematics and by our choice - determined partly by tradition - within the limits of the subject. The aim was to lighten the road with the bright lamp of logic, and so level out the difficulties, rather than to let the difficulties speak for themselves and to encourage the students to butt against them. We were rather successful, when assessed by the usual criteria: so many students passed the exams, were able to answer the questions - had attained goals that were formulated or could be formulated. Perhaps we did not do so badly - in most cases we did not kill young people's reason and common sense. It still happens that I meet former students of mine who talk with appreciation of our time together or of some textbook which relied on this faith in clarity as a pedagogical means.

In the somewhat more nuanced light of reflection some three decades later on, I wonder if we did not fall into the trap of clarity. In his book on Descartes, André Glucksmann says:

> When requiring not only clear but also distinct ideas, Descartes took the trouble to point out the trap of clarity and to tell that he was intent not to fall into it.[3]

Here the key word is *distinct*: to be able to distinguish the salient features - what is essential. In a recent book edited by J. C. Nyiri and Barry Smith, there are a couple of papers on the relationship between practical and propositional knowledge which are worth considering. Distinction - the ability to distinguish - belongs to the domain of practical knowledge. As one example of such a domain, the British legal tradition, The Common Law, is referred to. The common law builds on precedents rather than on written law. Roger Scruton says, that it 'has the character, not of a public pronouncement, but of a slow judicial discovery'. Scruton points out:

> when the barrister argues that the judge ought to *distinguish* the present case, he is arguing for a particular interpretation of the precedent.[4]

Thus distinction is about setting the present case into its proper context, to judge it as the basis for practical action.

In his paper 'Tradition and Practical Knowledge', the Hungarian J. C. Nyiri points to two positions with regard to the issue of practical knowledge:

> According to the first, this knowledge is a *practical abbreviation* within the texture or flow of knowledge as such, a device of paramount pragmatic importance perhaps, but not something whose discovery should basically transform our epistemological convictions. According to the second position, there is a layer or dimension of practical knowledge, which could in no sense be dissolved into knowledge of a propositional sort. Or perhaps - and this would be a stronger version of the same position - there is a hard layer of practical knowledge which serves as the bedrock on which *all* knowledge rests. Or indeed - to formulate a yet stronger version - all theoretical knowledge represents but an articulating, a spelling out, of a knowledge which is invariably irreducible to practise.[5]

Clarity as a concern of teaching, research and education should not be despised. All of us should be careful of the forms of what we want to say or show. But if clarity is blinding distinction, so that we do not see what is important or what is not, what is good or bad, then it turns into a trap. Such might be the case if we are required to ask only those questions that have clear answers, suited for formulation. In his *Metaphysical Horror*, the Polish philosopher Leszek Kolakowski remarks that according to Jean Piaget such questions as 'who made it?' (this mountain or that waterfall) correspond to the childish stage of human development. 'As yet', Kolakowski says, 'we do not grow up in the sense Piaget wishes us to'.[6] He continues that Enlightenment culminates in this injunction: 'stop asking such questions'. From where comes the supreme validity of the verdict which forbids us this search?

> Only from the fact that this civilisation - ours - which to a large extent has got rid of this search, proved immensely successful in some respects; but it has failed pathetically in many others.

Should not then humility bid us to be cautious not to reject questions on the only grounds that they are not clear or are impossible to fathom? Actually, they may concern us.

The Swedish Law of Higher Education provides that education (*utbildning*) at universities and colleges (*högskolan*) should be scientifically based. This paragraph was taken over from the earlier national University Statute. Compared to that statute, the present law implies two important differences which are related to the circumstances that the universities and colleges now comprise all kinds of post-secondary education and that they are organised in two separate fields of activity: research and education (*forskning och utbildning*). The University Statute referred to only a limited part of the present field of universities and colleges. The traditional university was divided into faculties, each of which was responsible for both teaching and research within its domain. The faculties decided themselves, within fairly wide limits, on the qualities of their activities: the interpretation of the term 'scientific' in the Statute was in the hands of those responsible for education. This is, in important instances, no longer the case.

It may be argued that the present provision of law was decided on upon remarkably little analysis. In the report by the 1968 Educational Commission, which was the basis of the 1975 decision of Parliament on the reform of higher education, the scientific character of education was not discussed. But there was an analysis of the connections between education and research, although without explicitly mentioning that scientific research was intended. The aim of connections with research was to add - or to ensure - a searching, questioning dimension of education, rather than to make connections to existing professional research. In the commission report there is a proposed formulation of a future Statute of Higher Education (which never came into being), in which one reads: '. . . undergraduate education is to be scientifically based . . .'. But this is mainly an unreflected matter of course. The critical training which is mentioned in the following sentence of the proposed statute, becomes a scientifically critical schooling. But there are problems if you want to turn such critical schooling into a criticism of the scientific basis. It remains an open question whether the commission understood 'research' as 'scientific research', although its possible intentions may be considered a thing of little importance twenty years later. The issue of the qualities of knowledge in modern society should now be raised in the perspectives of our time, including our experiences of the present universities and colleges and their rules and regulations.

The Swedish universities and colleges provide all types of qualified higher education. When the law states that their activities should be scientifically based, the only exception refers to artistic education. But even with this restriction, the prescription of the law is very inclusive - even if there is room for different interpretations. Its basic meaning seems to be that the scientific disciplines taken together constitute a sufficient basis for our culture, or at least for its more qualified manifestations, those for which universities and colleges are considered responsible. Or else the meaning of law is that qualified knowledge of the kind for which higher education is responsible has such a basis. What reasons may there be for such notions? The representatives of each individual discipline usually take care to emphasise the limits of the domain of validity of their discipline: astronomy is about the stars and linguistics is about human language. For many of us it sounds implausible that the union of all these (in themselves) limited disciplines could include all types of human knowledge in all their aspects. At most it might be a conviction with some people that such is the case, or that such might be the case, or that it would be a good thing if such were the case. When the Law of Higher Education provides that education at universities and colleges be scientifically based, this interpretation is evidence of an underlying conviction of our culture. This is a small step from other countries or other ages prescribing one religion for all institutions and all citizens. In any case, the provision of a scientific basis can have no scientific basis: '*car on ne fonde pas ce qui fonde*' - one cannot found that which founds - as Glucksmann says in his book on Descartes.[7]

For us who criticise the law of the scientific basis, it is obviously not a matter of eliminating the sciences. What is at stake is rather to extend this self-discipline (German: *Besinnung*) which every academic discipline exercises - at least when it is at its best - to the entire field of science. Not science as a vision or utopia, but as it actually exists. Also, we should draw conclusions from such self-discipline, both for our society at large, and for our schools and our higher education. It is my conviction that science, like all other types of knowledge, is for good and for bad, and that it runs the same risk as other orthodoxies - they may be papal or Protestant, capitalist or socialist - when they are provided as the only permitted belief, or are treated as the belief which is superior in all contexts and circumstances.

First, there is an obvious objection against the idea that the results of scientific research were, at any given moment, a sufficient basis for knowledge. The scientific community itself repudiates such ideas: further research would then be superfluous. But there is a trace of this thinking in the prevailing arguments, pleading that education should include the latest research findings: as if it were important, after one or two decades, whether the graduate of 1990 acquired the standpoint of science prevalent in 1980 or 1989. Behind the idea that the by no means unimportant ambition to follow the frontier of research is a concern of utmost significance, is the view of knowledge as information, as a commodity to be distributed from the scientific community, which decides on what should be considered the truth at each moment. But if knowledge is people's own knowing, the substance of which is tried out in responsible action, then it becomes obvious that the results of scientific research, however recent, must not be taken as imperatives, but rather as possibilities for us to try out, to accept or reject, or to make our own on our own conditions, with our own understanding and objectives. In this perspective the schooling of judgement is a more important issue than observing the frontiers of research.

But, so it is said, the important thing is not research findings but the scientific methods. There is a claim that *the* scientific method is the quintessence of higher education. There are also objections against this position. We become increasingly aware that the methods determine the results. If we take up a necessarily limited number of methods in education, one thing is certain: they are insufficient in those practical stations of life - in professional activities or elsewhere - that we later participate in. And, as Michael Polanyi (among others) has stressed, every scientific method must presuppose familiarity with the domain concerned.[8]

At the heart there is a skill, a mature distinction which is never transferred by formal education (*utbildning*) but in a process of formation (*bildningsgång*), which has more in common with an apprenticeship with the master than with information mediation in lecture halls or with the latest devices of information technology. There is no such thing as a method of learning to ask questions, as Gadamer says in *Truth and Method*, of learning to see what needs to be questioned. He continues: the art of questioning is that of being able to go on asking questions, thus it is the art of thinking. It is called dialectic, for it is the art of conducting a real conversation.[9]

The optimism greeting the new technique of interactive video is a good example of over-confidence in methods, or in *the* method. There is an idea that by storing pictures of various situations or facts in video discs, and by programming these so that they confront the viewer with consecutive options of choice, one would have a good teaching aid in a wide range of fields of knowledge. But this presupposes a programmer who together with a supposed expert decides what questions should be asked, and the formulation of these questions. Instead of developing a familiarity with the matter that calls forth the student's own doubt and trial in situations of responsibility, she or he is tempted to accept the programme's structuring of the issue and the expert's options of solution. This seems to be the opposite of the art of thinking as the art of asking further questions, simply because no real dialogues are to be had with a machine, whatever it may be called. Hannah Arendt remarks on the danger of thinking which arises out of the desire to find results that would make further thinking unnecessary.[10]

So, if interactive video as a teaching aid might be supposed to have dangerous secondary effects that make it a contribution of doubtful value to the education of young people, this should not prevent this technique from having important encyclopedic applications. But the bringing up and education of young people are no encyclopedic concerns. They start in practice. Only she or he who is familiar with the world can use the encyclopedia on her or his own conditions. Behind interactive video there is an assumption that only one logic exists, the logic of computers. But there are reasons to maintain a wider concept of logic, what Karl Jaspers calls *philosophical logic*. Jaspers says that this logic

> is no longer to be limited to the traditional formal logic or to methodology of investigation and proof in the sciences; these partial fields remain intact in their detail, though not in their total meaning.[11]

Jaspers speaks of different modes of knowing, each with its own consciousness, which encourages every mode to work itself out resolutely. Logic then is the form of honesty grown conscious. To Jaspers the value of scientific methods is as obvious as is their insufficiency. Every mode of knowledge has its own logic. This was brought forth by the old organisation of the university, where each faculty was a knowledge community with responsibilities for both learning and teaching. By now we have left the idea of the learning teacher and replaced her and him by the teaching researcher. However, the researcher's logic is the logic of a scientific discipline but not necessarily the students' logic or the logic of their knowledge communities.

There is one more aspect of the provision of scientifically-based knowledge that deserves emphasis. It concerns language. With some over-simplification it can be held that knowing, in order to be acknowledged in universities, has to be articulated in the language of a (doctoral) thesis. Mike Cooley describes in *Architect or Bee? The Human Price of Technology*,[12] how theoretical and practical knowledge were separated in the transition from the Middle Ages to the Modern Age. The master masons of the great cathedrals had been responsible for both building and design. They retained the qualitative and quantitative elements of work, the subjective and the objective, the creative and the noncreative, the manual and the intellectual, and the work of hand and brain, embodied in one craft. This unity was rejected by those who sought to show that theory was above, and separate from, practice. The growing academic elite resented the fact that carpenters and builders were known as masters, for example, *Magister Cementarius* or *Magister Lathomorum*. The academics attempted to ensure that *Magister* would be a title reserved for those who had completed the study of the liberal arts. Cooley points out that as early as the 13th century doctors of law were moved to protest formally at these academic titles for practical people. Régine Pernoud points at the same development in her book on the history of the bourgeoisie in France.[13]

We are quite familiar with this distinction which means that knowledge *of* something formulated in a language which claims generality, prevails over knowledge *in* the same field. It is not that practical knowledge has no language, but its languages are different, with other means of expression that are tied to the communities of practical knowledge - those of building, nursing or teaching. This same conflict can be found earlier than in the Renaissance. In his paper *The Socratic and Platonic Basis of Cognitivism*, Hubert L. Dreyfus says that Socrates:

> seems to want to elicit rules or principles from experts in each craft domain that would enable anyone to acquire expertise in that domain. . . . He seems to want a strict rule which can be used even by non-experts.[14]

But is this abstract language of rules - abstracted from the familiarity of practical knowledge - really a universal language, in the sense that it is available for all, and can be practised by everybody? Does it not, on the contrary, turn into the language of the academic elite, with its own norms and values, different from those of other people? Is not the allegedly universal language a tool for that division of labour that we associate with Taylorism and which could simply be described in the formula that some people think and others act?[15] Is this what Elias Canetti is speaking about when he says: 'A machine invents a world language. Since no one can understand it, it is accepted by all.'[16]

Scientific knowledge, which was intended to be knowledge available for everyone, acquires a singular relationship to human beings and human societies exactly by its ambition to objectivity and generality. There is a risk that people's own notions of what is evil and what is good, notions that lack objectivity and universality, wither away in face of the idea that only what is proved by science is valid. Our responsibility for our lives - and for life - will then also fade away and we run the risk of being reduced to receivers of information within bureaucratic or economic systems that share with science the claims of objectivity and universality. Theodor W. Adorno seems to express this when saying:

> Thoughts are drastically and fully brought under control by societal organisation. For every scientific assertion is on principle tested by every approved scientist of the discipline, irrespective of his mental ('*geistig*') constitution. And all spiritual activity should be repeatable afterwards by any other arbitrary individual.[17]

In an important paper the Finnish philosopher Lars Hertzberg criticises the general trend of our age of giving various professional roles a scientific touch.[18] Among other things he speaks of what he calls 'professional sciences' such as 'nursing science' and the 'science of teaching the mother tongue'. We have a notion, says Hertzberg, that scientific thinking is the pure form of rational thinking, and thus all forms of thought have to be dressed in scientific disguise in order to be taken seriously. We have got an elite that masters the symbolic skills, an elite whose position is founded on their being in possession of the secret of the apparent merit.

Hertzberg has very fittingly given his paper a motto coined by Joseph Butler, the 18th-century philosopher: 'Everything is what it is, and not another thing.' It is a call to sticking to the matters - to let each matter be what it is - rather than to objectivity, that objectivity which so easily turns into a guise for something else. Another quotation by Karl Jaspers is close at hand:

> Science, delivered to itself as only science, falls into neglect. The intellect is a whore, says Nicolas Cusanus, for it abandons itself to all sorts of purposes. Science is a whore, said also Lenin, for it sells out to every class interest.[19]

We are back in the relationship between practical and theoretical knowledge. If practice is the application of theory, if theory stands for itself, or rather, hangs in the mid-air, there is a great risk that we do not stick to the matters. What matters is familiarity with the matter. The only theoretical knowledge which is trustworthy is that based on practice, on one's own experience, on one's own responsible action. Practice should not be valued from the point of view of theory, but theory has to be valued in the perspective of practice. When it is said of the art of medicine that it should be based on science and practical experience, this may be so, but only if practice is the Alpha and the Omega, the beginning and the end, that all-embracing field in which knowledge is tried out. In *On Certainty*, Ludwig Wittgenstein says that practice has to speak for itself.[20]

If Nyiri is right in saying that there is a hard layer of practical knowledge which serves as the bedrock upon which all knowledge rests, then practical skill must be the main thread of education. English 'skill' has its roots in the old Norse word *skil*, which means 'distinction'. Skill has something to do with distinguishing the salient features, with observing and taking into account - or leaving out of account. Skill has to do with schooled judgment and is more than the mastery of various techniques. When we speak of knowledge and skills as two separate things, it is as if this dimension of distinguishing has faded away, because we have been tempted to separate that which must be kept together if vital knowing is to be possible.

Distinction has to do with responsibility and solidarity. It is being schooled, not in freely-floating communities of communication, but in the particular circumstances of every responsible action. It is not universal, and is thus alien to the claims to generality of the sciences. Instead it is tied to the world and the common sense of every human being. But, as André Glucksmann says, common sense, *le bon sens*, gets a bad press in *academia*: it is reduced to the absurd statement that all people's thinking about the same thing is equally good.[21] Rather the common sense - sound reason - becomes sound and healthy only by being tried and doubted, by being schooled in the art of distinction. Common sense resembles the Common Law in that it is in steady formation. It is built on precedents and is a slow discovery of the world. Therefore, its formation and education is incompatible with a view of knowledge which argues that research is entrusted to an elite, who is assigned the task of setting the goals of education for the many.

Chapter 9

The Research Connection
The Need for Argumentation in Teaching and Learning

Stefan Björklund

The law which since 1978 has governed all higher, i.e. post-secondary, education in Sweden stipulates that it 'must be grounded in research'. For study programmes in the traditional university sector, the link with research has long been a matter requiring little reflection, but in the case of other study programmes which in 1978 were made part of the unitary higher education system, the pedagogical implications of this provision have not been self-evident.

Evaluations have shown that a variety of conclusions have been drawn concerning the probable implications of the research connection.[1] I would like now, very briefly, to present four different interpretations before getting on with the real task of pleading for one particular interpretation and hinting at some of its pedagogical implications.[2]

The interpretation that most immediately springs to mind is that the content of education must agree with current research findings. Ideally, it must incorporate the latest of them. A research connection in this sense poses three requirements: well-read teachers, up-to-date teaching materials (which is also the teachers' responsibility) and the actual existence of research to tie in with the study programme, which brings me to my next point.

In the efforts to establish research connections for medium-length caring education programmes, prominence has been given to the development of research training opportunities. In some cases this has meant steering research students into subjects belonging to another research and study organisation. It is not always immediately clear what those subjects ought to be. There are instances of orientation towards both social sciences and scientifically-based medicine. But efforts in this quarter have also included the creation of a specific research field, caring research.[3]

The commonest definition of a research connection seems to be for instruction to incorporate training in scientific methods. But anybody setting out to construct a course of scientific method for a subject having no natural connection with research can expect to run into difficulties. There is not just one scientific method, there are many, and they vary from one research field to another. But the diversity of methods is not the biggest difficulty. It is more serious if methods are taught without any problems to refer to.[4] This reflection leads me to my next proposed definition.

The discussion of research connections often gives the impression of the latter being a coherent phenomenon. It has been said, for example, that the link with research constitutes the boundary between higher education and other parts of the education system. But the diversity of methods seems to give the lie to the notion of research connection as *one* phenomenon. The two remaining definitions, however, express ideals uniting the whole of the higher education system and constituting the foundation of its claim to autonomy.

In a book recently published by a research group at the University of Göteborg, together with British colleagues[5], and which ought to be read by every higher education teacher, results are presented which point to a fundamental paradox connected with learning. Learning, it is argued, is a by-product of comprehension of a text, which in turn is a by-product of interest in the text. If reading is governed by the intention of learning the text, then the reader overlooks or misunderstands the message of the text, with the result that the content will not stick in the memory.[6]

There are important pedagogical lessons to be learned from this finding. No matter how one organises the teaching situation, examination or external motivation, effective learning can only occur if there is a particular internal motivation. This motivation could simply be called curiosity. One cannot instruct the pupil to be curious. But the outer conditions can be organised to foster curiosity.

The incorporation of current research findings or methods courses cannot be the profoundest implication of the research connection. There are extensive fields of teaching having no research findings worthy of the name. And methods unrelated to problems lead nowhere. But the nature of internal motivation is an important link between research and studies. The definition of research connection which I am now considering boils down to an imperative need to facilitate an attitude to the subject matter.

This definition of 'research connection' may seem innocuous and of no practical consequence. And yet it lays down a boundary against the instrumentalism so highly characteristic of our social attitude. We doubtless benefit from our curiosity, but only as a side-effect, only as long as we are seeking knowledge for its own sake.[7] If we demote knowledge to a means, we will never find what we are looking for. As I have now defined it, research connection means that the content of an education cannot be wholly subordinated to demands of practical utility. And conversely, if we cannot afford this sort of extravagance in a programme of vocational education, we can stop talking about a research connection.

Down to the 1960s, influential philosophers maintained that the observation of phenomena in our world constituted the firm foundation of our knowledge.[8] The observations yielded data with the support of which we could construct theories about the workings of the world. Concepts had no meaning, it was said, unless they referred, directly or indirectly, to data provided by our senses.[9] Formal logic occupied a central position. This approach, often called logical empiricism, wanted to do away with loose speculations.

But there are difficulties involved in this approach. Studies of scientific work reveal that pure observation does not exist. Even in the everyday situation where we see a phenomenon with our eyes, our apprehension of what we are observing is subject to previous experience, experience tied together in general knowledge concerning basic characteristics of our surroundings. And things are worse still on the research frontier, where most phenomena are not seen at all. Observation is indirect, produced by instruments and intermingled with theories.

This led some theorists to turn logical empiricism upside-down. Theories, they said, were fundamental. Basic assumptions concerning reality, theories and rules of method made up continuous complexes called 'paradigms'. The individual observation implied, not a check in relation to an independent external reality, but a deduction from the paradigm. Rules of thinking and criteria of true and false were also governed by the paradigm. It was therefore impossible to decide, through observations of reality, which of two rival paradigms was preferable. There were no intellectual bridges between paradigms.

To the empiricists - just as to common sense - observation was the link serving to unite theory with the reality studied. Valid knowledge was conditional on the content of observation being determined by reality and not being influenced by anything else. Thomas Kuhn and his successors went to the opposite extreme. Observation, they said, was dependent on theory. Paul Feyerabend took the final logical step in this connection by maintaining that all ways of describing reality were equally valid. The knowledge possessed by the witch-doctor seems inferior to that of the medical scientist. But only from the perspective of science itself. The witch-doctor's criteria of truth are different and, viewed in his perspective, science is inferior. There is no point outside these two perspectives from which a comparative evaluation can be made.

Feyerabend argues: 'Arguments may retard science while deception is necessary for advancing it.'[10] These words show that it is not any specific scientific approach which is under attack, so much as the idea of our being able to convince one another by advancing arguments. Clearly, given Feyerabend's approach, it is futile to look for an unambiguous interpretation of the term 'research connection'. Indeed, not just futile but actually harmful, for - once again in Feyerabend's own words - 'a free society is one in which all traditions of knowledge have equal access to power'.[11]

The view of scholarly controversies, not as a battle between argument and counter-argument but as a power contest and a matter of social interests and socio-psychological motives, is typical of the epistemologists who are customarily known as 'relativists'.[12] My purpose in this essay is to assert that relativism is not the sole alternative to positivism and its belief in a single scientific methodology, and that the other alternative gives us exactly the general interpretation which we need of the concept of 'research connection'.

Michael Polanyi, who in several respects is a forerunner of Kuhn, refers at length to a number of ethnological studies, among them Evans-Pritchard's widely observed study of magic-related conceptions in an African tribe, the Azande. Evans-Pritchard found that every observation which, to him, decisively refuted one of these ideas could be explained away by means of other ideas in the Azande's intellectual system. No objections could take root, because Evans-Pritchard always had to formulate them in terms outside the language of the system of magic. The system, Polanyi says, was stable because it was circular. Arthur Koestler and Karen Horney, following their respective defections, have said the same of communism and psychoanalysis. But, Polanyi maintains, the same is also true of the scientific system of ideas. He quotes numerous examples from science to show how scientists explain away or ignore instances at variance with established ideas.[13]

Polanyi also attacks another line of thinking in the history of ideas in the western world, namely the notion that every idea must be called into question. According to René Descartes and John Stuart Mill, it is not until rational criticism has cleared away all groundless ideas that we have objective ground to stand on. This programme, Polanyi tells us, disregards the fact that every claim to knowledge on one point or another is depending on a 'personal commitment', i.e. acceptance without final proof. Ultimately, with the programme of radical criticism, nothing remains.

Can these two pictures be reconciled? Science as one of many creeds. The nihilistic end point of scientific rationalism. Polanyi juxtaposes them, but why not superimpose them one upon the other? The scientific approach is characterised by the union of faith and doubt.[14] Such a combination is improbable and fragile. It seems more natural to enclose successful intellectual systems, converting them into dogmas. But this in turn is the end of their success. Open systems in which conflict and instability are permissible are the only ones capable of changing and growing. The 'rational discourse' is a programme for systems of this kind.

The rational discourse is characterised by the burden of proof resting on the person propounding a thesis. Other participants in the discourse have to challenge the thesis until the respondent has established it in circumstances which cannot be refuted. The opponent must not believe in the thesis: he must not be overwhelmed by the respondent's eloquence, commitment or authority, his task is to doubt for as long as doubt can be reasonably maintained. In the rational discourse, I meet opponents who will not bow to anything but arguments but who on the other hand will not resort to anything but arguments. This procedure does not lead to results of unshakeable certainty, but it does lead to more than consensus between the participants, it leads to universally valid results.[15]

The essential thing about a research connection in this perspective is not really the incorporation of the latest research finding in teaching or the instruction of students in scientific methods. This way we have less to worry about if there is no vigorous research frontier connected with the field of education concerned. Instead the task should be described as that of opening the scholarly discourse to the student, inducing him/her to see as his own arguments the arguments for and against standpoints constituting the scientific exchange of opinion. I take issue with the relativists because they deny that reasons play any decisive part. To them, scientific disputes are won, not by superior arguments but by superior campaigning.

The failure of logical empiricism has taught us that there is no way of defining, once and for all, the boundary between scientific and nonscientific. There are no criteria whereby we can say in advance what an acceptable theory will look like, except that it must be open to criticism.[16] This takes away all restrictions on argument and makes power impossible. Social institutions do not automatically work this way. A social institution which is to be stable without distributing power between different roles requires a subtle balance. The art lies in maintaining an institution in which people think both freely and correctly, in which belief and disbelief are balanced, in which every argument is welcome but bad arguments are dismissed, in which every individual can nail up his theses but none will be spared an opponent. Cherishing this institution is the quintessence of the research connection.

Argument means maintaining that something applies *because* something else applies.[17] What happens in an argumentation is, first, a definition of the critical terms, to make sure that we are talking about the same thing.[18] This is rarely a simple matter of deciding what names we are going to give to different phenomena. Less time is usually needed to test the logic linking premisses and conclusion together. The rules of the discourse too - for example, what can be taken as proof of a statement, are also looked on by some philosophers as a kind of premiss which can be challenged and has to be defended.[19] The third and, in most discourses, dominant element is concerned with testing whether the premisses can be accepted - if any of them is untenable, we lose interest in the conclusion. A viewpoint is defended by showing that it follows from premises which in turn are valid conclusions from other premises.

One conceivable end to this chain of conclusions based on premises which are conclusions based on premises and so on, is the finding of premises which do not need to be proved. Epistemological rationalism tried to find a firm point of departure in that which reason perceives must necessarily be true. The alternative, empiricism, having had the upper hand during the 20th century at least in Anglo-Saxon philosophy, tells us that our observations of reality give us a solid foundation. But this view has few adherents today. One finds that absolutely pure observation, wholly independent of other assumptions concerning reality, is non-existent. Foundationalism is dead, there appear to be no firm foundations beneath the building.

Two questions now present themselves. If all premises are open to question, how can an opponent be silenced? And conversely, why does anybody bother to be an opponent since we know, right from the beginning, that the building is a castle in the air?

Hans Albert has coined the expression the 'Münchhausen Trilemma'. A trilemma is a dilemma with three horns instead of two. We seem, he argues, to be forced to choose one of the following three, equally unsatisfactory, alternatives when trying to meet the objections of a sceptical opponent. One alternative is for us to plead reasons for our reasons for our reasons and so on retrospectively ad infinitum. Another alternative is for us to call a halt and refuse to give any further reasons at some point in our argument. And the third alternative is the circular argument: A is pleaded as a reason for B which is pleaded as a reason for C which we have to resort to as a reason for A.[20]

The Münchhausen element of Albert's theory is the practical solution to the dilemma, a solution whereby we oscillate between the horns. The principle is that everything is open to question, but not everything at the same time.[21] To challenge an opinion we need access to at least one other opinion which is treated as above dispute. The second alternative, in other words, but only temporarily. The opinion beyond dispute can in turn be attacked, but from a new fixed point.[22]

Archimedes promised to lift the world with a lever if he could only find a fixed point outside it. That point does not exist. And yet we still contrive to extricate ourselves from the trilemma and lift the world. We rest the lever on opinion A so as to establish (lift) opinion B, which in turn lays the foundations of opinion C. Then we bear on opinion C to replace opinion A with D - or, in better keeping with the metaphor: to lift the opinion from point A to point D. This way we have completed a full revolution without moving in a circle. The circle has turned into a spiral. Münchhausen's trick is lifting one bootleg at a time.

I have described the quintessence of the research connection as a *disputation* between at least two people.[23] But, I now ask myself, is this truly an accurate picture? Don't I do most of my work alone, at my desk? That is where I read books, where ideas come to me, where I develop arguments and test objections. Without that work there can be no text to have a dispute on. In a word, I object to what I have just written: Haven't you - or rather, I - underrated the monologue?

Against this objection in turn I can offer the following defence. The 'monologue' to which the two of us (myself and myself) were just listening was in fact an internal dialogue.[24] There is reason to believe that it is copied from the 'outward', literal dialogues which have played an important part in my education. The crucial point, though, is not on this level but is connected with the idea of my thoughts as a coherent whole, a system. Suppose I have carried out an investigation and formulated the results in a thesis, an essay, a dissertation, etc. To achieve my results I have had to draw on a host of background knowledge concerning the nature of the world and the methods available for uncovering its secrets. I have to take this background knowledge seriously, and believe in it, in order for there to be any point in devoting time and commitment to the solution of my particular problem. The solution to the problem and the background knowledge I have managed to piece together into, as I see it, a consistent whole.

Can I at the same time be sceptical of the whole edifice? Yes, because I have learned to make the gesture: all our knowledge can be questioned. But actually and actively undermining the foundation of my thesis is another thing. What is still worse, I doubtless have difficulty myself in distinguishing properly all the premisses I take for granted and seeing where the weaknesses lie. If, as Dudley Shapere puts it, 'Progress in science consists partly in sharpening reasons for doubt and partly in making deeper assumptions explicit and therefore realistically open to examination . . .',[25] then all the indications are that effective doubt must be left to somebody who has not made a psychological investment in the thesis propounded.

In disputation the distribution of roles is central. The respondent brings forward a thesis and defends it against the attacks from the opponent. This makes disputation a kind of game, for example, like chess. Both games have a boundless amount of possible moves. That notwithstanding, chess is a zero-sum game - one in which the gains of one player are the losses of the other - and in which the matrix of the possible outcomes is simple in the extreme.

Some values in a matrix for disputation are easy to supply, when leaving out the fact that the respondent seldom brings forward only one thesis which has to be accepted or refuted in its totality.

Which outcome is the next best for the respondent: (a) to surrender to the arguments of the opponent, or (b) to maintain his thesis in face of all possible protests? It is easy to believe that the first alternative is the biggest set-back and then the matrix - with the exception of one small detail - will be identical with the matrix for chess. But this would be to misunderstand the main point of the entire game: to test whether there are sufficiently good reasons for a particular standpoint. In case (b) the arguments have come to grief and this is a failure for everybody. In case (a) the respondent, to be sure, has failed to defend his thesis but he has, after all, made the profit of coming to recognise the standpoint as a mistake.

Now the reader will probably say: well, let us for the sake of argument disregard that the disputants are real persons with real feelings and that the disputation at the same time is an examination. Still, is this not a perverse way of characterising a procedure which the parties have entered into of their own free will and from which they both derive benefit? My answer is no: even if we were talking about a zero-sum game it would not be perverse. The parties have a common interest in finding out whether there are strong enough reasons for a position. To achieve this end they submit to the rules of the game. The motives for play are outside the game. The point is that mutual benefit can be derived from playing even a zero-sum game, but that benefit cannot be read off from the matrix of the game. The fact of the white king and black king being mortal enemies does not prevent one playing chess with one's friends. A well-played match is rewarding even to the loser.

It is typical of an analysis of interpersonal relationships like games that one is not interested in knowing where the actors' preferences came from. It is immaterial where the respondent came by his idea or his motive for entering into the game. All the opponent bothers about is the strategies/arguments at the respondent's disposal. In the long history of disputation, this depersonalisation has sometimes gone so far that respondents and opponents have undertaken, respectively, to defend and attack theses quite regardless of what has previously been their true, personal convictions, the idea being that truth cannot be established on the basis of the assumptions and feelings of individuals. Truth emerges from the method, from the disputation.

The depersonalisation of the disputation can be seen as an expression of suspicion towards the subjective. The subjective is suspected of threatening rationality through wishful thinking and emotional reactions. Objectivity is viewed as a condition of truth and is a vital watchword in scientific contexts. And yet here, in a pedagogical and general human perspective, we have cause for reflection: shouldn't one encourage and support instead of attacking? And is not depersonalisation an enemy of personal attitudes like commitment and curiosity?

Conditioning an opponent's order of preferences is seldom a simple matter of revealing logical defects in his argument and is not always as simple as exposing incorrect information about actual conditions. Instead, Anatol Rapoport maintains, it involves influencing the opponent's way of looking at reality. Rapoport recommends a method whereby the opponent is invited to present his view and is helped to expound its consequences. The experience of being heard eliminates the feeling of threat associated with other standpoints, thereby opening his ears to what I, in turn, have to say. It is not possible to lay down any rules concerning how all this is to be done. That would be an invitation to formulate strategies and, accordingly, a regression from 'debate' to 'game'. The mechanism is not argument but empathy, i.e. capacity for entering into the opponent's way of seeing things. 'A debate', says Rapoport, 'is not resolvable by "rational" procedure', it is rather a question of 'conversion'.[26]

To me the word 'debate' seems to be unfortunate. Is not 'disputation', at least in ordinary language, some kind of 'debate'? And even more important is, that Rapoport against debate puts not one but several amalgamated forms of discourse. 'Conversion' may possibly also be characterised as a game but with a totally different distribution of roles. As in disputation, A wants to confer his own view to B. In conversion, on the other hand, B is not in an equal position. In conversion A chooses the strategy and B has no effective countermoves. For reasons I will discuss further below, I will call this form of discourse 'teaching'.

Rapoport's 'debate' seems to contain at least two additional forms of discourse. In disputation and in teaching A wants to bring over B to his standpoint. But the goal could just as well be the opposite: A wants to learn B's standpoint to make it his own. Let us call this form of discourse 'hermeneutical'.[27] Understanding B's point of view is no doubt important for successful teaching but then the empathy is a means to bring over B. In hermeneutical discourse the entering into B's point of view is not a means but an end in itself.

Rapoport's disclaimer of 'rational procedures' and the association of 'conversion' to 'conversation' leads the thoughts in the direction of a fourth kind of discourse. 'Conversation' is in fact one of the pet words of post-modernism. The word refers to the unplanned and unstructured form of discourse where everything can happen. In this discourse there is no place for propositions, rebuttals or arguments. Instead there are narrative and rhetoric. Furthermore, there is no obligation to stick to the subject; on the contrary, the conversation allows and encourages the unexpected and accidental. Irony plays an important role: to say one thing but leave open what your commitments are. Conversation excludes commitment because commitment is binding.

Disputation is an ancient method. It can be studied in the Dialogues of Plato. In *Gorgias* Socrates urges the other speakers to attack what he is saying, to test its truthfulness.[28] But even in this dialogue there is a tendency for the role of opponent to shift into that of teacher. Socrates is out to convert Gorgias the sophist. An extreme version of this form of dialogue can be studied in Boethius' *The Consolation of Philosophy* from the 5th century. This is a dialogue in the sense of 'me' conversing with the goddess of wisdom. But the goddess is no opponent scrutinising 'my' philosophical theses. She could equally well have been lecturing, because 'I' have no proposals and raise no objections. 'My' contribution is a number of questions and a host of assenting utterances as the goddess holds forth.[29] Thus the role of the interlocutor in *'The Consolation of Philosophy'* is not, as in the disputation, to attack the thesis, thereby testing its tenability, but to help in giving the thesis a clear, solid formulation. The partner is not an opponent but a teacher. This working method presupposes that the incomplete idea contains the embryo of a valid standpoint. Whereas the disputation institutionalises the quest for weak points of importance to the standpoint, the dialogue searches, benevolently and inquisitively, for material to underpin an initially fragile idea.[30] In disputation it is the task of the respondent to convince the opponent, whereas in the Socratic dialogue it is the teacher's task to help the pupil to search.[31] The latter is based on the idea of a basic consensus between the parties, the purpose of the conversation being to bring it into the open.[32] The consensus is fundamental in that, basically, the parties have an identical structure of ideas. The disputation demands something less: an overlap between the structures. This means that the disputation can only silence the opponent temporarily. One can always return to the attack from a new quarter.

As Alasdair Macintyre has pointed out, the hermeneutic dialectic is connected with the notion of harmony. States of conflict are viewed as morally unsatisfactory and possible to eliminate with the aid of discourse. This kind of approach can easily result in the pre-existing being refined and conserved. If there is a basic harmony and conflicts are evil, why not codify the harmony in a dogma?

Ludwig von Bertalanffy has pointed to the connection between harmony and homeostasis on the one hand and conflict and creativity on the other.

> If life, after disturbance from outside, had simply returned to the so-called homeostatic equilibrium, it would never have progressed beyond the amoeba which, after all, is the best adapted creature in the world - it has survived billions of years from the primeval ocean to the present day. Michelangelo, implementing the precepts of psychology, should have followed his father's request and gone into the wool trade, thus sparing himself lifelong anguish although leaving the Sistine Chapel unadorned.[33]

I have already questioned, however, whether the disputation should set the pattern for the teacher-pupil relationship. It is the teacher's task to support the pupil's motivation and stimulate his/her curiosity, taking up and pruning weak ideas, ideas which one day will be mature enough to be nailed up as theses. Without such work we can expect a poor supply of new respondents. Is the research connection compatible with sound pedagogics?

It might seem as though all pedagogical merits are to be found in a discourse characterised by empathy between the participants and that disputation can only be justified by the mechanisms of scientific criticism. But this is not the whole truth. The depersonalisation of the disputation means that attention is made to focus on the problem and its solution, not on individual achievement. For such an attitude to achieve complete domination is doubtless an unrealistic goal, a Utopia. Most of us, I think, experience a measure of personal failure after being clubbed down by an opponent. But the Utopia is worth cherishing for all that, because sociopsychological research has shown that creativity can be connected with commitment to the task for its own sake, as distinct from motivation focusing on appreciation and reward.[34] This suggests that the teacher must counteract a climate in which the central consideration is the cleverness of this or that person. The central consideration is the problem to be solved. It is important that the teacher himself should have this attitude to the subject matter, because his/her influence as a role example appears to make more difference than the choice of teaching method.[35]

Many people dislike the spectacle of contradictory goals for an activity, and they seek to resolve the contradiction by dismissing one of the goals or by trying, against all odds, to reconcile them. For my own part I believe one has to accept this as a genuine, inevitable conflict of values. Perhaps it can be used to sustain a form of creative activity, in the spirit of Michelangelo.

Argument and persuasion are both concerned with winning over the opponent to one's own opinion. But argument will only allow this to happen on certain definite conditions. *A* wants to convince *B* when he is working for *B* to embrace the opinion on the same grounds as *A* himself.[36] This means that *A* has to present his grounds and be prepared to defend them. The persuader does not submit to any such restriction of his scope for manoeuvre. He resorts to all the methods and dodges which will effectively influence the opposite number. There is nothing in the concept of 'persuasion' to imply that the opinion which *A* wants *B* to embrace is necessarily mistaken. *A* can very well be fighting in a good cause and persuasion is doubtless an inevitable ingredient of all upbringing (though it should not need to be so in advertising). But the words of the Higher Education Act regarding 'capacity for critical appraisal' must be taken to mean that persuasion is excluded from higher education pedagogics. And examinations must also be designed in such a way that the teacher can rely on the examinee's answers not being a product of persuasion.

Earlier I referred to the so-called relativism which, in various quarters, has succeeded the positivist theory of science. Relativism tells us that apparent truth is entirely dependent on the socially determined position of the observer in the world of existence and that arguments appropriate to one perspective are ineffective in another. The shift of paradigms, Thomas Kuhn said, is a conversion, a revolution, not something which happens because one is convinced by arguments. Parallel to the advent of relativism, there has been a growth of interest in rhetoric, with certain philosophers seeing in rhetoric a respectable instrument of scientific communication.[37]

Rhetoric comes in four different guises. Firstly, it is an adornment of the presentation of comprehensive, coherent arguments. This is a fairly, but not entirely innocent form of rhetoric. The purist may allege that the adornment conceals what is important - the content of arguments.

The next step is to look on rhetoric as an infill for a discourse whose nucleus consists of arguments but is not strictly held together by them.[38] As a result, the discourse mingles persuasive and argumentative components. Whether we like it or not, this situation is inevitable when arguing with the aid of the natural language, as I am now doing. That language is an outstandingly flexible, many-sided instrument, due in fact to its relative lack of precision. By using old words in new ways we can - very occasionally - formulate new and unexpected ideas. The dilemma of the purist is not only that he bores his readers or listeners, but also that there are any number of things which he is unable to say in his exact but inflexible language.

The opposite of the purist is the person who refuses to admit to any difference between argumentation and persuasion. Jacques Derrida believes himself to have unmasked the false pretensions of argument to supremacy.[39] We have already had occasion to refer to Paul Feyerabend. From this third variant of rhetoric it is only a short way to the fourth, that which attaches importance, not to the content of the message but to its form alone. The step is a short one because the persuader tries to make the listener so fascinated by the form that he/she will swallow the content unscrutinised, and accordingly the persuader demotes content in deference to form.

When this form of rhetoric invades a discussion the latter degenerates into something that neither wants to convince nor to persuade. Instead, the discussion turns into a *'conversation'*. Conversation is, as I indicated above, one of the catchwords of Post-modernism.[40] The freedom from every rule or any agreed structure is described as a revolt against everything that binds and oppresses. The simple fact is, however, that beyond the rules and structures there is *not* freedom but emptiness. In my discussion on the foundations of game theory I tried to show that only agreed-upon rules and structures can create options for actions, i.e. freedom. Furthermore, a closer look at the systems theory will convincingly show that total openness must eventually lead to self-obliteration.

Derrida does not defend rhetorics, he applies it. When somebody criticises his texts he talks about something else, because to answer would actually mean that he accepts precisely the rules he has abandoned. A reader who is expecting to meet a consistent argumentation becomes frustrated. Instead, the proper attitude when reading Derrida should be analogous to that which is often recommended when confronted with an abstract painting: don't look for concrete representation or formal excellence but let your stream of associations flow![41]

Richard Rorty is decidedly more accessible. He is propounding the case for rhetoric in a traditional discursive form. Rorty's point of departure is that every attempt to create universal foundations for our discussions have failed. The concepts and basic ideas we use when we describe, explain and evaluate the world are all historical contingencies. There is no language beyond the traditional and natural forms of language, which we use to chose our concepts and basic ideas. The thought that the objective reality in some way gives us some kind of master-matrix is illusory, according to Rorty, precisely because when construing the matrix we are compelled to use the same kind of language we initially wanted to understand and control. This is the reason why the task of philosophy - if it still has any - is to explain, by telling the story, how the 'contingencies' emerged. The narrative gives us a possible chance to interpret and reinterpret our own situation, and thus also a chance of emancipation. Emancipation or freedom is more important than rational discourse and hence is Derrida's way of responding to his critics, impossible to refute.[42]

Rorty's mild form of anarchism does not prevent him from understanding that total freedom could become a threat to human co-existence. We create and uphold our social and political institutions precisely because we want our transactions of goods, services and opinions to be as efficient, peaceful and fair as possible. The critical rational discourse developed in scientific and scholarly argumentation is such an institution. But Rorty, being an anarchist, and not a liberal as he maintains, does not need any institutions. Instead, it is a fundamental compassion that ultimately guarantees a decent human co-existence, and compassion cannot be the result of philosophical discourse. It is rather the great authors like Vladimir Nabokov or George Orwell, who through their narratives strengthen and expand compassion and sympathy.[43]

It seems as if Rorty's freedom is freedom in a vacuum. To be free means generally to have an optimal numbers of options to chose from. Rorty has certainly torn down almost every restriction but in doing so he has also destroyed all options. When sitting down at a chess board I have a number of options, which are indeed immense but still limited, and at the same time also *created*, by the rules of the game. Rorty's kind of freedom is achieved literally if I smash the board. By doing this I don't have to follow the rules, but I have simultaneously also lost the possibility of making *one* single move. In short, I have lost all the options the rules of the game actually offered. Of course, I am free to behave as I please at the chess board, provided I am prepared to pay the price. For my own part, I am definitely prepared to choose and uphold the institution of chess. In reaching such a decision I don't need, contrary to Rorty's suspicions, to be convinced that the rules are absolutely valid - beyond all boundaries of time and space. It is sufficient to treat them *as if* they were.[44] Once again, the rational discourse is an institution quite comparable with that of chess, even if its determinates and delimitations are a little bit more abstract.

What is the truth of the matter, is the difference between persuading and convincing a persuasive distinction? It is a linguistic and cultural fact of the same kind as the rules of chess that we distinguish between what is said and how it is said. Form, indeed, is not without significance, for without form there can be no content. But content, as we normally view the matter, is supreme. Form exists for the conveyance of content and good form is form which conveys content effectively. But the institution of 'communication', just like the institution of 'chess', is made up of people's intentions and actions. Intercourse is what we make it - disputation or conversation.

It has been amply shown that people's notions and values concerning the world around them, and accordingly the rules governing discourse, vary from one culture to another. But the thesis of the impossibility of arguing across such linguistic boundaries presupposes that languages are different right down to the last letter. This is not self-evident where different cultures are concerned, and unlikely in the case of different classes within the same culture, and very unlikely in the case of men and women. As long as there is any overlap between languages, i.e. in people's way of structuring their experiences, there is also a chance of building argumentative bridges.[45]

Clearly, the smaller the overlap the more arduous and time-consuming the procedure will be. It is arduous and time-consuming enough, even in the normal teaching situation in higher education, for a great deal of what the teacher says to be viable in practice to function as persuasion without the teacher himself noticing it - the location of the limit will be recalled: the pupil must be induced to embrace the teacher's opinion on the same grounds as the teacher himself.

But if persuasion is so much more economical, why object to it? Well, the economy, of course, is in the short term. Easy come, easy go. Nor is persuasive belief a viable foundation on which to continue searching for knowledge. However, there is also a more overriding reason. Argument has another characteristic which makes it more attractive than persuasion. If *A* tries to convert *B* to his opinion but does not care whether *B* does so on the right grounds, i.e. the grounds convincing *A* himself, then he is not treating *B* as an equal. *A* is not acting as if *B* were a rational subject like himself. Instead

B is to *A* simply an object to be influenced. This endows argument with a general human quality which is often worth the high price which has to be paid for it.

The exercise of power is a form of influence. Persuasion and argument are also forms of influence. Ergo: an argument is the exercise of power! Somewhat flippantly, this kind of false deduction may be said to characterise the comprehensive survey of research into power and communication undertaken by C. R. Berger in his *Handbook of Interpersonal Communication*.[46] I have no objection to 'persuasion' being made part of the concept of 'exercise of power'; in both cases *A*, who is powerful, has a resource which he *uses against B*. But in argument, *A* has a resource which he *transfers to B*. The resource in this latter case is an insight which, to begin with, is possessed by *A* but not by *B*. If the argument is successful, that is, if *A* can present good enough reasons, then *B* will be made the richer by this insight. The exercise of power is inevitable even in a democracy. But the ideal is for intercourse between people to be characterised by equality. And so it is not only in teaching that we need to distinguish between argument and persuasion.

The moral superiority of argument may perhaps appear self-evident on a trivial plane, but it is worth noting that there are circumstances of a moral nature which appear to speak in favour of radical relativism. Seeing one's own claims to knowledge as dependent on one's own place in life implies humility in relation to other people's claims to knowledge. This makes it less tempting to interfere and influence others. The western world has been criticised for lack of humility towards cultures in other parts of the world.[47] It is true that there are situations where consideration for the other person suggests that we should refrain from trying to influence him. Writing in a somewhat different context, David Hume maintains that if the other person is 'incapable of all resistance, and could never, upon the highest provocation, make us feel the effects of her/his resentment, the necessary consequence, I think, is that we should be bound by the laws of humanity to give gentle usage to her/him . . .'.[48] But if communication still takes place, and often it has to take place, then relativism and its companion rhetoric are referred to an attitude towards the opposite number which is not one of respect.

If both sides try to influence one another, the person trying to convince his or her partner shows greater respect than the person trying to exercise persuasion, because the former puts forward his grounds for critical appraisal and is prepared to defend them against attack and, if his defence is unsuccessful, to give up his opinion. The persuader does not give the other person's opinion any chance of influencing his own opinion. When the radical relativist decides that any one opinion is as good as another, he cuts off the possibility of taking his humility to the lengths of assuming that the opponent's opinion might be better. This very humility is shown by the person who argues. But on the other hand he cannot take his humility to the extent of a priori admitting that the opponent's opinion is just as good as his own. This would mean the psychological self-contradiction of embracing an opinion which one considers to be unfounded.[49]

Note the difference between 'consideration' and 'respect' present in my argument. Attacking another person's opinions can be an expression of brutal lack of consideration. It is typical of such situations for the parties not to be on an equal footing. But it is never an expression of respect to leave another person in peace with his wrongful opinions.

In my belief, the connection between argument, respect and equality presents an educational moral. The atmosphere in the classroom must not imply that the pupils are more stupid than the teacher. Unless the teacher conveys the impression that the pupils are his/her equals in the sense of being capable of grasping the grounds which he/she presents as the basis on which opinions are to be learned, an incentive will be lost and teaching will degenerate into persuasion. Higher education pedagogics should be based on respect rather than consideration.

The German philosopher Jürgen Habermas is perhaps the best-known exponent of the idea of the rational discourse. He asks: How are we to ensure that political decision-making will be a forum for establishing the common best instead of an arena in which egoists struggle for a maximum of personal advantage? He believes that if the decision-makers are put in a situation where they are forced to convince one another, they will also be forced to plead universal principles in support of their standpoint.[50] Does not Habermas' discourse with a view to the achievement of unity give the whiphand to those who are strong in argument? Does the ideal of equality allow us to accept this? Are not the genuine interests of the weak better protected by putting things to the vote, before the silent ones have been overwhelmed by the eloquent?

Jon Elster is disposed to answer these questions in the affirmative.[51] To that answer one can object with one of his own arguments. Contrary to Habermas, he maintains that political discussions, for lack of time and for other practical reasons, can seldom continue long enough for unity to be achieved. But for other practical reasons, it is also uncommon for a vote to take place in conditions where discourse is banned. So the question is whether the interests of the disadvantaged are better protected by half-told tales. It seems more credible to me that the interests of the disadvantaged are best protected by a procedure in which all arguments are put on the table and subjected to scrutiny.

My assumption is based on the following train of thought. I noted that different people have different capacities for argumentation. This actually involves two different components: knowledge of facts and other circumstances *and* the capacity for self-expression. Presumably there is a certain correlation between these two capacities. Knowledge of a matter is likely to enhance one's capacity for expressing an opinion on it. But a knowledgeable person cannot always find the right words. And, conversely, we all know people who are fluent in their expression of opinions without having particular good insight. It is the latter group who abuse the power of speech and who have more prospect of succeeding in the uncompleted discourse. Loose talk does not have the staying power of firm knowledge.

Elster's answer is plausible only as long as we assume that we are dealing with pure questions of interest, i.e. questions which I can decide exclusively on the basis of my preferences. But political questions are by no means always (and scientific questions seldom) questions of interest. If anything, the rule is that they include a greater or lesser element of assessments of fact. What does reality actually look like? What means do we have at our disposal of transforming reality in one or the other desirable direction? Somebody with a bad map is more liable to get lost and miss his destination. The ignorant is more liable to vote in a manner which does not accord with his interests. The more ignorant a decisionmaker is to begin with, the greater is his need for a discourse which will closely illuminate the facts.

Now, perhaps somebody will object, it may well be that assessments of factual conditions are frequent elements of political decision-making, but it is principles summed up in terms like 'liberty' and 'justice' that are dominating the decisions taken. On these points, where no expertise is consulted, the discourse has no part to play and the ballot is the best guarantee of the decision being characterised by the decision-maker's genuine opinion as to what is right and proper. These, of course, are rhetorical questions. It cannot be perfectly clear to me from the very beginning, for example, how a moral principle is to be defined for translation into the decision of a particular question or how a conflict between two principles is to be resolved.

Anyone feeling at this point that élitism is rearing its ugly head should be reminded of the difference between trusting somebody's word and being convinced by somebody's argument. In the uncompleted discourse, in which we do not have time to expound all arguments, I have to appraise the person's credibility. But in the complete discourse, authorities evaporate; it is the content of the arguments that I assess. If any élitism remains, this is it: there is no equality between arguments. That élitism is something we will have to live with if we are to fashion our future with reason.

But is the complete discourse a realistic idea? Suppose the question is one of the structure of the galaxies. Without knowing enough physics and mathematics, the rest of my life would be insufficient for a discourse fully acquainting me with the arguments. Evidently, then, I have to take the astronomer's word for these things, do I not? This example shows that there is no sharp boundary between being convinced by authorities and being convinced by arguments. But boundaries can still exist without being sharp. The astrologer too is an expert in his field. I am not at all convinced by him. I have not penetrated his arguments in detail, but I know how he evaluates data when drawing conclusions and what overriding theory he embraces, and I am not convinced on any point. The fact of the astronomer, and not the astrologer, convincing me is based on an assessment of their arguments, not on points of detail but in general terms.[52]

Suppose that, by dint of great care and exertion, we have arrived at an opinion of the true nature of things. Then why bother about an opponent? Why not dismiss him or her right from the beginning? The answer becomes apparent if we watch the disputation unfold in a context of systems theory.

A belief system is a system in which symbols of phenomena, symbols of values and concepts are organised by being tied to each other.[53] The outlook orients the individual in relation to the world around him, makes possible an exchange of messages with other individuals and caters to mental needs.[54] This is done by the belief system receiving information from and transmitting information to other systems. The information is intended to eliminate a dissimilarity between two systems. But a certain similarity between the systems is essential in order for a flow of information to be possible. The elements of the systems must to some degree be identically organised. No communication can take place without structure on the part of both sender and receiver.

A system, then, has to have a certain structure. But at the same time a certain instability is necessary. A system receiving information changes in doing so. In this process the information represents a much smaller quantity of energy than the change which is brought about. In order for the insignificant amount of energy to produce the change, the system must have a certain degree of instability. A system which is absolutely ordered cannot receive information. A system of that kind is dead.[55] And so a good belief system occupies the borderline between completely disorganised ideas about reality and ideas which are organised unshakeably. From this we may conclude that the degree of structure alone is not a serviceable yardstick of a good belief system. We have to take into account the necessity of a belief system being open.

When the 'systemness' of a system increases, i.e. when its structure becomes firmer and its boundaries against the outside world more sharply defined, this means greater stability. The terminal phase is absolute delimitation and an absolutely firm structure. This marks the end of growth; the system has ossified. There is a vital difference between asserting that a system - in this instance a person's view of the world - has actually attained this stage of equilibrium and asserting that there is a tendency towards a higher degree of 'systemness'. This tendency is no mystical force. It is actually rational, because it creates a firm basis for action and because it is a prerequisite of communication.[56] It does not become irrational until it excludes feedback from the environment. And so it is not unreasonable to suppose that human development may have promoted such a tendency.

The individual receives information from any number of different quarters, and that information is frequently contradictory. If the individual does not exclude this information, then new instability is constantly imparted to his belief system. This prevents the tendency towards consistency ending in an absolutely firm structure, in rigidity.[57] Openness prevents the 'systemness' of a belief system achieving rigidity. A belief system which, logically, is absolutely consistent but is totally mistaken in its ideas must be completely enclosed. System theory teaches us to view our ideas as a complicated network in which one idea is tied up with several others. The network forms a sphere in which certain ideas occupy the surface and can be altered without extensive changes in the rest of the network, while ideas close to the centre - logical, for example - cannot be altered without far-reaching consequences to other parts of the structure.[58]

The different ideas in the network are never really in harmony, and the lack of harmony is a sign of disorientation in relation to the world around us. To improve our orientation we are anxious to make such changes that will eliminate tensions. But great changes involve heavy expenditure in the form of intellectual realignment, and we cannot cope with tearing up essential parts of the structure day after day. If an interlocutor presents an observation which does not immediately fit in with my structure of ideas, it is less trouble for me to alter ideas close to the surface. But if this is not sufficient and ideas close to the centre come into the danger zone, I feel a greater need to oppose him.

For my own part I am more disposed to doubt my ability to check with my own eyes everything which happens on stage than to believe that the magician actually pulls a rabbit out of the hat. If the magician wants me to accept his thesis that rabbits can be produced from hats, my opposition will be based on the prohibitive expenditure on the part of both of us, in the form of losses of other ideas deep down in the structure. But suppose the magician lets me stand so close to the operation that all the time I can see the inside of the hat and the back of the table and the respondent still stands there, all of a sudden, with a rabbit in his hand. The task of the opponent will now be more difficult. In my desperation, perhaps I am tempted to resort to a radical scepticism, arguing that we can never put the least amount of trust in our sensory impressions. But in this case I am the one who is throwing expensive parts of the structure overboard. And since it is one of the rules of the game in disputation, and this is an important point, that both respondent and opponent must be serious and prepared to take responsibility for those parts of the structure which they demolish, I would avoid this move and instead attack along the lines of 'suggestion' or 'hypnosis'.

It is impossible to formulate a rule of debate showing the point where sensible debaters will stop questioning. What is included in the premisses of one conclusion is also included in the premisses of other conclusions. If in an argument one demolishes one premiss, this has implications for other arguments. The further back in the chain we go, the greater will be the losses, i.e. the amount of well-established ideas we have to sacrifice. This is what limits the extent to which we are prepared to take our doubt. But one must not give up too early. Persevere as long as calling into question can open up the possibilities of new knowledge and interesting new perspectives. Science is typified by an effort to follow the chain deep in towards the centre. Sometimes it is even useful, as an experiment, to dispute premises which, in one's heart of hearts, one cannot doubt, just to see what the consequences will be.[59] If the consequence is that we are forced to give up things which we feel certain of knowing, this speaks in favour of the premisses which have been called in doubt.

Both the alternative epistemologies - rationalism and empiricism - define, in different ways, *a priori* rules about what may be said in the course of discourse. Disputation, called Dialectic by some, contains no such rules of *content*. But this is not to say that the door is open to the irrational, to chaos. The disputation lays down strict rules of *procedure*, and the roles of respondent and opponent are fundamental to that procedure.[60]

A method which first establishes premises and then works its way ahead to conclusions is well-suited to the monologue. The reverse order, with the thesis being formulated first, and its tenability then tested by exposing and attacking the premises, invites more participants. The first method does not make it impossible to tolerate objections, but the second method welcomes them. The person most anxious to come closer to the truth has most reason to listen to those who claim that he is mistaken. But listening is not the same thing as implicitly accepting every objection.[61] It is this subtle balance between obstinacy and open-mindedness which is difficult to achieve except through a disputation.

The Swedish Higher Education Act prescribes not only a connection with research but also the adjustment of studies to the requirements of working life. This in turn encompasses a wide variety of demands.[62] In addition to acquiring theoretical knowledge, prospective dentists and violinists also have to learn a sophisticated manual craft. A caring attitude to clients and patients has to be instilled in social workers and nurses. Budding architects have to develop their artistic perceptions. The debaters who have been perturbed by the demand for a research connection have feared that all these other values will succumb in an over-intellectualised environment where only the empirically verifiable and verbally expressed can be accepted.

Needless to say, the term 'research connection' cannot cover all aspects of teaching in higher education. But this does not necessarily imply that it poses a threat to those other values. In the remainder of my essay I will try to hint that the research connection, given the interpretation I propose, is also naturally applicable in the aesthetic field.

The Swedish poet Esaias Tegnér assured us that truth, right and beauty are eternal. Today, many of us call into question the possibility of anything at all to be able to count on eternity. But there is another way too in which Tegnér's idea may seem outmoded. Statements of facts, i.e. statements concerning what is true, belong, in a diluted sense, to the realm of eternity. It often happens that something which we believed to be true yesterday proves false today, but this only means that we made a mistake yesterday. If we know for sure that something is true, then it is true yesterday, today and tomorrow. But this is not so with verdicts concerning the good (moral judgements) or the beautiful (aesthetic judgements). Moral judgements perhaps acquire, through tradition and law, a certain authority, but they are ultimately founded on subjective values, as is quite clearly the case with aesthetic judgements. This is how many people, scientists and others, would seem to view the matter.

A strict segregation of the descriptive and explanatory (empirical) on the one hand and the evaluative and ascriptive (normative) on the other, has long been a central rule of the methodology of social sciences. It is not possible, the rule tells us, to deduce that which *is* from that which *ought to be* - or vice versa. For normative enterprises, this is a serious distinction. Unlike statements of facts, for which one finds a firm, objective foundation in observations of reality, normative pronouncements do not have an objective foundation. Normative statements are always, in the ultimate analysis, dependent on values, and values are produced by a subject. And so the next rule in the book tells us that science cannot decide value questions. In practice, however, there have been many bridges over the gap between 'is' and 'ought to be'. There is a great deal of normative scientific work to be done whereby recommendations are deduced from goals which are taken for granted without proof because they are based on general and assumed values, and from investigations of causal connections and other empirical relations.

It is also well-known that everyday language does not obey any strict rules of method. 'It's beautiful weather over Värmeln today,' Gustaf Fröding, another famous Swedish poet, proclaims. Is this a description or does the proclamation, as one might suspect from the adjective, also declare the speaker's meteorological values? I do not believe there is a conclusive answer to this question. For one thing 'beautiful weather' in our language means 'sunny weather' - I suspect this may not be quite the case with the languages spoken in the Sahara. On the other hand, most people in our northern climes like the sun and there are good reasons for believing that the statement also expresses the speaker's gratification. Those who are cheered by rain ought, for the avoidance of misunderstandings, to choose another adjective. Sometimes it has been hoped that scientific purity can be defended by avoiding the terms of everyday language. But can political science avoid words like 'liberty' and 'democracy'?

But, as social scientists have realised, there is worse to come. We cannot investigate everything. We train our empirical interest on that which is important and relevant. To the natural scientist this means making a selection from all the phenomena of which reality is composed, and the focus of our interest is governed by several factors. If she is an epistemological realist, i.e. a person who supposes that there is a world independent of our experience, the selection does not affect phenomena in themselves. To the social scientist, on the other hand, the matter is more complicated. It is, to a great extent, our view of what is important and relevant that constitutes social phenomena. Unlike galaxies and atoms, chess does not lead an independent existence. It is people's activities which have given it a place in the world. Democracy, similarly, is a social phenomenon because we attach importance to the question of whether we ourselves decide matters affecting our lives.[63] And so the simple distinction between the subjective, that which people feel like doing, and the objective, that which exists in the world outside their feelings and opinions, comes unstuck. The game of 'chess' is not independent of people's intentions and actions and ought therefore to come on the subjective side of a dichotomy. But chess has evolved in the course of human relations going a long way back in time. As a result, the game has acquired an 'objective' character. The king and the king-related concept of 'mate' are a central part of the game's make-up. I can choose to refrain from playing chess, but I cannot choose to play chess without a king.

Some human actions are meaningful outside a social context, for example, the ingestion of vitally necessary foodstuffs (there is justification for this awkward turn of phrase: the simple word 'eat' has a considerable accretion of social determinants). But other actions only acquire meaning within a social structure. Moving a piece of white, carved wood from one square to another only acquires a meaning when the piece of wood symbolises a 'bishop' and there are other pieces of wood/symbols on other white or black squares in one or another configuration. If the bishop next to the white king in a particular configuration is moved four steps diagonally to the left, this is a move in an opening which has been known since the 16th century. Nothing can be done or expressed with the bishop alone, which incidentally can look quite different from the standard bishop but still be identified because of the very structure surrounding it. It is the wholeness, its symbols and rules, which makes it possible for the actor to do things with the piece of white, carved wood.

It is true that an argumentation regarding values presupposes some kind of premises accepted *bona fide*: i.e. accepted in spite of their lacking absolute foundation. But that, as we already have seen, is also the case as regards argumentations on matters of fact. In both cases one is in principle trapped in the 'Münchhausen Trilemma' and there is only one way out: to leave a number of basic, reasonable premises uncontested - if not forever at least for the time being. It is an obvious fact that we usually feel on much safer ground in argumentations on matters of fact. This, however, is just because we - as a contingent property of our culture - leave a lot of empirical premises, but very few moral or aesthetic premises uncontested. To be sure, this makes an important practical difference.[64] Even if he was wrong about eternity Tegnér was in principle right in another respect: truth, goodness and beauty are all rocking in the same boat.

According to one school of thought which has been influential not least in Swedish philosophy, there is no objective foundation for moral judgements. What we consider to be good and evil is ultimately a question of feelings. The emotivist does not need to abandon his attempts to induce others to embrace the same feelings of good and evil as himself. But substantial arguments do not get him very far; basically, the question is one of persuasion. In recent years the pendulum has swung over and several publications have attempted to lay objective foundations for moral judgements. Best-known of them all is John Rawls' great work *A Theory of Justice* from 1971. Other examples are Thomas Nagel's *The Possibility of Altruism* and Brian Barry's *Theories of Justices*. All these books have the same basic idea. Consent to ascribe the same importance to other people's interests as to my own is a structurally necessary part of an ethical inquiry. I cannot claim 'this is fair' without taking what Nagel calls 'the impersonal standpoint'. I can of course refuse to talk about justice, thereby relinquishing all claims to rights, but I cannot speak of justice and at the same time claim that what is right is a question of what I feel.

This is not a new idea. In *A Treatise of Human Nature* we find David Hume writing as follows:

> When we form our judgments of persons, merely from the tendency of their characters to our own benefit . . . we find so many contradictions to our sentiments in society and in conversation, and such an uncertainty from the incessant changes of our situation, that we may seek some other standard of merit and demerit, which may not admit of so great variation . . . This is far from being as lively as when our own interest is concerned . . . nor has it such inference on our love and hatred: but being equally comfortable to our calm and general principles 'tis said to have an equal authority over our reason and to command our judgment and opinion.[65]

The immensely wide-ranging debate on Rawls' theory has shown that he has not succeeded in finding an absolutely indisputable definition of Hume's 'general views'. But the dialectical model does not demand any secure foundations. What is needed is for arguments, of whatever kind they may be, to have premises which in turn are based on premisses etc, which are united in a structure which is not entirely private but overlaps between the participants in the discourse.

The exclamation; 'What a nice cup of coffee this is!' can possibly be put into a rudimentary argument ('after all, it's the first cup since yesterday'), but there is little scope for opposition because the exclamation rests essentially on a private experience. And there is little temptation to oppose it. I can accept the exclamation without it causing the slightest disorder in my structure of ideas. A comparison with moral questions shows that they definitely cannot be subjective in this sense. Acceptance of a moral judgement has repercussions which deeply affect my structure of ideas, and so the very slightest shortcoming in the judgement will provoke opposition. On the other hand, there is a great likelihood of our finding overlaps in our respective structures.

In debates on empirical or moral issues, one eventually comes to a point where a premiss appears so patently obvious that any further discussion would seem to be a waste of time.[66] Can't you see for yourself that this is the way of things? Can you really question the intrinsic value of human life? It is not unreasonable to put an end to the discussion on reaching this point, but it is possible to continue the discussion further.

In the ambition to avoid the anarchy of subjectivism, one has in the philosophy of arts, sometimes tried to establish a very early and definite restriction. Thus it has been maintained that an object of art has an irreducible value. One perceives it immediately and one cannot connect it with any extrinsic quality. The disadvantage of an early restriction is obvious. If one does not instantly agree with a statement you cannot test it by looking at its premisses. Either you accept the statement or you don't, there is no room for improving your opinion through an elucidating discussion.

At the other extreme, the philosophers have tried to let the premiss of utility and nothing else ground claims for artistic value. The artistically valuable is identical with what people actually like. This includes two major disadvantages. First, whose taste will be allowed to decide the matter - that of the majority, the expert's or mine? The second disadvantage is that, here again, the argument will capitulate at an early stage. As the saying goes, there can be no disputes over taste.

This is a situation which makes reductionism tempting, i.e. the deduction of artistic value from benefit, which is not the same thing as the former alternative, because we cannot be sure that somebody who benefits from something is actually aware of doing so. But the paternalistic ambitions lead either to the disappearance of 'artistic value' into the bargain - as, for example, in Jeremy Bentham's theory, equating benefit with 'pleasure' (physiological satisfaction, in principle quantifiable) and where 'pushpin' proved to be every bit as good as 'poetry', or else 'benefit' has to cover everything we value, in which case the reduction is illusory, depriving us of the ability to explain why pushpin and poetry are valued in different ways.[67] All in all, to reduce artistic value to utility does not seem promising to an argumentation-minded person.

Quite another possibility is to look on 'artistic object' as one of the fundamental categories with the aid of which we in our culture view and structure reality.[68] 'Individual' is one such category. We think in such categories every day, which makes it easy for us to forget that they are not self-evident. In the philosophy based on Hinduism, the Whole is what counts and the individual is a painful accident. The aim of yoga is to obliterate one's individuality so as to merge with the eternal, unchanging universe. Compare this with the Christian belief in Paradise, which teaches us that we will be resurrected more or less as we stand and walk today, though with not quite the same infirmity. Dante easily recognises the features of friends and enemies on his pilgrimage from Inferno up to Paradise. This is the kind of intellectual tradition which creates a language with expressions like 'individual rights' or 'power'. Of course, the alternative I am now describing is also a kind of relativism; its categories do not exist independently of time and space. But it is a relativism totally without subjectivism:[69] once the categories have been established there is no scope for the caprice of individuals or groups. It is not the opinion of the majority, of the experts or of myself that decides what is aesthetically valuable, any more than it is the opinion of the majority, expertise or myself which makes a true statement truthful. The earth moved before Copernicus. And Bach's *St. Matthew Passion* was one of the greatest works of music long before Felix Mendelssohn retrieved it from oblivion. If you do not agree with these two statements and can see better arguments, you always have the possibility of challenging both the majority and the experts. But to succeed you will need very good arguments indeed.

F. H. van Eemeren and his co-authors maintain, in their survey *The Study of Argumentation*, that the term 'argumentation' is only applicable to verbal exchanges.[70] I question this. In *Art and Illusion*, E. H. Gombrich provides a fascinating survey of the history of pictorial art. He rejects the idea of an evolution from naïve inability to perceive what reality really looks like to sophisticated ability to reproduce our visual impressions undistorted by any preconceived opinion. In order to represent reality in a picture, the painter must resort to established formulae based on what he *knows* of reality.

But the elements in a formula also represent reality, and eventually it came naturally to try and make them resemble what the painter saw from his position at the easel, to create an illusion of the picture being a window on to reality. But when those efforts culminate with the impressionists, the paradox becomes obvious. No perception, Gombrich tells us with numerous references to psychological research, is independent of expectations, of formulae and unconscious theories. The innovative artist works in a field of tension between conventions on the one hand and observations and experiments on the other. A great 'scientifically' experimental landscape painter like John Constable studied not only nature and its shifting colours but also the works of predecessors. 'I fancy I see Gainsborough in every hedge and hollow tree,' he says on one occasion. But the poles of convention and visual impression are not fixed for all time.[71] The successful artist makes us alter our formulae, causing us to take a new look at reality. Gombrich puts this beautifully:

> Whatever the initial resistance to impressionist paintings, when the first shock had worn off, people learned to read them. And having learned this language, they went into the fields and woods, or looked out of their window on to the Paris boulevards, and found to their delight that the visible world *could* after all be seen in terms of these bright patches and dabs of paint. The transposition worked. The impressionists had taught them, not, indeed, to see nature with an innocent eye, but to explore an unexpected alternative that turned out to fit certain experiences better than did any earlier paintings.[72]

Cannot the impressionists be said to have driven home an argument? An argument, after all, means joining old elements together into a new and convincing whole.

So far, so good. But does this also apply to the post-impressionist period, to expressionists, cubists and surrealists, to abstract painting? Romanticism has persuaded us to believe that the work of art can spring straight from the emotional life of the genius, an immaculate conception unbesmirched by rules and conventions. Gombrich does not share that view. Many 20th century painters have derived their vision, not from their surroundings but from their inward being. But to express that vision they have still been thrown back on the stock of symbols and formulae, which can be augmented and refashioned but never eliminated.

Gombrich says that the main purpose of his book is to investigate the limitations of the choice open to the artist and his need of a vocabulary. But Gombrich also seeks to establish that, contrary to what one tends to believe, those limitations are not a weakness but if anything a source of strength. Where everything is possible and nothing unexpected, communication breaks down. It is because art employs styles governed by technique and by the formulae of tradition that representation has been able to serve as an instrument not only for information but also for expression.[73]

Art, Gombrich tells us, is communication. Communication is dependent on a structure of rules and symbols. Starting with communication, we can pronounce on what is better and worse and we can criticise the individual work of art. If we destroy the structure, communication dies and art with it. But a structure can also ossify, becoming a prison to thought. It has to be kept open and alive. A high-class work of art can deliver convincing criticism of the structure and bring about its transformation. There is nothing mysterious or irrational about the idea of a structure being amenable to reform from the inside and by degrees. Within the framework of an open, reformist structure, we can acquire and convey to one another new, unexpected and fantastic experiences.

Gombrich maintains that there are no innocent eyes. Looking at the world around us, we are always stuffed full of theories and formulae and preconceived opinions, i.e. everything which I summarised in an earlier section in the word 'system'. Preconceived, close-knit opinions can be a weakness, a sign that the system is no longer open. But old, well-established knowledge and old pictures are also a precondition of our being able to distinguish anything at all of the world around us.[74] Without it we cannot discover anything new. The romantic tradition likes to view scientific and artistic breakthroughs as mysterious inspirations of genius. But Gombrich the art historian and Shapere the historian of science both agree: behind the breakthroughs one can often discern a chain of good reasons and of trial and error.

It is common to try and break down public opposition to the avant-garde by appealing to the public to look and listen open-mindedly, without preconceived opinions. But this is impossible. That which, to the trained musical ear, is a musical structure is just noise to the person who has no preconceived opinion, even though, on account of the veneration enjoined towards the Work of Art, he may conceal this embarrassing fact from others and from himself. At the première of Stravinsky's *The Rite of Spring* in Paris in 1913, the audience rose in rebellion. This narrowmindedness usually moves us to supercilious mirth, fully enlightened as we are nowadays. But perhaps that audience was still better than an audience which, for fear of looking reactionary, listens to everything with the same impersonal respect. The best audience is the one which has a preconceived opinion but is capable of changing its mind.

Nothing can be new to us if we do not possess anything old. Inevitably, what we have inherited by tradition gives us the criteria without which we cannot distinguish, still less judge what is new. If everything is permitted, the Parisian audience can be criticised for its indignation. But it cannot be criticised for having been mistaken. If so, its disgust at *The Rite of Spring* carries as much weight as our appreciation. If, on the other hand, the Parisian audience is to be criticised for having been mistaken, it cannot be criticised for having taken a stand.

But isn't this a manifesto of hidebound conservatism? If I am correct in my thinking, why are we so interested in anything over and above what already tallies with our models? From our analysis of the term 'system' we have learned that a system with great capacity for constantly improving its information about its surroundings can build up and defend a more complicated structure and will put a premium on active searching, i.e. curiosity. A life devoted to searching for ever-new aspects of the world and our existence is a better life.

The observation that we tend to see what we expect to see is no recommendation or defence of conservatism. On the contrary. To correct and develop our view of the world, we need to be contradicted. A discourse which does not rest content with the immediate image apparently conveyed by our senses but critically tests their credibility, is a precondition for our view of the world being capable of change and improvement. Homeostasis occurs in fields where the subjective is protected from disturbances, from being called into question and from demands for good reasons.

Debates on empirical conditions avoid circularity by the arguments being intermittently rooted in our observations. Those observations, it is true, are stuffed full of theory, but they still bear a relation to the world out there which, in the words of Gunnar Myrdal 'kicks back' if we disregard it. Objective grounds of this kind for debates on empirical conditions may seem to imply that they occupy a different and better position compared with debates on moral and aesthetic questions. But tradition also offers an 'objective' basis for debates. Moral and aesthetic values, admittedly, have emerged from people's activities, but this does not make them subjective.[75] The moving of pieces of black and white wood over 64 black and white squares does not necessarily add up to chess. A concatenation of letters of the alphabet does not automatically make a poem. A work of music cannot sound just as you like. This observation is no judgement on free creativity. On the contrary. Alternative courses of action only exist within the frame-work of structures, and creating something new must necessarily imply refashioning something already given. On the other hand, this observation represents a rejection of the opinion that the moral and the aesthetic are beyond the range of rational discourse.

Allow me to recapitulate. I have proposed that 'research connection' should be translated into practice as 'disputation', i.e. critical rationalism plus dialogue. I have also mentioned a number of other values which might be harmed by 'scientification', among them the aesthetic values which are an important component of many higher education study programmes. As far as I can understand, those apprehensions are not borne out by events. On the contrary, 'the disputation' as a model for research connection is very appropriate in this context as well.

A work of art (a poem, a painting, a work of music etc.) is a link in communication. Perhaps it might be objected that so many poems, paintings and works of music never reach an audience or are even intended to do so. But this is a secondary phenomenon. The fact of our, more or less audibly, putting our thoughts into words even when we are alone, does not prevent language primarily being a means of conveying wishes and observations to others. The 'work of art' category is a social phenomenon. It has evolved in the course of human society and cooperation but is not subject to our subjective caprice. It comprises a delimited, independent part of the world in which we live.

The point of communication is to say something unexpected, something which has never been said before. This sounds like an impossible requirement. There are few of us to whom it is granted at any time in our lives to say something thoroughly unexpected (which also meets the requirements I shall mention presently). But small innovations should not be belittled; they too are worth the trouble of listening to.

But for communication to materialise, surprise is not enough. A measure of recognition is also needed. To identify what is communicated (the message), the recipient must recognise its components. It is impossible to communicate anything which is new through and through. Free creativity does not mean being unrestricted by all the old rules and all the old material. Creativity means creating something new on the basis of the old.[76]

The minimum requirement, then, is for the recipient to understand the message, and this can be trouble enough if the artist - or researcher - has something very unexpected to say. But this is not all. As a general rule the artist and researcher also want to convince the listener, the reader, the spectator or the colleague. Convincing means overcoming resistance. The recipient must clear a space in his system of ideas.

The general argument in this tentative essay is one of ongoing reformist and disputatious change of the inherited store of ideas. This is not a trivial picture. The natural tendency is to look on what has been handed down as something firm and good and to defend it against attacks by cementing it into dogmas.

Chapter 10

Research Training and the State
Politics and University Research in Sweden, 1890-1975

Birgitta Odén

The educational sector in a society is usually characterised in hierarchical terms, beginning with preschool; then lower-level or primary school; high school or 'gymnasium'; undergraduate college or university studies; and graduate studies. All these levels of the educational hierarchy have been the subject of intense research during the past few decades, while the educational system itself has simultaneously developed and been the focus for critical evaluation. Weakest of all scientific interest has been that devoted to graduate education - 'the highest education' - to adopt a term used by the English educationalist, Ernest Rudd.[1]

Since the mid-60s, considerable political interest has been tied to research and the politics of research. Thus, the theme of graduate education and politics takes on a special interest as a topic for analysis.[2] How have the political authorities dealt with the sensitive issue of the training of researchers in a society that has officially proclaimed its adherence to the ideal of freedom for research?

In a more extensive work, I have surveyed the graduate educational programmes in Sweden for the period 1890-1975, of four different academic subjects: history, political science, cultural geography and economic history.[3] In that work, the main focus centres upon describing and analysing the environment contexts of graduate educational programmes, and the conceptual parameters that guided the responsible authorities for the respective disciplines.[4] In the short study presented here, another perspective has been adopted: that of graduate education as an issue of university politics.

The topic of my article - the politicisation of graduate and doctoral programmes in Sweden - implies both a *relation* between two entities of society, the political body and the community of scholars, and a *historical process* which has changed that relation. This process can be identified as a growing interest on the part of the sphere of politics in graduate education, both in its organisation and its outcome. Hence, politicisation in my context does not mean political interference in the actual research process.

What then are the different interpretative frameworks which can be used to describe the relationships between politics and the highest level of education, and which simultaneously allow us to gain insight into the dynamics of the processes of change?

In Sweden as in other nations, we have a highly regarded tradition within the history of science that describes this relationship in terms of a struggle for freedom: the scientific community has performed, and continues to perform an unrelenting and, until the Second World War, successful struggle against the State. From this perspective, the production of knowledge is viewed primarily as a process internal to the scientific community. A historical perspective is used to show that every infringement on the part of the State, either through its establishment of disciplines to serve its own ends, or through the appointment of professors against the wishes of the scientific community, or still yet by interfering with the administrative organisation of research and education - every encroachment has had dire consequences for the research community.[5] In this model, demands are implicitly made upon the autonomy of the university.

In my own opinion, this interpretative framework contains some serious weaknesses. Clearly, it is guided by a wish to legitimise an interest of the scientific community in preserving its own self-identity and freedom of action. However, counter-examples from university history demonstrate just as clearly that the opposite can also be true: namely, that political interest in research and education has had a stimulating effect on the formation of the disciplines and on our development of knowledge, even when decisions have been made against the wishes of some members of the scientific community. In part, the formation of the research councils constitute one such example.

A more serious weakness of this model is that it overlooks the overlapping membership of scientists. In their professional practice they belong to the scientific community, but as citizens they belong to society and have to defend its interests. Every society has a latent need for knowledge, which in the case of the historical sciences comprises interpretative frameworks and forms of understanding of our present situation. No historians can - whether they admit it or not - work uninfluenced by the needs of their own time. Examples of demands for changes of the universities for the sake of the larger society, by researchers who have also been social activists, include the medical professor in Lund Georg Kahlson's programme for the reformation of medical research and medical studies during the 1940s, and the world famous economist Gunnar Myrdal's demand for a reformation of the universities during the same time period.[6] However, these demands did not lead either of them to give up the notion of scientific freedom for research as a consequence.

There exists, however, a second interpretative framework which is the opposite of the freedom-seeking model, namely, the administrative model. Here, the university's history is described and explained as a series of administrative reforms. The polarisation of the State and the university is thus toned down. Through administrative procedures, the State directs the form and the design of research and education. In principle, the content of research and education is left to the university. The historical process of change is seen as a gradual and incremental one, where the role of scientists is reduced to an irritating murmur.[7] In opposition to research governed by the scientific community, within this second interpretative framework, we have what may be conceptualised as 'socially-steered' or 'socially-governed' research.

But this model too has obvious weakness, primarily in its lack of attention to the value of the accumulated experiences of the scientific community. It seeks to legitimise political measures by identifying the production of knowledge with the production of goods in a planned economy.

In 1983, Katrin Fridjonsdottir, a young sociologist at the University of Lund, introduced a third interpretative framework which I have found very useful. Fridjonsdottir describes the relationship between the political body and the community of scholars as a *changing contract*.[8] Thus, normatively, the desirability of *negotiation* emerges. Within a Swedish model of societal regulation, this process of negotiation takes the form of investigative committee work by the State and referral to the universities for consideration before the parliament makes a decision, which in turn is implemented and supervised by the independent, civil service department, i.e., the National Board of Universities and Colleges (NBUC), formally the Chancellor's Office.

Inherent in the notion of contract is a recognition that both parties have a common interest. Fridjonsdottir's point that the contract is not permanent but that it is changing, means that negotiation, or bargaining, becomes the central focus. As a sociologist, Fridjonsdottir examines the pre-conditions of today's contract, the structural framework of the bargaining, and she illustrates her thesis empirically with analyses of the politics of the Swedish national research councils. My task as a historian is to examine the effects of these successive negotiations, the process of change, and my study area is graduate education. The link between us is the theoretical framework - the idea of a changing contract.

Sweden has a long and successful history of collective bargaining between the employers and the employees of the labour market. We speak of the 'spirit of Salt-sjöbaden', of that atmosphere which has dominated and promoted the historical development of a comparatively peaceful process of change, instead of an open power struggle between capital and labour. The basis for the evolution of a positive climate of negotiations has been a generally recognised common interest of the deliberating parties to reach a solution. The changing contracts have emerged from negotiations that have been built upon an exchange theory, where the demands of both parties should be at least minimally satisfied, without, however, endangering the common interests of the negotiating parties.

Can we then apply this interpretative framework - at least as an elucidating metaphor - to relations between the State as employer, and the scientists as employees? It is apparent that there is a generally acknowledged common interest, both for the political and for the scientific community in the area of graduate educational programmes. The larger society needs both well-educated researchers and good research. And the scientific community needs resources to satisfy *their* need for educational capacity and for the growth of knowledge. There may, of course, be disputes concerning the interpretation of 'well' and 'good', but this is, in my opinion, more a question of different emphasis than of a genuine disagreement. Thus, the fundamental theoretical prerequisites are in place which can provide an empirical model of future action.

However, this is not to say that in its practical application, the model will produce positive results. There are two risks that the bargaining model will not work well. First, there may be weakness in the interpretations of reality that constitute the very foundation for the intended reforms. Second, it is obvious that changes in an educational system take a long time to achieve, since their implementation often entails painful changes in mature and responsible persons' mentalities and capabilities for action.

Graduate Education as an Independent, Political Sphere

First, a few words about when graduate education became a subject of political interest, i.e. about when it was transformed from a sphere of non-decision-making to an arena of current political interest. In other words, about the historical context in which graduate education was politicised.

Graduate education today is evidently a highly political subject in the Western world. If primary education for all was the great political problem of the educational sector from the 1820s to the 1940s, then university education is the most burning issue of the post-World War II period. Both these focuses of political interest have been followed by a scholarly interest in them - first for research on the schools, and later for research on university undergraduate education. The researchers have behaved as 'citizens' in that the political problems have inspired their choice of study area. Since the 1960s, we have seen a strong political interest in graduate education. And it is not difficult to predict a flourishing of scholarly interest in graduate education during the coming decades.

Does this then mean that graduate education was *not* of political interest before? A historical search for occasions when graduate education was the focus of political interest reveals traces of such interest far back in time.

When the famous and prototypical Berlin university was established in 1810, with the Humboldt brothers as its most important inspirators, both research and graduate education were central issues of the educational programme.[9] Within the discipline of history, it was the educational programme of Ranke that developed into the first organised graduate educational programme. Leopold von Ranke, who was the world's foremost historian for more than six decades, and who educated both German and American professional historians, was installed in his office in Berlin against the recommendation of the faculty, and upon the explicit order of the political authorities.[10] But once he had been installed in his office, his professorial chair became a Mecca for historians from all over the world.

In contrast to Germany, France shows a long period of resistance among professors, both towards giving doctoral training and towards developing a programme of graduate education. But after the French defeat in the Franco-German war in 1871, a process of critical self-examination started in the Department of Education which was primarily aimed at its very lack of graduate education programmes.[11] The French Minister of Education sent the young historian, Gabriel Monod, to Germany to study their doctoral training programme. A similar programme of graduate education was developed in Paris during the latter part of the nineteenth century. The local universities, however, stubbornly continued to resist this new requirement that professors should educate new researchers. This was a mentality or ideology which lingered long, not only in the historical sciences, but in other disciplines as well. To become a researcher was not a process of training, but a process of personal maturation.

When, in the late 1950s, De Gaulle's government began to confront the problem of a growing technological gap between the United States and France, it was because of these historical antecedents that the attention of political authorities once again was directed towards graduate education. French professors had a humanistic resistance towards doctoral training which had to be broken and the educational system re-formed.[12]

In Great Britain, throughout the 1980s such bodies as the Advisory Board for the Research Councils (ABRC) and Select Committees of the House of Commons and the House of Lords drew attention to the problems of graduate training. No systematic attempt was made, however, by government or other central bodies to tackle these issues.

I have taken up these examples because amongst the myths of academia, graduate education is usually described as a sanctuary of academic freedom. But upon several critical occasions, it appears that this area has been of considerable interest to the body politic as well. Graduate education has come to be regarded as a key issue for a nation that wishes to promote its interests in relation to those of the surrounding world. Politicians have come to regard good scientists as a scarce resource. And this has given the scientific community a favorable bargaining position.

Developments in Sweden

I will now attempt to illustrate how the politicisation of the graduate and doctoral programmes has occurred in Sweden, and I will do so by describing the course of events as a bargaining process.

In a 1982 article in the Social Democrat journal, *Tiden*, Bo Gustafsson (Professor of Economic History at Uppsala) demonstrates that the national university statutes of 1876 entailed a right of the universities to formulate their own educational goals, and that it is not until the 1960s that one begins to notice a politicisation in graduate education.[13] This is a correct description if one remains within the framework of the statutory regulation. Yet the State demonstrated its interests for special graduate training early on through the creation of stipulations for a degree of Licentiate of Philosophy (*filosophie licentiat*) in 1870. Delving to the level of negotiations, one can note a centrally-oriented interest in developing phases of graduate training already long before the 1960s.

When, in the middle of the nineteenth century, some Swedish scholars brought back from Germany ideas about doctoral training as a part of the educational programme of the university, such training took place through the establishment of seminars, which were to be the equivalent for the humanities, of the laboratories of the natural sciences. The seminars were to develop through the establishment of specialised libraries and through series of publications of the students' research. They were meant to constitute forums for the learning of scientific methods and argumentation. Those teachers who tried to adopt this innovation according to the structure of the German seminars encountered strong opposition from their colleagues. Despite this resistance, this educational form was adopted by some disciplines. Among them was my own speciality, history, which, during the latter part of the nineteenth century attracted greater numbers of students to graduate education than any other university discipline.

When the Chancellor, as mediator between the State and the university, issued a statute for the nation's universities in 1891, it was specified as mandatory that every discipline should have a seminar. This 'contract' was the result of negotiations between the university and the political authorities - but between a progressive minority at the university and the political authorities. Resources were to be given by the State, while the universities were to conduct doctoral training through the establishment of seminars.

Turning now from the contracts to reality, two types of departures from the dictates of the contract become apparent. The resources allotted for the seminars by the State were very small, and hence the Swedish seminars were a sad copy of the flourishing seminars of the German universities, with their own buildings and large staffs. But neither did the scientific community accept their share of responsibility for the activities of the seminars. It is evident from the remaining source material that an overwhelming number of disciplines never developed research seminars. Even if they did exist in official programmes, they often failed to function as forums of doctoral training, but instead focused on discussions of more general problems, i.e. they were seminars, but not research seminars.

However, the reason for the university's breach of contract should not be seen as obstruction or as a struggle for academic freedom. Many teachers within the social sciences and humanities shared the conviction of their French colleagues that one simply cannot be trained to become a scientist. One becomes a scientist through one's own work, which builds upon a foundation of inborn talent.[14]

Two distinct ideologies of doctoral training can consequently be distinguished in the historical material: one humanistic-hermeneutic, which regarded graduate education as a deep shaping of one's personality and as an individual maturation process; and a natural science-positivistic ideology, which regarded doctoral education as a methodological process of learning and a collective process of professionalisation.

For a long time, doctoral training in Sweden was conducted according to the 1891 contract. Until the 1950s, this part of the university's activity was affected by a frustrating disharmony between these two ideals. Measured both in terms of quantity and quality, the results of graduate education in Sweden were uneven and dependent upon the competence of one's professor.[15] There were, however, no internal discussions at the universities about the means and goals of graduate education. Doctoral training was regarded as the sole affair of the professors, as *'Lehrfreiheit'*.

Led by the leader of the Conservative Party group in the First House, Ernst Trygger, (Professor of Law at Uppsala) the 1933 Drafting Committee on University Matters initiated a discussion about how professors could maximise the effectiveness of their inducting and train a new generation of scientists. But the reproduction of the few professors existing at the time, around 200, was no great problem. No specific measures were implemented.

With the political scientist Georg Andrén as Chairperson and the historian Erik Lönnroth as chief secretary, the 1945 Drafting Committee on University Matters signalled a change in this respect. For the first time, there is a distinctive, explicit demarcation in the directives from the political side that indicate that it would be desirable that professors devote more of their time 'to advising the more advanced students'. The Drafting Committee's recommendation of licentiate and doctoral student scholarships for all disciplinary branches led to fundamental changes in the prerequisites for graduate education. A special political allocation of resources was created for the support of graduate students and for the printing of dissertations.

Due to the tremendous increase in public education that developed in Sweden, as in other western countries, during the decades following World War II, the interests of the body politic in the universities up to 1960 focused upon the problems of undergraduate education.[16] The problems surrounding graduate education were temporarily solved by the 1955 Drafting Committee for University Matters which called for relieving the professors of the duties of undergraduate education so that they could devote more of their time to graduate training and to the advising of graduate students. In the 1959 motion, these modest recommendations were postponed until a later date. However, the economic conditions of graduate students were improved through the creation of new training positions and funds to cover degree candidates' expenses.

A whole new situation was created in 1962. The Social Democratic Party's Student Association took up an initiative which aimed at putting graduate education in the foreground. The initiative was rapidly carried to the highest political level by the then Prime Minister, Tage Erlander. Conferences were held and a governmental investigative committee was established. While this committee had a majority of scientists, other participants included labour union representatives, students, and representatives of business and parliament. Political guidelines were issued by the Social Democratic Minister of Education. The stated political goal became the achieving of more effective graduate education and a faster flow of doctoral students. In a bargaining process which began inside the committee, the politicians' offer to the scientific community consisted of new positions at the university and new basic resources for the graduate programmes. The specific 'trade unions' looking after the interests of the different professional groups at the universities, took a very active part in the bargaining process, demanding that the job-security of university employees be solved simultaneously with the construction of a new employment structure. The student organisations made clear that *their* goal was economic security for doctoral students at a level to which I have found no counterpart in any other country. They wanted full support without teaching obligations during four years for everybody, who was accepted as a doctoral student.

The cards in the bargaining process had been dealt. The game could begin.

However, before I proceed to a description of the outcome of the negotiations, I would like to give some attention to the question of why graduate education became a political priority question at this particular point in time. How is one to explain that the political body appears as the active and driving agent of change of something so genuinely academic as the education of doctoral students?

During the 1950s and the beginning of the 1960s, the Swedish political climate was strongly optimistic regarding economic development, and deeply convinced that it was through research and applied science that the nation would be able to maintain its position as one of the highest-ranking welfare states in the world. The kinds of research that politicians were committed to included not only the natural sciences, technology and medicine, which had long been nursed and supported by them; but also the social sciences, because they were needed for 'the social engineering' of the Swedish welfare state. Social science-oriented disciplines within the humanities, of the kind that could prepare humanity for a technological society were also considered important. Disciplines as social history, philosophy, ethnology and drama could fulfil such a function. The goal was now not only to get young, doctorally-trained people into the school systems as before, but also - and perhaps foremost - to get them into state and local government administration.

The emphasis lay upon *youth*. It was not middle-aged researchers who were to be integrated into society. Research findings were to be socially relevant, and society's separate administrative units were instructed to develop what we call 'sector research', that is, research that is socially-directed and aimed at solving concrete social problems.[17] It was easy to understand that with this long-term ambition of solving society's emerging problems through science, the short-term goal had to be to train researchers rapidly, who could then work as the problem-solvers of the administrative bodies - in a manner similar to doctorally-trained technologists involved in new products development in the business world.

In his autobiography, Tage Erlander has written an illuminating description of the optimistic climate of the development, and the positive attitude toward science that characterised both parties in the bargaining process:

> It was not as beggars that scientists came to the politicians' table. All of them were aware of the crucial role that their science would be able to play in the building of a future society.

The politicisation of graduate education was thus described by Tage Erlander neither as a struggle for academic freedom, nor as political encroachment, but precisely as a negotiation between equals.

Various possibilities for promoting scientific progress were discussed. 'However, foremost of all measures was support for all persons who showed an exceptional capacity for scientific research,' reports Erlander. In the same way that it was to help France move out of a crisis and towards a brighter future, both in the 1870s and in 1950s, so graduate education in Sweden became the very key to our future society.

The New Graduate Education

The result of the committee's study was a plan for reforming doctoral training, the intention of which was to place the Swedish graduate degree on a par with those of Germany and the United States. The model that was used, both for the required standards, and for the content of the training programmes, was the American PhD - or rather the blueprint for an American doctoral degree - not this degree in reality. What the participants in their bargaining process overlooked was a deep-seated conflict within American doctoral programmes in the humanistic sciences. This was a conflict between the two educational philosophies: the one inspired by the natural sciences, with its positivistic educational programme in which doctoral training consisted of a technical learning process; and the other a hermeneutically-inspired educational programme for which doctoral training consisted of a human maturation process. The politicised Swedish plan became associated with the positivistic notion of a unity of the sciences, and with demands to adapt doctoral programmes in the humanities and the social sciences to the design of the natural sciences.[18] There was total agreement in the committee on this point.

Coupled to this new degree was a whole new career system for scientists, where the selection of future university employees would be made at the post-graduate level, and where all who thus extended their careers would be guaranteed life-long and secure support within the walls of the university. For those who did not survive the selection process, there was supposed to exist an expanding public sector - which constituted the very foundation of the political visions of change in the graduate educational programmes.

From a political perspective, this initiative was a good one. It created the conditions both for greater academic effectiveness and for the greater security demanded by union representatives. The economic bases of support for students were also to improve.

When the committee's plan was complete, the bargaining process continued. The plan was sent out for consideration to university faculties, to the counties' political and local governmental bodies, to the most influential trade unions, and to the student organisations. Their answers were used to modify the committee's original plan. Since the government and parliament hold the real power over the allocation of resources to the universities, it was essentially the politicians who could decide how a politically acceptable graduate education programme would be formulated. At the same time, however, the political powers were constrained by the fact that their interests were identical to those of the scientific community that constituted the other bargaining party. The interest shared by both parties was in the need for good researchers and high-quality research. Any changes in the educational system that might endanger the achievement of this common goal are naturally neither desirable, nor are they politically sound. For this reason, governmental modifications of the proposals often came to be tied to the university referral committees' refusals to sanction motions and to their repudiations. The bargaining process worked.

The 1969 government bill concerning graduate education and the subsequent parliamentary decision can be characterised - in Katrin Fridjonsdottir's terms - as a contract. Government and Parliament pledged to increase the number of positions tended for post-doctoral studies and to make available basic resources for research. However, the national financial budget did not allow for as large an increase in resources as the committee planned. The political body also listened to the university's complaint about the proposed new scientific career. In the name of academic freedom, it delegated a great deal of responsibility to the university for shaping the goals of research, for the size of the graduate schools, for selection of researchers and for the development of each university department's course offerings.

The universities were commanded to shorten the time needed for completion of the doctoral degree, from eight years to four years. In order to continue to achieve good results, without lessening the overall quality of research, it was intended that graduate research in the humanities and social sciences should change from being individually-oriented, to becoming more of a collective enterprise. 'Team-work' in research became the key word. And the then Minister of Education, Olof Palme, recommended that the doctoral dissertation should no longer be an individual's life work, but should instead represent a qualifying test of research capability.

Formally, the design of the graduate programme was directed by the politicians, the content by the university. But practically, the problem becomes whether a far-reaching change in design can be carried out without influencing the content.

The question we can now ask is: Was the contract fulfilled? If not: Who was responsible for any breach of contract? Or are we confronted with processes of change which lie outside the parameters of the contract, and which have altered the very preconditions for its fulfilment?

On one point, it is obvious: The political party in the negotiation process has not been satisfied with the results of current academic activity, as indicated by several politically-directed investigations of our graduate educational system. Statistically, one can easily demonstrate that the universities are not fulfilling the contract. We have not taken upon ourselves the unpleasant task of using a rigorous selection process to promote those who ought to be given an opportunity to pursue graduate studies. We fail to attract talented individuals to all disciplines. Some disciplines now face a risk of not being able to fill their professors' chairs at the turn of the century. Despite the lower quantitative expectations of Ph.D. dissertations, graduate training takes as much time as before. Students prefer to do a 'lifework' than a 'qualifying test'. Finally, only a few educational environments within the humanities or social sciences have accepted team-work as a method of achieving qualitative results collectively, rather than individually.

But the universities also feel cheated by the bargain. Resources which were earmarked for expansion of the important post-doctoral level were primarily placed at the disposal of the research councils, and not the universities. Happenstance, in the form of research projects accepted by the research councils, rather than the universities' own careful selection process, thus governs the recruitment to a university career. It is becoming more and more difficult for younger researchers to pass the boundary between educational and career positions as positions are few and new doctors abundant.

The scientific labour market, which was supposed to need employees with rapidly-completed doctoral degrees, appears to many disciplines as something of a myth. Not even the universities are eager to take care of those with a PhD degree. Among students, the doctoral degree has begun to be viewed as a burden, rather than a desirable goal. Eagerness on the part of the students to complete their graduate education has declined drastically, and teachers' possibilities of altering the process are, of course, limited. Students' so-called 'completion rates' have deteriorated. The complaints are formulated in the grant proposals and promemoria of the research councils and academies, perhaps most sharply in the Royal Swedish Academy of Sciences report of 1985.

Perhaps one can characterise today's relations between the political body and the community of scholars as mutual suspicion concerning the opposite party's ability and desire to fulfill the previously negotiated contract. Perhaps one can speak of a potential conflict situation, a point where the bargaining relation between the political body and the academic community has ceased to operate. 'Win back the universities from the State' became a rallying cry for the universities' professors in the 1980s.

At this point, two questions demand to be answered: First, is it the politicisation of the graduate programmes that is the source of the current crisis situation in Swedish graduate education? Are the propagators of the freedom-seeking model correct in that threats to research emanate from any form of political infringement upon academic freedom?

And the second question: Is it possible to save Swedish graduate education that is based on the 1969 contract? Or - to quote a pronouncement by a then young Social Democrat in the radical Social Democratic journal *Tiden* - must we confess our mistakes and return to the starting point?[19]

Viewing the relationship between the State and the scientific community in terms of a bargaining process, one is not convinced that it is politicisation in itself that is the villain in this drama. The repeated changes and revisions in the system of graduate education indicate a considerable desire on the part of the politicians to meet and accommodate the critiques levelled by the universities. Neither is it realistic to return to an earlier system. It, too, contained considerable weaknesses and would hardly have managed better to solve the problem of a diminishing job market for PhDs and a clearly unbalanced recruitment of doctoral students to certain disciplines, especially the modern languages, where students seem to avoid research and prefer jobs outside the universities.

However, despite intensive efforts to reform the system of graduate education through negotiation, some considerable difficulties remain. Clearly, the original conception of a uniform graduate education for all the disciplinary branches emanated from a positivistically-derived simplification of reality, which only impeded its implementation. The reform was also to be encumbered by the fate of having been launched at a time when reality took a turn toward an unpredictable new situation: the number of graduate students increased while the employment market for MAs and doctorates stagnated. The climate for theory of science in Sweden, which thus far had been calm, was shaken by revolutionary crises in the sense of Kuhn that heralded important reorientations of great significance to the socially - and society-oriented disciplines. The optimistic belief in progress through science faded away.

Nor is it possible to rule out a certain reluctance or resistance to undergo mental reorientation. The graduate students were unwilling to work solely for a PhD likened to an apprentice's examination, i.e., a thesis that demonstrated a working competence, but no more. Instead, they continued to be committed to something they believed in. The sensitive role of advisers that had been called into question now became the focus for reorientation; and research conducted through project financing by the research councils was more precarious than anyone had anticipated. At Lund University, Professor Olof Wärneryd, Dean of the Faculty for Social Sciences, expressed what many had experienced: 'To train researchers is not an art - it is an impossible mission'.

The Future of Graduate Education in Sweden

When one applies a bargaining model that is borrowed from the labour market to analyses of graduate education, one is gradually made aware that *one* important element is missing in the negotiations between the State and the university: an element which *is* present in negotiations between employers and employees. This element consists of the negotiators' perception of risk - the risk of immediate economic collapse. This makes the two parties more willing to accept each others' argument.

In academic bargaining, the element of risk is not very well articulated. The risk that good research and qualified researchers will be compromised is something that only becomes evident after a very long time. And these long-term risks do not appear as threatening enough for the negotiating parties. Hence, what we need are *valid indicators* of quality that can tell us in which direction we are headed, that is, how the system operates in historical perspective. Only then can the negotiating parties work under conditions which make cooperation as necessary as it once was for the employers and employees at *Saltsjöbaden*.

How then were the qualitative aspects of graduate education dealt with at the political level?

Signed into law by a liberal-conservative government, the first, so-called 'research political' bill of 1981/82 included a few suggestions concerning graduate education that had been adopted from the so-called 'Andrén-committee' (former university chancellor) recommendations. The Liberal Minister of Education Jan-Erik Wikström suggested a qualifying review for acceptance into graduate programmes, written evaluations of theses, an expanded certifying thesis committee, as well as improved economic support for graduate studies, and graduate student positions paid by the research councils. The recommendations and experiences of the universities were to have greater impact. To resolve the issue of quality, a return to the earlier system of control of academic standards for completion of graduate studies had been recommended.

With the former Prime Minister Olof Palme as the first signee, the Social Democratic bill rejected both the strengthening of the certifying committee and detailed evaluations of theses, because these two measures were judged to prolong the average length of graduate studies. The qualitative test must come later, upon application for a senior lectureship (*docentur*). The argumentation coincides with the 1969 governmental bill in which Swedish graduate education as it exists today took shape. The Social Democrats, however, were also prepared to further increase the advisory capacities of the universities and the number of paid graduate student positions. On the issue of quality control, the Social Democratic platform won.

The research political bill of 1983/84, signed by the deputy Prime Minister Ingvar Carlsson, included an introduction that focused on two areas: What was needed was to improve the quality of scientific achievements, and to recruit younger researchers to important areas. A concern for the recruitment issue had already been expressed in the investigative committee report, entitled *Continued Higher Education*, presented under the leadership of Arne Gadd, a prominent Social Democrat from Uppsala. Importantly, the focus upon quality is a new subject in the debate about graduate education. The bill promulgated the now familiar phrase: 'Poor research is worse than no research at all'.

The greatest impetus to the concern for quality was an intensive debate in the mass media surrounding the issue of the alleged declining quality of Swedish doctoral dissertations. This debate was apparently stimulated by reports that were circulating about some foreign university libraries that had refused to accept Swedish doctoral theses.

The mass media, however, had overlooked one important factor. When the Swedish doctoral degree was placed at a level somewhat above the older licentiate degree, it was uniformity with international standards, particularly those of the United States and West Germany, that was being sought. In the fervour of the debate, what was forgotten was the fact that American and German doctoral theses are not published to the same extent as are Swedish ones. Elsewhere it is only the very best theses, i.e., the ones that publishers believe they can sell, that are printed; the remainder gather dust on the shelves of departmental archives. Thus, a library-based comparison between foreign theses and Swedish ones is very unfair: the *elite* of foreign theses is compared to the *totality* of Swedish thesis production. The reaction of some of the foreign libraries could actually have been predicted, and can hardly be used as a reliable indicator of the general quality of Swedish theses.

The next research political bill, that of 1986/87, and also signed by Ingvar Carlsson, increased the amount of support to the graduate students. In this bill, efforts to promote recruitment are included, while the concern for quality appears to have subsided somewhat. In particular, the generally positive evaluation awarded by the OECD to Swedish research led to a general impression that the problem of quality was no longer as acute. Instead, what was emphasised was the issue of recruitment, and of structural limitations to research careers. However, since the Swedish universities and academies were simultaneously applying pressure over the issue of the quality of research, it suddenly became urgent to seek out more systematic methods of evaluating Swedish research of the kind that the Research Council of the Natural Sciences had been carrying out since the end of the 1970s.

Thus, there appears to be reason to pose the question, to what extent have evaluations through 'peer-reviews' of research within the various disciplines been able to uncover grounds for the suspicion that Swedish graduate education fosters qualitatively poor results?

The two evaluations that were recently conducted, for sociology and history, assess graduate education primarily from a quantitative point of view. However, if one reviews the analyses of the scientific results with an eye as to whether or not the assessed works are dissertations, then it is possible to discover that many doctoral theses are not merely 'apprentice exams', but have the ambition of presenting new and creative research results.[20]

In fact, most of the assessed works are doctoral theses. Both of the disciplines reviewed are among those subjects that have a high rate of acceptance to graduate studies and a long period of graduate education. Despite these facts, what is obvious is that quality, whether measured in terms of creativity, vitality, or international orientation, has not suffered. One might even venture the suspicion that it is the many graduate students that constitute the very milieu for the qualitatively high results of the disciplines where, due to the few academic positions, it is otherwise difficult to create optimal conditions for graduate training.

The continual bargaining process between the universities and the State authorities concerning both formal and informal aspects of graduate education, yields a consistently negative picture. The completion rate for graduate students is too low; in a simple cost-benefit analysis the effectiveness is too low; the length of education is too long; advisory capabilities are inferior; and quality is constantly at issue. One investigation after another is undertaken in an effort to find solutions to these problems. Drafting committees for research matters discuss the problems, and the NBUC has once again been given directives for conducting a new investigation of the graduate education system.[21]

In my opinion the choice of perspective is wrong. Some of the problems that have been identified are actually structural problems that will always be an inherent component of a demanding education that concerns mature women and men in the prime years of family building and the height of intensity of their careers. Other problems relate to the assault of the baby-boom generation, i.e., the 1940s generation born in the post-World War II period, on the academic institutions and the labour force, and will fade away over the long term. What is clear is that most of the identified problems are also found in other graduate educational systems than the Swedish one.

Under these circumstances, perhaps a more positive approach would solve many of the snarls of contemporary negotiations. The investigatory committees should strive to identify those environments that foster creativity, as well as those that achieve constant completion rates and guaranteed recruitment.[22] Such environments exist, but they need to be identified and analysed. The sociologist Göran Jenses' six sociological studies of graduate students' educational experiences within various disciplinary branches at Lund University was a step in the right direction.[23] However, it should be completed by qualitative analyses of the results. Jenses' studies indicated that the long average periods required to complete graduate studies are based upon a variety of reasons that differ from discipline to discipline. He also showed that these lengthy study periods should not always be viewed as obstacles from the point of view of society. The older doctors have often an early connection with the labour market.

All politics of reform build upon the assumption that the conceptions of the desired goals are adequate. My hypothesis is that we actually know less about how a good critical and creative graduate education programme should be construed than what is needed in order to begin the task of a constructive politics of reform in this area. Eva Österberg, Professor of History at the University of Lund, says of graduate student advising that in practice it is a matter of 'time and trust'.[24] What is needed is further research on the form and content of milieux that stimulate high-quality graduate studies, more knowledge of how they are maintained, and how they continue to foster creativity. This is the *time* dimension. Simultaneously, we need knowledge of how fragile human relations may be fostered and strengthened: relations that may be described in terms of *trust* between mutually creating colleagues in a collective, knowledge-building endeavour.

Chapter 11

The Exceptionalism of American Higher Education

Martin Trow

Introduction

In this paper I would like to discuss some differences between the system of higher education in the United States and those of other advanced industrial societies. Obviously, there are great difficulties in generalising to the whole of western Europe and Japan. (I exclude discussion of East European countries since their basic assumptions regarding the role and function of education at least were fundamentally different from those in the West.) And any generalisation to the educational systems of societies as different as Sweden and Japan, Italy and Great Britain, are necessarily very broad and inevitably distort the picture of any particular system. Nevertheless, taken together, the higher education systems of western Europe and their outposts elsewhere in the world (including Japan) differ enough from that of the United States to throw into bold relief the 'exceptionalism,' the uniqueness, of the American system.

Differences between the United States and other countries in their forms and structure of higher education are obscured by the fact that we tend to call elements of our systems by similar names. We all have professors and lecturers, colleges and universities, research institutions and laboratories; we all award academic degrees that resemble one another if they are not identical. In addition, our differences are not only obscured but diminished by the international scope of science and scholarship. The fundamental building blocks of teaching and learning in colleges and universities throughout the world are academic disciplines which have an international presence. A sociologist in the United States speaks easily to one in Paris or Stockholm or Tokyo; they read the same books and deal with the same problems. And that is true, on the whole, for physicists and philosophers and economists as well. There are national characteristics that mark the work of any scholarly community, but these bear much the same relation to a discipline as it exists internationally as a regional dialect bears to the common language of a nation. Thus, to describe and understand some of the activities of academic life, particularly the developments of modern science and learning, the products of research and scholarship, it is possible to subordinate (if not wholly ignore) the differences between national systems, and the unique social and historical circumstances out of which those differences arise.

Nevertheless, for many purposes the differences between American and European systems are very large, and cannot be ignored. I will look briefly at ten ways in which American higher education differs from that of most other systems of higher education.

Attitudes Regarding Higher Education

First there is the American belief in education for its own sake. We have a broad national commitment to education for everybody for as long as people can be persuaded to attend formal institutions of education. Our youngsters are constantly being warned about the costs and dangers of dropping out of high school, and are encouraged over television and on the backs of matchbooks to attend college, 'the college of their choice.' Americans have an almost religious belief in the desirability and efficacy of postsecondary education for almost everybody; no other nation in the world makes that commitment or holds that belief. We back that belief with the provision of postsecondary schooling somewhere for everyone who wants an education beyond high school, most notably in a broad system of community colleges which admit students without reference to their high school diploma.

The United States made its commitment to mass higher education, and created the structures that would permit its growth to its present size, long before large numbers were enrolled. By 1900, when only four per cent of Americans of college age were attending college, we already had in place almost all of the central structural characteristics of American higher education: the lay board of trustees, the strong president and his administrative staff, the well-defined structure of faculty ranks, and, in the selective institutions, promotion through academic reputation linked to publication and a readiness to move from institution to institution in pursuit of a career. On the side of the curriculum the elective system, the modular course, credit accumulation and transfer based on the transcript of grades, all were in place by 1900, as were the academic departments covering all known spheres of knowledge, and some not so well known. Underpinning all was the spirit of competition, institutional diversity, responsiveness to markets (and especially to the market for students) and institutional autonomy marked by strong leadership and a diversity of sources of support. The United States already had the organisational and structural framework for a system of mass higher education long before it had mass enrollments. All that was needed was growth.

What has happened since to American higher education? Of course, there has been growth - an enormous expansion in the numbers of students, institutions, staff, research support, and everything else. But apart from expansion and growth, the most important structural change in American higher education this century has been the development of the community college system, and the way that has tied the four-year institutions and their degrees to the world of continuing and vocational education. Academic freedom is more firmly and broadly protected than at the turn of the century, thanks in part to the American Association of University Professors (AAUP). In addition, there is now broad federal support for student aid in the form of grants and loans, and this has supplemented rather than replaced other and earlier forms of student aid. Federal agencies support university-based research at a level that could hardly have been imagined 90, or even 50, years ago. The machinery of fund-raising, the organisation of alumni and the associated development of big-time sports has gone further than one would have imagined, though the roots of all that were already in place at the turn of the century. And there are faculty unions in some hundreds of colleges and universities, though not in the leading research universities. But what is impressive about American higher education in the early 1990s is not how much it differs from the system that existed at the turn of the century, but how similar it is in basic structure, diversity, mission, governance and finance.

The question may be raised of how it came to be that a century ago the United States had already created a preternaturally precocious system of higher education with an enormous capacity for expansion without fundamental structural change. Part of the answer lies in the weakness of central government in America throughout the nineteenth century, and a federal constitution which gave to the states the primary responsibility for the provision of education. This translated into the absence of a national academic standard, which elsewhere has prevented the rapid expansion of higher education by preventing the creation of new institutions which could not meet that standard. By contrast, the many colleges and universities which have been established in this country since the Revolution were granted charters by the states without having to meet high academic standards. As a result, a few decades after the Civil War England was serving a population of 23 million with four universities; the state of Ohio, with three million, already boasted 37 institutions of higher education.[1] By 1910 the United States had already established nearly 1,000 colleges and universities, with a third of a million students, at a time when 16 universities in France enrolled altogether about 40,000 students, a number nearly equalled by the number of faculty members in American colleges and universities.

In most European countries, including England, enrollment rates in higher education just after World War II ran from three to five per cent of the age grade. With the exception of the United Kingdom, the four decades after World War II have seen a growth in enrollment rates in Western Europe to somewhere between 25 and 35 per cent, depending on the country and how one counts. Britain enrolls about 14 per cent of the age grade in degree-granting institutions or courses, a figure roughly stable for the past decade. The enormous post-war growth in higher education in every European country was of course initiated and planned by government; there is almost no private higher education in Europe - some church-related universities and a few linked to the business community are relatively small and do not affect overall national policy. Throughout Europe, central governments provide most of the funds for the support of higher education, both for teaching and research.

The sources of the post-war growth in Europe were many, but private initiative was not one of them. Throughout Western Europe, the end of World War II saw a broad growth of democratic sentiment, reflected (among other things) in demands for a wider access to both secondary and higher education. The expansion of secondary education and the growth of the welfare state both increased the demand for people with some kind of postsecondary education. Moreover, European governments came increasingly to believe in the contribution of education, and especially of higher education, to economic development and thus to military strength. This led in many of these countries to forms of manpower planning which depended heavily on investment in higher education.

Despite the post-war growth of higher education throughout the world, the American system remains much larger and more diverse than any European system. Its 3500 accredited colleges and universities and 14 million enrolled students represent about 50 per cent of the 'college-age' cohort; since opportunities for continuing education are widely available, the proportion of Americans who ultimately take degree-credit postsecondary study is over 50 per cent.[2] The size of American higher education is not determined by central government planning or policy, but by the demand for postsecondary education in the society at large, and by decisions regarding admissions standards and tuition costs made by or for the institutions of postsecondary education.

Public and Private Sectors

America's colleges and universities are a mixture of public and private institutions with the privately-supported institutions present at every level of excellence and in every category of function. While it is true that nearly four out of five of our students are currently (1991) enrolled in public institutions, the private sector remains enormously important as models for the public sector. For example, of the ten leading research universities, eight are private; of the top 20 research universities, 15 are private institutions. And the best undergraduate four-year colleges are also part of the private sector. Many private institutions are regional and more modest in their aspirations, but at all levels of selectivity there is easy movement of students and faculty, and ideas about teaching and learning, between the public and private institutions. This relationship is almost unique in the world of advanced industrial societies. (Japan is a partial exception among industrial societies in having a very large private sector of higher education, though with the state-supported 'national' (formerly 'Imperial') universities on the whole at the top of the hierarchy.) By contrast, for a variety of political and historical reasons, European countries discourage private institutions of higher education by withholding charters, support, and institutional autonomy or discretion. Currently, although in a number of European countries support is being sought for higher education in the private sector, less than five per cent of operating costs in European higher education comes from private sources.[3]

Perhaps the crucial difference in the United States is not the existence of a large and prestigious private sector, but rather the multiplicity and diversity of funding sources for both private and leading public institutions. Overall, American higher education is currently (1988-89) spending about $135 billion in operating expenses, roughly 2.7 per cent of the gross national product.[4] Government at all levels together provides nearly half of all current revenues for American higher education, not including federal aid given directly to students, which shows up for the most part in tuition and fees. The federal government provides only about 25 per cent of the total funds for higher education, including its support for research and development in the universities, but excluding the aid it provides directly to students, currently running at about $10 billion in a combination of student grants and loans. State and local governments (mostly state) provide one-third of the funds for higher education, including federal aid they have received, and the institutions themselves about 15 per cent from their endowments and other sources. If federal aid to students is counted as federal support, it increases the federal contribution to about 23 per cent of total, and reduces the student contribution to about the same percentage. About six per cent is provided by individuals, foundations, and private business firms in the form of gifts, grants, and contracts.[5]

These proportions differ between public and private colleges and universities, of course, though it must be stressed that all American colleges and universities are supported by a mixture of public and private funds. For example, while in 1985-86 public colleges and universities got 45 per cent of their operating budgets from state governments, private institutions got less than two per cent of theirs from state sources. (On the other hand, private colleges got a slightly larger proportion of their support funds from the federal government than did public four-year institutions, one per cent versus 11 per cent.) Another big difference between public and private institutions lies in the much greater importance of student tuition fees and payments for services (monthly room and board) in private schools: they account for less than one-third of the revenues of public institutions but nearly two-thirds of the support for private institutions.[6] These proportions differ sharply among even finer categories of colleges and universities - for example, as between public research universities and public four-year colleges.

But even in the public sector, among the leading research universities like Berkeley, state support may be only half or less of operating expenses, the rest coming from federal research grants, gifts, endowment income, fees and tuition, and payment for services, as, for example, from patients in university-operated hospitals.[7]

In the United States, the diversity of funding sources has increased in past decades with federal aid to students, tuition payments and private gifts all growing rapidly. During the same period, since World War II, the diversity of funding sources in the UK has until very recently been decreasing, as central government has taken over tuition payments and student support. Where central government in the UK provided only about a third of operating expenses for the universities just before World War II, and about two-thirds just after it, that figure grew to about 90 per cent by the mid-1960s.[8]

'General Education' as Part of the Curriculum

American higher education is marked by a commitment to the idea of a 'liberal' or 'general' education for all (or at least most) undergraduates. Elsewhere, with few exceptions, a broad liberal education in our sense of the word is gained, by the minority who get it, in the upper secondary schools which prepare for universities; and beyond that, outside of the formal curriculum altogether. Higher education in Europe is for the most part highly specialised and oriented toward professional or pre-professional training. American colleges and universities provide a good deal of 'general education' that elsewhere is done in the upper secondary schools, in part because of the broad comprehensive nature, (and in European terms) consequent academic weakness of our secondary schools, which are designed to bring as many young people as possible to the end of secondary schooling so that they can qualify for entry to higher education. Currently, about 75 per cent of American students finish high school and are qualified for entry to some kind of college or university. By contrast, about 30 per cent of the age group in France are qualified to enter higher education, and in England the proportion is under 20 per cent. The proportions of the age grade who actually do enter some form of higher education are, of course, lower - in Britain currently around 14 per cent, in France about 25 per cent, as compared with roughly 50 per cent in the United States.

The Elective System, the Modular Course, and the Unit Credit as Academic Currency

Another unique characteristic of American higher education is the phenomenon of the modular course with its attached 'credits,'[9] and the definition of the requirements for a degree in terms of the accumulation of course credits rather than, as elsewhere, through success on an examination or the presentation of a thesis. The unit credit is the currency of American higher education. Credits which can be accumulated over time and transferred between institutions and between different major fields of study within colleges and universities make it relatively easy for students to 'stop out' and return at a later date, with their past work not wasted but safely 'banked' on their transcripts. In addition, the credit system greatly facilitates the transfer of students from one institution to another, and makes possible links between continuing education and earlier studies.

But while this kind of academic currency introduces enormous flexibility into our system and allows students to change their institution or fields of study two or three or more times before earning their degrees or credentials, it also tends to reduce the socialising impact of a concentrated period of study in a single university.

The Academic Profession

There are marked differences between the academic profession in the United States and that of most other countries. In Europe, on the whole, academic departments have been characterised by a single professor and many assistants. In the traditional European university, from the early or middle nineteenth century until World War II, the central figure in the university was the chairholder. In Germany the *ordinarius* professor represented his discipline in his university, and in his several roles he not only taught, directed and carried on research, but together with other chairholders, also governed his own faculty, and the university through the election of a rector from among their midst. Since World War II, and especially since the middle '60s, the 'junior' (non-professorial) teaching staff in European universities have gained more power along with the students in the governance of departments and universities. This governance system is formalised in various boards and committees on which are found representatives of the professors, junior faculty, students, and sometimes non-academic 'staff', each elected by the 'estate' which its members represent. In many European societies these elections are contested along the lines of the national political parties and are thus deeply politicised; the political divisions within the society are thus brought directly into the heart of the academic institutions.

In Britain the professor did not have quite the same overwhelming power and authority as did his counterparts on the Continent, largely due to the power of the college fellows in Oxford and Cambridge who actually govern the colleges which were (and are) the units of those ancient universities. While professors have been much stronger in the University of London and in the provincial universities than in Oxbridge, the tradition of 'a democracy of gentlemen' impeded the emergence of a professorial oligarchy of the kind found in Continental universities. In the UK, as on the Continent, professors still comprise only a fraction (in the UK about 10 per cent) of all university teachers, and the rank is not the normal terminal career grade of the academic profession. The United States is almost alone in having a relatively flat academic hierarchy: the ranks of lecturer, assistant professor and associate professor are understood to be stepping stones to the final career grade of full professor. Since all young entering assistant professors can expect to become full professors in time, they tend not to see their interests as opposed to those of the full professors, but acquire the values of their seniors in the course of becoming professors themselves. And thus they are not represented in university government as a special interest group - the 'non-professorial staff' - as in most Continental countries. Moreover, American departments are more egalitarian both in the autonomy given to assistant and associate professors and in the parts they play in departmental and university decisions.[10]

Governance Structures

There are basic differences in the governance of American colleges and universities as compared with their counterparts in England and on the Continent. England aside, everywhere else a ministry of education or its equivalent plays a central role in (a) the appointment of academic staff, especially professors; (b) the allocation of budget among and within universities; (c) the criteria for access to universities; and d) the determination of the standards - the examinations or theses - required to earn a degree. In most cases this ministry is located in central government; in Germany the state governments have primary responsibility for higher education, with some powers, especially for the support of research, reserved to the Federal ministry in Bonn. As a result, the administrative staffs for higher education are typically located in the ministry rather than in the institution itself. By contrast, in the United States there is no federal ministry of education - our Department of Education plays a very small role in relation to higher education, apart from administering substantial programmes of student grants and loans. In American private colleges and universities, the whole of the administrative apparatus is located within the institution and is an arm of the university president. In public institutions most of the administrators also serve the president, though some decisions are held in the hands of a state department or commission (and this varies among the states and between different classes of institutions). Whether the administrative staff lies inside or outside the university has great consequences for the kinds of decisions it can take, and thus for its autonomy.

Academic Leadership

In the United States the president of a college or university is both the head of 'the administration' and also the academic leader.[11] He serves by appointment of a lay board of trustees and is responsible only to them. So long as he has their confidence and support the American college president has a very high degree of power and authority within his own institution. By contrast, European institutions (again Britain aside) have no lay boards of governors, and ordinarily their chief academic officer is a weak rector, formerly elected by the full professors, and more commonly now by a vote of the various estates of the university. The rector (by whatever name) ordinarily is only the chairman of the various governing committees and serves a relatively short period of time, returning thereafter to his professorial chair. On the Continent he has alongside him a permanent administrative official appointed by the ministry and responsible for the finances and most of the internal administrative decisions. This administrative officer - the *Kurator* in Germany - is a civil servant on long-term appointment, and commonly comes to exercise a very large amount of authority and power within the university. The weak rector cannot make decisions, as American college presidents can, about the internal allocation of funds, most academic matters, or ultimate decisions on academic personnel.

The Lay Board

The American college or university invariably has a lay board, which at once ensures its ultimate accountability to its local, regional or national constituencies in the broader society, but also insulates it from the direct management and intervention of the government of the day. Such boards ordinarily have the ultimate legal authority over the institution, and come to identify with it and its interests even though appointed, in the case of most public institutions, by the governor of the state. In European countries the direct accountability of the institution to the broader society is ensured by the authority of the ministry and its officials over the institution. The autonomy of European universities is a function of traditional restraints on government from interfering directly in academic affairs, thus permitting a high measure of academic freedom, discussion and debate within the walls of the institution. Apart from the freedom to teach and to learn, the university rarely has much authority to manage its own size and shape, its entry or exit requirements, or its broad character and functions. As in many other respects, the UK stands somewhere between the United States and the Continental countries in this respect. British universities, with the exception of Oxford and Cambridge, do have lay boards, but they are weaker than their American counterparts, and the instruments of central government, the Department of Education and Science and the newly created statutory funding bodies increasingly play, or threaten to play, a more *dirigiste* role, similar to their counterparts in France and Germany.[12]

'Vocational' and 'Technical' Studies and Continuing Education

Almost every European country has created a variety of non-degree-granting postsecondary institutions, largely committed to vocational and technical education. These 'postsecondary' institutions are very often not included in the category of 'higher education;' access to them is through different routes than to the universities, and there is almost no movement of students from those institutions to the institutions of higher education, since they provide shorter courses, and do not offer the same degrees as the universities and their counterparts. Most of these institutions have been created since World War II to provide easier access to forms of postsecondary education that are responsive to local and regional interests, and that offer technical and vocational studies that have difficulty in expanding within the traditional universities, or are not offered there at all.

In the United States many of the functions of these institutions are provided by community colleges, with the big difference that the community colleges are understood there to be part of the broad system of higher education. Credits within them are transferable to degree-granting institutions, and their faculty members are trained in the four-year colleges and research universities. Community colleges in the United States, and many four-year colleges and universities, both public and private, also provide a good deal of 'continuing education' for adults seeking to keep up with their fields, or to change them, or to extend their education in directions that are not vocationally oriented. In Europe the continuing education of adults has not on the whole been provided in the traditional institutions, but in other institutions which ordinarily have few links with the traditional institutions of higher education.

Service to the Society, as well as to the State

Alongside its commitments to research and to teaching American higher education has a broad commitment to service to almost any organised interest that asks for it, and can pay for it. This is necessarily so since American colleges and universities are supported by the society broadly and not just by the state. They need student tuition, private gifts, and public and private research support as well as subventions directly by the state to state-aided institutions. By contrast, European universities do not have this same kind of general commitment to serve society; they are creatures of the state and do what the state asks them to do in return for full funding (or near it) by state agencies. From the early nineteenth century until very recently European universities have been largely (though not exclusively) engaged in the preparation of graduates for public service of various kinds (including teaching, and in Protestant countries, the established churches). And student numbers have on the whole been constrained by the limited demand for state employees. As recently as 1976-78, in West Germany between two-thirds and three-quarters of jobs open to graduates were in the public sector; in Sweden and Denmark, about two-thirds; in France, three-quarters of the arts graduates and 60 per cent of the science graduates went into the public sector and only 17 per cent into the private sector. In 1978 in Great Britain, 44 per cent of the graduates went into public administration, teaching or the nationalised industries while 45 per cent took further coursework, did research or continued in academic careers.[13] Even in Italy, with its enormously inflated university enrollments, public service was and is the goal of most graduates. But in recent years, the sharp decline in the number of positions available in the public sector, and especially in teaching and research, together with the democratisation and expansion of European higher education, has greatly attenuated that link between the universities and public service, and has forced graduates to look elsewhere than to the civil service for employment; in some countries this has accelerated the professionalisation of business management.

But since their conceptions of service have been so dominated by their relations to the state, European universities have not been highly responsive to the emergence of new needs and interests in the society that are not yet reflected in public policy or in the directives of ministries. Moreover, their full funding has given them less incentive to be responsive to local and regional interests, particularly in business and industry. In the past few years some European nations have shown considerable interest in encouraging their institutions of higher education to develop closer ties with industry, with varying degrees of success. In some cases, governments, as in the UK, have cut the budgets of the universities so as to force them to seek support from business and industry. This has been dramatically 'successful' in some universities (eg, Salford) where the cuts were very deep. But it is a less effective strategy where the university does not have the resources to serve local interests, or where it has not built up a network of links of service and attitudes of responsiveness over decades.

There are, of course, many exceptions to this generalisation, and more all the time; the 'Americanisation' of European higher education reflects itself not so much in broader access or a less specialised curriculum as in a growing sensitivity to the needs of business and industry in return for increasing levels of support by the business community. This is clearest in some British universities and polytechnics, in the 'petit grandes écoles' in France, which are often directly sponsored by local chambers of commerce, and in such institutions as the University of Turin, known colloquially as 'Fiat University' for its close links to that large firm.

This is by no means an exhaustive inventory of unique characteristics of American higher education. Other features of the system flow from those cited above. For example, the relative youth of American students, the great distances that so many have had to travel to college from home, and the early and continuing religious ties of so many colleges and universities, all have led American colleges and universities to accept a greater responsibility for their students' physical and moral welfare, *in loco parentis*, than most European universities. This in turn has led to the growth of very large and highly professionalised student services in such areas as health, counselling, halls of residence, intramural sports, among others, staffed for the most part by nonacademic professionals. These large staffs are directly responsible to the college or university president, and give him direct control over resources, of people and money, that his European counterparts do not have.

Or to take another example of the way unique characteristics generate others: the large measure of institutional autonomy in American higher education, the modular course and the absence of national examinations together make it relatively easy to create new courses, new departments and professional fields, interdisciplinary courses, and educational innovations of all kinds.

This last point suggests a broader or more general way of looking at the specific differences that I have enumerated above. This more general perspective pivots around the distinction among 'elite,' 'mass,' and 'universal access' systems of higher education.[14] On the whole, until World War II, European systems of higher education supported elite systems of higher education, offering access to no more than three or four or five per cent of the university age grade. Since World War II, all European systems of higher education have expanded very considerably, moving toward structures which allow the entry of 15, 25, and even 35 per cent of the age grade.

This transformation from an elite to a mass system involves not merely the expansion of small institutions into bigger ones, or the creation of many new colleges and universities. It involves profound changes in attitudes toward higher education on the part of students and teachers; in its organisation, finance and governance; in the structure of secondary education, in the criteria for admission to higher education; in the recruitment and education of faculty; in curriculum, physical planning, and much else. But the history of European higher education since World War II has been the story of their efforts to grow in size and in functions without radically transforming their institutional structures, and of the ensuing difficulties all European systems have encountered in trying to accommodate mass numbers and mass functions within structures designed for elite higher education. These efforts have been marked by very great strains and difficulties, and have been only partially successful. The difficulties became especially pronounced when most European systems began, some 15 years ago, to accept more than 15 per cent of the age grade in degree-granting institutions of higher education. (The British have held their proportion to just under 15 per cent, in an effort to preserve the forms, structures and standards of elite higher education in all their degree-granting institutions.) By contrast, the organisational structure of mass higher education in the United States was already in place 100 years ago. American higher education has many problems of its own, arising directly out of its broad access and relaxed standards - the recurrent discussions about the quality of undergraduate education are a case in point.[15]

But on the whole we have a precocious system, without many of the problems, and weak solutions, that mark contemporary European higher education. How we have come to develop such a unique, and uniquely adaptive and responsive, system is the subject of the next section, in which the question is raised in the context of a comparison with the history and organisation of higher education in the UK. Many, but not all, the comparisons made in that section would apply to Continental countries as well. But Britain has its own forms of 'exceptionalism'; American higher education differs in different ways from the higher educational systems of different countries.

Trends and Countertrends: 'The Americanisation' of European Higher Education

The issue of American exceptionalism can be looked at in a number of different ways: the nature and extent of differences between American and other countries, institution by institution, or as societies; the sources of those differences in history, geography, demography, culture and values, or whatever; and trends toward the convergence or divergence of America and other nations in specific or general respects. In this last section I will point to what I take to be trends in most European societies toward American-style forms and structures, which I see as inherent in their move toward mass higher education. But I do not assume that these trends will result in an absolute narrowing of the differences between American and European higher education over the next few decades, for several reasons, among these the strong resistance built into European countries and their educational systems to an expansion and differentiation of higher education on the American model, and the continuing evolution of mass higher education in the US.

In any event, I close by pointing to three broad trends in European systems of higher education toward American patterns which may (or may not) narrow the differences between our systems over the next few decades.

1. The first is the *tendency in all European countries toward the further differentiation of function among institutions of higher education* - a continuing differentiation between and sometimes within institutions that reflects the increasing heterogeneity of students in their social origins, their academic preparation and abilities, their ages, their experiences while in higher education, and their future careers. This increasing differentiation is a concomitant of the move from elite to mass forms of higher education, and the consequent growth both in the number and variety of students and what they study.

This tendency toward diversity does not proceed without resistance in some countries, especially those in which the state has a monopoly, or near-monopoly, over higher education. Diversity causes problems for central state management. It is more difficult to administer different kinds of institutions, with different costs, functions, admissions policies, standards of instruction, variety of courses, etc. Moreover, with diversity inevitably comes inequalities among institutions and sectors - in student achievement, staff/student ratios, status and prestige in the larger society - inequalities which are natural concomitants of the different activities and functions of the institutions and of the kinds of people they recruit, both as students and as teachers.

But while these inequalities are inherent in diversity, they are extremely awkward when the state has a monopoly over the higher educational system. Public authorities are embarrassed by inequalities among institutions which formally have equal status; governments tend to try to reduce those inequalities by applying common standards for entry and for degrees, common salary schedules for staff, common funding formulas, common formulas for support of research, building and capital investment. These central efforts are in part a response to the tendency of bureaucracy to standardise its treatment of all dependent units, but also reflect norms in almost all societies which require that states treat institutions that are dependent on them equally and 'fairly.' These tendencies toward equality, which are inherent in the nature of public authority and bureaucratic management, run contrary to the inherent tendency of diversity to generate differences which can be perceived as inequalities.

It is possible for state authorities to plan for a certain measure of diversity within the state system - as for example the maintenance of three or four distinct strata of institutions of higher education. Examples are the differences between universities, polytechnics, and institutions of further education in England; in France the sharp differences between the *grandes écoles*, the universities and the IUTs; and in California, the differences between the University of California (with its nine campuses), the California State University system (on 19 campuses), and the 120 community colleges. In each case this formal differentiation, and the legitimation of marked differences in treatment among the sectors, is a partial response to the pressures for diversity in a system of mass higher education. But in each case there are strong pressures for equality between institutions *within* the same sector and, in some European nations, other pressures to reduce the differences in character, mission, and level of support *between* different segments (as, for example, between the universities and the polytechnics in the UK).

There is another reason why state authority has difficulty encouraging the emergence of a really wide diversity of institutions, and that is the political expectation that it make decisions, and correct decisions, in the face of alternatives. It is hard for political authorities to confess that they do not know which of a variety of forms of higher education ought to be the model for future development, or to say that all of them should be encouraged. The response of their political opponents is likely to be: 'It is your responsibility to decide which of these forms of development is best and to choose it; anything else is to waste resources when resources are scarce, and when such waste is reprehensible or worse.' How can a government defend itself against the charge that it is so indecisive it cannot even decide what form and shape an emerging publicly-supported system of higher education should take, and continues to support some forms which almost certainly will be shown to be ineffective and inadequate? The only problem is that at the time these innovative institutions or programmes are launched it is not at all clear *which* of them are likely to be successful. But politically this need to assert omniscience, and to show decisiveness and a mastery of events, is almost mandatory for political authorities who face opposition and criticism. That need to appear to be strong, wise, all-knowing and decisive forces public authorities to act with more conviction than they must feel in the design of educational systems. Or looked at another way, if they were to support a wide diversity of institutions on public funds, it could be charged that the government was consciously supporting institutions that would probably fail. That charge would be true, except that no one at the time could know which of them would in fact fail.

Americans accept, as on the whole Europeans do not, that competition in higher education, as in other areas of organised social life, is the most effective way of planning for an unpredictable future, on the ground that despite the appearance of waste, it creates a diversity of institutions some of which will be better fitted for future, as yet unpredictable, conditions and demands than any that can be designed by a central state authority. One illustration of what unrestrained market forces and competition in continuing education in the United States looks like is provided by Grand Rapids, Michigan, an industrial and market city of about 250,000 population, with about 400,000 in the broader metropolitan area. It is a leading centre in the United States for the manufacture of office furniture.[16] The city is served by a strong state-supported regional college, Grand Valley State College, which offers work through the Master's but not the doctoral degree to some 9,000 students, mainly traditional-aged studying full time. This college has a beautiful campus a few miles outside of town, and modest facilities in Grand Rapids itself, where it currently provides some continuing education in graduate study in social welfare, education, public administration and business studies. However, also present in Grand Rapids and also offering continuing education in all kinds of subjects, mostly in rented space, are the following institutions:

1. Michigan State University - a branch of the big land-grant state research university;

2. Western Michigan University, a regional state university;

3. Ferris State College, a regional state college, like Grand Valley;

4. Aquinas College, a private Catholic institution;

5. Davenport College, a proprietary college offering a bachelor's degree in Business Studies;

6. Jordan College, a proprietary college;

7. Grand Rapids Community College, offering degree credit courses at the level of the first two years of the baccalaureate, plus many non-credit vocational studies;

8. Calvin College, a private church-related college;

9. Grand Rapids Baptist College, a private church-related college; and

10. Kendall School of Design, a proprietary college.

One might think that that would be provision enough. But, no, Grand Valley State College has been given $30 million by the State of Michigan to build a large building in Grand Rapids as a facility for a major expansion of its provision of continuing education. The college's engineering departments will be moving there, together with the department specialising in the study of work environments, primarily offering degree level and post-graduate engineering programmes to adult employed learners. Moreover, there is little planning or coordination among these providers.

So in this representative American town we see a nearly free market for the provision of continuing education, some of it wholly self-supporting, some of it partly subsidised. One might ask: Why this fierce competition? The answer seems to be that for each institution, more students mean more money either from their fees, or through enroll-ment-driven formula budgeting from the state, or from both. In addition, continuing education is yet another service that engenders support in the broader community for the provider. Thus the providers are all highly motivated to recruit students, that is, to create a learning society, and they are all highly sensitive to the consumers' interests. Above all, behind all this lies the assumption that 'supply creates demand'.

To many Europeans this picture of continuing education in America is marked by unnecessary diversity, lack of coordination or central control over quality, inefficient duplication, waste, and the absence of continuity. The standard American answer to all these criticisms is the answer of the market: 'We cannot be inefficient and wasteful, or we would not be able to survive.' And such an appeal to the 'unseen hand' reduces the need to develop a more elaborate educational, political, or philosophical rationale; if students continue to enroll and pay, then the provision seems evidently needed and desirable.

That story, it seems to me, illustrates five characteristics of American higher education which are not shared in most European countries, and which help explain the peculiar form that continuing education takes in the US:

1. The high measure of autonomy attached to our individual institutions, and their ability to go into the market without seeking approval elsewhere, in a ministry of a regional board.

2. The broad assumption in the US, very widely shared, that education is intrinsically a good thing, and that everyone should get as much of it as they can be persuaded to enroll for.

3. The fact that there is no cap, no upper limit to the number of students who can be enrolled in the state's public institutions of higher education. There are, of course, limits on entry to specific colleges or universities, but not to some institution in the system.

4. Most public institutions and systems are funded on a per capita basis, and thus have a continuing incentive to enroll as many students as possible.

5. A substantial part of continuing education in the US (depending on how it is defined) is supported by student fees. That means that much continuing education in the US is not felt to be competitive with other public goods like welfare, other levels of schooling, roads, health care, and the like, but rather with the students' own private consumption. Public policy issues ordinarily arise when some decision has to be made about the allocation of scarce public resources among competitive claims for different public services. Insofar as continuing education is self-supporting, or is treated as if it were, it does not have to justify expansion.

European systems have refused to go down this road of uncontrolled market driven competition. Nevertheless, the next decades of higher education development in many countries will be marked by strong tensions between diversifying forces within institutions and between them, tensions arising out of the growing diversity of students and the explosion of knowledge on the one hand, and the constraining forces of public authority on the other.

Of all the issues in higher education policy currently being debated in Europe there is the broadest consensus on the importance of extending access to mature students, for reasons both of social justice and of technological advancement and economic growth. Nevertheless, the resistance to continuing education is strong, especially in the traditional universities and faculties, which see the education of mature part-time students as very clearly not a characteristic of elite education as it was known in the nineteenth and most of the twentieth century.

It may be that continuing education in Europe will take alternative forms which will show their relative merit in their capacity to respond effectively to fast-changing and unpredictable conditions in society and industry - introducing diversity through the back door, so to speak. But meanwhile, American higher education will continue to change during these next decades, among other things incorporating more part-time continuing education into our traditional colleges and universities, while further blurring the lines between university and society, life and learning, as more part-time education for degree credit is offered by business firms and the military.[17]

2. *The growth and democratisation of higher education leads, among other things, to the development of closer organisational ties between universities and various non-university forms of postsecondary education.* In every country these latter take many different forms: higher vocational colleges, teacher training institutions, schools of music, art, drama, nursing, agriculture and fisheries, administration and management, and other specialised vocations; extension services and other forms of continuing education; and open universities. In many countries these institutions have grown up in somewhat haphazard ways over the years in response to the efforts of a special interest or a powerful politician; sometimes they offer certificates, sometimes an academic degree, though usually a different one than the universities offer. The courses that they offer often overlap both with one another and with courses offered in university. Often these institutions, at least those in the public sector, are under the supervision of different ministries, sometimes with each government ministry having its own training institution. But rarely do these institutions provide access to the university sector; they are not, as we say, well articulated.

Governments may make efforts to rationalise this sector of postsecondary education - at least the public institutions in it - by bringing them into regional groupings and other administrative relationships, as in Sweden. But again, the special interests which created these institutions, and the ministries which sponsor them, will resist this rationalisation, usually successfully.

I have noted that these institutions currently rarely provide access directly to the universities. That may change. One well-documented finding of recent studies in many countries is that people who want to continue their education as adults are more likely to be those who already have had a lot of it.[18] Wanting more education is an acquired taste, acquired through education itself. If that is so, then the graduates of many of these non-university colleges and institutes will increasingly want to continue their higher education, and will seek higher academic degrees and the advanced study that the university offers. These opportunities exist now in most places for exceptional individuals. I anticipate that as this demand grows it may be made easier for mature students to 'transfer' to the university, and to earn the university degree.

The increase in the number of mature students in the university - we can already see this trend in many places - will have effects of various kinds on university education itself: on the curriculum, on modes of instruction, on student financial support, on the relations between student and teacher. Resistance to this trend from the universities lies in the traditional link between elite forms of higher education and the education of *young* men (and more recently women) usually from upper or upper-middle class origins, at a time when their minds and characters are being shaped and formed. Mature students are often of lower social origins (that is often why they didn't go to university directly from secondary school); they seek to increase their skills rather than to undergo character formation; they may not be interested in the university's notion of what constitutes appropriate higher education; and they tend to make a university look increasingly like a technical or polytechnical institute, with the loss of status that implies.

Nevertheless, I believe that the movement of mature students, many with prior experience in non-university forms of higher education, into the university will continue, and that universities everywhere will change and adapt to this trend. Here again, private institutions (where they exist) will have the advantage of their greater adaptability to change.

3. *Another trend I think we are seeing in many European countries is toward stronger university presidents*, whatever they may be called in different countries and institutions. This trend arises out of the tendency toward diversity that I've already spoken of, and also out of the rapidly changing environments in which higher educational institutions will be finding themselves. To turn to the last point first: where the characteristics and mission of 'the university' is clear in the society, and where all of the universities in the society are similar, except for their age and distinction, then state authorities can manage them from outside the institution in a fairly routine and predictable way; the intellectual life of the institution goes on with a certain measure of continuity, while the civil servants in the ministries manage the relatively simple administrative and financial affairs of the institution from outside. Or in another setting where institutions have relatively clear and stable functions, they can be governed from inside by committees of academics, as in Oxford and Cambridge, or by committees of chairholders and full professors, with a weak elected rector, as in many European universities in the past. Both of those arrangements depend on relatively slowly changing external conditions and a broad consensual agreement on what the mission of the institution is. But as institutions of higher education become more varied in character, and as their relation to their environments changes rapidly, they have to be more responsive to new situations. And this requires the kind of decisiveness and discretionary power at the centre that we find in effective business organisations, which also have to act quickly and decisively in response to changing market and financial conditions. A strong chief institutional officer, I suggest, is the only authority who can point an institution of higher education in a new direction, who can seize opportunities when they arise and give an institution the leadership along various dimensions - academic, political, managerial, symbolic - that it needs for success in the competitive academic world that is emerging.[19]

I do not underestimate the very strong cultural and institutional resistance to this tendency in European systems. Neither state authorities nor the powerful academic guilds look with kindness on strong administrative officers at the head of their institutions, nor do the strong academic, staff and student unions that have emerged as actors in the governance structures of many European institutions over the past few decades. So I am very far from suggesting that the strong university president will be common outside the United States very soon, especially in the public sectors of European higher education. But we can see it already in many countries outside of Europe, especially in the private sector, where institutions have the freedom to create their own governance arrangements.[20] And I think it is one of the organisational characteristics that will give private institutions a marginal advantage over public institutions in the decades ahead. Private universities not only are able to create a strong executive at their head, but they *need* a strong executive in order to survive in a world that may not give them the guarantees and subsidies that it does to public institutions.[21] Insofar as governments give publicly supported colleges and universities more autonomy and more responsibility for their own support and functions, they must also give more power and discretion to college and university presidents.

Conclusion

In this paper I have been exploring some of the differences between American higher education and the form it takes in other modern societies. I have also touched on some of the historical sources of our 'exceptionalism,' in the course of which I have suggested some of the ways in which the peculiar characteristics of American society and government gave rise to and sustained its unique system of higher education. But a third aspect of this topic has been almost wholly neglected in this paper: the impact of American higher education on American society and on American democracy. For example, much research supports the assertion that higher education has substantial and enduring effects on the attitudes of those exposed to it.[22]

And those changed attitudes in a population in turn make possible real changes in social relations, if and when they are accompanied by changes in law and institutional behavior. For example, in the US the years after World War II saw a steady decline in hostility toward black Americans, and a growing readiness on the part of whites to give blacks equal treatment and fair access to education, housing and jobs. These changes in attitudes were strongly correlated with exposure to higher education. I believe that the considerable progress the United States made in race relations after World War II was made possible by the growth of mass higher education, and the marked decline in racial prejudice that accompanied it. If that is true, then it represents a very great contribution of American higher education to the life of the society. And the 'affirmative action' policies of American colleges and universities may have helped to create and expand a black middle class, policies that could not have been pursued in a society with high national standards for university access.

But this is merely one illustrative example of the effects of American higher education on American society. An institution now so broadly and deeply implicated in so many aspects of American life must have effects on it of many kinds, political, economic and cultural, both for good and ill. It may be that it is those connections between higher education and the institutions of American society that are of greatest relevance to this theme of 'American exceptionalism'.

Chapter 12

Swedish Research on Higher Education in Perspective
Eskil Björklund in Conversation

Thorsten Nybom (ThN):

The Swedish *Research on Higher Education Programme* was inaugurated in 1971. It would be interesting to know the general and specific preconditions of Swedish research policy preceding the Programme's establishment, which initially influenced its conditions, aims and organisation. What, for example, were your own ideas about research policy in the early 1960s?

Eskil Björklund (EB):

Before 1963 I had not really thought in such terms as research policy. After having graduated in practical philosophy, I had previously had two main jobs. First, at the Departments of Sociology at the Universities of Stockholm and Uppsala I had been working as one of the Swedish coordinators of two international, comparative sociological studies. Later, I came to the Institute of Military Psychology, where I was occupied primarily with test construction and the training of interviewers, along the lines established by its first Director, the Professor of Education at the University of Stockholm, Torsten Husén.

But in 1963, I was invited to participate in the creation of a new organisation for school research at the National Board of Education *(NBE)*. A year later, I also became part-time secretary at the Social Science Research Council *(SSRC)*. Through these new assignments I was suddenly deeply involved in research policy-making and planning. These jobs also meant the beginning of a long-lasting partnership with one of Husén's collaborators at the Teacher's College in Stockholm, Professor Nils-Eric Svensson, presently Director of The Bank of Sweden Tercentenary Foundation - the largest independent sponsor of research in Sweden.

ThN:

I remember that Svensson, when I interviewed him two years ago, stressed the importance of the sector's own inherent dynamics in the emergence of what later became relatively extensive Swedish school research. Can you comment on this and also say, whether your respective professional backgrounds made any vital difference to the future focus and organisation of school research?

EB:

There were two main background factors behind the new school research organisation. First, there were the various school commissions that had been actively working for more than 20 years. Secondly, there were the experimental activities which had been going on all through the 1950s in order to prepare for the introduction of the new comprehensive school system. In this experimental work, the role of the NBE had been that of chief coordinator. And so, when Svensson and I joined the NBE we were expected to continue - and further intensify - this kind of work.

But we had our own ideas about future activities. Above all, we wanted to initiate different kinds of studies about the internal life of the schools. The 1962 Comprehensive School Bill had emphasised the importance of encouraging the pupils' ability to work independently, and one of the tasks of school research, *and* of the NBE, as we saw it, was to pave the way for such changes. Getting to your question though, about the impact of our professional backgrounds, I don't think they really had more than a marginal effect on the focus of school research. There was in the 1960s a strong political ambition to individualise school instruction, and in order to achieve this it seemed reasonable to build partly on the experience that came out of constructing school tests.

The school research efforts gradually came to include a number of projects in which Departments of Education, in cooperation with school teachers and publishers of text books, developed various educational aids for self-directed studies. *Our* role in this connection, though, was to make sure that there was a substantial amount of research in these combined research, development and publishing endeavours. Naturally, I also tried to supplement this mainly psychological and educational research with more sociologically-oriented studies of school and society.

ThN:

Some have described what Svensson and you built up at the NBE as not just *one* part of the specifically Swedish variety of research organisation, which later was to be dubbed 'sectorial research'. It has been argued that school research in fact came to function as *the prototype* for this particular way of organising applied social research. How would you describe your role in this connection? To what extent was school research an integral part of a general development in social science research, and in what way did it include a genuine innovation in research organisation and research policy?

EB:

As I mentioned earlier, in addition to my job at the NBE I was also a secretary at the SSRC. In 1964, I succeeded Nils-Eric Svensson in that post, while he remained in the council as a regular member. In fact, I retained that position right up to 1978. At the SSRC I worked to a great extent on stimulating debate on the organisation and policies of social science research, especially in the disciplines of psychology, education and sociology. This was done by means of conferences, seminars, internal study groups, informal get-togethers etc. These discussions mainly centred on the organisation of applied social research, and, not least, on the role of the Council in this process.

As a contribution to this general discussion I published two articles on *The Situation of the Social Sciences* and *The Development of the Social Sciences*. The first of those essays was written when I was participating in a series of seminars on research policy, organised by the Academy of the Engineering Sciences, in 1964-65, with the legendary Stevan Dedijer as moderator. In these two papers I was propounding the thesis, that social science research, just like research in the natural and engineering sciences, ought to be expanded *both* as funded *and* as commissioned research:

> To be able to expand and yield valuable results, all kinds of research needs to have suitably designed contacts with its field of application. If this is correct it must also be valid for the social sciences.

Among the various forms of social science organisation I discussed were research and development (R&D) units at different government offices, applied research institutes in, for example, social work and education, an institute for basic social science research and an academy of the social sciences.

In this connection, of course, the school research we were then in the process of building up served as an example of how to organise applied research. It seemed obvious to me that these organisational innovations and readjustments should be based on close interaction between scholars and the funding agencies, and that new research organisations should be developed through a dialogue between traditional social science as represented by the SSRC and potential users of research, as, for example, the NBE.

ThN:

This deliberate intermingling - manifested by yourself and Nils-Eric Svensson - of the expanding sectorial research and the traditional university-based research, was evidently not felt to present any fundamental problems of principle? You apparently saw no difference between what the 'new' social sciences should do and the tasks posed for research funded by the SSRC? Did you rather believe this to be a joint societal project for social science research?

EB:

Yes, we looked on it as a common cause. It seemed natural to me that the SSRC should play its specific role, while the other official research sponsors fulfilled *their* clearly specified responsibilities. What we wanted to do was partly to discuss how applied social research should be designed and organised, and partly to awaken interest among politicians in creating the resources needed for research in various sectors of society. My main argument was that a society which allocated vast resources for thoroughgoing reforms in, for instance, the social and educational sectors, should also invest in the knowledge necessary for their success, in on-going assessment of these reforms, and in the evaluation of their actual outcomes.

The question to me was not *whether* but *how* this necessary investment should be brought about. Even though we did not consider it to be entirely without problems, the essential task for us was to establish new principles and drum up the necessary resources. Above all, we wanted to point to the opportunities for research and usually did not put all that much emphasis on possible complications. There *were* indeed also complications, but that is another, later story.

ThN:

To my mind, your description here is fundamental to a proper understanding of the origins and development of Swedish sectorial research. Personally, I have repeatedly maintained that this development was on the whole at the initiative of the researchers. The idea emanated from the scholarly community - such as the SSRC - and not, as has frequently been claimed, from the growing insistence by politicians and bureaucrats that research must be directly linked to a demonstrable instrumental benefit. For example, when reading the accounts of the state and future development of the social sciences which various disciplinary groups at the SSRC produced in 1967 at the request of the Swedish government's Research Advisory Board, one finds that all the academic chairholders had an instrumental and applied approach to research. It was almost exclusively with reference to immediate social usefulness that they asked for more money for their university departments and disciplines. Not even these prominent scholars appear to have seen any fundamental differences, or complicating dimensions, between applied and basic social research. What you just said seems to confirm this picture.

EB:

I want to comment on this by saying that social science in the early 1960s was living on very small external grants, mainly from the SSRC. At the same time there was a strong conviction that if you wanted a substantial expansion of social research in the universities, it must be done through other resources coming through different channels. Where such resources could come from was illustrated by school research. Nils-Eric Svensson and I were not the only ones who thought that you had to turn to new providers and sponsors, that social science research could only expand in collaboration with the society outside higher education. At the same time though, we felt that this collaboration must be based on conditions and principles acceptable to the researchers. They should be ready to place their competence at the service of building a better society, but only on condition that they themselves would continue to be in complete command of their methods and results. The inherent problems and dysfunctions in these developments appeared only later, when it gradually became more apparent how - and to what extent - sectorial research tended to be steered by political and administrative values.

ThN:

I wonder if this initial inability or reluctance to perceive various complications and problems in the new research developments could be partly due to the fact that you and others regarded scientific quality and freedom as primarily related to considerations about scientific methods, techniques, and the presentations of results etc, rather than to normative issues having to do with the basic epistemic preconditions of science and its role in society? When I once put this question to Nils-Eric Svensson, he was disposed to answer in the negative.

EB:

With the benefit of hindsight, I think I would be inclined to confirm your observation. As I remember, many of us were at the time relatively unreflecting in our theories of science and research policy. We did not see the further and deeper implications of a change in the organisation and funding of research. Ever since the 1950s there had existed a rather simple and implicit faith in the potential of science and research as a means for societal change and improvement. Among behavioural scientists, with whom I had most dealings, this simplistic view of the role and meaning of science was, as I remember it, rather widespread.

ThN:

The period we have been talking about so far is an essential and necessary background to the expansion of sectorial research. Since the Research on Higher Education Programme was part of this general development, I would like you to summarise the political and scientific 'research ideology' that pervaded when you and Svensson started that work, in 1970-71. Had, for example, the 'sectorial principle' been accepted by both the research community and research policy makers as the obvious 'royal road' of modern research organisation?

EB:

In the mid-1960s, when we were discussing questions of this kind within the SSRC and in our Advisory Group at the NBE - who, by the way, were largely the same people - we were still engaged in rather open-ended and fundamental discussions. Among other things, we discussed the possibilities of independent research institutes having no or few ties to either universities or national authorities. Our models were, for instance, the Swedish Defence Research Institute, the Norwegian Institute of Social Research in Oslo, and the various Swedish industrial research institutes, jointly financed by industry and the state. The main idea was that this kind of 'neutral' institute might be better in balancing and coordinating the scientific demands and interests of the researchers with those of the interested users of social research.

Relatively soon though, the newly established sectorial agencies in ministries and national authorities started to live a life of their own, and the idea of building some form of independent research organisation gradually vanished in a reality where the sectorial agencies not only controlled the money, but also decided upon the future directions of applied research and on the matters concerning 'relevance' and 'quality' norms. In this process, the NBE and its Research Planning Bureau probably played a crucial role.

In the latter part of the 1960s, school research expanded rapidly and it also increased in societal influence and political reputation. As a consequence, the NBE soon not only came to dominate the funding of school research, but also threatened to gain control of the research agenda and determine the cognitive interests of the discipline of education. In addition, we soon discovered yet another area of conflict in that the NBE often wanted to introduce teaching aids and other innovations, before they had been subjected to any really scientific scrutiny. Rather often we heard the school bureaucrats say that they 'could not afford to wait for definite research results'. The ambitions of the central authority (and the ministry), *not* research quality or research results, gradually became decisive for policy. As a consequence, Nils-Eric Svensson and I began to question the integrated school research organisation in the NBE.

So, when I came to the *University Chancellor's Office* we were convinced of the necessity to create an independent research programme which was *not* attached to the daily work and long-term reform agenda of the central authority. *This* was, as I see it, *the* most important conclusion regarding research policy that we drew from the status and character of school research as it stood at the end of the 1960s.

ThN:

I would like to return briefly to the research institute problem. In many countries the independent or university-based research institute had become the 'obvious' way to organise large-scale social research, whereas in Sweden it was very early on almost completely removed from the research political agenda. Not least, the traditional academic community opposed this solution. In academic circles the obvious and eternal truth was that independent research institutes posed a 'threat to the very heart of the university'. Your account here verifies my own impression of a specific 'Swedish model' for the organisation of social research. The influence of international impulses and models seems to have been negligible. Instead, the close ties of social research to powerful central bureaucratic and political authorities became a somewhat uniquely Swedish characteristic.

EB:

Returning once more to the 1950s and 60s, one can see that in the build-up of Torsten Husén's Department of Education at the Stockholm Teachers' College, with its specific tasks, such as the construction of standardised achievement school tests etc, and with its typically strong links to the school bureaucracy, his previous Institute of Military Psychology served as a model. Nils-Eric Svensson, for instance, has pointed to the fact that at the Teachers' College the researchers saw themselves more as an important part of the school sector than as a part of a university-based research community.

The Research on Higher Education Programme was, however, established within the University Chancellor's Office, which at the time was a new and rather weak central authority for the universities. Partly because of this fact, but partly also because of the peculiarities of the university sector itself, it became possible to get acceptance even for such an odd idea as a more or less free-wheeling research programme, which gradually and eventually emancipated itself from the bureaucratic settings in which it was born.

ThN:

But these were still genuinely Swedish ideas about how to organise applied social sciences?

EB:

Yes. In the case of research on higher education we had from the start, as far as I can remember, practically no international contacts. These did not develop until the mid 1970s. The situation in school research was similar. While in school research there were many international contacts already in the 1960s, no foreign *organisational* models existed. It is true that some of our international partners like, for instance, the secretariats of the education and the science committees of the OECD, and the Schools Council in England, were also involved in studies of teaching and learning, but their missions and organisational patterns were quite different. In England, the Schools Council was not a national authority, it was an independent foundation which cooperated with individual, interested teachers. In Sweden, both school research and later the - quite different - research on higher education were organised and functioned on a national level.

ThN:

Before we start talking about the establishment and organisation of the Research on Higher Education Programme, I would like you to pursue the international thread a little further, and discuss Sweden's traditionally close relations with the OECD experts. It is a well-known fact that Swedish school research very early on aroused a great deal of international interest, due both to its size, its findings, its political standing and impact on policy, and, last but not least, to its generous economic resources. The question is, whether this international appreciation of Swedish school research did not primarily reflect the preferences and interests of politicians and bureaucrats rather than its outstanding scientific quality. One gets the strong impression that the relations between Swedish school research and the OECD gradually turned into a 'closed circular system', where Sweden soon became the 'pet child' of the OECD experts and the Swedish school establishment, in turn, repeatedly pointed to the OECD experts' opinion to confirm their obvious 'success'. This mutual appreciation had very little to do with undisputed scientific eminence. It was - as usual in the case of OECD, one is tempted to say - a matter of shared ideological preferences, and it could be seen as an excellent example of the well-known phenomenon in politics and economics of 'coordinated prejudices.'

EB:

On the whole, I agree with this description. But one must remember that Swedish school reforms had attracted international attention since the 1940s, not least on account of their political content and implications. Besides, Swedish school commissions had traditionally included a strong element of research and of qualified policy analysis. From 1963 onwards this was institutionalised through the NBE as a permanent school research programme. It is within this special political context that one must understand the wide appreciation of Swedish school research. But the basic criteria of the OECD were, of course, mainly political and administrative, and not scientific quality.

ThN:

Turning now to the Research on Higher Education Programme, I would like to begin by referring to the fact that its establishment coincided with the period 1968-77, which is alternately referred to as the reorganisation, or the ultimate destruction, of Swedish higher education and which is best summarised in the term 'U68'. To what extent is the Research Programme to be viewed as part of a particular 'U68-Ideology'?

EB:

I want to remind you of the fact that this Programme originated within a unit of the University Chancellor's Office which had been created in 1969, called the Educational Development Unit *(ED)*. Its main task - following the example set by the school development work - was to intensify educational development work in the universities and colleges. During the first year and a half, Nils-Eric Svensson and I worked mainly on establishing ED units at the different universities. To this end, we identified and selected individual university teachers who might function as ED consultants. It was the Committee on University Pedagogics, chaired by Torgny Segerstedt, Professor of Sociology and Vice-Chancellor at Uppsala University, and with Torsten Husén as one of the members, which had initially proposed that there should be one ED Unit at the central office, and one at each university. In the spirit of sectorial research, this committee also proposed that a specific sum should be reserved for educational research and development activities, but not for independent, basic research.

The latter idea was introduced when I moved to the University Chancellor's Office in February 1970, and it immediately won the approval of my two superiors - Nils-Eric Svensson and the Chancellor, the former Under-Secretary of State for Education and Director-General of the NBE, Hans Löwbeer. Beginning in 1972 we brought a number of advisers to the Research Programme, mostly professors of educational psychology and sociology, as well as two practitioners - Lars Ekholm, Head of Division at the Chancellor's Office, and Gunnar Bergendal, Principal Secretary of the 1968 Education Commission *(U68)*, and Professor of Mathematics at the University of Lund. The composition of the group suggests that the link with U68 came to be more important than that with university pedagogics. In addition, it was the University Chancellor Löwbeer himself who had recommended that the secretary of the U68 ought to be included in the Research Programme's Advisory Group, for the very purpose of ensuring that its activities were broadened to include the role and impact of higher education in society at large.

ThN:

I wonder whether Bergendal not only represented a personal connection with U68, but also a political legitimation for a broadened Research Programme and a guarantee that the Programme should be understood as an integral part of the reforming approach and the ideas represented by U68? Bergendal's engagement in the Programme meant that its direction and relevance could hardly be questioned, either by people from within the Chancellor's Office or by the representatives of university pedagogics?

EB:

That is probably correct, and I can add that this also coincided with my own ambitions. When I first broached the idea of a special research programme, I was thinking of something far transcending the limited teaching-learning area. Gunnar Bergendal shared this ambition to a great extent, and represented a powerful interest group demanding studies in which higher education was viewed as an integral part of modern society, a point which had not been stressed by the Committee on University Pedagogics. In this way, my own interest in emphasising the scientific aspects and broadening the field of study of the Programme coincided with Bergendal's and Löwbeer's interests in taking into account the specific issues of the U68 Commission. Right from the outset, then, the Research Programme had three main subthemes: 'The structure of higher education and its role in society', which very much corresponded with the central perspective of U68, 'The organisation and forms of work of higher education' and 'Evaluation: control of functions and results'.

ThN:

Let's for a moment turn to the period 1971-1975. It would be interesting if you could specify the tasks that the Programme set for itself. For instance, in what direction did its activities and decision-making develop during the first years, both with regard to its relations with the government office to which it belonged, and with the researchers whose interest it depended on? Then we can also talk about the principles and criteria which determined the Programme's selection of projects.

EB:

The central ED Unit initially handled three different programmes and therefore consisted of three separate groups, working parallel to and supplementing each other. The 'Group for research projects' was just one part of the new unit, the others being the 'Group for inservice training of teachers', and the 'Group for development projects'. The third group was to concern itself with short-term planning and policy issues, while the Group for inservice training would handle further training of university teachers and other staff. The ED Units at the universities were, of course, important partners for these two groups. The Group for Research Projects, on the other hand, would build up a Research on Higher Education Programme.

At that time hardly any such research existed apart from a few studies commissioned by the U68, and a number of projects with strong elements of development work, supported by the Committee on University Pedagogics. Our task was therefore to get such research under way. According to an early memorandum, the Research Group's work schedule included mapping out what research was needed, stimulating researchers to initiate studies in the field, following and evaluating these projects, and disseminating their results. Additionally, it included developing procedures and securing resources for research, as well as following developments at research and other 'for this area important' institutes in Sweden and abroad.

Almost immediately we invited researchers to send their grant applications and distributed money once a year to a limited number of projects. Already in 1971 we distributed 1.5 million SEK, most of which went to projects in educational psychology. We soon initiated and organised conferences, which we called 'problem area meetings', where different researchers could present their own conceptions of different problems. These meetings were occasions when such accounts could also be discussed with the 'planners' - a designation we used for people like Hans Löwbeer, Gunnar Bergendal and Lars Ekholm - who, in turn, were supposed to set forth what they - and hence the sector as well - considered to be the most urgent problems.

The Research Programme was soon directed towards building up a substantial foundation for long-range planning in higher education. Another task we took up was the establishment of contacts with representatives of other disciplines besides education. One of the first disciplines we approached was political science, and here Professor Olof Ruin at the University of Stockholm was one of our earliest contacts. At a meeting at Linköping in 1973, Ruin and his young assistant Rune Premfors, as well as a number of distinguished disciplinary representatives from other universities - Pär-Erik Back (Umeå), Lennart Lundquist (Lund) and Hans Meijer (Linköping) - participated. This group showed a genuine and immediate interest in the field, and, as a direct result, several rather major studies materialised in Stockholm and Umeå.

As early as 1972 I got in touch with two economists, Ingemar Ståhl (Lund) and Bengt-Christer Ysander (Stockholm), which resulted in two major studies. At roughly the same time, the first historian - Professor Birgitta Odén (Lund) - became involved through a conference on graduate studies and doctoral research training. Odén's engagement gradually developed into the first research study of the Programme with a genuine historical perspective. In this way, relations were established and developed with a number of professors in the social sciences and the humanities. A few years later, in 1977, twelve different disciplines - eight in the social sciences and four in the humanities - had started smaller or more ambitious projects within the Research on Higher Education Programme.

Since about the same time the group of scientific advisers to the Programme has also regularly consisted of one professor from each of five disciplinary groups: philosophy/theory of science, history/history of ideas and learning, economics/economic history, education /psychology and political science/sociology. This broadening of the disciplinary competence in the Advisory Group has, as I see it, proved to be one of the Programme's most important research political innovations.

ThN:

Was the Research Programme already from the start linked with the cognitive interests and specific problems of traditional research, or was the selection of projects in these early days determined more by bureaucratic and policy priorities? In other words, was the sector not only client/financier, but also 'problem formulator'? Were proposals rated chiefly with reference to their anticipated administrative usefulness or to their intradisciplinary relevance and quality? Another, and somewhat delicate, question in this connection would be whether the initially strong position of the discipline of education was due to the actual state of its scientific competence or to the Research Programme's specific priorities and focus of interest?

EB:

Taking your second and smaller question first, during the early years we took over and supported a number of projects initiated by the Committee on University Pedagogics. One of the researchers involved here, by the way, was the Professor of Education at the University of Gothenburg, Ference Marton. These projects were almost exclusively pedagogical, and so, during the first three years, more than 70% of the money went to education and psychology. It was for the very purpose of redressing this bias, that we got in touch with representatives of other disciplines. They were expected to shed light on the more general, societal problems of higher education, which also had been raised by U68.

But it took some time before we received qualified applications from these virgin fields of study. For the evaluation of research proposals we naturally tried to apply the same criteria as the SSRC used. But there was a complication here. Whereas the SSRC had only one criterion, that of scientific quality, the Research Programme had another criterion which carried just as much weight, namely 'practical relevance'. Even though these two criteria in principle should complement each other, I think it is fair to say that in the first years of the Programme practical relevance took priority. A research project which was rated high as regards practical relevance was sometimes accepted even if there could be some doubts about its scientific quality.

One should also bear in mind that in the early years there were rather few highly qualified researchers who wanted to get into this comparatively new field of research. Hence one of the main tasks of the Programme was the building up of a basic fund of competence among researchers. This necessarily meant that many of the early projects had the character of doctoral training projects, with a fairly high element of risk. As you very well know yourself, it is very difficult to make a realistic assessment of the capacity of a doctoral student, even if the competence of the applying professor/supervisor could be appraised. And so the outcome of such investments varied quite a lot, with some of the projects turning out to be successful and others ending in failure.

Another comment I want to make in this context is that at the beginning of the 1970s Swedish researchers often had rather respectful attitudes towards top civil servants. Even in the Research Programme the researchers and advisers felt as if they were sitting in the lap of the authorities. One certainly knew that the final decision on individual projects ultimately rested with the national authority.

ThN:

If you should try to summarise the essential characteristics of the Research Programme during the period 1971-75, what specific aspects would you emphasise? Do you remember if you already had a clear ambition of breaking free from dependence on the national authority? If not, when did you first understand that by admitting active scholars into decision-making within a formal bureaucracy and thereby initiating a process of 'scientification', you were also going to build in tensions that would eventually become acute and end up either in an autonomous research council or a complete bureaucratic take-over?

EB:

As I pointed out earlier, the emancipation of the Research Programme from its bureaucratic setting was a gradual process over a long period of time. From the beginning we had explicitly stated that the Programme should 'not function as a research council which awards grants on the basis of applications'. And this was then seen as a very crucial characteristic. Hence it was not until the mid 1980s that it was possible to publicly admit that the Programme's advisory groups in fact had begun to function as a research council already in the latter part of the 1970s. There were at *that* time some important changes in the Research Programme, including everything from its actual content to its status. And in this process, the changes of content preceded those in status. I believe these transitions could only be understood if we take two seemingly unrelated factors into account. The most important was the general upheaval in Swedish higher education caused by the U68 reform proposals. The other was the considerable freedom of action the Chancellor had given to the new ED Unit in his Office. This unit was not to be a part of the regular bureaucratic line organisation, and the Research Programme could, *in its turn*, be independent within this relatively autonomous unit.

Having said this, however, one must repeat the strong dependence of the Research Programme in the first part of the 1970s. It was primarily through later developments that the Programme gained its independence. Not until the second part of the 1980s did the Research Programme come to be formally governed by an autonomous research council with a majority of researchers and a few vice-chancellors and rectors instead of the 'planners'.

ThN:

Moving on to 1975, I would like to know what happened at about that time to make you mark that year as a turning point. Were the changes you are talking about primarily organisational, or did they also include aims and content?

EB:

The changes in the Programme included all these aspects. Besides, I guess it's fairly natural that after some years of a programme you try to evaluate what has been achieved, and you start thinking of how to carry on in the future. Accordingly, in 1975 we undertook a fairly radical appraisal of our actual selection procedures. In a memo I summarised the criticisms that had been made of various aspects of the activities of the Research Programme. It included points like:

(a) The proportion of doctoral training projects was too high.

(b) The studies were governed more by pure research interests than by sectorial needs.

(c) The researchers had difficulties in delivering on schedule.

(d) Certain professors participated both in the capacity of applicants and of reviewers/advisers.

(e) The selection of projects was made without due regard to scientific quality.

(f) The selection didn't take sufficient account of the most urgent problems in higher education.

(g) Projects were often poorly connected with international research and tended too much towards general investigations and policy studies.

On all those - partly contradictory - points I thought the criticism to be, by and large, well-grounded. So, in the Advisory Group we began to discuss what measures could be undertaken to deal with the shortcomings. The internal discussion led to a number of changes: from then on, the research applications had to be specified in the same way as when applying to the traditional research councils. We also introduced a system of peer-review by outside researchers. Furthermore, we demanded that our research advisers use the same criteria of quality as the research councils, and that each of them also present a written evaluation of the applications coming from her/his own discipline. All in all, these changes made the Advisory Group function like a research council, though it was still not a research council in the proper sense of the word, since the formal decisions on grants were still taken by the Chancellor's Office.

Another event in 1975 which made this year a turning point was that through the agency of Torsten Husén I got to know the American sociologist Martin Trow at Berkeley, California. On a tour of the USA I visited a number of institutes for research on higher education. The journey proved important, because I then understood that there was, on the whole, little true research in this field in the US either. In fact, most of the studies in higher education actually being done there were policy studies or 'institutional research'. They were typically local investigations aiming directly at the improvement of the daily activities of the university concerned. No coordinating agency of any kind was to be found for the limited scientific research being done in the field. Instead, it was based on the interest of a few eminent researchers who devoted part of their efforts to the problems of the universities. Among those were, for example, Burton Clark (Yale/UCLA), James March (Stanford), Robert Merton (Columbia) and Martin Trow (Berkeley).

These scholars, however, did not see themselves as 'higher education researchers', but rather occupied central positions in their various parent disciplines. The specially designated 'departments of higher education' that I visited at some of the universities were, on the other hand, more concerned with the training of university administrators than with basic research.

My new-found insights from this journey also resulted in Martin Trow's participation in our first international conference later that year. In the fall he also served as Visiting Professor at the University of Stockholm, and undertook a study of the Research on Higher Education Programme. All this taken together - the Advisory Council, the disciplinary orientation and the internationalisation - make it natural for me to treat 1975 as a year of definite change.

ThN:

Do you see these qualitative transformations as elements of a single and integrated process?

EB:

Yes, and in this connection I would also like to stress the importance of Trow's report on the Research Programme. In it he made an illuminative analysis of the best way to stimulate the development of knowledge about higher education. What Trow underlined, and this certainly made a deep impression on me, was that to further promote the development of knowledge and inquiry in *any* field of study, the single most important thing to do was to create an active research community. A working community of the researchers concerned was far more important than the selection or outcome of any individual project. To illustrate the principal points of the reorientation, and why I thought it crucial that the Programme be led by researchers instead of planners, I want to quote from one of Trow's many articles, published already in 1965:

> If you look to science for certainty you are likely to make the scientists cautious and trivial. Since, if they cannot risk being wrong they are not likely to be right about anything really important. That, I think, is what happened to much of what is called 'educational research', which has been paralysed by its assumption of responsibility for action.

But to remind you, once more, of the actual situation in Sweden, I would also like to quote from a letter I wrote to Trow in December 1975:

> We are here presently working much more on building an innovation and development community, and the idea that we also need a research community on higher education is not so easy to sell.

That was the general situation in the fall of 1975, and from 1976 onwards I saw it as a main task of the Research Programme to build up a working research community. And in these efforts I continued to have a very constructive working relationship with Martin Trow both through his visits to Sweden and through my own visits to his university.

ThN:

But the lack of quality and international orientation you were referring to, and which was also mentioned in your overall assessment of the development of the Research Programme down to 1975, was nevertheless only *one* type of criticism put forward. There was also the opposite kind, referring mainly to the Programme's lack of connection with 'the sector's problems and acute interests'. What happened to these objections in a situation where you were actively advocating Trow's 'disciplinarisation' strategy? To me, at least, his arguments seem to have been a vigorous rebuttal of the possibility of identifying any kind of administratively defined 'sectorial interest'. Instead, the relevant problems, according to Trow, are formulated by good researchers in a viable research community. The fact that Trow, just like yourself, was realistic enough to understand that this research community could never be built up in direct opposition to the presumptive financiers in politics and the bureaucracy, alters nothing in this connection.

Perhaps I could formulate my question as follows; was it then, in 1975, that you and some others associated with the Research Programme first came to understand that one cannot expect politicians and bureaucrats to be capable of adequately formulating the long-term knowledge needs of a particular sector of society? Instead, this task is best performed by - *and is indeed the duty of* - active researchers. Was this also the time when you began to hope that the responsible politicians and administrators would eventually realise that this division of labour probably is the one most likely to meet the demands for long-term practical relevance as well?

EB:

Yes, this is roughly what some of us thought to be the way in which the Research on Higher Education Programme should develop. What you call Trow's 'disciplinary strategy' was of course, what was characteristic of my parallel work at the SSRC. But as I said before, with the Research Programme we saw it as our task to create new and different conditions and frameworks for the distribution of grants. In the beginning we had, as you know, a rather crude conception of these issues. In the Newsletter from the ED Unit, of January 1973, we published something called 'The Chancellor's problem list', which we expected would serve as a guide in the planning and selection of relevant studies. It is true that this 'wants list' was based on a number of conferences between researchers and planners, but its character was, nevertheless, that of a very simple 'laundry bill'.

Gradually though, we became somewhat more sophisticated. There were certain planners, like Ulla Åhgren-Lange, Head of Division at the Chancellor's Office, who tried to formulate longer and more coherent problem overviews from a specific planning perspective. These surveys were meant to function as a kind of check-list for researchers who wanted to formulate their topics of inquiry in response to the demands of practice. On the other side we also encouraged a number of interested researchers to produce overviews of knowledge and literature, drawing on their own discipline-based theories and concepts. These different kinds of overviews, together with the reports from our many 'problem area meetings', were seen as important points of departure for the continuing work.

The central importance of these 'guides' distributed in the 'Reports from the Chancellor's Office', was never questioned, because we were still more or less convinced that it was through meetings and dialogue between researchers and planners that the most relevant problems in the sector would be articulated. Later, in the early 1980s, there was a further shift of emphasis when we began saying that it was only by promoting truly scholarly studies that one could provide a plausible frame of reference for the future direction of the Research Programme. This was openly stated, for instance, in the Programme's 1985 overview Newsletter:

> The theses that theoretically significant research is also practically useful and that it is important also in the human sciences to reformulate practical problems so that they can be studied scientifically, were accepted as basic preconditions for this Programme. The long-term aims of such efforts, quite simply, is that of greater self-understanding in the universities and colleges (The Programme should be 'higher education's own research concerning the foundations of its own activities.').

This insight, of course, implied that the criteria of relevance now had more to do with knowledge and understanding than with administration and planning. One consequence was that we - the researchers, advisers and Programme secretariat - began to make more conscious efforts to integrate ourselves into the international research community, through conferences, comparative studies and publishing.

ThN:

Would you like to extend your comments a little on how this 'scientification' and internationalisation of the Programme actually came about, and perhaps also comment on its simultaneous emancipation from the national authority?

EB:

I could perhaps illustrate this process by describing the international conferences, and how they changed over time in both organisation and content. At the first two conferences - 1975 and 1978 - a Head of Division at the Chancellor's Office was chairman of the organising committees. In the former case, publishing was done by a Dutch publisher, with a substantial Swedish printing grant. That conference was, by the way, organised in collaboration with the Council of Europe. The 1978 conference, on the other hand, was published in the *National Board of Universities and Colleges (NBUC)* series of monographs in English. (In 1976, The Chancellor's Office had been renamed the NBUC).

Political planning and administration were the main themes of the 1978 conference, just as it had been in the previous one. Sweden's ambitious reforms in higher education formed a very stimulating background for the debates at these conferences. But they were at the same time conferences, characterised by the manner of asking questions and giving answers typical of some of the humanistic and social science disciplines mentioned earlier. Among the papers given there was, for instance, a seminal one by Professor Tony Becher of the University of Sussex and Professor Maurice Kogan of Brunel University, on *Process and Structure in Higher Education System*, which two years later was expanded into a book under the same title. (A second revised edition will appear in 1991.) The discussions at this conference, and later also among the researchers and advisers of the Programme - Gunnar Bergendal must be mentioned as one of the most active - led to a number of studies on the inner life of higher education, focussing specifically on the development of knowledge traditions in different disciplines, as well as in some of the professional and semi-professional schools.

By contrast, if we then go to the conference of 1983, it was the political scientist, Professor Olof Ruin from Stockholm, who chaired the organising committee. Ruin had, for a few years in the late 1970s, also been Deputy Chancellor of the NBUC. The rewritten papers were published in three volumes, each summarising a particular subtheme of the conference. The books were edited by the researcher in charge, in the NBUC monograph series. At the 1987 conference the Uppsala historian, Professor Rolf Torstendahl, chaired the programme committee, and hosted the conference. The responsible researchers for each subtheme are editing the volumes, but these will shortly be put out by two leading international publishers - one British and one American.

Over time then, there has been a transition from policy discussions to problems and issues generated by research. At the same time, the international conferences have become more central to the Research Programme's development. This, of course, is not only reflected by the conferences mentioned, but also through many other, usually discipline-based, meetings abroad which the Programme's researchers nowadays regularly attend. Research on higher education in Sweden, even though it started as an integral part of Swedish sectorial research, has gradually become an active member of the international research community.

ThN:

Is there a connection between the Programme's capacity for resisting pressures from its bureaucratic and political environment, and its firm establishment in the international research community? Is it - to put it plainly - the case that the growing autonomy of the Research Programme is partly a result of the fact that the Programme's continued development is no longer only a Swedish concern? In other words; Swedish research on higher education, today, is not just a recipient, but also an active contributor within an international scholarly network?

EB:

You certainly have a point here. With a slight touch of sarcasm, it is sometimes said that the Research Programme is actually more popular abroad than at home and that the Swedish Government and the NBUC, after losing control over the Programme, became less interested in its activities. But I don't think that this description is correct. If, for instance, one moves to the last couple of years, one finds that both the present University Chancellor (the former Vice-Chancellor of The Royal Institute of Technology, Professor Gunnar Brodin), and the Government, through the Minister of Education and the Under-Secretary of Higher Education, have recently asserted that the special value of the Research Programme is closely linked to its independence. The authorities have openly and repeatedly conceded that regular contact with the international research front, and institutional autonomy, are both crucial to the Programme's capacity for generating relevant knowledge on higher education and research systems. They have also agreed that the introduction of new ideas and theories from the qualified international research debate is very important in Sweden with its traditionally more practice-oriented discussions. I personally looked upon the recognition of the Programme's character and autonomy in the 1988 Budget Bill as final confirmation that we had developed appropriate forms for the Research Programme and its activities.

ThN:

But doesn't this also illustrate another important point, namely, that the particular form of internationalisation chosen by the Programme was rather new and unique in the Swedish context? Instead of a close affiliation with politico-bureaucratic organisations like the OECD, which traditionally had been the obvious international collaborators for Swedish education and science policy-making, there was suddenly a government agent developing close relations with a community of active scholars?

EB:

Yes, and here I think you are touching on something that has been particularly important in the development of the Swedish Research on Higher Education Programme. As you know, the OECD played an important - and sometimes detrimental - part in the formulation of university and science policy in many of its member countries by introducing a new, broader research concept in the early 1970s: 'Enlarged Science Policy'. In the Swedish context this came to be called 'Sectorial Research' or 'R&D Research' (!). This particular way of integrating 'research' in the various societal sectors, and deliberately blurring the boundaries between research, development work, policy studies, official inquiries and practical reform work, was strongly recommended by the OECD, especially from the early 1970s. But even if this conception of research became very popular in Sweden, the Research on Higher Education Programme soon made it a special point to question precisely this integrated type of 'R&D Policy'.

On my initiative, we organised a conference in 1976 - in cooperation with The Bank of Sweden Tercentenary Foundation, the NBUC, the NBE and the SSRC - about different ways of relating science and research to practical applications. After that these questions were made a priority field in the Research on Higher Education Programme. A number of studies were published and some of them were, I dare say, both highly relevant and of great scientific importance. The impact of these studies did a great deal to secure the institutional autonomy of the Programme. They were also seminal in giving Swedish research on higher education a marked profile in international research. At the same time, and independently of the research activities, Swedish politicians and, of course, administrators responsible for higher education continued taking part in the OECD and in other international policy-oriented organisations and activities. As regards the Research Programme, though, I must repeat that from now on it became far more important to acquire the frames of reference for research from leading scholars in different key disciplines than from leading politicians and administrators in the sector.

ThN:

Let's return, for a moment, to the period 1975-79 when this 'scientification' started. I know that this process was by no means unproblematic. As I understand it, these years were, if anything, a period of protracted disputes about principles. Your difficulties in securing the autonomy of the Programme were probably connected with the fact that you no longer had the immediate support of Nils-Eric Svensson. In January 1975 he had left the ED Unit to become Director of The Bank of Sweden Tercentenary Foundation. But probably more important than the change in personnel was the general impact of a very special research policy climate. Could you briefly characterise how this conflict became manifest in various circles: the NBUC, the Advisory Group, and the research community?

EB:

One must understand that this conflict had at least two dimensions, even in the NBUC. Partly, it had reference to the growing tensions and intensified disputes within the R&D Unit (the ED Unit had been renamed in 1976). There was, for example, the problem of presenting results and publishing. Not until the fall of 1983 did the Research Programme get its own Newsletter. Before that, it had a joint periodical with the other programmes of the R&D unit by the guaranteed obscure title of *R&D for Higher Education*.

But as you said earlier, the growing tensions derived largely from the fact that an autonomous research programme must, after all, form a part of a research community, not of an organisation for planning and policy studies. So there was a conflict between what the NBUC considered to be its well-founded and legitimate interests, and the necessary 'antibureaucratism' of an autonomous, if still centrally funded, research programme. When looking back on what happened, I can well understand why my colleagues in the NBUC insisted that this conflict should be resolved by an integration of the activities in the R&D Unit, including closer affiliations to the NBUC. In the spirit of sectorial research they, of course, considered my 'separatism' to be both inadequate and dysfunctional. It would obviously have been much easier for the R&D Unit to deal with its environment in the *NBUC* if it had agreed to be an integrated and 'bureaucratically intelligible' organisation. That is why I can perfectly well understand those who pursued the 'integration strategy'.

To illustrate their basic standpoints and arguments, I would like to quote one of my sharpest - and therefore, in a way, most helpful - inhouse critics, Bertil Östergren, former chief-negotiator for The Central Organisation of Swedish Academics, who later became political editor of *Svenska Dagbladet*, the conservative Stockholm daily. At a conference in 1977, he went straight to the point by saying:

> Unlike Eskil I cannot see any meaning in making a distinction between development and research projects. I have worked with both but never understood why such a delimitation should be drawn.

Östergren, and the many who thought like him, wanted no independent programme for research. Instead they wanted to organise innovatory sectorial activities in large, combined projects of limited duration. These projects were supposed to integrate all kinds of research and development activities - long and short-range research, development work, policy studies, the training of personnel, etc. It was probably very much due to my own personal convictions and persistence that this particular line of action did not prevail. And as the battle went on I was, of course, made aware of the fact, that my restiveness caused much irritation, both in my immediate surroundings and in the rest of the NBUC, sometimes also including the University Chancellor himself!

But even if my ideas at times were met with fairly solid resistance, I was also often supported by a number of people in the NBUC, including one or two of my closest colleagues and not least, usually also by the University Chancellor. I was also backed by the Advisory Group where, among others, Gunnar Bergendal - by now Rector at the Teachers' College in Malmö - continued to be influential. Additionally, there was now the support of a research community which already had begun to establish itself nationally and internationally. This support gradually became more apparent. One of the earliest expressions of this new 'research front' was at a conference in 1977, where these matters were discussed, and where Bertil Östergren also participated.

ThN:

I would like to add something to your description of the 'Östergren strategy' as a natural, and from a social psychological point of view understandable, administrative perspective. In my opinion this attitude, emanating essentially from the sector's short-term needs and long-term preferences, is also to a prominent degree a reflection and expression of the dissolution of the traditional research concept, which the expanding sectorial research in Sweden had actually entailed. The new sectorial concept maintained that for almost every type of inquiry one could use the label 'research'. The notoriously amorphous concept of 'R&D Research', advocated by Östergren and others, was not only an inherent consequence of bureaucratic functionalism, but also a question of what the Professor of Theory of Science in Gothenburg, Aant Elzinga, later came to speak of as 'epistemic drift'.

EB:

Yes, and as I said earlier, the Research Programme's own difficulties in administering autonomous research from within a central bureaucracy were instrumental in making the interplay between research and planning a special field of study in the Programme. Those studies, some of which were partly 'self-analytical', and the discussions which they helped to initiate, gradually influenced opinion among centrally-placed administrators and politicians in such a way that the particular nature and position of the Research Programme was more and more accepted as an established fact of life. One of the consequences of this development was that in December 1987 the University Chancellor finally formally delegated all decisions on the content of the Programme and the distribution of its money to an independent council consisting of some of the leading Scandinavian scholars in the field. The Research Council, which also includes a few vice-chancellors of Swedish universities and colleges, is sovereign in its decisions and selects research projects on their scientific merits.

The autonomy of the Research Programme was now not only accepted, but seen as the necessary precondition for the new role assigned to it. This role was not to produce the knowledge needed for political planning and reform, but rather to increase the universities' and the research communities' own understanding of the fundamental characteristics and dimensions of higher education and research. As a consequence, the actual content of the Programme changed so much that by the mid 1980s it seemed natural to change the name of one of its central problem fields from 'The governance and organisation of higher education' to 'The development and organisation of knowledge'! More and more the nature of knowledge and learning as such came into focus. The centre of interest became the inner lives of research and higher education rather than, as previously, their external administrative framework.

The impact of these changes can also be seen in the allocation of resources. During the 1980s scholars in the humanities - philosophy, theory of science, history, history of ideas and learning - received 42 per cent of the grants allocated, as against the 11 per cent allotted to them in the previous decade. A corresponding relative reduction occurred in the behavioural sciences. The share allotted to education, psychology and economics went down from 65 to 31 per cent. The third major group of disciplines -

political science and sociology - on the other hand, retained their share - 24 and 27 per cent respectively - during these decades. The Programme has also changed character in the sense that today a large part of the money goes to a number of established research groups, while the steering Research Council and its Secretariat have reduced their role to that of stimulating cooperation between the different groups, and serving as their discussion partners.

The staff of the Secretariat has gradually been reduced to a minimum, while the research groups themselves carry the full responsibility both for publishing and conferences. The political and administrative authorities of the higher education system are, of course, still present, but now rather in the role of interested supporters and critical readers of the publications that the research generates. As I just said, from 1987, the responsibility for the direction and activities of the Programme is entirely vested in its research council and in the community of active researchers.

Publishing by the researchers involved in these studies has expanded quite rapidly, during the 1980s. For instance, between 1984 and 1989 the number of publications listed in the Programme's Newsletter grew from 69 to 133 per year. The published material mainly consists of traditional monographs and papers in established scientific journals, but it also includes a growing number of articles in daily papers and popular science magazines. Furthermore, the publishing today is almost equally balanced between English and Swedish. Written contributions to the Programme's conferences and seminars have also undergone a distinct change of character, both through a relative increase in the output of the humanities, and also an increasing number of eminent contributions from invited foreign scholars.

To summarise: the Research on Higher Education Programme has in various ways developed and prospered in the 1980s, mainly because of an intensified disciplinary orientation, a strengthened research control and a conscious ambition to internationalise. These changes in a new and relatively small field of research would probably not have been possible had there not been a simultaneous change in Swedish policy in general. Briefly put, this change of research and science policy in the 1980s can be said to have marked a halt to the expansion of sectorial research, and a shift of the centre of gravity back to the universities. Scientific leadership, disciplinary rootings and international standards have become three of the watch-words in Swedish research policy generally, and as far as now can be judged, they will remain so for the foreseeable future.

Chapter 13

The Academic Critique of the OECD Research Policy Doctrine
A Discursive Essay

Sverker Gustavsson

An organisation which has outlived its usefulness seldom disappears. Instead it usually finds itself a new job to do.

Of course, this is not always the case, but at all events it is what happened when the Organisation for European Economic Cooperation (OEEC) was converted, in the autumn of 1961, into the Organisation for Economic Cooperation and Development (OECD). The earlier organisation had been set up in 1948 as part of the Marshall Plan. Within its framework the governments of Western Europe had been able to formulate and administer the programme for the recovery of their war-ravaged economies which the United States had pledged itself to finance. That task had now been completed. Governments on both sides of the Atlantic maintained that the organisation was still needed all the same, though it should include more countries and be given wider responsibilities.

As so 'European' was deleted from its name and 'Development' substituted. The United States and Canada (and later on, Japan, Australia and New Zealand as well) were then able to join. Gone was the initial post-war campaign against 'hunger, poverty, desperation and chaos'.[1] What was now needed was economic policy in a much wider and more forward-looking sense.

From the viewpoint of each of its 22 member governments, the OECD provides a meeting point and, in some respects, a kind of informal superior example, at least in the continental European context. Under the direction of a 1700 strong Secretariat, stationed in Paris, committees go about their duties, surveys are conducted and conferences arranged. These efforts are aimed at supplying the member countries with policy assessments and recommendations in various fields. All this forms part of a basic approach centring round three essential ideas: maximum lasting growth and employment combined with the maintenance of financial stability; healthy economic expansion both in member countries and in developing countries; and a development of world trade on a multilateral, non-discriminatory basis.

The general mood of optimism in the late 1980s was less evident than it had been twenty-five years earlier. This has not meant any falling off of demand for the kind of experience interchange offered within the OECD. On the contrary. The Vietnam War, the oil crisis, stagflation, the political resignation of the 1970s, the debt crisis of the developing countries, the growth of environmental awareness and the great nuclear accidents have all shed vivid light on the old concept of the Fall of Man. As a result of the many setbacks encountered by leading ideas of the industrialised world in both the last two decades, it is seen in our present-day OECD perspective to be not *less* but *more* essential than ever to encourage the development of science, technology and a rationally founded organisation of society. For those who have once tasted the fruit of the Tree of Knowledge, there is no return.

Schools, universities and technical progress in the employment sector have constantly received special attention from the organisation. Its experts were already telling us in 1963 that historical studies show research and education to be more influential factors than the levels of labour and capital, in accounting for the growth of production. Research and education lead to *better* labour and *better* efficiency of capital equipment.[2] This goes without saying. But translating these qualitative determinations into quantitative expressions and practical recommendations has proved more easily said than done.

The OECD plays an important part in science policy the world over. That is obvious. At the same time one cannot help noticing the critical attitude taken by current university opinion. The doctrine of integrated planning of research and a consequent undermining of research autonomy, which in all essential respects has evolved within the OECD and dominates the debate between its member governments, has hardly any support at all among those immediately affected. Quite simply, according to leading scientific opinion the world over, it is not all that cogently thought out.

The advocates of the 'modern' view, for their part, do not take the objections of the academics all that seriously. Criticism of this kind is only natural, they say. Researchers and teachers feel that their privileges are threatened when policy relating to their activities comes to be framed more rationally and democratically.

The arrogance of this latter attitude does not improve things. When in the everyday run of things, researchers and university teachers comment on the OECD doctrine, it is only too often that their remarks conclude with an ironic grimace. Bureaucrats and politicians are merely intent on increasing their own power. That's all there is to it, the argument goes. Such is the way of the world. But, for goodness sake, let's put a good face on things or we might sabotage our own funding.

This is not a very edifying approach, least of all in relation to the rising generations of scientists and teachers. And so I feel it is important to ask how much justification there is in the criticism of the OECD's doctrine of science policy. Perhaps the slight practical impact of university opinion is connected with the quality of its arguments? Perhaps the current academic standpoint is less solidly based than pretentious attitudes would give us to believe?

To be generous to research opinion, one should take as one's starting point an essay from 1985, written by an eminent American university historian, Roger L. Geiger.[3] The central portion of his argument is notably lucid.

True to the manner of modern analysts of ideas, Professor Geiger pins down the topic of his investigation by means of an abbreviation. He refers to the conviction under consideration as ESP, short for 'enlarged science policy'. The expression is taken from one of the OECD's most widely noticed reports from the mid-1970s. That report termed it essential for research and development to be regarded as an integral whole. Member governments, it was said, should adopt 'an enlarged view of what such a policy might be'.[4]

Summing up the implications of the OECD doctrine, Geiger concentrates on three aspects:

- what ESP is aimed against

- ESP's positive aims

- the practical consequences of ESP.

ESP, Geiger begins, is aimed at undermining - that is, undermining the authority uniting the labours of qualified researchers. Careers are made in this historically evolved scientific community entirely on the strength of intradisciplinary qualifications. Universities and research councils obstinately refuse to pay any attention to extradisciplinary factors. Both these attitudes are in the long run bound to have a devastating effect on the growth of a society dependent on science, and they must therefore be combated according to an orthodox advocate of ESP.

Expressed in positive terms, ESP derives its special character from the fact of its perspectives reflecting the will to a holistic approach. Ideally speaking, one single ministry should be in charge of all research. Or, more correctly, everything termed research in different sectorial fields should be compared. Otherwise there will be no optimum distribution of resources. A fixed amount of the community's resources is presumed to be at the disposal of 'research', for distribution between different community purposes. But not only this. The government's overall assessment should also permeate work at other, non-central levels of administration. The historically-given tendency for assessments to differ between universities and research councils on the one hand and politically controlled authorities and economically controlled companies and organisations on the other does not have a future. Instead the future belongs to a system in which all factors take account of the development of society as a whole.

One curious point in this connection, Geiger emphasises, is the way in which ESP is pleaded for, compared with what its advocates actually prescribe. To support their case, they plead the shortage of resources. All forces of good must cooperate. At the same time they call on member governments to take risks. New and untried ideas, academically unrecognised subjects and hitherto unknown organisational arrangements are taken, in principle, to be preferable - not in spite of, but because of the limited resources available.

This makes the most important point. ESP is the wrong solution to a serious problem at a worrying time. Geiger sums up by saying that the undermining of the authority of the research community, coupled with the holistic view advocated, will have two quite palpable practical consequences. One of them is that ESP will result in priority being given to every imaginable form of applied study at the expense of primary research. The second consequence can be perceived at the university department level, where there will be an ongoing reinforcement of the wrong incentives. More importance would attach to things gaining recognition within the discipline.

The problem of the future, as Professor Geiger sees it, is how to substitute vitalisation for the tendency to intellectual stagnation caused by ESP. All we need do, in his opinion, is to realise that the involvement of

'non-scientists in purely scientific decisions, the further bureaucratisation of science, and the intrusion of third-party planning, are all antithetical to the normal operations of the basic scientific community. For this reason it should be evident that the university is not the proper arena for an enlarged or interventionist science policy. Rather, the university should provide a home for practitioners of the basic disciplines and thus the seat of the national scientific community . . . Achieving this may not prove easy, given current conditions, but if this goal is clearly recognised the choice of possible strategies would be greatly clarified.'[5]

The OECD science policy doctrine is fundamentally counterproductive. There is widespread conviction on this point in the universities. Researchers, as a rule, are deeply concerned and, on the personal plane, often noticeably upset. They are tormented by being regarded as reactionaries for defending a line which, ever since the eighteenth century has been considered essentially forward-looking. At the same time they are basically optimistic. This goes with the job. With the great tradition of the Enlightenment behind one, even 25 years' misguided theorising on the part of the politicians and bureaucrats becomes supportable. The short-term tactic is that of putting a good face on things. The more long-term strategy is that of persuasion.

This being so, I feel that the criticism by the research community requires elucidation on three points in particular, otherwise the opponents of ESP run a serious risk of their message continuing to fall on deaf ears.

First of all, it is the part of the discussion relating to the *authority* of the research community that requires elucidation. I am struck by the ease with which Professor Geiger passes over what must be termed the gut question. He vigorously emphasises the way in which ESP undermines the source of significance, meaning and respect between researchers. Yes indeed, an orthodox defender of the doctrine will reply, but that is exactly the point. In other words, the question is not *whether* ESP undermines authority but *why* there is reason *not* to do so. With Geiger's approach, this latter point is never brought into the debate. The reader is not forced to work out the problem thoroughly in his own mind. All he has to do is take sides - one side or the other - in the battle over 'professorial rule'.

As I see it, there are two distinct kinds of reason for strengthening the academic system of norms instead of undermining it. What is good for research as such is important enough. Scientific work demands mutual criticism. Quite simply, research will be better and more efficient, if the verdict is decided by intradisciplinary viewpoints.

But science is also an ideal in terms of the policy of ideas and cultural philosophy. Research is one of those aspects of human life deriving their value from the appraisal of their products independently of the light in which they appear as a result of the values we put on other parts of our existence.

In St Paul's Epistle to the Galatians, we read: 'There is neither Jew or Greek, there is neither bond nor free, there is neither male nor female: for ye are all one in Christ Jesus'. During the Enlightenment, this fundamental Christian idea took on a worldly as well as a religious significance. In courts of justice, at the polling station and in a large number of other situations, the individual and his argument should be judged on relevant merits, regardless of his or her attitude in respects other than those constituting the relevant sphere of human culture and human progress.[6]

Scientific discourse, subject by subject, constitutes a seminal ideal of this kind, contributing towards the definition of what we call progress and culture. Scientific respect and scientific authority are one of the few fundamental values concerning which we can say that 'no social good x should be distributed to men and women who possess some other good y merely because they possess y and without regard to the meaning of x'.[7]

This makes it hard to understand how it could ever occur to anybody to see progress in counteracting the fundamentally democratic rules of association applying to the interaction of archetypally working researchers.

This, in my opinion, is how one should defend the principle of scientific authority. The essential point is that we are concerned here with something independent, something apart and something fundamentally democratic - a Utopia if you will, but in that case a Utopia which is not calculated to remain only a dream.

This, however, is not the only aspect of criticism of ESP which can be improved on. I am also struck by the lightness with which our American university historian passes over another closely related issue. Why must maintenance of the authority of the scientific community presuppose essential *unconcern* with subjects of practical importance? Professor Geiger hints at a profounder insight into the matter when, parenthetically and cryptically, he declares the ability of the universities to 'accommodate many other things, including applied research'.[8] But he does not enlarge on this view. It is as though he finds it of marginal importance in this context, which - logically - it is not.

What I am alluding to is the error historically attached to the debate on research. Time and time again, arguments are propounded for and against research which is controlled, practical and useful. In contradistinction we are shown research which is independent, theoretical and pursued for its own sake. There is an implied antithesis here, clear and distinct, between liberty and utility.

Sometimes this mistake is made by the critics as well as the advocates of ESP. Exaggerating somewhat, the advocates of liberty seem to believe that they must not be useful. The advocates of utility, conversely, seem to believe that practically-oriented research does not require quality and integrity.

This idea is not only illogical, it is - in my opinion - also unrealistic. The fact is that universities do not confine themselves to theoretical subjects. Medicine, technology and agricultural research have been institutionalised for almost a hundred years now. Activities in these subject fields do not differ from those of the natural sciences and humanities. There is, I feel, something fundamental to be learned from this fact.

In principle, university research can be limitlessly useful. This does not require the slightest infringement of the principle of scientific authority. One only has to realise that there is an organisational problem involved here in two particular respects. There is the way in which research is organised in an external, administrative respect. Is it an assignment on somebody's behalf or work on one's own programming responsibility? Another issue concern the internal, intellectual character of the problems which research sets itself. Are these socially defined or are they a matter of primary research?[9]

Thirdly and finally, the critics are notably superficial in their analysis of the concept of *bureaucracy*. It is as though mere mention of the word sufficed to evoke the association required for agitatory purposes. This, in my opinion, is by far the least developed point of criticism against ESP, which is a pity. For wrapped up in this part of the current negative attitude, there is a thought which it is supremely appropriate to liberate and refine. I would like to end by hinting at the way in which this might be done.

Professor Geiger is a well-meaning, forward-looking and in other respects extremely acute university representative. And yet something is missing. One notices this in the third part of his argument. There, as I see it, he wishes to call to mind one, two or possibly all three of the following different meanings of the word 'bureaucratisation':

- The relative number of persons in universities not personally involved in research and teaching grows progressively larger with the passing of time.

- The quantity of irrelevant paper work and unnecessary meetings grows as a result of excessively detailed regulation combined with lack of determination and ability on the part of those most immediately affected to assume direct responsibility.

- The number and weight of extra-disciplinary considerations increases in the making of research policy decisions at different levels.

A great deal could be said about each of these three interpretations. For example, it is hardly a matter of indifference whether the growing number of 'bureaucrats' consists of research engineers, computer programmers, librarians and the kind of skilled financial administrators needed in order for a research group to be able to operate on a basis of dynamic interaction between public authorities, universities and manufacturers of new research instruments. In this case, bureaucratisation is connected with the increasing sophistication of research as such, and its need of increasing material support of various kinds. Similarly, it has to be made clear whether bureaucracy is self-imposed or not. It is often the lack of mutual trust in practical cooperation between different professional groups that increases the flow of paper and the number of unnecessary meetings. If so, the cure lies in increasing rather than reducing internal specification. And as I have just intimated, the 'extra-disciplinary' can be perfectly legitimate. This can mean medical research with a view to the development of clinical nursing, or studies actually commissioned by national authorities, organisations and companies.

But the question is whether we are not concerned here with a more fundamental tendency. What I have in mind is the great appreciation of the three fundamental values of efficiency, flexibility and justice which has become increasingly apparent during the 20th century. Resources should be distributed so as to be able to put them to the best possible use, and - it is felt - one should be able to steer them in the direction of the right researcher. It is hard to see how such innocent turns of phrase could be aimed at anything startling, but I maintain that they are.

Research, in the high-flown academic sense, is a community. Within its bounds there is a free interchange of ideas and critical viewpoints between equal-ranking academic citizens, none of whom can 'pull rank' on the others. The argument counts for everything. What is tenable is decided in an international market for ideas, where nobody pays any regard to name, background and prestige. Even the most respected and celebrated are believed capable of making mistakes. Even those who are completely unknown are believed capable of contributing an observation or a discovery which will confirm received doctrine, elucidate it or turn it upside down.

In practical terms though, research must always include the exercise of authority. Marks have to be awarded for exams and theses. Statements have to be written as a means of ranking the applicants for appointments and research grants. In principle, though, this is a necessary evil. The *State* character of research is the exception confirming the basic rule. Essentially, research must have the characteristics of a community. Otherwise it betrays its idea.

The muted hostility towards 'bureaucracy' which is so widespread in the university world has, I would venture to claim, an explanation which has for the most part eluded both the advocates and the critics of ESP. In practice, there is too wide a gap between high academic principles and what actually goes on in the everyday run of things. That is my thesis. Hence the cynicism, the frustration and the absurdly derisive attitude of teachers and researchers at universities in the OECD countries.

The quality of a country's overall policy on research and higher education can, I believe, be discerned from the desk diaries of students, teachers and researchers. The more time they devote to reading, writing and discussion of proper books and essays, the better. And conversely: the more time they spend writing, reading and discussing applications, statements and peripheral papers of various kinds, the worse things will be. In politics and administration, this latter form of activity *is* the activity. It is work in laboratories, libraries and seminars that makes a university - not the activities of all its constituent bodies in administrative terms.

In other words, contrary to what advocates and opponents of ESP commonly suppose, the fundamental problem is not the balance between primary and applied research but the balance between structural support and marginal support. Historically speaking, the balance has gone wrong. I maintain that over the years we have come to pay far too heavy a price for flexibility, efficiency and justice. Too much time is spent filing administrative papers. This is what researchers and teachers are doing instead of, in the high-flown sense, developing, testing and criticising their own ideas and other people's. What ought to be a scientific community in which the exercise of office occurs only occasionally is developing, step by step, into a total scientific state in which the exercise of office is all that goes on.

The entire system needs to have its balance redressed. That is my thesis. If the balance in today's Swedish university system is 30-70 (typically, there are no statistics on this particular point), it ought instead to be 70-30. Applications, statements and evaluations are official exercises which, in the light of high-flown principles, should be in the nature of exceptions. But as things have developed over the years, this kind of work is actually pre-empting a progressively larger share of the working week of an increasing number of people. And this, I emphasise, is happening without very many people protesting. Psychologically it is connected with the possibility of exerting more power in a superficial sense by writing statements than by researching, teaching and reviewing.

Researchers and teachers have cause to reproach themselves for not having sounded the alarm much earlier. Year after year they have neglected to make active efforts to redress the balance of research support across the board - from marginal support to structural support. Neither government and parliament nor public opinion have received the right signals. The message conveyed through official channels is liable to be a different one, guided by more cynical calculation and lack of self-respect than will prevail as long as researchers and teachers speak privately and in confidence with each other.

Chapter 14

The American University and Research
A Historical Perspective

Roger L. Geiger

Inventing the American University

Higher education began in the USA just over 350 years ago when instruction commenced at Harvard College (1638). For the next 250 years, however, such education was largely confined to the collegiate level. The United States lacked places of higher learning that deserved to be called universities - institutions where teaching would reach the existing limits of knowledge, where future scholars could be formed, and where contributions to the advancement of knowledge would be encouraged.

For the last century of this span, at least a few Americans were conscious of this lack. Benjamin Rush in 1787 called for this lacuna to be filled by a 'national university'; and George Washington was sufficiently inspired by this notion to leave a bequest to this conjectural entity. Another founding father, Thomas Jefferson, dedicated his last years to designing an ambitious plan for the University of Virginia (1824). But the realities of this creation soon belied its founder's enlightened hopes. Still later, Henry Tappan made great progress in attempting to develop a university in Michigan (1852-63). He established, among other things, an observatory and a genuine Master's Degree; but the backlash attending his efforts caused him to be fired and further progress was postponed. Before the Civil War no lasting organic connections were made between the higher learning and American collegiate education.[1]

The generation that stretched from the Civil War to 1890 was a transitional one for American higher education which witnessed the protodevelopment of universities as well as the establishment of other new institutional forms. Numerous possibilities for linking collegiate and advanced studies were tried during these years, but none was yet able to become dominant. The first American PhDs were awarded at Yale in 1861 for work done within the Sheffield Scientific School. This unit had developed in order to accommodate applied sciences and advanced studies in a separate setting where it would not disturb the pedagogy and social relations of Yale College. The following year Congress passed the Morrill Land Grant Act, which specified that agriculture and the mechanic arts would be taught in conjunction with liberal studies - in effect, the antithesis of the segregation practiced at Yale (even though Sheffield, paradoxically, was the Connecticut recipient of Land-Grant funds). In New York State the combination of philanthropy and Morrill Act funds produced in Cornell University an early prototype of the land-grant university. Utilitarian and liberal education were offered on the same level, and before long research was cultivated there as well.[2]

A more radical experiment was begun in Baltimore in the following decade. Impressed by the prestige and accomplishments of German universities, the trustees of the will of Johns Hopkins endeavored to create a German-style university in the United States, one that would for the first time institutionalise research and graduate education. The president designated to implement this design, Daniel Coit Gilman, chose only scholars as the first professors - three Americans with German PhDs and three foreigners. It admitted relatively few, well-prepared undergraduates, and conducted them to an advanced level of study in just a three-year course. Most of its students were postgraduates, some supported by university fellowships. Johns Hopkins University burst into a void in American higher education. Its teachers organised the disciplinary associations for history, modern languages, and economics; they also founded the major disciplinary journals in chemistry, mathematics, philology, archaeology, psychology, and modern languages. By 1889 it had conferred almost as many PhDs as Harvard and Yale combined. In that time it had done more than any other institution to shape an American academic profession. But Johns Hopkins could not fill the void. It remained a small and circumscribed institution. After 1884 its available resources were devoted to establishing a medical school - an equally remarkable innovation. The university proper, however, found few means for augmenting its activities. For others, moreover, it was unclear whether or not Johns Hopkins represented the pattern of the American university. Charles W. Eliot, President of Harvard, remained sceptical: 'as yet we have no university in America - only aspirants to that eminence,' he opined in 1885.[3]

Within a short time, aspirants and experiments proliferated. Both Clark (1889) and Catholic (1887) universities attempted to follow the Hopkins model, only in purer form, by opening as all-graduate institutions. Stanford University (1891), on the other hand, adapted the Cornell model, which meant offering liberal, professional, and utilitarian curricula with a smattering of graduate work. In Chicago, William Rainey Harper beguiled John D. Rockefeller into bankrolling an elaborate university enterprise (1892), dedicated primarily to advancing knowledge, but also designed to bring instruction and edification to a broad slice of the population. Established institutions also experimented in search of a formula for true university work. The Columbia School of Political Science was founded by John Burgess on the assumption that the American college was outmoded. The school recruited students at the senior year of college and led them to the PhD in three years of study.[4]

These different institutional innovations had different destinies. The dream of a purely graduate university at Clark under G. Stanley Hall proved ephemeral: it failed to hold the backing of its principal benefactor, nor did it win support elsewhere. It persisted as a truncated institution on the income from its initial gift. Catholic University abandoned this chimera and soon admitted undergraduates. Chicago was the most spectacular success as an institution, catapulting into the forefront of American universities. Certain of Harper's many innovations were rapidly copied - particularly summer schools and academic departments; but the University of Chicago as a whole remained an idiosyncrasy, its eccentricity made possible by Rockefeller philanthropy. At Columbia, the School of Political Science reverted to the normal pattern. Instead of new departures, the evolutionary path proved in the long run most compelling.

At Harvard, Charles Eliot had experimented unsuccessfully with special graduate lectures at the beginning of his tenure. Abandoning that approach, he organised a graduate department (1873); however, since it offered no separate courses, students were still largely left on their own. Not until the success of Johns Hopkins became apparent did the inadequacy of Harvard's ad hoc arrangements force a change. The faculties of Harvard College and the Lawrence Scientific School were combined, and this new entity, Faculty of Arts and Sciences, became responsible for the reorganised Graduate School (1890). A set of courses 'primarily for graduates' was now offered. For the first time, the immense resources of Harvard were organised and available for graduate work. And Eliot was at last satisfied.[5]

A graduate school superimposed upon a vigorous undergraduate college had several inherent strengths. A large body of undergraduates permitted the maintenance of a numerous and specialised faculty. It was such a faculty, in turn, that made graduate education and the conduct of research possible. Moreover, it was principally the college that attracted support from American society, whether from state legislatures, alumni or philanthropists, to finance this costly enterprise.

Graduate education in the United States remained a modest industry prior to the First World War. Some 300 PhDs were graduated annually by the end of the 1890s, and that figure rose to over 400 a decade later. But undergraduate enrollments boomed after 1890, and the research universities grew even more rapidly than the system as a whole. During this era bigger was better for universities, and both public and private research universities followed this course. From 1905 to 1915 the fourteen universities that Edwin Slosson called the 'Great American Universities' enrolled one of every five students in American higher education. These institutions had the resource base to sustain to varying degrees a research capacity.[6]

The characteristic American pattern that crystallised after 1890 was that of a multipurpose university which combined liberal and professional education with graduate education and research.[7] It was the size and the wealth of the enterprise as a whole that allowed these institutions to afford the critical and costly inputs to the latter activities - eminent and highly paid professors with time for research, libraries, laboratories, and other types of support. Conversely, it was the inability to afford these inputs in sufficient amounts that prevented numerous other aspiring institutions from participating meaningfully in the university research system at this time. The American university research system was thus steeply and inherently stratified. But even among successful institutions, this pattern of the American university had one serious limitation. Because most university revenues were associated with its other activities, there were few resources available for the direct costs of research *per se*. After 1900 this became an increasing problem due to the rising costs of research in the natural sciences. Previously, American universities had relied upon gifts and endowments to support their purely scientific work in separate observatories and museums, but philanthropy could not be relied upon to support the ongoing investigations within university departments. The American university prior to World War I lacked external backers for its considerable research ambitions.[8]

The Interwar Years: Emergence of a Research Economy

The most momentous change of the interwar years was the emergence of regular, recurrent sources of funding explicitly for research - a university 'research economy'. These funds came from private sources, primarily from foundations and to a lesser extent from industry. The sums involved were not large in relation to the entire university enterprise, but their effects upon university research were profound.[9]

The great foundations of the era, essentially the repositories for major portions of the wealth of Andrew Carnegie and John D. Rockefeller, moved haltingly into the role of patrons for academic research. Immediately after the war the giant Rockefeller Foundation envisioned founding an independent research institute for the natural sciences. When the scientific community could not come to agreement about this plan, it decided instead to create a programme of postdoctoral fellowships that would be administered by scientists through the National Research Council. At the same time, the General Education Board undertook a programme of assisting private colleges with matching grants for endowment. It soon became disillusioned, however, with the prospect of significantly bolstering the financial underpinnings of the nation's private sector. In 1923 several of the Rockefeller trusts embraced the mission of advancing knowledge through assistance to universities.

Beardsley Ruml, new director of the Laura Spelman Rockefeller Memorial, undertook to build knowledge of society by promoting social science research and graduate training. From 1924 to 1928 he committed $20 million to these efforts, most of which went directly or indirectly to the research universities. Almost simultaneous with the arrival of Ruml, Wickliffe Rose became head of the General Education Board and an especially created counterpart, the International Education Board. He embraced the advancement of basic science, and also focused on furthering research for the most part within universities. Rose committed $30 million to American science before his retirement in 1929, and almost all of that flowed to the research universities.

Both Ruml and Rose sought to advance knowledge by strengthening institutions, and for that reason they concentrated their support upon the best existing science programmes - 'to make the peaks higher' was the apt phrase associated with Rose's approach. Their efforts consequently redounded to the benefit of the established research universities. With few staff to assist them, they parcelled out support in rather large grants to university programmes that possessed their confidence. Some grants provided research capital for buildings, endowed institutes, or endowments earmarked for research-related purposes. Other large grants created multi-year support for research at a university in broadly defined areas. In such cases university scientists would themselves determine how the funds would be spent. The foundations also supported intermediary organisations like the Social Science Research Council and the National Research Council. Such funds were spread more widely through small grants-in-aid and fellowships. Only in the 1930s, when foundation assets were squeezed by the Depression, would they attempt to target their research support more narrowly through individual project grants.[10]

In the interwar period support from industry for university research was less salient (and somewhat less respectable), but it nevertheless played an important role in certain fields. Dupont exhibited the postwar spirit of cooperation with academe by establishing fellowships for graduate work in chemistry. This was the field in which ties with industry were most readily made. A number of universities with strong engineering departments established 'engineering research centres' specifically to perform work for industry. Food companies and later pharmaceutical firms also turned to university scientists to investigate specific topics.[11]

For the research universities, the 1920s began in dismal fashion with high inflation and a postwar recession; but the last half of the decade brought their greatest prosperity to date. In place of a single strategy for building research capacity, two tracks emerged. For the state universities bigger was still better. They expanded enrolments, called upon a larger contingent of graduate students to teach introductory courses, and were rewarded by their legislatures with larger appropriations. The private universities, however, faced with a shortage of capital early in the decade, restricted their enrolments and concentrated their resources. When prosperity returned, in the form of generous gifts from alumni and the foundations, they were able (again, to varying degrees) to augment substantially their investment in each of their students. This affluence allowed the hiring of eminent scholars and scientists who would carry comparatively light teaching loads.

The existence of a privately funded research economy profoundly affected the university research system. The most immediate impact of the capital grants was to create thriving pockets of research at the most favoured institutions and in chosen fields. The leading private research universities gained the most, with Chicago easily topping the list. State universities received few large grants during the 1920s. The overall effect, then, was to enhance the stratification of American research universities. The funds that were distributed through the SSRC and the NRC were diffused more widely throughout the university community. In particular, the institution of postdoctoral fellowships made a vital contribution by firmly directing the most promising young scientists into research at the start of their academic careers. In general, foundation support for research had its intended effect in terms of institution building and in raising the stature of American science.

The indirect effects of the research economy were nevertheless also important. The stratified nature of the university research system did not seem to produce discouragement among the less favoured, but rather inspired emulation. One important factor in the pattern of the American university had been changed. Research was no longer simply a fiscal burden; it was potentially a source of support as well. Foundation giving, in particular, had the effect of raising the priority of research in relation to the university's several other roles. Research and graduate education thus became ingrained aspirations of the nation's leading institutions and indelibly associated with university prestige. As the relationship between universities, with their intramural research capacity, and the extramural research economy were developed during the interwar years, the full consequences of dependence on external funders were not yet realised. Academic science was largely directed by a closed oligarchy of eminent scientists who shared a number of ideological convictions: university research should be supported by society because of the unforeseen benefits that basic scientific discoveries would bring; funding should be directed to the best scientists, who would produce the most fruitful results; only scientists of established reputation could determine who the best scientists might be; and, private support was preferable to that from government in order to preclude the taint of politics in these delicate decisions. During the Ruml-Rose era, it suited the purposes of the foundations to operate in a manner consistent with these values. They placed their trust in the membership of the research councils or other individual scientists in whom they had confidence. But afterward, it proved difficult to expand support for research under those conditions. An attempt to enlist industry to finance a National Research Fund, which would have been distributed by scientists, failed to elicit the needed backing. Later, during the New Deal, an attempt to induce the federal government to support university research under similar arrangements also failed. By the end of the 1930s it was becoming evident that the privately funded university research economy was not generating adequate resources for the expanding capacity of universities to perform research. Yet there was no appreciation in the research system of how the interests of the funders of research might be accommodated with those of the performers of research.

The Postwar Era: Federal Support and Programmatic Research

Academic science demonstrated its usefulness to the country during World War II, and it was continued usefulness that was demanded from universities by the federal government in the years following the war.[12] Prior to 1940, the only significant amounts of federal support for university research were directed to the agricultural extension stations. Afterward, this form of aid was joined by four other distinct channels to comprise the federal component of the university research economy:

1. military research continued to be supported on a broad range of subjects, with the largest amounts going toward research related to radar, fuses, and rocket propulsion;

2. the Atomic Energy Commission *(AEC)* assumed the mantle of the Manhattan Project, and with it control over all research involving radioactive materials;

3. the Public Health Service assumed the outstanding contracts of the wartime Committee on Medical Research and began building the National Institutes of Health *(NIH)* empire; and

4. last and certainly least was the implicit government responsibility of supporting basic university research for the advancement of knowledge. This was to be the function of Vannevar Bush's national research foundation; but, unlike the other channels, Congress failed to pass the enabling legislation in the crucial months of 1946. Instead, the Office of Naval Research *(ONR)*, with far more funds and fewer constraints, became the patron of much basic research until the early 1950s.[13]

By 1954 the university research economy had the configuration shown in Table 1. Quite apparent from these figures is the applied cast of university research, even though it was apparently less in 1954 than immediately after the war. Federal contract research centres claimed almost half of federal research funds, and the Department of Defense provided almost 50 per cent of the funds for university research. This state of affairs was disturbing to many scientists and university leaders. Harvard's James B. Conant, for one, argued that the distinction between basic and applied research was not really the crucial issue; rather, the system had become dominated by programmatic research - 'a research programme aimed at a specific goal' - to the neglect of 'uncommitted' or disinterested research, aimed at advancing knowledge without respect to ulterior goals.[14] The problem facing the university research system was that, while all applied research was programmatic in nature, much of the basic research being supported was as well. The principal federal supporters of basic research - NIH, AEC, and even the much-lauded ONR - all had practical missions. There seemed to be comparatively little support for the kind of unfettered investigations that had long been regarded as the true mission of the university.

The dominant presence of the federal government in the postwar research economy produced a research system that was heavily skewed toward programmatic ends. Some fields flourished, particularly physics and engineering; while in others research funds remained difficult to obtain. Funds were also lacking to 'grease the wheels of science' by supporting fellowships, exchanges, meetings, and publications. Probably most serious was the absence of programmes to support the strengthening of the research capacities of universities.

Table 1: University Research Economy, 1954: University Expenditures for Separately Budgeted Research by Source of Funds ($ millions):

Total, Univ. only	205.5	
Total Federal	141.7	
Defense		101.2
HEW (largely NIH)		19.2
AEC		16.6
NSF		1.4
other federal		3.4
Institution/State/Local	17.5	
Foundations	22.7	
Industry	18.6	
Private gifts & other	5.0	
	(not included above)	
Agriculture	74.2	
Federal	13.5	
State & Local	60.7	
FFRDCs (federal research centres)		130 (20 centres)

Source: National Science Foundation, *Scientific Research and Development in Colleges and Universities: Expenditures and Manpower*. 1954

In the immediate postwar era the universities were tossed by some confusing cross-currents. The influx of students as a result of the GI Bill partially revitalised institutional finances after the ravages of the Great Depression and the deprivations of the war years. This forced overenrolment pushed real per-student spending figures to extremely low figures. For universities in general, the decades of the 1930s and 1940s were ones of low investment in physical capital. The 1950s brought first the uncertainties of the Korean War, accompanied by renewed inflation. Not until the mid-fifties was higher education able to benefit from a strong economy and a normal financial environment.

State and private universities were affected somewhat differently by these conditions. The research-oriented state universities expanded their budgets in order to accommodate the veterans, and then largely retained these gains as enrolments subsided. By 1955 they had considerably increased their instructional spending (and expanded their faculties). Private universities generally suffered from the diminished purchasing power of their endowment income and from a dearth of capital for improvements and additions. Voluntary support, on which they depended for capital, did not surpass the peak levels of 1928-31 until after 1955. Improvements in research capacity prior to 1955 were made from exceedingly low levels, except perhaps at the most favoured centres of research. Thus, even in the mid-fifties faculty were generally underpaid and virtually every university had a long wish list of badly needed facilities. The situation was epitomised in the medical schools, where there was an abundance of research funding, while the schools themselves were on the brink of insolvency. This financial weakness at the institutional level, together with the concentrated nature of the research economy, combined to produce the characteristic qualities of the university research system in the postwar era.

Immediately after the war there was an intense, and not altogether healthy, competition for the services of scientists, especially atomic physicists. They naturally tended to cluster at the leading universities which offered them the most propitious conditions for research. At the same time, the continuation of wartime laboratories assured that certain fields would be dominated by the institutions at which they were located. These two factors alone were sufficient to account for the high concentration of postwar research. In fact, the concentration of research funding declined rather steadily from the postwar years to the present. In 1952, the first ten universities received 43.4 per cent of federal research funds (not including FFRDCs); whereas their share currently is close to half that figure. Even in 1955, when FFRDCs are excluded, only perhaps six universities were expending more than $10 million on organised research - MIT, Chicago, UC Berkeley, Michigan, Illinois, and Columbia.

Table 2: Concentration of Funding: Fed. R&D Obligations
to first Ten Univ. (%)

1952	1958	1968	1975	1987
43.4	37.0	27.7	25.8	21.9

Agencies that supported Little Science through modest, short-term grants - ONR, NIH, and later NSF - distributed their funds fairly widely, even considering the concentration of research talent. Elsewhere, however, the system was characterised by quasi-permanent relationships between large university laboratories (and especially FFRDCs) and their mission-agency patrons. These latter relationships accounted for the vast bulk of funds. There was a fair degree of pluralism in the postwar research economy if one took into account the several federal patrons; however, the funding possibilities for individual fields were often quite circumscribed. The postwar statesmen of science - Bush, Conant, and Karl Compton, among others - had been concerned to preserve the pluralism of American university research by maintaining viable private alternatives to federal funding. In the natural sciences, though, just what they had feared came to pass. The overweening presence of federal support caused private foundations to withdraw from the field. In the life sciences the picture was more mixed. The foundations committed to this area were gradually overshadowed by the growth of NIH, but private funders remained and sought out unfilled niches. Only the social sciences continued to rely upon the private foundations for research funding, although the Ford Foundation came to dominate this area by the mid-fifties.

Universities responded to the expanding research economy with exasperation and apprehension, but in hindsight their adaptations reflected pragmatism and flexibility. The arrangements for accounting for organised research, which had been quite casual before the war, had to be regularised and eventually confided to a separate administrative unit. The most prominent organisational difficulty was created by the hypertrophy of research in selected areas of the university. As research became an end in itself, with its own continuing financing, the complementarity of teaching and research, upon which the academic departments were predicated, was superseded. Three kinds of adaptations were evident. In medical schools and sometimes in physics departments regular faculty positions were decoupled from departmental finances: permanent faculty were hired on 'soft' money. In other areas the demands of research were often met by creating

Organised Research Units (ORUs). Such units were not new to American universities, but the extensive reliance upon them was.[15] The universities that had the largest amounts of research funding - notably MIT and Berkeley - also had the most ORUs. The federal contract research centres were a direct outgrowth of the war. For at least a decade a sorting process took place which tended to isolate some types of research in this kind of institutional quarantine (for example, Lawrence Livermore). For a time federal funding for FFRDCs nearly equalled all federal support for university research proper, but after the 1950s they exhibited much slower growth. The dynamics of FFRDCs reflected the state of the particular fields in which they operated, as well as the prosperity of their patrons. Their relationship with their respective universities, however, was in most cases tenuous.

The Sputnik Era, 1957-1967

The transformation of the university research system began in the mid-fifties. Prosperity brought a marked expansion of the research economy: expenditures for research in universities proper grew by 60 per cent from 1954 to 1958, that is, before the effects of Sputnik were felt. Increases were roughly comparable in both federal and nonfederal funding, but within the federal component two opposed tendencies were evident. Funding from the armed services became decidedly more pragmatic as military budgets came under some unaccustomed pressure. The result seems to have been greater use of FFRDCs in preference to research in universities proper. Elsewhere, funding was increased considerably by the NIH and the AEC, while the NSF finally became a significant funder of university research. With these changes the proportion of basic research in the university totals rose from 62 per cent to 70 per cent. The growth of research funds was greatest in the life sciences (114%), reflecting the prosperity of NIH and private funders. The physical sciences also did well (+76%), as the AEC expanded its on-campus support. Engineering (+6%) reflected the armed services' preference for FFRDCs.

These years also witnessed a dramatic improvement in university research capacity, particularly at the major private institutions. In general, public research universities made greater improvements in per-student expenditures before 1955 (partly because of enrolment growth thereafter), and private universities, capitalising on propitious financial conditions and considerably higher levels of voluntary support, generally registered their greatest increases in the decade after 1955. Because of changes in the research economy, university research became less concentrated. Whereas in 1954 only 11 universities expended more than $5 million on separately budgeted research (not including agriculture and FFRDCs) by 1958 20 institutions had crossed that threshold. The ten leading recipients of federal research funds in 1954 received 46 per cent of the total (again, excluding agriculture and FFRDCs), but in 1958 their share had dropped to 37 per cent (these exclusions reflect NSF bookkeeping).

In the years prior to Sputnik, the university research system was evolving away from the cast that it had taken immediately after the war. It was encouraged in this respect by a campaign extolling the virtues of basic research that was orchestrated by NSF, and conducted by university scientists and administrators. This trend was impeded by the frugality of the Eisenhower Administration and the increasingly pragmatic orientation of the armed services. Sputnik resolved this debate in favour of basic research. Within a few years the system was transformed into the antithesis of what it had been in the postwar era.[16]

The US responded to Sputnik with new and substantial commitments to Space, Science, and Education. New programmes in each of these areas redounded to the benefit of the research universities. The preoccupations with space resulted in the creation of NASA. Although the ultimate thrust of NASA was toward Big Science and engineering, it forged numerous links with university research during the 1960s. As a newcomer agency, eager to build a network with academic science, it was in a position analogous to ONR in the late 1940s. It provided generous funding on lenient terms to selected groups of scientists at many institutions. By 1966 NASA was supplying almost 10 per cent of federal funds for academic R&D; and some 36 universities were receiving more than $1 million from the agency.

The National Defense Education Act (1958) was the beginning of regular federal support for graduate students, foreign languages and area studies. The federal government thus undertook to support the research role of universities in ways other than the funding of research.

The most spectacular gains were nevertheless made in precisely this last area. The federal government committed itself unequivocally to supporting basic research in the universities for the sake of advancing knowledge (and also besting the Soviets). From 1958 to 1968 federal funds for basic university research rose from $178 million to $1251 million - a seven-fold increase during a decade of relatively stable prices. This was by far the most significant component of growth in an expanding research economy. Moreover, it tilted the balance of basic research into university laboratories: the national budget for basic research grew by $2400 million during these years; university-based research accounted for $1400 million of this increase; and federal funds comprised $1100 million of that. Whereas universities expended 32 per cent of the funds for basic research in 1958, they spent 57 per cent of the total in 1968. This was a golden age for academic science.

Table 3: Indicators of Change in University Research Role.

	Gross National Product	National Basic Research	% GNP	Total Univ. R&D	% GNP	Basic Univ. Res.	% Nat. Basic	% Univ. Res.
1953	364,900	441	.12	255	.07	110	25	43
1960	506,500	1197	.24	646	.12	433	36	67
1964	637,700	2289	.36	1275	.20	1003	44	79
1968	873,400	3296	.38	2149	.25	1649	50	77
1986	4291,000	14163	.33	10,600	.24	7100	50	67

The expansion of the research economy was accompanied by the recognition of the need to strengthen the infrastructure for university research. A report from the President's Science Advisory Council (Seaborg Committee) recommended in 1960 that the number of research universities in the nation should be doubled - from 15-20 to 30-40.[17] The Ford Foundation had already begun a programme of upgrading selected universities, and federal programmes eventually followed at the principal agencies supporting university research. During the 1960s for the first time the federal government provided capital funds in substantial magnitudes to enhance the research capacity of universities. By 1968 the government was supplying almost one-third of the capital funds expended by universities - compared to a proportion of about one-eighth in the 1980s.

Federal support for infrastructural needs, together with greater financial support from other sources, rectified one of the conditions that lay behind the substantial concentration in the university research system - the restricted research capacity of all but a few institutions. The growing abundance of funds for research, especially investigator-initiated projects, ended another limitation. Finally, as the graduate schools turned out an increasing number of research-oriented PhDs, the number of university researchers greatly increased. By 1968, 41 universities were receiving more than $10 million in federal R&D obligations, and the share of the total claimed by the first ten had declined to 27.7 per cent.

By the mid-1960s the post-Sputnik accretions to the research economy had over-grown the configurations of the postwar-era research economy. Comparing 1958 and 1968, the additional funding to NIH and NSF, plus the net addition of NASA, comprised more than 60 per cent of federal funding for university R&D. By the latter year it appeared that an 'Academic Revolution' had taken place, that the values of the graduate school had gained ascendancy in American universities.

The domination of investigation by disciplinary paradigms even became the object of criticism: a crisis of 'relevance' was perceived in the university curriculum, and perhaps in the conduct of research itself. Meanwhile, much of the programmatic research sponsored by the Department of Defense was deemed unfit for university campuses.

The 'new' federal funds in the research economy were spread far more widely than the 'old' funds had been, thereby furthering the decentralisation of the research system. This, in turn, enhanced competition. University leaders and academic scientists greeted the new regime with alacrity. The emphasis given to basic research allowed them to do what they felt universities ought to be doing, and without the misgivings about secrecy, continuity, or external control that had plagued them during the preceding era. Thus, universities readily adapted by increasing their emphasis on research and its attendant values. This meant aggressively recruiting productive scholars and scientists, and devoting their own discretionary funds to building research capacity. This was the rational course. For perhaps the first time in university history, research seemed to be a remunerative activity for a substantial number of institutions. Not only did the federal government stand ready to assist universities to meet the high overhead expenses associated with efforts to maintain and extend research capacity, but that capacity could now assuredly generate a continuing flow of project funds and indirect-cost reimbursements.

In this heady environment, few expressed real concern over the attenuation of pluralism. The Seaborg Committee had pronounced that the federal government, and only the federal government, was responsible for expanding the system of university research. During the 1960s each discipline in turn defined its absolutely indispensable research needs, and then, in effect, presented the bill to the public.[18] The federal contribution to academic R&D rose from 53 per cent in 1953, to 63 per cent in 1960, to a peak of 74 per cent in 1966; and then remained above 70 per cent for the remainder of the decade (Table 4).

Private contributions to university research (industry and nonprofits) fell as low as 8.7% (1967-69). At this juncture universities finally were forced to face the consequen-

Table 4: Federal Dependence: University R&D supported
by Federal Funds (%)

1953	1960	1966	1976	1987
53	63	74	67	63

ces of overdependence on a single source - the condition that had worried university leaders during the preceding postwar era.

The Stagnant Decade, 1968-77

The momentum imparted to academic science by the launch of Sputnik lasted for ten years. 1968 represents a kind of apogee for the university research system in terms of real expenditures and federal support for research. This was not solely a university phenomenon; research expenditures for the country as a whole peaked in 1968 as well. The university research economy remained roughly stable in real terms for the next seven years, through 1975, while the national research economy actually declined by nearly 10 per cent. Significant growth in university research did not occur again until 1978. The system thus experienced a decade of stagnation, which in some cases brought outright retrenchment.

Despite the transition from expansion to stagnation, the university research system changed only slowly during this decade. The federal contribution to university research fell somewhat to 67 per cent. Applied research fared somewhat better than basic, so that the proportion of the latter declined from 77 per cent (1968) to 69 per cent (1977). Still, despite evident dissatisfaction with purely disinterested academic research, there was little movement toward a more programmatic orientation. The proportions of academic science obligations awarded by NIH and NSF remained about the same, although both agencies altered their policies by devoting significantly more of their funds to actual research. This behavior maintained the pool of project funds, but had an additional, adverse impact on universities. During the 'Stagnant Decade' federal support of the kind that bolstered university research capacities was severely curtailed. Funds for R&D plant peaked at $126 million in 1965, but averaged just $35 million annually during the 1970s (current $). Federal fellowship support reached a high figure of $447 million in 1967, but stood at only $185 million a decade later. Universities were asked to do more on their own to sustain their research roles, and they were hard-pressed to meet this challenge.

These years were difficult ones for university finances. The private universities, in general, had tended to overcommit themselves during the late 1960s, and as a result concentrated on putting their budgets back into the black during the early 1970s. State research universities came under increasing pressure during the early 1970s to justify their high costs to egalitarian-minded legislators. From about 1968 it was virtually taken for granted that a major new federal programme would have to be initiated in order to rectify the financial conditions prevailing in higher education. When it came in 1972, however, Congress provided expanded forms of student financial aid instead of institutional aid that would have been of immediate succor to the research universities. Under these conditions, few institutions were able to augment their research capacities during the 1968-1977 period. Their problems were not just with income, which in most cases continued to rise, but also with the rapid growth in non-instructional demands, such as energy costs, administrative requirements, and the necessity of meeting federal regulations. Research was in fact severely crowded as an institutional priority by other concerns.

Decentralisation nevertheless continued as the proportion of federal research funds received by the top ten universities declined from 29.1 per cent in 1967 to 25.8 per cent in 1975. It seemed, however, that the stagnation in research funding and the persistent financial difficulties facing universities would now favour the leading institutions.[19] As the competition for research funds became more intense, the advantage of those universities with the highest peer-rated faculties ought to have become more pronounced. Sustaining a research commitment also seemed to demand a larger investment of institutional funds. At the second-tier research universities, however, a deemphasis of research seemed apparent. Insofar as institutions were adapting to this situation, they appeared to be contemplating a withdrawal from research commitments - either to turn toward undergraduate and professional teaching, or to abandon broad research/graduate programmes for more specialised undertakings. It consequently appeared that the country could not sustain as research universities the number of institutions that had aspired to that status in the 1960s and that the secular trend toward decentralisation of university research was about to be reversed.

The Current Era: 1978-1988

In actuality, the university research system neither continued to stagnate nor contracted toward the peak institutions. Instead, the system renewed its secular expansion beginning about 1978. In ten years (1977-87) it grew 56.5 per cent in real terms - not a bad showing for a mature system that experienced little growth in students or faculty. Moreover, in a largely unforeseen development, support for the increase in research came disproportionately from nonfederal sources. Federal funds for university R&D increased by 10 percentage points less than the average, while nonfederal sources grew by twenty points more. The fastest growing single source of university research support was private industry, which funded 6 per cent of the 1987 total. That six per cent figure, in fact, understates the rising importance of university-industry ties. A good part of nonprofit support of academic research (perhaps another three per cent of the total) probably comes from corporate or industry-related foundations; and some state support is now directed toward subsidising university-industry linkages. The expansion of research support from nongovernmental sources has increased the actual and perceived pluralism of the system. No longer are the research universities considered to be wards of the federal government: When Robert Rosenzweig and Barbara Turlington wrote of this in 1982 they deliberately referred to *The Research Universities and Their Patrons.*[20]

The current decade has been reasonably prosperous for the research universities generally; their instructional budgets grew by roughly 30 per cent in real terms (1974-76 to 1984-86). This figure most likely understates the improvement that has taken place in their financial positions. The privatisation of university income has almost certainly been more pronounced than that for just research funds. The great gains of the 1980s for universities have come from increased tuition (the delayed payoff from the expansion of student aid) and voluntary support. Without a doubt, many universities have used these funds to enhance research capacity; but it has also been common to bolster those aspects of the university that most directly affect its ability to attract students and raise money - admissions, development, student aid, and perhaps those structures that most appeal to students and alumni. Unlike the 1960s, universities have acted conservatively toward creating new faculty lines.

The financial conditions of the 1980s have been especially beneficial to the leading research universities. They have well-established channels for raising voluntary support and a surplus of applicants with little sensitivity to price. Despite these factors, and despite the continued stiff competition for federal research funds, the leading research universities have by-and-large not kept pace with the growth of total R&D expenditures. The proportion of federal R&D funds received by the ten largest recipients declined to 22 per cent in 1987; their share of total R&D expenditures was even less - 19 per cent. Between 1974-76 and 1984-86 the most highly peer-rated universities fared as follows:

slightly increased research share	*slightly decreased research share*	*decreased research share*
Cornell	MIT	Michigan
Stanford	Yale	Berkeley
Texas	Illinois	Princeton
Caltech	UCLA	Wisconsin
	Minnesota	Harvard
		Penn
		Columbia
		Chicago

The share of university R & D of the largest performers has changed as follows:

Table 5: Change in Market share of large R&D Univ., 1974-76 to 1984-86

	positive			negative		
Change:	>20%	10 to 20%	0 to 10%	0 to -10%	-10 to -20%	< -20%
University Performing >2.0% in 74-76	0	2	1	2	5	2
University Performing 1.0-2.0% in 74-76	4	1	3	8	0	4

By implication, the smaller research universities, or at least some of them, have been increasing their share of research funding. It is difficult to characterise these advancing institutions with any precision. They include many state institutions from Sunbelt states where, at least until recently, economic growth has provided the underpinning for increases in enrollment and state support. Also prominent are public and private universities with close ties to industry, especially engineering schools. For the former group, the old formula of more students and higher appropriations seems to have translated into greater research capacity. For the latter group, links with the fastest growing segment of the research economy have produced above average growth. More generally, this pattern would indicate that the growth in the research economy during the 1980s has been due substantially to the initiative and adaptation of individual institutions.

Conclusion

The university research system of the United States has retained its fundamental features despite a century of growth and the superimposition of significant additional components. Most importantly, the research capacity continues to depend in large measure on the vigor of individual universities, while the amount of research performed depends upon funding from the extramural research economy. Secondly, these external funds represent a shifting balance between support for disinterested basic research in the academic disciplines and programmatic research in keeping with the interests of funders. The dynamics of the university research system, past and present, can be portrayed in terms of these two dichotomies.

The dependence for research capacity upon the resources of individual universities has in one sense been a traditional weakness of the American system. Only in the decade after Sputnik did the federal government assume the responsibility to enhance research capacities across a wide range of universities. Today, when the litany of problems confronting research universities is recited, most of the items can be associated with this issue: the lack of support for infrastructure, including instrumentation; and the impossible demands upon research university libraries. The inadequate support for graduate students, and the consequent concern about the pipeline for future scientists, would also belong partly with this list.[21] In addition, the heterodox efforts of a few universities to lobby Congress for special appropriations would seem to be a pathological expression of these university needs - and university aspirations.

In another sense, the continued decentralisation of university research conveys a different message. A growing number of research universities are clearly managing to expand their research capacities. The decentralisation of university research is not a result of federal pressures to spread research funding more widely: total expenditures for research are more decentralised than expenditures from just federal funds. Research has increased as a university priority since the stagnant years of the 1970s. The result, despite relatively little assistance from the federal government, has been to augment the research capacity of American universities.

The research economy has grown moderately during the 1980s, but the current fear is that federal budgetary restrictions will preclude a continuation of this expansion, which is necessary to maintain the overall health of the university research system. The positive side of this situation is that the system has been growing less dependent upon federal funds. Decentralisation has tended to increase the pluralism of funding sources. Most likely, advancing research universities have been able to tap local sources of support for their research. By and large, however, this has meant a greater proportion of programmatic funding.

There can be little doubt that the 1980s has witnessed a disproportionate growth in programmatic support for academic research. Not only has funding from industry been the fastest growing component, but it has been supplemented by numerous federal and state programmes designed to promote technology transfer and closer links between universities and industry. In one respect this trend represents an overdue correction to the attitude of disdain for applications and business that reigned during the post-Sputnik decade. But it has not been an unmixed blessing. Critics have worried, much as they did in the postwar era, about the diversion of scientists from basic research and about the possible perversion of essential elements of scientific communications. In addition, programmatic support cannot substitute in most fields for disinterested disciplinary research. Above all, it is necessary to maintain the vigour of the basic research goose if the golden eggs of technology are going to be gathered.

On the whole, though, the current balance may be a healthy one. The research universities today may be more responsive to the needs of American society than at any time in the past. If so, this happy state is not the result of any particular policy. Rather, it stems from the habits of flexibility and adaptability that have well served American universities throughout the first century of their history.

References

Introduction, Martin Trow

A slightly revised version of a Paper read at the seminar 'Universitet och Samhälle' (University and Society) to mark the retirement of Dr Eskil Björklund as Director of the Research on Higher Education Program, sponsored by the Chancellor of the Swedish Universities, Stockholm, May 30-31, 1989.

1. E. Björklund, 'Research on Higher Education: Long Term Development of Knowledge', in *R&D for Higher Education*. NBUC/Stockholm 1983:2, pp 4-5.

2. E. Björklund, *A Program Overview comparing the 1970s with the 1980s*, in *Studies of Higher Education and Research* (SHER) 1988:1, p 1 (Björklund 1988).

3. For the most recent and comprehensive example, see E. Björklund, *Two Decades of Swedish Research on Higher Education*, in *SHER* 1989:2.

4. Björklund 1988, p 4.

Chapter 1, Nils Runeby

1. In N. Runeby, 'Ett otidigt och okärt främmande'. Om den lärde, studenten, universitetet och vår utbildningstradition, in *Lychnos* 1988 (Runeby 1988), I have tried to summarise this development in Sweden. C. Ahlund in his recent analysis of the Scandinavian university novel, has also discussed the situation at the 19th century Scandinavian universities and in the Scandinavist movement; C. Ahlund, *Den skandinaviska universitetsromanen 1877-1890*, Skrifter utgivna av Litteraturvetenskapliga institutionen vid Uppsala universitet 26. Uppsala 1990 (*Ahlund 1990*).

2. C. Graña, *Bohemian versus Bourgeois. French Society and French Man of Letters in the 19th Century*. New York & London 1964, pp 67. Also the standard work by H. Kreuzer, *Die Boheme. Beiträge zu ihrer Beschreibung*. Stuttgart 1968 (Kreuzer 1968).

3. P. L. Thorslev Jr, *The Byronic Hero. Types and Prototypes*. Minneapolis 1962, p 18.

4. See chap. 'Fausts laboratorium', in I. Holm, *Industrialismens scen*. Stockholm 1979, for references on the Faustian tradition. The most famous versions of the Prometheus and Faust themes combine the elements of revolt and reconciliation; in Goethe's re-interpretation his understanding of Prometheus can easily be reconciled with the Christian worldview of Faust, eg, J. Duchemin, *Prométhée. Histoire du Mythe de ses Origines orientales a ses Incarnations modernes*. Paris 1974.

5. For the quoted pamphlets of I. Hwasser, '*Om vår tids ungdom*'. Uppsala 1842, and '*Om äktenskapet*'. Uppsala 1842 (2d ext. ed.), see Hwasser, *Samlade skrifter*. On Hwasser, S-E. Liedman, *Israel Hwasser*, Lychnos-Bibliotek 27, Stockholm 1971, esp chapters 4-5 (Liedman 1971).

6. Hwasser, *Om äktenskapet*, pp 24.

7. Hwasser, *Om vår tids ungdom*, pp 1,16,26 also p 34,43 and pp 48.

8. Hwasser, *Om vår tids ungdom*, pp 45.

9. M. Stirner, *Der Einzige und sein Eigenthum*, is here quoted from J. Carroll (ed), *Max Stirner: The Ego and His Own*. New York/Evanston/San Francisco 1974, pp 94. In his ed. Carroll is using the translation of S. T. Byington (1907). On the vagabond concept and Stirner, also Kreuzer 1968, pp 8.

10. P. Wende, *Radikalismus*, in O. Brunner et al (eds), *Geschichtliche Grundbegriffe 5*. Stuttgart 1984.

11. W. H. Riehl, *Die bürgerliche Gesellschaft*. 1851 (10th ed., 1907) (*Riehl 1851*). I have used P. Steinbach's abridged ed. (Frankfurt/Main 1976). On Riehl, see the introduction in *Steinbach (ed) 1976*, and K. Bergmann, *Agrarromantik und Grossstadtfeindschaft*. Meisenheim am Glan 1970. (*Bergmann 1970*). On Riehl's 'Fourth Estate', also Kreuzer 1968, pp 291: '(Riehl's) interpretation is correct so far as the German proletariat to a great extent got its revolutionary consciousness through the mediation of intellectuals as well as their interpretation of history and society, but the influence of the critique from the "demagogues" was of course, due to the existing social injustices. Further, it must be noted that the intellectuals protested not only because of their proletarian existence: among the "demagogues" there were also "renegades" ("Abtrünnigen"), coming from good social conditions or with brilliant expectations, ie people living under proletarian conditions (eg in exile) just because they were dissidents.' (my transl.).

12. For the following, Riehl, pp 227-38, and Steinbach, Introduction, in Steinbach (ed) 1976, pp 35.

13. For this reason, Riehl is more afraid of the civil servant and white collar proletariat than of the 'literati'. The civil servants, because they are 'überstudiert', indulge in false expectations, and even the most decent Philistine can become a frustrated democrat and communist. This particular proletariat is not dependent on the market and has to be kept in check by sheer and open repression .

14. On diversion, M. Murray, *Utbildningsexpansion, jämlikhet och avlänkning. Studier i utbildningspolitik och utbildningsplanering 1933-1985*. Göteborg 1988.

15. Bergmann 1970, p 49.

16. C. V. A Strandberg's address is printed in *Svenska Akademiens Handlingar ifrån år 1796, 38*. Stockholm 1864 (loc. cit. pp 8). In his memorial speech on Hwasser, in *Svenska Akademiens handlingar ifrån år 1796, 36*. Stockholm 1863, Strandberg talks with compassion and understanding about the ageing professor's growing isolation and despair. Generally, see the important study by K. Monié, *Den etalerade vetenskapsmannen. Gustaf Ljunggren - svensk litteraturhistoriker*. Stockholm 1985, where she is analyzing both the transition from the 1840s to the 1850s, and the problems discussed in this essay.

17. The following is entirely founded on the report: *Studentmötet i Kristiania 1869*. Lund 1871. References to pages have therefore been considered unnecessary. The volume also contains a long section on the Folk high schools in the Scandinavian countries and detailed descriptions of different journeys, excursions, and receptions. The proceedings and speeches are rendered partly as summaries by the editors, partly as reprinted newspaper articles or manuscripts from the participants. On the Student meeting, also F. B. Wallem, *Det norske Studentersamfund gjennem hundrede aar*. Oslo 1916, pp 570; B. Odén, *Ärestoder och minnesfester i Skåne*, in *Ale* 1976:2: and *Ahlund 1990*, pp 199. In the essay I am using the expression 'close to the people' as a translation of the Swedish word 'folklighet'. I borrowed the term from Liedman, *Civil Servants Close to the People: Swedish University Intellectuals and Society at the Turn of the Century*, in *History of European Ideas* 1987. In his essay Liedman is discussing the meaning of the concept, which is relevant also in my context, even if Liedman is using it for somewhat different purposes.

18. On Eilert Sundt as a social scientist, esp the articles by A-L. Seip, *Forholdet mellom 'Capitalen og Arbeidet' i gruvesamfunnet Röros 1851*, in *Norsk Historisk Tidsskrift* 1974; *Eilert Sundt og vekstideologiens dilemma*, in *Norsk Historisk Tidsskrift* 1975; and *Eilert Sundt. A Founding Father of the Social Sciences in Norway*, in *Scandinavian Journal of History* 1986. C. V. Rimestad's interest in the urban workers and their education is easily understood. He was at the time deeply involved in the much noticed, and occasionally also successful, activities of the Arbeiderforeningen in Copenhagen, which he himself had initiated. C. Rosenberg, a man of the 'radical' 40s, can perhaps be seen as a 'free-floating' literate, because his writings had forced him to resign from the civil service. His 'vagabondage' had however its limits. He deeply disliked Georg Brandes and rejected socialism. He was rather belonging to the left wing of the National Agrarian, Christian Grundtvig movement. See U. Andreasen and C. S. Pedersen, in *Dansk Biografisk Leksikon 12*. Köbenhavn 1982.

19. B. Grandien, 'Landskap och människa. Om den litterära och konstnärliga fotvandringen under 1800-talet', in *Historiens vingslag. Konst, historia, ornitologi. Festskrift till Allan Ellenius*. Stockholm 1987, also Grandien, *Rönndruvans glöd. Nygötiskt i tanke, konst och miljö under 1800-talet*. Stockholm 1987.

20. Ch. Skoglund, *Vänsterstudenter, kulturradikalism och bildningsideal i sekelskiftets Sverige*, Idéhistoriska uppsatser/Stockholm 1987, pp 31.

21. V. Rydberg's address is printed in *Svenska Akademiens Handlingar ifrån år 1796, 53*. Stockholm 1878 (loc cit, p 129,135 and pp 47,152).

22. The quotations from Rydberg, *Bilder ur Goethes Faust*, are taken from K. Warburg (ed), *Rydbergs Samlade Skrifter II*, pp 316-28.

23. *Runeby 1988*, pp 4.

24. The A. Schopenhauer quotations can be found in Schopenhauer, '*Ueber die Universitäts-Philosophie*', in Schopenhauer, *Parerga und Paralipomena*. 1851 (Schopenhauer 1851). The Nietzsche quotations come from F. Nietzsche, '*David Strauss, der Bekenner und der Schriftsteller*'. 1873, in Nietzsche, *Unzeitgemässe Betrachtungen*. Here, Nietzsche is also using the factory metaphor (loc cit, Paragraph 8).

25. J. Schmidt, *Die Geschichte des Genie-Gedankens 2*. Darmstadt 1988, pp 156. Nietzsche's apotheosis of youth is formulated on the last pages of Nietzsche, '*Vom Nutzen und Nachteil der Historie für das Leben*'. 1874, in Nietzsche, *Unzeitgemässe Betrachungen*.

26. The B. Bauer quotations are taken from Bauer, *Russland und das Germanenthum*. 1853. I have used the excerpts published in K. Löwith, *Die Hegelsche Linke*. Stuttgart/Bad Cannstadt 1962. The concept 'critical nihilism' is also Löwith's, see Löwith, *Von Hegel bis Nietzsche*. Zürich/New York 1941. A comprehensive presentation of the different views on Bauer cannot be undertaken here, but Kreuzer, is anxious to stress the general scepticism towards the 'technical' civilisation: 'Bauer's ideas are not founded on an eg anachronistic agrarian traditionalism, supposedly explicable through the specific character of German intellectuals and the 'retarded' political and ideological developments in Germany. Instead, we find a typical reaction to industrial society from a kind of intellectual that was both reflective and outspoken antipatriarchal. ' (my transl.), Kreuzer 1968, p 277. Ahlund has emphasised, that a deep disappointment with university life is a characteristic feature of the university novels: 'The by far most dominating impression of the university novels is one of revolt, opposition and dissociation.', Ahlund 1990, p 198. In the German summary of his book Ahlund makes an interesting point on how the acute conflict is solved: 'The hero leaves the university, goes into politics, becomes a free writer or engages in practical work serving society. His ambition to promote popular education plays here an important role.', Ahlund 1990, pp 300.

27. Quotation from Schopenhauer 1851.

28. H. Böhme and E. Sundermann, 'Aspekte preussischer Kulturpolitik zwischen reformerischen Elan und staatstragender Reaktion', in M. Schlenke (ed), *Preussen. Beiträge zu einer politischen Kultur 2*. Reinbek b. Hamburg 1981, pp 267.

29. K. Jarausch, *Deutsche Studenten 1800-1970*. Frankfurt/Main 1984, p 59.

30. For the following, S. Wieselgren, *Vårt Uppsalaliv. Minnen från 1860-talet*. Stockholm 1907. In the 1880s and 1890s Wieselgren wrote novels about the students in Uppsala. Even here Wieselgren gives a fairly rosy picture of the intellectual standard of the university and the students, see Ahlund 1990, chap. V.

31. P. Hellqvist, *Att tänka fritt och att tänka rätt. Seminariet och universitetsreformen 1891*, in Liedman and L. Olausson (eds), *Ideologi och institution. Om forskning och högre utbildning 1880-2000*. Stockholm 1988 (*Hellqvist 1988*), also R. Torstendahl, *Disputation eller information. Den pedagogiska linjen i Historiska föreningens verksamhet*, in *Hundra års historisk diskussion. Historiska föreningen i Uppsala 1862-1962*. Stockholm 1962 (*Torstendahl 1962*), and J. Weibull, *Lunds universitets historia IV*. Lund 1968, pp 59. The 'turn' towards research can also be illustrated by the textbooks written for the 'Gymnasium', see G. Andolf, *Historien på gymnasiet. Undervisning och läroböcker 1820-1965*. Stockholm 1972.

32. The relations between W. E. Svedelius and M. Weibull is discussed in Torstendahl, *Källkritik och vetenskapssyn i svensk historisk forskning 1820-1920*. Stockholm 1964 (Torstendahl 1964). Svedelius was

professor of Political science in Uppsala, 1862-1881. I am quoting from Svedelius, *Avsked från studenterna*. Uppsala 1889 (3d ed), loc cit p 4, and pp 7 (Svedelius 1889). On Svedelius and Hwasser, see Liedman 1971, pp 227.

33. Svedelius 1889, pp 13 and 24.

34. Svedelius 1889, p 38 and pp 80.

35. Torstendahl 1962, pp 14,18 and p 32.

36. Torstendahl 1964, pp 117, p 124,141, pp 236 and p 247 also Hellqvist 1988, pp 82.

Chapter 2, Rolf Torstendahl

1. A first version was presented at a conference on 'Knowledge elites, the process of professionalisation and changes in communication systems' arranged by the European Science Foundation's standing committee for the social sciences in April 1988 in Uppsala.

2. For further discussion of professions as knowledge-based groups, Torstendahl, *Essential properties, strategic aims and historical developments. Three approaches to theories of professionalism*, in M. Burrage and R. Torstendahl (eds), *Professions in Theory and History. Rethinking the Study of Professions*. London 1990 (Torstendahl 1990a).

3. Torstendahl, *Introduction: Promotion and Stategies of Knowledge-based Groups*, in Torstendahl and Burrage (eds), *The Formation of Professions: Knowledge, State and Strategy*. London 1990 (Torstendahl 1990b).

4. A. Giddens, *Elites in the British Class Structure*, in P. Stanworth and A. Giddens (eds), *Elites and Power in the British Society*. Cambridge 1974 (*Stanworth-Giddens 1974*).

5. From the vast literature on the place of nurses in the professional environment, eg A. Etzioni, *Complex Organizations*. New York 1969; A. Abbott, *The System of Professions. An Essay on the Division of Expert Labor*. Chicago 1988, pp 71, and p 96 (*Abbot 1988*); E. Freidson, *Professional Powers. A Study of the Institutionalization of Formal Knowledge*. Chicago 1986, pp 165 and 188.

6. Esp. in France, but the question was raised also in Germany. Several contributions in A. Grelon (ed), *Les ingénieurs de la crise. Titre et profession entre les deux guerres*. Paris 1986 treat this question; also cf *Technik, Ingenieure und Gesellschaft. Geschichte des Vereins Deutscher Ingenieure 1856-1981*. VDI-Verlag 1981, pp 305-11 (*VDI 1981*).

7. The literature on 'the legal profession' seldom discusses this split into different professions seriously, cf Abbott 1988, pp 247-79, esp pp 265-67.

8. Torstendahl, *Bureaucratisation in Northwestern Europe 1880-1985: Domination and Governance*. London 1991, ch. 2, and B. Stråth and R. Torstendahl, *State theory and state development: States as a network structure in change in modern European history*. Uppsala 1988 (ms).

9. Esp. D. S. L. Cardwell, *The Organisation of Science in England*. London (1957) 1980.

10. For this development there is an overwhelmingly rich literature: eg T. Shinn, *L'Ecole Polytechnique 1794-1914*. Paris 1980 (Shinn 1980), R. Fox and A. Guagnini, *Britain in perspective: The European context of industrial training and innovation, 1880-1914*, in *History and Technology* Vol. 2, 1985, pp 133-50. For a more extensive discussion Torstendahl, *Engineers in Sweden and Britain 1820-1914. Professionalisation and bureaucratisation in a comparative perspective*, in W. Conze and J. Kocka (eds), *Bildungsbürgertum im 19. Jahrhundert*, Vol 1. Stuttgart 1985, pp 543-60 (Conze-Kocka 1985).

11. K. Åmark, *Öppna karteller och sociala inhägnader. Konkurrensbegränsningsstrategier bland professionella yrkesgrupper i Sverige 1860-1950*, in S. Selander (ed), *Kampen om yrkesutövning, status och kunskap. Professionaliseringens social grund*. Lund 1989, pp 96-101; cf K. Åmark, *Open Cartels and Social Closures: Professional Strategies in Sweden, 1860-1950*, in *Burrage-Torstendahl 1990*, pp 104.

12. W. D. Rubinstein, *Men of Property: Some aspects of occupation, inheritance and power among top British wealthholders*, in *Stanworth-Giddens 1974*, p 163.

13. C. J. Hewitt, *Elites and the distribution of power in British society*, in *Stanworth-Giddens 1974*, p 64.

14. F. & J. Wakeford, *Universities and the study of elites*, in *Stanworth-Giddens 1974*.

15. For the historical aspect, *Shinn 1980*; for the 1960s and 70s, E. Suleiman, *Politics, Power and Bureaucracy in France. The Administrative Elite*. Princeton 1974, E. Suleiman, *Elites in French Society. The Politics of Survival*. Princeton 1978 (*Suleiman 1978*) and P. Birnbaum et al., *La classe dirigeante francaise. Dissociation, interpénétration, intégration*. Paris 1978; for a recent, more journalistic discussion and critique of the situation, A. Wickham and S. Coignard, *La nomenclatura francaise. Pouvoirs et privilèges*. Paris 1986.

16. Suleiman 1978, pp 69-71.

17. Conze-Kocka, in *Conze-Kocka 1985*; Kocka, *Bürgertum und Bürgerlichkeit als Probleme der deutschen Geschichte vom späten 18. zum frühen 20. Jahrhundert*, in J. Kocka (ed), *Bürger und Bürgerlichkeit im 19. Jahrhundert*. Göttingen 1987, pp 21-63; Kocka, *'Bürgertum' and professions in the 19th century: Two alternative approaches*, in *Burrage-Torstendahl 1990*, pp 62-74; P. Lundgreen, *Zur Konstituierung des 'Bildungsbürgertums': Berufs- und Bildungsauslese der Akademiker in Preussen*, in *Conze-Kocka 1985*, pp 79-108 .

18. H. Siegrist, *Professionalization as a process: Patterns, progression and discontinuity*, in Burrage-Torstendahl 1990, pp 177-202.

19. M. Burrage, *Unternehmer, Beamte und freie Berufe. Schlüsselgruppen der bürgerlichen Mittelschichten in England, Frankreich und den Vereinigten Staaten*, in H. Siegrist (ed), *Bürgerliche Berufe. Zur Sozialgeschichte der freien und akdemischen Berufe im internationalen Vergleich*. Göttingen 1988, pp 53-62 (Siegrist 1988); Burrage, *Beyond a sub-set: The aspirations of manual workers in France, the United States and Britain*, in *Burrage-Torstendahl 1990*, pp 151-176, esp pp 165.

20. On the associations and the professionalisation process of French engineers, Shinn, *Des Corps de l'Etat au scteur industriel: Genèse de la profession de l'ingénieur, 1750-1920*, in *Revue francaise de sociologie*, Vol. 19 1978, pp 39-77 (Shinn 1978).

21. Eg *VDI 1981* and N. Runeby, *Teknikerna, vetenskapen och kulturen. Ingenjörsundervisning och ingenjörsorganisationer i 1870-talets Sverige*. Uppsla 1976 (*Runeby 1976*).

22. Eg H. Siegrist, *Bürgerliche Berufe. Die Professionen und das Bürgertum*, in Siegrist 1988, pp 11-48; Torstendahl 1990a, pp 56-60.

23. On this question, further *Shinn 1978* and Torstendahl, *Engineers in industry, 1850-1910: Professional men and new bureaucrats. A comparative approach*, in C. G. Bernhard et al. (eds), *Science, Technology and Society in the Time of Alfred Nobel*. Oxford 1982, pp 253-70.

24. Further Torstendahl, in Conze-Kocka 1985.

25. This was an effect of Beuth's planning of the *Gewerbeinstitut* in Berlin, though not his primary aim, see H. J. Straube, *Chr. P. Wilhelm Beuth*. Berlin 1930. It was more of an aim to Nebenius in Baden, when founding the Karlsruhe Polytechnic, see F. Schnabel, *Die Anfänge des technischen Hochschulwesens*. Karlsruhe 1925. Only when some schools were transformed to *Technische Hochschulen* in the 1870s a true division of levels became stabilised, R. Rürup, *Die Technische Universität Berlin 1879-1979: Grundzüge und Probleme ihrer Geschichte*, in Rürup (ed), *Wissenschaft und Gesellschaft. Beiträge zur Geschichte der Technischen Universität Berlin 1879-1979*. Berlin 1979, pp 3-47, esp. 10-12.

26. Torstendahl, *Teknologins nytta. Motiveringar för det svenska tekniska utbildningsväsendets framväxt framförda av riksdagsmän och utbildningsadministratörer 1810-1870*. Uppsala 1975, pp 167-82; Runeby 1976, pp 195-279.

27. On the transformation of physicians in the 19th century in a continental European context, eg C. Huerkamp, *Der Aufstieg der Ärzte im 19. Jahrhundert. Vom Gelehrten Stand zum professionellen Experten: Das Beispiel Preussens*. Göttingen 1985 .

Chapter 3, Olof Ruin

In this essay I have restricted my references to works published by members of the 'Group for the Study of Higher Education and Research Policy', at the Department of Political Science at the University of Stockholm. Of course, there are a number of other researchers - in Sweden and abroad - who have studied these and related questions and made important contributions.

1. B. Wittrock and S. Lindström, *De stora programmens tid*. Stockholm 1984.

2. O. Ruin, *Studentmakt och statsmakt*. Stockholm 1979 (Ruin 1979). On the national planning of the 1960s, see B. Lindensjö, *Högskolereformen. En studie i offentlig reformstrategi*. Stockholm 1981.

3. On Sweden in a comparative perspective, see R. Premfors, *The Politics of Higher Education in a Comparative Perspective*. Stockholm 1980.

4. On 'democratisation' in Swedish higher education, see Ruin 1979 and O. Ruin, *Sweden: External Control and International Participation. Trends in Swedish Higher Education*, in H. Daalder and E. Shils (eds), *Universities, Politicians and Bureaucrats*. Cambridge 1982.

5. On 'corporativisation', see above note 4 and R. Premfors, *Facklig högskolepolitik. De fackliga organisationeras program och aktiviteter*. Stockholm/FRN 1981.

6. On UHÄ (NBUC), see O. Ruin, *UHÄ- en ny typ av verk*, in *Forskning om utbildning* 1979:4. For a comparative perspective, see A. Bladh, *Decentraliserad förvaltning. Tre ämbetsverk i nya roller*. Stockholm 1987. On 'decentralisation' as a dimension of the higher education reform of 1977, see Y. Myrman, *Sjösättningen av högskolereformen i Sverige*. Stockholm 1979 och 1985.

7. On the growing interest in research and research training, see R. Premfors, *Svensk forskningspolitik*. Lund 1986, also O. Ruin, *Reform, Reassessment and Research policy: Tensions in the Swedish Higher Education System*, in B. Wittrock and A. Elzinga (eds), *The University Research System. The Public Policies of the Home of Scientist*. Stockholm 1985.

Chapter 4, Thorsten Nybom

1. The flow of books and articles makes it almost impossible to have a reasonable command of the sources. The initial discussion in the Summer/Fall of 1986 with its 100 or so articles was already (1987) followed by an 'anthology phase', which was superseded by an 'evaluation and conference phase' in 1988. Each of these two latter produced an enormous amount of books. Not least due to the political changes, there are apparent signs of a coming reorientation in German historiography - and a renewed stream of books. For a survey eg; *'Historikerstreit'. Dokumentation einer Kontroverse um die Einzigartigkeit der national-sozialistischen Judenvernichtung. Munich* 1987 *('Historikerstreit')*; D. Dirner (ed), *Ist der Nationalsozialismus Geschichte? Zu Historisierung und Historikerstreit*. Frankfurt am Main 1987 *(Dirner (ed)1987)*; D. J. K. Peukert, *Wer gewann den 'Historikerstreit'? Keine Bilanz*, in P. Glotz (ed), *Vernunft riskieren. Klaus von Dohnanyi zum 60. Geburtstag*. Hamburg 1988. For contributions from two of the main adversaries; E. Nolte, *Das Vergehen der Vergangenheit. Anwort an meine Kritiker im sogennanten Historikerstreit*. Frankfurt am Main 1987, and H-U. Wehler, *Entsorgung der deutschen Vergangenheit? Ein polemischer Essay*. Munich 1988 *(Wehler 1988)*. For a leftist view; R. Kühnl, *Vergangenheit die nicht vergeht: Die Historiker-Debatte. Darstellungen, Dokumentation, Kritik*. Cologne 1987. For a right-wing contribution; R. Kosiek, *Historikerstreit und Geschichtsrevision*. Tübingen 1987. For an anti-Habermas contribution; I. Geiss, *Die Habermas Kontroverse. Ein deutscher Streit. Berlin 1988*. For comments from the international community; K. H. Jarausch, *Removing the Nazi Stain? The Quarrel of the German Historians*, in *German Studies Review (GSR)* 1988, pp 285-301 *(Jarausch, GSR 1988)*, also R. Evans, *In Hitler's Shadow*. London 1989 *(Evans 1989)* and esp. C. S. Maier, *The Unmasterable Past. History, Holocaust, and German National Identity*. Cambridge/Mass 1988. *(Maier 1988)*. (The central 'progressive' figure of the 'Historikerstreit', Jürgen Habermas, Professor of Philosophy at the Johann Wolfgang Goethe University in Frankfurt am Main (1929), is not only one of the most influential philosophers of our time and the spiritual heir of the 'Critical Theory' of Theodor Adorno and Max Horkheimer. The former student at the Frankfurt 'Institut für Sozialforschung' is also a towering figure

in German and international scholarly and political debate. For an intro to Habermas' thinking; Th. McCarthy, *The Critical Theory of Jürgen Habermas*. Cambridge/Mass. 1981, also note 10 below.).

2. In the German tradition my concept 'Cultural Sciences' includes both the humanities and the social sciences.

3. For an intro, G. C. Iggers, Introduction, in Iggers (ed), *The Social History of Politics. Critical Perspectives in West German Historical Writing since 1945*. Heidelberg 1985 (Iggers (ed) 1985), pp 1-48. On history today eg Wehler, *Das neue Interesse an der Geschichte*, in Wehler, *Aus der Geschichte lernen?* Munich 1988, pp 26-33 (*Wehler 1988a*).

4. *Jarausch, GSR 1988*, p 290.

5. For an initiated but slightly partisan view, see Wehler 1988, pp 131ff. For a political interpretation; G. Eley, *Nazism, Politics, and the Image of the Past: Thoughts on the West German Historikerstreit, 1986-1987*, in *Past and Present* 1988:121, pp 171-208 (*Eley, PaP*).

6. For an exception, see Hans Mommsen; eg, H. Mommsen, *Verordnete Geschichtsbilder? Historische Museumspläne der Bundesregierung*, in *Gewerkschaftliche Monatshefte* 1986:1, and H. Mommsen, *Stehen wir vor einer neuen Polarisierung der Geschichte in der BRD?*, in S. Miller (ed), *Geschichte in der demokratischen Gesellschaft*. Düsseldorf 1985, pp 71-83. On H. Mommsen note 93 below.

7. H. Mommsen, *Suche nach der 'Verlorenen Geschichte'?* in *'Historikerstreit'*, p 168, and H-A. Winkler, *Auf Ewig in Hitlers Schatten? Zum Streit über das Geschichtsbild der Deutschen*, in *Frankfurter Rundschau (FR)* Nov. 14. 1986. Also G. Hartman (ed), *Bitburg in Moral and Political Perspective*. Bloomington/Ind. 1986, and *Maier 1988*, pp 13.

8. Kohl used the expression 'die Gnade der Spätgeborenen' in an interview with A. Hillgruber, in the German conservative daily '*Die Welt*' Oct. 1. 1986. See also the row after the speech delivered by Philipp Jenniger (CDU), the speaker of the Bundestag, on Oct. 9. in memory of the so-called 'Reichskristallnacht' which started off the systematic persecution of the German Jews; the German liberal weekly *Der Spiegel* 1988:46.

9. Above note 7, also J. M. Markham, 'German Book Sets off New Holocaust Debate', in *The New York Times*, Sept. 6. 1986, and J. Miller, *Erasing the Past: Europe's Amnesia about the Holocaust*, in *New York Times Magazine* Nov. 16. 1986, also C. S. Maier, *Immoral Equivalence: Revising the Nazi Past for the Kohl Era*, in *The New Republic* Dec. 1986.

10. von Wiezsäcker, *A Voice from Germany*. London 1987.

11. For a discussion, Habermas, *Die Neue Unübersichtlichkeit*. Frankfurt am Main 1985, and Habermas, *Der philosopische Diskurs der Moderne. Zwölf Vorlesungen*. Frankfurt am Main 1989, also Habermas, *Die nachholende Revolution*. Frankfurt am Main 1990.

12. For an illuminating account, *Jarausch, GSR 1988*, pp 285-301 (Konrad H. Jarausch, Lurcy Professor of European Civilization at the University of North Carolina at Chapel Hill, has written extensively on 20th century German history and is an eminent judge of modern German historiography.).

13. Wehler, *Geschichtsbewusstsein in Deutschland. Entstehung, Funktion, Ideologie*, in *Wehler 1988a*, pp 19-25. (Hans-Ulrich Wehler (1930) Professor of History at the Bielefeld University, and his former Bielefeld colleague (presently Professor of Social History at the FU Berlin), Jürgen Kocka (1941) are often described as spiritual leaders of the 'progressive' or 'critical' school in German historical research. Even if this is not entirely correct, Kocka and Wehler - due to their professional standing, in modern German and American social and political history, and polemical sharpness - have played a decisive role in recent German historiography, and not least in the 'Historikerstreit'. For an intro; R. Fletcher, *Recent Developments in West German Historiography: The Bielefeld School and its Critics*, in *GSR* 1984:7.).

14. Kocka, *Wider die historische Erinnerung, die Geborgenheit vorspiegelt*, in *FR* 1988:2 (*Kocka, FR 1988:2*) and Wehler, *Geschichtbewusstsein in Deutschland*, in *Wehler 1988a*, p 23. Also R. Bichler, *Das Diktum von der historischen Singularität und der Anspruch des historischen Vergleichs. Bemerkungen zum Thema Individuelles versus Allgemeines und zur langen Geschichte deutschen Historikerstreits*, in K. Acham and W. Schulze (eds), *Zum Verhältnis von Einzel- und Gesamtanalyse in Geschichts- und Sozialwissenschaften*. Munich 1990, pp 169-91 (*Bichler 1990*).

15. K-F. Werner, *Die deutsche Historiographie unter Hitler*, in B. Faulenbach (ed), *Geschichtswissenschaft in Deutschland*. Munich 1974, also W. Schulze, *Deutsche Geschichtswissenschaft nach 1945*. Munich 1989 (*Schulze 1989*).

16. Wehler, *Geschichtsbewusstsein...*, in Wehler 1988a, and esp Schulze 1989.

17. This perspective has not least been discussed by Kocka, eg *Kocka, FR 1988:2*; Kocka, *Kritik und Identität. Nationalsozialismus, Alltag und Geographie*, in *Neue Gesellschaft Frankfurter Hefte* 1986:10 (*Kocka, NGFH*); Kocka, *Deutsche Identität und historischer Vergleich*, in *Aus Politik und Zeitgeschichte. Beilage zur WochenZeitung Das Parlament (APZ)* 1988:40/41 (*Kocka, APZ 1988:40/41*), and Kocka, *Geschichte als Aufklärung?*, in J. Rüsen (ed), *Die Zukunft der Aufklärung*. Frankfurt am Main 1988 (Rüsen (ed) 1988). Also Bichler 1990, p 191.

18. Eg, *Kocka, FR 1988:2*, and esp. Rüsen, *Historische Aufklärung im Angeschicht der Postmoderne: Geschichtswissenschaft im Zeitalter der 'neuen Unübersichtlichkeit'*, in *'Steitfall Deutsche Geschichte'*. Essen/Hibbing 1988 (*Streitfall 1988*), also Maier 1988, pp 168.

19. This does not apply exclusively to the discipline of history but includes the entire rational discussion of science and knowledge. The modern 'value-nihilism' or extreme relativism has - referring to the trivial fact that science and the scientific discourse has obvious social connotations - wanted to deny that science or scholarship has any specific qualities and binding rules. Usually, is done by referring to Th. Kuhn and P. Feyerabend. See S. Björklund, below pp. 122 and 128-9 (Björklund 1991).

20. The 'Alltagsgeschichte' is a very heterogenous group of historians, ranging from critical social historians to politically dedicated members of local 'History Workshops'. One of the common denominators is perhaps their interest in local social, economic and cultural life. Contrary to the critical social historians they are usually turning to anthropology, ethnology and 'semiotics' for inspiration and support; note 25 below.

21. Pronouced in Stürmer, *Dissonanzen des Fortschritts. Essays über Geschichte und Politik in Deutschland*. München 1986 (Stürmer 1986). For further references; Wehler 1988, pp 69 and 171.

22. Note 19, also H. Lübbe, *Über den Grund unseres Interesse an historischen Gegenstände. Kulturelle und politische Funktionen der historischen Geisteswissenschaften*, in H. Flashar (ed), *Geisteswissenschaften als Aufgabe. Kulturpolitische Perspektiven und Aspekte*. Berlin 1978, pp 179-93. Also *Kocka, NGFH*, pp 890; *Kocka, APZ 1988:40/41*; and Wehler 1988, pp 171. For a sharp criticism of 'everyday history', Wehler, *Alltagsgeschichte: Köningsweg zu neuen Ufern oder Irrgarten der Illusionen*, in Wehler 1988a, pp 130-51. Wehler maintains that the new-conservative 'revisionists' and the 'green' everyday historians represent the same kind of antirationalism. For a more nuanced 'progressive' criticism, Kocka, *Klassen oder Kultur? Durchbrüche und Sackgassen in der Arbeitergeschichte*, in Merkur 1982. For a positive view, *Eley, PaP*, p 201.

23. For an intro, W. Conze, *Evolution und Geschichte. Die doppelte Verzeitlichung der Menschen*, in *Historische Zeitschrift (HZ)* 1986:242. Also *Kocka, FR 1988:2*. Curiously enough, those who have criticised the 'critical' social historians don't seem to understand that *critique* in a theoretical context does not necessarily have negative connotations, but rather means 'to investigate the fundamental foundations', Björklund 1991.

24. See the first editorial of the journal of the 'progressive' school *'Geschichte und Gesellschaft' (GuG)* 1975:1.

25. For this particular strategy, see eg the German linguist G. Bauer, *Ett spektakel högt över historien*, in *Ordfront Magasin (Bauer, OM)* Stockholm 1988:6.

26. This does not include theoretically sophisticated social historians of an anthropological vein such as K. Tenfelde and D. J. K. Peukert; eg Peukert, *Alltag und Barbarei. Zur Normalität des Dritten Reiches*, in *Dirner (ed) 1987*, and Peukert, *Inside Nazi Germany. Conformity, Opposition, and Racism in Everday Life*. London 1987.

27. E.g. F. Brüggemeir and J. Kocka (eds), *Kontroversen um die Alltagsgeschichte*. Hagen 1985.

28. Pronouced in K-H. Bohrer, *Unzusammenhängende Notizen über Geschichte*, in Merkur Sept 1987 (Bohrer, Merkur), also Fleischer, *Zur Kritik des Historikerstreit*, in *APZ* 1988:40/41 (Fleischer, *APZ* 1988:40/41), further; Rüsen in Streitfall 1988.

29. Bohrer, Merkur.

30. Esp. Fleischer, *APZ* 1988:40/41, pp 7-10.

31. Bohrer, Merkur, also Lübbe, *Politischer Moralismus. Der Triumph der Gesinnung über die Urteilskraft.* Berlin 1987; and Fleischer, *APZ* 1988:40/41, pp 11-14.

32. This is one of the most common arguments against the 'progressive' or 'critical' social historians, for a discussion, Jarausch, *GSR* 1988, for an example Fleischer, *APZ* 1988:40/41, pp 11-14.

33. Eg Fleischer, *APZ* 1988:40/41, pp 8.

34. Habermas, *Historical Consciousness and Post-Traditional Identity. Remarks on the Federal Republic's Orientation to the West. Copenhagen May 14. 1987*, also Wehler 1988, pp 7.

35. The title of Habermas' first article was: *Eine Art Schadensabwicklung. Die Apologetischen Tendenzen in der deutschen Zeitgeschichtsschreibung* (A kind of 'discounting the damages'. Apologetic tendencies in modern German historiography), in *Die Zeit*, July 6, 1986.

36. Habermas, *Vom öffentlichen Gebrauch der Historie. Das offizielle Selbstverständnis der Bundesrepublik bricht auf, Die Zeit* Nov. 11. 1986. The Mommsen-quotation is from A. Heuss, *Theodor Mommsen und das 19. Jahrhundert.* Kiel 1956, p 224.

37. Eg, H. Möller, *Es kann nicht sein, was nicht sein darf*, in *'Historikerstreit'*, pp 322-30, and Th. Nipperday, *Unter der Herrschaft des Verdachts*, in *Die Zeit* Oct. 17. 1986. These allegations against Habermas et al. seem all the more irrelevant, as esp. Nolte's attempts to place the genesis of Auschwitz in Stalin's 'Gulag' and in the persecutions of the Kulak-farmers, and his unprecise hints of a declaration of war from the international Jewish community were immediately dismissed on solid empirical grounds, see Eberhard Jäckel, *Die elende Praxis der Untersteller*, in *Die Zeit*, Sept. 12. 1986. (*Jäckel, Die Zeit*) (On Thomas Nipperday, the brilliant, traditionalist Prof of Modern History at the University of Munich, (1927), *Wehler 1988*, pp 116, and *Maier 1988*, pp 12 and 34.

38. Nolte, *Zwischen Geschichtslegende und Revisionismus? Das Dritte Reich im Blickwinkel des Jahres 1980*, in *'Historikerstreit'*, pp 15-35 (Eng. version, in H. W. Koch (ed), *Aspects of the Third Reich*. London 1985), and Nolte, *Vergangenheit die nicht vergehen will*, in *Frankfurter Allgemeine Zeitung (FAZ)*, June 6. 1986. (Ernst Nolte (1923), Prof. of Modern History at FU Berlin, started out as a pupil of the philosopher Martin Heidegger and has remained somewhat of an outsider in the discipline. He established himself as an expert on fascism through his work *'Der Faschismus in seiner Epoche'*. Munich 1963. According to Nolte this book is the first part of an exposé of modern political ideologies. The 2nd volume is called *'Marxismus und Industrielle Revolution'*. Stuttgart 1983, the 3rd *'Deutschland und der Kalte Krieg'*. Munich 1974, and the last *'Der Europäische Bürgerkrieg 1917-1945: Nationalsozialismus und Bolschewismus'*. Berlin 1987. Already in some reviews of the earlier volumes Nolte was accused of the same apologetic tendencies that to an eminent degree started off the 'Historikerstreit', eg, F. Gilbert in *American Historical Review (AHR)* 1976:81, and the introduction in P. Gay, *Freud, Jews and other Germans*. New York 1978. For a devastating criticism of the last volume, H. Mommsen, *Das Ressentiment als Geschichtsschreibung. Anmerkungen zu Ernst Noltes 'Der europäische Bürgerkrieg'*, in *GuG* 1988: 495-512 (*H. Mommsen, GuG 1988*), and W. J. Mommsen, *Waren die Bolschewisten an allem Schuld*, in *Kölner Stadtanzeiger* 1988:9, p 1. For Nolte's own account of his particular type of 'philosopical history'; Nolte, *Philosophische Geschichtsschreibung heute*, in *HZ* 1986:4. For a critique, W. Schieder, *Der Nationalsozialismus im Fehlurteil philosophischer Geschichtsschreibung. Zur Methode von Ernst Noltes Europäische Bürgerkrieg*, in *GuG* 1989:1, pp 89-114.

39. For such allegation against Habermas; *Fleischer APZ 1988:40/41*; and Fleischer, *Die Moral der Geschichte. Zum Dispute über die Vergangenheit, die nicht vergehen will*, in *'Historikerstreit'*, pp 123-31. Also J. Fest, *Die geschuldete Erinnerung*, in *FAZ* Aug. 9. 1986, and K. Hildebrand, *Die Zeitalter der Tyrannen*, in *FAZ* Aug. 11. 1986 (*Hildebrand, FAZ*); H. Schulze, *Fragen die wir stellen müssen*, in *Die Zeit* Sept. 26 1986, and Möller in *'Historikerstreit'*, pp 322-30. (Joachim Fest (1926), is the author of a famous Hitler biography and one of the editors of the prestigous conservative daily 'Frankfurter

Allgemeine Zeitung' (FAZ). Helmut Fleischer (1927), is Prof. of Philosophy at the Technical University in Darmstadt, and was earlier an influential Marxist theoretician. Hagen Schulze (1943) is Professor of Modern History at the FU Berlin and one of the 're-inventors' of 'Geopolitics' in modern German history.).

40. For sharp criticism, *Jäckel, Die Zeit*. Also Kocka, *Hitler sollte nicht mit Pol Pot verdrängt werden*, in *FR* Sept. 23 1986 (*Kocka, FR Sept. 86*), and *Kocka, NGFH*.

41. Esp. Jäckel, *Die Zeit*, and H. Mommsen, *GuG* 1988, also Kocka, FR Sept. 86.

42. (Michael Stürmer (1938) Prof. of Modern History at the University of Erlangen, presently Director of a well-financed think-tank, 'Die Ebenhausen Stiftung Wissenschaft und Politik', is first and foremost a specialist in the history of the German Empire; eg, '*Regierung und Reichstag im Bismarckstaat*'. Düsseldorf 1974; (ed), *Das Kaiserliche Deutschland*. Düsseldorf 1977; '*Die Reichsgründung*'. Munich 1984 and '*Bismarck*'. Munich 1987. Stürmer started out as a pronounced 'critical' or 'progressive' historian in the 60s. From the so-called 'Tendenzwende' in the mid-70s he turned to what the Germans call 'Cultural History' (18th century), and in the early 80s he appeared as one of the more prominent ideologues in the immediate entourage of Chancellor Kohl. In later years he has been trying very hard to reinstate the geopolitical theories of Rudolf Kjellén, Klaus Haushofer et al, from the turn of the century, and particularly the thesis of the so-called unfortunate German 'Mittellage'. He is also frequently appearing as a 'philosopher' of history and advocating the thesis that the primary duty of historical research is to create and reinforce 'national identity'. He is also propounding the view that the West Germans have a particular lack of historical 'consciousness' and 'identity'. According to Stürmer this is partly due to the activities of the 'critical' school; eg, Stürmer, *Geschichte im Geschichtslosen Land*, in *FAZ* April 25. 1986, on Stürmer, see eg *Maier 1988*, pp 43.

43. Wehler 1988, esp. pp 174. Also Kocka, NGFH and Maier 1988, pp 115.

44. For an exposé of geopolitics from Kjellén and Treitschke via Carl Schmitt and Karl Haushofer to the American historian David Calleo, Wehler 1988, pp 174.

45. Andreas Hillgruber (1925-1989) was Professor of Contemporary History at the University of Cologne and 'doyen' among the traditional historians of World War II, specialising in military and political history; eg '*Hitlers Strategie. Politik und Kriegführung 1940-41*'. Frankfurt am Main 1965; '*Der Zweite Weltkrieg. Strategie, Politik und Kriegsziele der grossen Mächte*'. Stuttgart 1982. Hillgruber turned early and definitely against the ambitions of the 'critical' social historians, and advocated a traditional type of political history with foreign policy as the 'prime mover'; eg, Hillgruber, *Politische Geschichte in moderner Sicht*, in *HZ* 1973:216. On Hillgruber, H. H. Herwig, *Andreas Hillgruber: Historian of 'Grossmachtspolitik', 1871-1945*, in *Central European History* 1982:15.

46. Habermas in *Die Zeit July 6. 1986*, and *Eley, PuP*. Also *Maier 1988*, pp 19 and *Evans 1989*. The title of Hillgruber's book is '*Zweierlei Untergang. Die Zerschlagung des deutschen Reiches und das Ende des europäischen Judentums*' (Double destruction. The crushing of the German Reich and the end of the European Jews). Berlin 1986.

47. Kocka, NGFH, and Kocka, FR 1988:2.

48. For an example of this particular 'strategy', Nipperday, *Die Zeit*.

49. On the simplistic leftist view of a 'rebutted conservative conspiracy', Jarausch, GSR 1988, pp 288, for an example, Kühnl 1987, pp 282-86.

50. The fourth of Habermas' named adversaries, Klaus Hildebrand (1941) Professor of Modern History at the University of Bonn is hardly of the same professional stature as the other. He is sometimes - slightly unfairly - labelled as 'Hillgruber's butler'. He has nevertheless, gained a rather influential position as a conservative publicist (FAZ, Die Welt) and in research policy. Hildebrand is an ardent adversary of the 'critical' social history, eg, '*Geschichte oder Gesellschaftsgeschichte*', in *HZ* 1976:223. He is also a passionate critic of the 'Sonderweg' thesis, and was earlier, among other things, propounding the opinion that the only 'special German case' was Hitler; eg, 'Monokratie oder Polykratie? Hitlers Herrschaft und das Dritte Reich', in G. Hirschfeld and L. Kettenacker (eds), *Der Führerstaat: Mythos oder Realität*. Stuttgart 1981 (Kettenacker (ed) 1981), and 'Deutscher Sonderweg und Drittes Reich', in W. Michalka (ed), *Die nationalsozialistische Machtergreifung*. Paderborn 1984 (Michalka (ed) 1984). Now he is rather

advocating some kind of Noltean 'totalitarianism' theory; *Hildebrand, FAZ*. On German scholars; Kürschner, *Deutscher Gelehrten-Kalender*. Berlin 1987.

51 Wehler 1988, pp 197, also Jarausch, GSR 1988, p 249, and W. J. Mommsen (interview with Th. Nybom, Uppsala March 29. 1989).

52. For an intro. to Stürmer's thinking, Stürmer 1986, and Stürmer, *Das Ruhelose Reich 1866-1918*. Berlin 1983, also Stürmer, *Das industrielle Deutschland*. 1982. For a critique of Stürmer's geopolitics, V. Berghahn, *Geschichtswissenschaft und Grosse Politik*, in *APZ* 1987:11, also H-J. Puhle, *Die neue Ruhelosigkeit. M. Stürmers nationalpolitische Revisionismus*, in *GuG* 1987. (Ironically enough, 'geopolitics' could in a way be said to have constituted the *original* and positive 'Sonderweg' thesis of German 'Kultur' versus Gallic/Anglosaxon 'Civilization' before WWI. It got its most brilliant expression in Thomas Mann's famous '*Betrachtungen eines Unpolitischen*' in 1918).

53. Stürmer 1986, p 196.

54. Stürmer, *Kein Eigentum der Deutschen*, in Stürmer 1986 and Nolte in '*Historikerstreit*', pp 13-35. Also Hildebrand, *FAZ*, and Hildebrand's review of Nolte's article in H. W. Koch (ed) 1985, in *HZ* 1986:242.

55. Hillgruber 1986.

56. Iggers in Iggers (ed) 1985, pp 1-48.

57. Eg Wehler, *Max Webers Klassentheorie und die neuere Sozialgeschichte*, in *Wehler 1988a*, pp 15, and Kocka, *Max Webers Bedeutung für die Geschichtswissenschaft*, in Kocka (ed), *Max Weber der Historiker*. Göttingen 1986, pp 13-27.

58. Eg Wehler 1988, pp 143, and Wehler, *Was ist Gesellschaftsgeschichte?*, in Wehler 1988a, pp 115-29. Also Kocka, NGFH, and Kocka in Rüsen (ed) 1988.

59. Nipperday, 'Historismus und Historismuskritik heute', in Nipperday, *Gesammelte Aufsätze zur neueren Geschichte*. Göttingen 1976, pp 59-73. Also Wehler 1988, pp 116, and notes 21 and 22 above, also Iggers in Iggers (ed) 1985, pp 38 for further references.

60. Stürmer 1986, passim. For a detailed comment, Wehler 1988, pp 69-79 and 171-74, and Maier 1988, pp 44 and 142.

61. On Treitschke and the 'Bourussianism', A. Dorpalen, *Heinrich von Treitschke*. New Haven 1957.

62. For two different but equally interesting examples; Möller in '*Historikerstreit*', pp 322-30, and Fleischer, APZ 1988:40/41.

63. ibidem.

64. Fleischer, APZ 1988:40/41.

65. Iggers in Iggers (ed) 1985, pp 44.

66. If one limits oneself to the so-called 'classics' who have discussed similar problems one could mention; Barrington Moore Jr, *Social Origins of Dictatorship and Democracy* (1966), Rolf Dahrendorf, *Society and Democracy in Germany* (1965/67), David Schoenbaum, *Hitler's Social Revolution* (1966) and *Nolte 1963*(!). For a recent 'progressive' contribution, see J. Herf, *Reactionary Modernism: Technology, Culture and Politics in Weimar and the Third Reich*. Cambridge 1984. For a discussion of the theories of fascism Kühnl, *Faschismustheorien*. Hamburg 1979 (Kühnl 1979). For an overview of the research on the Third Reich, I. Kershaw, *Der NS-Staat. Geschichtsinterpretationen und Kontroversen im Überblick*. Reinbek 1988.

67. Kocka, *Der 'deutsche Sonderweg' in der Diskussion*, in *GSR* 1985:2 (Kocka, GSR 1985) and Kocka, APZ 1988:40/41, also the discursive essay by Jarausch, *Illiberalism and beyond: German History in Search of a Paradigm*, in *Journal of Modern History* 1982, pp 268-84, and H. Grebing, *Der 'deutsche Sonderweg' in Europa 1806-1945. Eine Kritik*. Stuttgart 1986..

68. Iggers in Iggers (ed) 1985, pp 44.

69. For a discussion, Maier 1988, ch4, pp 100-20.

70. For a discussion on the 'domination of Politics' in the 1930s, T. Mason, *Der Primat der Politik. Politik und Wirtschaft im Nationalsozialismus*, in *Das Argument* 1966:41 and Nybom, *The Swedish Social*

Democratic State. A Tradition of Peaceful Revolution, in D. Ashford (ed), *New Perspectives of Comparing Public Policies across Countries*. 1991(fc).

71. Th. Veblen, *Imperial Germany and the Industrial Revolution* (1915); J. A. Schumpeter, *Social Classes and Imperialism* (1927); and A. Gerschenkron, *Bread and Democracy in Germany* (1943).

72. F. Stern, *The Politics of Cultural Despair*. Berkeley 1961; G. L. Mosse, *The Crisis of German Ideology*. New York 1964.

73. For an illustration of the span of the 'progressive' discussion; eg H. Kaelble, *Der Mythos von der rapiden Industrialisierung in Deutschland*, in *GuG* 1983, Wehler, *Wie bürgerlich war das deutsche Kaiserreich?*, in Kocka (ed), *Bürger und Bürgerlichkeit im 19. Jahrhundert*. Göttingen 1987 (*Kocka (ed) 1987*), also Kocka, *Bürgertum und Bürgerliche Gesellschaft im 19. Jahrhundert. Europäische Entwicklungen und deutsche Eigenarten*, in Kocka (ed), *Bürgertum im 19. Jahrhundert im europäischen Vergleich*. Munich 1988.

74. On the Marxist-Leninist standpoint, H. J. Steinbach, 'Die Theorie des "Organisierten Kapitalismus" als antimarxistisches Konzept zur Darstellung des staatsmonopolistischen Kapitalismus in der Sozialge-schichtsschreibung in der BRD', in *Jahrbuch für Geschichte* 1978, pp 339-72.

75. On this new 'coalition', Iggers in Iggers (ed) 1985, pp 44, and Maier 1988, pp 105.

76. Above pp 308 and 311.

77. Evans (ed), *Society and Politics in Wilhelmine Germany*. London 1978; Evans, 'The Myth of Germany's Missing Revolution', in *New Left Review* 1985:149 and G. Eley and D. Blackbourn, *The Peculiarities of German History: Bourgeois Society and Politics in 19th Century Germany*. Oxford 1980(85).

78. On the implications of the attacks on the 'Sonderweg'-thesis, Iggers in Iggers (ed) 1985, pp 45, also W. J. Mommsen, 'Weder Leugnen noch Vergessen befreit von der Vergangenheit. Die Harmonisierung des Geschichtsbildes gefährdet die Freiheit', in *Historikerstreit*, p 309, and Kocka, APZ 1988:40/41, pp 22-28. Also Maier 1988, pp 105.

79. Eg, Wehler's debate with Eley in the German Journal *Merkur* (May, June, Aug.), and Wehler in Kocka (ed) 1987.

80. For a discussion Kocka, GSR 1985, and Kocka, *The Debate about the German 'Sonderweg'*, in *Journal of Contemporary History* 1988:23. Also Craig, *The German Mystery Case*, in *The New York Review of Books (NYRB)* 1986:1. On German liberalism, J. J. Sheehan, *Der deutsche Liberalismus 1770-1914*. Munich 1983, and D. Langewiesche (ed), *Liberalismus im 19. Jahrhundert. Deutschland im europäischer Vergleich*. Göttingen 1988.

81. Kocka, APZ 1988:40/41, p 26, and Maier 1988, p 109.

82. H. A. Turner, *Big Business and the Rise of Hitler*, in *AHR* 1969; Turner, *Faschismus und Kapitalismus in Deutschland*. Göttingen 1972; Turner, *Hitlers Einstellung zu Wirtschaft und Gesellschaft vor 1933*, in *GuG* 1977:1; and Turner, *Die Grossunternehmer und der Aufstieg Hitlers*. 1986.

83. Eg, R. Neebe, *Die Verantwortung der Grossindustrie für das Dritte Reich*, in *HZ* 1987:224, also Kocka, *Ursachen des Nationalsozialismus*, in *APZ* 1980:25.

84. Kühnl 1979.

85. Kühnl 1979, and W. Abendroth, *Sozialgeschichte der europäischen Arbeiterbewegung*. Frankfurt am Main 1965 and Abendroth, 'Das Problem der sozialen Voraussetzungen der Faschismus', in *Das Argument* 1970:58.

86. J. Falter, *Wer verhalf der NSDAP zum Sieg? Neuere Forschungsergebnisse zum parteipolitischen und sozialen Hintergrund der NSDAP-wähler 1924 33*, in *APZ* 1979:28/29; R. Hamilton, *Who voted for Hitler?* Princeton 1982; Kater, *The Nazi Party: A Social Profile of Members and Leaders, 1919-1945*. Cambridge/Mass 1983; Kater, *Medizin und Mediziner im dritten Reich*, in *HZ* 1987:244; K. H. Jarausch, *The Unfree Professions: German Lawyers, Teachers and Engineers between Democracy and National Socialism*. New York 1988 (*Jarausch 1988*); D. Hänisch, *Sozialstrukturelle Beststimmungsgründe des Wahlverhaltens in der Weimarer Republik*. Duisburg 1983. See also the various contributions in Kettenacker (ed) 1981.

87. The theory existed already in 30s (Theodor Geiger), before Lipset reformulated it, Kühnl 1979, pp 90-110.

88. Below note 90.

89. Above note 85, esp. Kater 1985, and Jarausch 1988.

90. For Borchardt's rather controversial theses, Borchardt, *Wachstum, Krise und Handlungspielräume der Wirtschaftspolitik*. Göttingen 1982. For a discussion, G. D. Feldman, *Die Nachwirkungen der Inflation auf die Geschichte 1924-33*. Munich 1986. For criticism, C-D. Krohn, '"Ökonomische Zwangslage" und das Scheitern der Weimarer Republik. Zu Knut Borchardts Analyse der deutschen Wirtschaft in der 20er Jahren', in *GuG* 1982, and C. S Maier, 'Die Nicht-Determiniertheit ökonomischer Modelle. Überlegungen zu Knut Borchardts These von der "kranken Wirtschaft" der Weimarer Republik', in *GuG* 1985, pp 275-94.

91. P. Stadler, 'Rückblick auf einen Historikerstreit. Versuch einer Berurteilung aus nichtdeutscher Sicht', in *HZ* 1988:247, pp 23.

92. Iggers (ed) 1985 (Henry Turner is also a long standing member of the editorial board of the central journal of the 'critical' school (*GuG*).

93. M. Broszat, *Plädoyer für eine Historisierung des Nationalsozilismus*, in *Merkur* May 1985, and Broszat, 'Was heisst Historisierung des Nationalsozialismus?', in *HZ* 1988:247. Martin Broszat (1926-1988) was Director of the prestigous Munich Institute for Contemporary History (Institute für Zeitgeschichte) and one of the major historians of the Nazi state. Brozat's insistence on the institutional continuities within German history and hence also including the Nazi state resembles the analysis of Hans Mommsen (1930), Professor of Modern History at the Ruhr University in Bochum, who has been propounding the thesis of 'the leaderless state', eg the Third Reich as a battlefield between different competing bureaucracies. H. Mommsen is an eminent scholar of the history of the Weimar Republic and the Third Reich. In 1989 he published the 'definite' history of the Weimar Republic. On H. Mommsen's contributions to the 'Historisation' debate; H. Mommsen, in *'Historikerstreit'*, pp 156-73, and H. Mommsen, *Die Realisierung des Utopischen: Die 'Endlösung der Judenfrage' im Dritten Reich*, in *GuG* 1983. For a discussion, Saul Friedländer, *Überlegungen zur Historisierung des Nationalsozialismus*, in Dirner (ed) 1987, pp 34-50. (Heinrich-August Winkler (1938) Professor of Modern History at the University of Freiburg, is an eminent historian of 19th and 20th German history. He has among other things written extensively on German liberalism and published a three volume work on the German labour movement in the Weimar Republic.).

94. 'But isn't historisation natural and necessary? Shouldn't history look for parallels, integrate the singular phenomenon within the complex and general pattern of a narrative in which the singularity loses its sharp characteristics? Indeed, but this does not mean historisation - at any cost', cit S. Friedländer, '"A Past that refuses to go away". On recent historiographical debates in the Federal Republic of Germany about National-Socialism and the Final Solution', in *Zeitschrift für Religion und Geistesgeschichte* 1987:39, p 99. About the post-modern type of 'historisation', Maier 1988, pp 168, and Jarausch, GSR 1988, p 290, also Friedländer in Dirner (ed) 1987, pp 34, and Kocka, FR 1988:2. For illustrations eg Fleischer, APZ 1988: 40/41, and Bauer, OM.

95. H. Mommsen in *Historikerstreit*, pp 157.

96. This lumping-together becomes perhaps most absurd in the case of Christian Meier (1929), the moderate Professor of Ancient History at the University of Munich who among other things has published a seminal book of politics in ancient Greece. The then chairman of the German Historical Association (Verband Historiker) tried, without being unclear about his fundamental views, to reconcile the scholarly community, Meier, *Kein Schlusswort*, in *Historikerstreit*, pp 264-74, also Meier, *40 Jahre nach Auschwitz. Deutsche Geschichtserinnerungen heute*. Munich 1987. Richard Löwenthal (1908) is Directory member of the 'Forschungsinstitut der deutschen Gesellschaft für Auswärtige Politik' in Bonn and a long-time friend of the former Chancellor Willy Brandt. Kurt Sontheimer (1928) is Professor of Political Science at the University of Munich, and a prominent figure in West German public debate. As regards Wolfang Mommsen and H-A. Winkler - even though they in certain ways are representatives of the 'critical' school - have both repeatedly stressed their 'non-alignment' to any of the existing 'schools'.

97. The Lamprecht Controversy at the turn of the century was really about the legitimacy of a historical discipline that also included social, economic and cultural dimensions, and of a discipline which used theories and methods from the expanding social sciences. These attempts were met with fierce resistance

from the ruling elite of traditional, conservative political historians, R. von Bruch, *Wissenschaft, Politik und Öffentliche Meinung. Gelehrtenpolitik im wilhelminischen Deutschland*. Husum 1980, (Bruch 1980) and P. Seifert, *Der Streit um Karl Lamprechts Geschichtsphilosophie*. Augsburg 1925, also B. vom Brocke, *Kurt Breysig: Geschichtswissenschaft zwischen Historismus und Soziologie*. Lübeck 1971 and Bichler 1990, pp 171-83.

98. One indication of the changes in the opinion after the 'Historikersteit' was the election of Wolgang Mommsen as the new chairman of the prestigious 'Verband Historiker' 1988. Wolfgang J. Mommsen (1930) Professor of Modern History at the University of Düsseldorf, and former Director of the German Institute in London is a scholar of a very wide range. He has written extensively on imperialism and international politics, and is *the* outstanding expert on the life and work of Max Weber and on Wilhelmine intellectual life. He has also made numerous contributions on German historiography.

99. I am not least referring to the position and activities of the German historical discipline before World War I, see e.g., W. J. Mommsen, *Deutsche Geschichtswissenschaft im Kaiserreich*. 1989 (ms). In recent time one could perhaps contemplate the fate of economics!

100. A. W. Johansson, *Den nazistiska utmaningen*. Stockholm 1988, p 13.

101. E.g. the editor of *Der Spiegel*, Rudolf Augstein, 'Die neue Auschwitz-Lüge', in *Der Spiegel* Oct. 6. 1986. The possible exception would be Nolte, H. Mommsen, *GuG* 1988 and Julius H. Schoeps, 'Treitschke redivivus. Ernst Nolte und die Juden', in *Tagesspiegel* Dec. 1. 1988.

102. Maier 1988, and Craig, *Facing up to the Nazis*, in *NYRB* 1989:1. (Charles S. Maier, Prof. of History at Harvard University has not only written what I consider to be the still unsurpassed account and analysis of the 'Historikerstreit', he is also an eminent scholar in 20th-century European history. Among his works, see the path-breaking *Re-casting Bourgoise Europe: Stabilization in France, Germany, and Italy in the Decade after World War I*. (Princeton 1975).

Chapter 5, Björn Wittrock

1. For an extensive treatment of these aspects eg P. Wagner, *Sozialwissenschaften und Staat: Frankreich, Italien, Deutschland, 1870-1980*. Frankfurt am Main 1990; P. Wagner, C. H. Weiss, B. Wittrock and H. Wollmann (eds), *Social Science and Modern States: National Experiences and Theoretical Crossroads*. Cambridge 1991 and P. Wagner, B. Wittrock and R. H. Whitley (eds), *Discourses on Society: The Shaping of the Social Science Disciplines*. Dordrecht 1991 (Wagner, Wittrock, Whitley), but also D. Rueschemeyer and T. Skocpol (eds), *Social Knowledge and the Origins of Social Policies* (fc) and P. Manicas, *A History and Philosophy of the Social Sciences*. Oxford 1987 (Manicas 1987).

2. An interesting account of the deeply politically implicated German ethnographic-linguistic research focusing on Eastern Europe and German-speaking minorities is given in M. Burleigh, *Germany turns Eastwards: A Study of 'Ostforschung' in the Third Reich*. Cambridge 1988.

3. This argument has recently been advanced by L. Trädgårdh, 'Varieties of Volkish Ideologies: Sweden and Germany 1848-1933', in B. Stråth (ed), *Language and the Construction of Class Identities*. Göteborg 1990 and B. Wittrock and P. Wagner, *The Discursive Constitution of Policy: State-Centered Societies in Transition*, in D. Ashford (ed), *Comparing Public Policies*. Pittsburgh 1991. An excellent overview of the discussion of the German 'Sonderweg' is given in J. Kocka, 'German History before Hitler: The Debate about the German "Sonderweg"', in *German Studies Review*, Vol. 23:1 1988, pp 3-16 (Kocka 1988).

4. The sheer disbelief, not to say cultural shock, with which the events of the late fall of 1989 were received by many a West German intellectual of the post-war generation is nicely captured in P. Süskind's little article 'Deutschland, eine "Midlife-crisis"', in *Der Spiegel* 1990:38, pp 116-25. Süskind reports how, sitting in Paris, he cannot believe that the opening of the wall is not just the signal to a long-awaited democratisation of the GDR much like that already underway in Poland, Hungary and Czechoslovakia but to a transformation of Germany. The concomitant and instantaneous shift in acceptable political rhetoric appears to him as nothing short of incomprehensible; how could politicians who for years had said that reunification was maybe something for the next century but certainly not for this one, and who

had always gone to great lengths in avoiding even the slightest slip into nationalistic rhetoric of a type which would have been considered as normal in any number of Western countries, and who had brought up a generation of young West Germans to take this to be the only acceptable political style, enthusiastically change all of this almost overnight?.

5. For an interesting analysis of the societal and cultural consequences of this type of continuity in the Swedish case see S. Strömholm, Self-doubt in Uniform, in *The Times Higher Education Supplement* 13-07-90. Hans-Ulrich Wehler's review of Horst Möller's history of Germany between 1763 and 1815 is characteristically called '*Deutschland? Aber wo liegt es?* (Germany? But *where* is it?), in *Die Zeit* 1989:42.

6. An overview of the 'Fischer controversy' is given in J. A. Moses, *The Politics of Illusion: The Fischer Controversy in German Historiography*. London 1975. For the more recent 'Historikerstreit', see eg H-U. Wehler, *Entsorgung der deutschen Vergangenheit. Ein polemischer Essay zum Historikerstreit*. München 1988 (Wehler 1988); K. H. Jarausch, *Removing the Nazi Stain? The Quarrel of the German Historians*, in *German Studies Review* 1988, pp 285-301 and Th. Nybom, *Humanities as a Mirror of Society. The 'The Battle of the Historians' in the Federal Republic of Germany in the late 1980s*, above pp 59-75. See also Kocka 1988. Although recognised in general terms, Germany's position as an intellectual lead nation in the late 19th and early 20th century has, when it comes to the histories in specific fields and individual disciplines, often been subjected to a kind of whiggish history writing. Thus the exemplary role of German universities in this period is more or less generally acclaimed, e.g. A. Flexner, *Universities: American, English, German*. London/Oxford/New York (1930) 1968 but also for a contemporary German view F. Paulsen, *Wesen und geschichtliche Entwicklung der deutschen Universitäten*, in W. Lexis(Hg), *Die deutschen Universitäten. Für die Universitätsausstellung in Chicago 1893*. Berlin 1893, and F. Paulsen, *Die deutschen Universitäten und das Universitätsstudium*. Berlin 1902, also T. H. Ellwein, *Die deutsche Universität. Vom Mittelalter bis zur Gegenwart*. Königstein 1985. However, the fact that for instance early American political science was thoroughly imbued with German notions about the role of the state has been more or less conveniently forgotten but for painstaking and detailed recent scholarship, eg J. G. Gunnell, *In Search of the State: Political Science as an Emerging Discipline*, in Wagner, Wittrock and Whitley but also Manicas 1987.

7. A classical analysis of the waning economic power of Germany in Central and Eastern Europe in the wake of the defeat in the First World War and of the efforts to resurrect that power under Nazi rule is A. Teichova, *An Economic Background to Munich: International Business and Czechoslovakia, 1918-1938*. Cambridge 1979.

8. F. Ringer, *The Decline of the German Mandarins*. Cambridge 1969; F. Ringer, *The German Mandarins Reconsidered*. Berkeley/Center for Studies in Higher Education, Occasional Papers No. 20 1981, and F. Ringer, 'Differences in Cross-National Similarities among Mandarins', in *Compative Studies in Society and History*, Vol. 28 1986:1, pp 145-61 (*CSSH 1986:1*), also S-E. Liedman, 'Institutions and Ideas: Mandarins and Non-Mandarins in the German Academic Intelligensia', in *CSSH 1986:1*, pp 119-44 and S-E. Liedman, *Reply* (Ringer), in *CSSH 1986:1*, pp 165-68.

9. F. Meinecke, *Die deutsche Katastrophe. Betrachtungen und Erinnerungen*. Leipzig/Wiesbaden 1946.

10. In many ways the major wartime works of the authors mentioned - Hesse's *'Das Glasperlenspiel' (The Glass Bead Game)*. Zürich 1943, Jünger's *'Auf den Marmorklippen'* (On the Marble Cliffs). Erlenbach/Zürich 1939), Popper's *'The Open Society and Its Enemies I-II'*. London 1945 and Adorno-Horkheimer's *'Dialektik der Aufklärung'* (Dialectic of Enlightenment). New York 1944 - may be read as just so many reinterpretations of the very possibility of classicist Germanic-European culture, as epitomised by the 'Mandarins', against the background of the Nazi disaster. Ironically it would seem that Popper's liberal and anti-historicist political philosophy and Jünger's deeply conservative and purely literary and metaphorical analysis represent two archetypal efforts to save parts of that heritage, whereas Hesse, Adorno and Horkheimer, in their whole style so much a product of 'Mandarin' culture, represent the most radical intellectual break with that culture in ways which by decades foreshadowed debates which came to characterise the intellectual discussion in the West in the latter part of the 20th century, whether during 'the student rebellion' of the 1960s and 70s or the debate about 'post-modernism' in the 1980s and 90s.

11. Needless to say, on a personal level the returning emigre intellectuals testify to this dilemma and in some cases, such as the famous author Alfred Döblin ('Berlin Alexanderplatz'), found no way out of it except renewed emigration.

12. See eg Th. Nybom, above pp 59-75 for an overview of this debate but also Wehler 1988 and J. Habermas, *Die nachholende Revolution*. Frankfurt am Main 1990 (Habermas 1990).

13. S. Meuschel, 'Kulturnation oder Staatsnation? Zur Renaissance der Suche nach nationaler Identität in den beiden deutschen Staaten', in *Leviathan* 1988, pp. 406-35 (*Meuschel 1988*) and M. R. Lepsius, '"Ethnos" und "Demos": Zur Anwendung zweier Kategorien von Emmerich Francis auf das nationale Selbstverständnis der Bundesrepublik und auf die Europäische Einigung', in *Kölner Zeitschrift für Soziologie und Sozialpyschologie*, 1986:38, pp 751-59.

14. For an interesting discussion, H. Wagner, 'Die politische Dreieinigkeit von Nation, Staat und Europa. Erwägungen zur Identitätskrise der Deutschen', in H. Wagner, A. Schwan and R. Hahn (Hg), *Fragen und Antworten zur deutschen Identität*. FU Berlin/Fachbereich Politische Wissenschaft, Occasional Papers No. 19 Mai 1987, pp 1-28.

15. A series of the key policy documents pertaining to this development are reprinted in P. Longerich (Hg), *Was ist das deutsche Vaterland: Dokumente zur Frage der deutschen Einheit 1800-1990*. München/Zürich 1990. For an interesting discussion of the more recent developments see Meuschel 1988, also W. Schulze, 'Die zweigeteilte Geschichte', in *Die Zeit* 1990:36.

16. Some reactions are nicely captured in G. Hofmann, 'Die Entdeckung der Bundesrepublik. 'Wir' und das Kontrasterlebnis DDR: Seit zehn Monaten denken die Westdeutschen neu über sich nach', in *Die Zeit* 1990:31.

17. Eg Habermas 1990 and N. Luhmann, 'Dabeisein und Dagegensein: Anregungen zu einem Nachruf auf die Bundesrepublik', in *Frankfurter Allgemeine Zeitung* 22-08-90.

18. E. Gellner, *Nations and Nationalism*. Oxford 1983 (Gellner 1983) but also R. Torstendahl, *Transformation of Professional Education in the 19th Century*. Paper at the 1987 Research on Higher Education Program International Conference. Stockholm 1987.

19. For interesting analyses along these lines Gellner 1983 and J. Habermas, 'Historical Consciousness and Post-Traditional Identity: Remarks on the Federal Republic's Orientation towards the West', in *Acta Sociologica*, Vol. 31 1988:1.

20. See the classic by Octavio Paz '*El Laberinto de la Soledad*'. Fondo De Cultura Economica. 1959.

21. This process is extensively discussed in Gellner 1983 and A. Giddens, *The Nation State and Violence*. Cambridge 1985.

Chapter 6, Rune Premfors

1. Th. Anton, 'Policy-Making and Political Culture in Sweden', in *Scandinavian Political Studies* 1969:4, p 94.

2. Th. Anton, *Administered Politics. Elite Political Culture in Sweden*. Boston 1980, esp. pp 13.

3. Eg A. Elzinga, 'Research, Bureaucracy, and the Drift of Epistemic Criteria', in B. Wittrock and A. Elzinga (eds), *The University Research System. The Public Policies of the Home of Scientists*. Stockholm 1985.

4. It ought to be mentioned that the questionnaire was distributed in 1983 - although I think little has changed since then with respect to matters discussed in this essay.

5. Actually they were 197 since three of the 'top bureaucrats' were identical with three of the 'R&D managers' - cf further below in the text - who had already responded to the questionnaire.

6. In the parliament ('Riksdag') elected in 1982 34 per cent among the Members had a basic higher education degree. For data on the educational background of Ministers and Junior Ministers, see H. Bergström, *Rivstart? Om övergången från opposition till regering*. Stockholm 1987, pp 232 and pp 249.

7. A. Mellbourn, *Byråkratins ansikten*. Stockholm 1979, pp 93.

8. Admittedly, virtually all studies in this vein have focused on the use of social science research knowledge, not on research knowledge in general. For the pioneering study, see N. Caplan et al, *The Use of Social Science Knowledge in Policy Decisions at the National Level*. Univ. of Michigan: Institute for Social Research. 1975; and for the best work to date, see C. Weiss, *Social Science Research and Decision-Making*. New York 1980 (Weiss 1980).

9. The proportion reporting that research knowledge is of great or very great importance among respondents with personal experience of doing research is 70 per cent, while among those having no such experience the comparable figure is 60 per cent.

10. This somewhat odd expression is of course due to a peculiar feature of Swedish governmental organisation: the Ministries proper are very small bodies (about 200 professionals on average) while the bulk of central government consists of more than a hundred autonomous central agencies - each of whom, however, 'belongs' to a particular ministry.

11. Weiss 1980, Chapter 1.

Chapter 7, Burton R. Clark

1. An outstanding comparative analysis of the German, French, English and American national systems of higher education as primary international models or centers of learning may be found in J. Ben-David, *Centers of Learning: Britain, France, Germany, United States*. New York 1977. In three central chapters, Ben-David compared these systems in respect to general-liberal education, professional education, and research and research training. The latter chapter in particular has stimulated my current research and the central concerns of this paper.

2. A three-year, five-country study that would be intensive as well as extensive was made possible by a generous 1987 grant from the Spencer Foundation. The grant has helped support both field research and sustained analysis in each of the five countries, particularly in the American case. 'We' - the ten or so scholars most centrally and continually involved - are grateful to the Spencer Foundation for its generous support.

3. Centrally involved colleagues were: for Germany, Claudius Gellert; for Britain, Tony Becher, Mary Henkel, and Maurice Kogan; for France, Guy Neave and Richard Edelstein; for the United States, Patricia Gumport; and for Japan, Morikazu Ushiogi, Tatsuo Kawashima, and Fumihiro Maruyama. I was responsible for the overall coordination of the study. Two small working-party conferences held at UCLA during the summers of 1988 and 1989 helped measurably to direct our efforts along common paths, while allowing for different configurations of thought and effort appropriate for quite varied national contexts.

4. The concept of 'substantive growth' is developed in W. Metzger, 'The Academic Profession in the United States', in B. R. Clark (ed), *The Academic Profession: National, Disciplinary, and Institutional Settings*. Berkeley/Los Angeles 1987, pp 123-208 (Metzger 1987). The conceptions of members of disciplines as 'tribes' and their respective bodies of knowledge as cognitive 'territories' are developed in T. Becher, *Academic Tribes and Territories: Intellectual Enquiry and the Cultures of Disciplines*. Stony Stratford/(Milton Keynes) 1989.

5. The concept of 'high knowledge components' is take from C. Kerr, 'A Critical Age in the University World: Accumulated Heritage Versus Modern Imperatives', in *European Journal of Education (EJE)*, Vol 22, No 2, 1987, pp 183-93.

6. The concept of reactive growth, in contrast to substantive growth, is developed in Metzger 1987. Metzger saw reactive growth as growth that follows from increases in student numbers, that is, pressures on the input side of the higher education system. I have here extended the concept to include reaction to increases in labour market demands - the demands of training that play upon the output side of the system.

7. Kerr, in *EJE*, esp pp 188-89.

8. Eg the work of the Institute for Scientific Information (ISI), Philadelphia, Pennsylvania, as expressed in their new (1989-90) newsletter *Science Watch: Tracking Trends and Performance in Basic Research*. ISI has constructed an elaborate Science Indicators Database that is internationally available for quick-and-

ready use. As of 1989, its Database tracks more than '8,200 currently active specialty areas in science'! Also very active in monitoring national scientific performance, and more broadly in research forecasting, is The Science Policy Research Unit, University of Sussex, England. See John Irvine and Ben R. Martin, *Foresight in Science: Picking the Winners*. London 1984.

9. For basic categories that distinguish among disciplines and specialties on the basis of their cognitive domains and related styles of research, see Becher 1989.

10. T. N. Clark, *Prophets and Patrons: The French University and the Emergence of the Social Sciences*. Cambridge/Mass. 1973; and Guy Neave and Richard Edelstein, *The Research Training System in France: A Micro-Study of Three Academic Disciplines*, in B. R. Clark (ed), *The Research Foundations of Graduate Education: Germany, Britain, France, United States, and Japan* (fc).

Chapter 8, Gunnar Bergendal

1. J. B. White, *Heracle's Bow. Essays on the Rhetoric and Poetics of the Law*. Madison/Wisconsin 1985, p 31.

2. H-G. Gadamer, *Truth and Method*. London 1955. p 12 (Gadamer 1955).

3. A. Glucksmann, *Descartes c'est la France*. Paris 1987, p 154 (Glucksmann 1987).

4. J. C. Nyiri & B. Smith (eds), *Practical Knowledge: Outlines of a Theory of Traditions and Skills*. London/New York/Sydney 1988, pp 68 and 70 (Nyiri 1988).

5. Nyiri 1988, p 23.

6. L. Kolakowski, *Metaphysical Horror*. Oxford 1988, p 118.

7. Glucksmann 1987, p 80.

8. M. Polanyi, *Personal Knowledge. Towards a Post-Critical Philosophy*. London/Melbourne/Henley 1958.

9. Gadamer 1955, pp 329-30.

10. H. Arendt, *The Life of the Mind*. New York/London 1971/1981, p 176.

11. K. Jaspers, *Reason and Existenz*. London 1956, pp 133-4.

12. M. Cooley, *Architect or Bee? The Human Price of Technology*. London (Paperback) 1987, p 56.

13. R. Pernoud, *Histoire de la Bourgeoisie en France*. Paris 1960/1981, pp 289 and 294.

14. H. L. Dreyfus, *The Socratic and Platonic Basis of Cognitivism*, in *AI & Society*. Vol 2, 1988:2.

15. H. Arendt, *Totalitarianism*. SanDiego/New York/London 1966, p 23.

16. E. Canetti, *The Human Province*. London 1986, p 245.

17. T. W. Adorno, *Against Epistemology*. Oxford 1982, p 44.

18. L. Hertzberg, *Vetenskapens auktoritet och människans uppgifter*, in *Finsk Tidskrift* 10/1987. (Swedish - my trans).

19. K. Jaspers, *Über Bedingungen und Möglichkeiten eines neuen Humanismus*. Stuttgart (1951) 1962, p 13 (My trans).

20. L. Wittgenstein, *Über Gewissheit/On certainty*. Oxford 1969, par 139.

21. Glucksmann 1987, p 208.

Chapter 9, Stefan Björklund

This essay is part of a larger manuscript, that hopefully, will soon appear as a book.

1. M. Aldskogius, *Samverkan för anknytning till forskning och forskarutbildning inom vårdområdet. En sammanfattning av läget 1987*. 1988 (mim). Also B. Abrahamsson, *Forskningsanknytning. Om sambandet mellan forskning och grundutbildning*. UHÄ (NBUC)-rapport 1977:10, and the commission by the

government to the NBUC, 24-07-86, as well as the subsequent pronouncement of the NBUC: *'Samverkan för forskningsanknytning'* 28-06-88.

2. G. Wallén (ed), *Omvårdnad som vetenskap och ideologi*. Rapport från institutionen för Vetenskapsteori Nr. 140/Göteborg 1983.

3. For a discussion see J-J. Jensen, *Forskning og undervisninmg på universiteterne. Et samspil?*. Esbjerg 1986.

4. L. Laudan, *Progress and its Problems. Towards a Theory of Scientific Growth*. Berkeley 1978, p 12. It might sometimes even be difficult to distinguish the method from the object of study, P. Whitley, *The Intellectual and Social Organisation of Sciences*. Oxford (1984) 1987, p 133.

5. Compare P. Scott, *Ideologies of the University*, in G. Bergendal (ed), *Knowledge Policies and the Tradition of Higher Education*. Stockholm 1984, p 44 (Bergendal 1984): 'The university has ceased to be an academic community, except in vacuous rhetoric, and has instead become a shared administrative environment.'

6. F. Marton, D. Hounsell and N. Entwistle (eds), *Hur vi lär*. Stockholm 1986, pp 74 and 123 (Marton et al. 1986).

7. *Forskning om Högskolan*. UHÄ (NBUC)-Rapport 1986:14. On this kind of side-effects, see also J. Elster, *Sour Grapes. Studies in the Subversion of Rationality*. Cambridge (1983) 1985, pp 43.

8. For my discussion on the theory of science, see esp. W. Newton-Smith, *The Rationality of Science*. Boston 1981, and D. Shapere, *Reason and the Search of Knowledge. Investigations in the Philosophy of Science*, in *Boston Studies in the Philosophy of Science, Vol 76*. Doordrecht 1984 (Shapere 1984).

9. B. Kanitscheider, *Analytic and Synthetic Philosophy*, in G. Andersson (ed), *Rationality in Science and Politics*. Doordrecht 1984, p 159 (Andersson 1984).

10. P. Feyerabend, *Against Method. Outline of Anarchistic Theory of Knowledge*. Atlantic Highlands 1975, p 195. For a more positive interpretation of Feyerabend, see P. A. Roth, *Meaning and Method in the Social Sciences. A Case for Methodological Pluralism*. Ithaca 1987 (Roth 1987), pp 98.

11. For sympathetic references, see Bergendal, *Several Dimensions or Only One?*, in Bergendal 1984, pp 81, 120 and 127.

12. B. Barnes and D. Edge (eds), *Science in Context. Readings in the Sociology of Science*. Milton Keynes 1982, pp 2 and B. Barnes, *Scientific Knowledge and Social Theory*. London 1974, p 455.

13. M. Polanyi, *Personal Knowledge. Towards a Postcritical Philosophy*. Chicago (1958) 1962, pp 287 (Polanyi 1962), and K. Popper, *Normal Science and its Dangers*, in I. Lakatos and A. Musgrave (eds), *Criticism and the Growth of Knowledge*. Cambridge 1970, p 55.

14. In reality, Polanyi is also talking about co-existence between faith and doubts. But he does it to show how the necessity of 'Committment' in spite of the persisting doubts. Hence, the sub-title 'postcritical' of his book, see Polanyi 1962, pp 294 and 374, also D. F. Norton, *David Hume. Common Sense Moralist, Sceptical Methaphysician*. Princeton 1982, pp 279.

15. A. Rescher, *Dialectics. A Controversy-Oriented Approach to the Theory of Knowledge*. Albany 1977 (Rescher 1977), p 123, and M. Barth and E. C. W. Krabbe. *From Axiom to Dialogue. A Philosophical Study of Logics and Argumentation*. Berlin 1982 (Barth, Krabbe 1982), pp 23.

16. W. W. Bartley, *Logical Strength and Demarcation*, in Andersson 1984, pp 69.

17. Harman is making a distinction between 'arguments' where the 'rule of implication' is present and which is cumulative, on the one hand, *and* 'reasoning' where the 'rule of inference and revision' is present, on the other. Harman's distinction is not incompatible with my position, but I am using the concept 'argument' in a more colloquial and everyday meaning of the word, see G. Harman, *Change in View. Principles of Reasoning*. Cambridge/Mass. 1985, pp 3 (Harman 1985).

18. This is not synonymous with the futile demands, that all concepts and terms must be defined, see P. T. Gearch, *Reason and Argument*. Oxford 1976, p 38 (Gearch 1976).

19. Shapere 1984, p 178 and pp 235. For a discussion on Toulmin, see T. Nilstun, *Moral Reasoning. A Study in the Moral Philosophy of S. E. Toulmin*. Lund 1979, pp 78. For Quine, see J. Dancy, *Introduction to Contemporary Epistemology*. London 1985, p 94 (Dancy 1985) and Roth 1987, pp 6.

20. H. Albert, *Traktat über kritische Vernunft*. Tübingen 1968, p 13, also K-O. Apel, *The Problem of Philosophical Foundations in Light of Transcendental Pragmatics of Language*, in Baynes, K., Bohman, J. and MacCarthy, Th. (eds), *After Philosophy. End or Transformation*. Cambridge/Mass. (1987) 1989 (Baynes et al 1989), p 251.

21. Apel in Baynes et al 1989, p 263 and R. E. Flathman, *The Philosophy and Politics of Freedom*. Chicago 1987, p 136 (Flathman 1987).

22. The Rawlsian 'reflexive equilibrium' with its oscillating between our moral intuition and rational construction, can be seen as an application of this idea, see J. Rawls, *A Theory of Justice*. Cambridge/Mass. 1971, p 20.

23. This is called 'dialectics', see Rescher (1977) and Barth and Krabbe (1982), also F. H. Eemeren, R. Grootendorst and T. Kruiger, *The Study of Argumentation*. New York 1984 (Eemeren et al 1984).

24. The whole truth is, alas, that not even this my operation could be labelled an 'inner dialogue' in the proper sense of the word. Instead I am actually reproducing my colleague Olof Petersson's critique of a previous paper, at a seminar in Uppsala.

25. Shapere 1984, pp 223, also M. Buchmann, *Improving Education by Talking: Argument or Conversation*, in *Teachers College Record*, Vol 86:3 1985, pp 441, and M. Buchmann, *Maximizing the Effectiveness of the Educational System*, in E. Goodlad (ed), *The Ecology of School Rewards: 86th Yearbook of the National Society for the Study of Education*. Chicago 1989, pp 170 (Buchmann 1989) Buchmann sees the problems very much the same way I do, but like Rapoport she is still suspicious of 'argumentation'. Compare her emphasis on communication, not just of beliefs but of justifications of beliefs, loc cit.

26. A. Rapoport, *Fights, Games and Debates*. Ann Arbor (1960) 1970, p 273 and pp 285.

27. R. Rorty, *Philosophy and the Mirror of Nature*. Princeton 1970, p 218: 'For hermeneutics to be rational is to be willing to pick up the jargon of the interlocutor rather than to translate it to his own'.

28. Plato, *Dialoger, Gorgias*. Stockholm 1965, p 95.

29. Boëthius, *Filosofins tröst*. Stockholm 1987, p 28, where the Goddess is chasing the Muses of poetry away and takes hold of the philosopher.

30. H-G. Gadamer, *Truth and Method*. London (1965) 1981, p 330b.

31. A. MacIntyre, *After Virtue. A Study in Moral Theory*. London (1981) 1987, p 163 and Eemeren et al 1984, p 263, also L. Lövlie, *Det pedagogiske argument. Moral, auktoritet og selvprövning i opdragelse*. Otta 1984, pp 61.

32. This is a dimension in Habermas' thinking which has led to his being accussed of 'fundamentalism' - against his own vehement protests, see S. K. White, *The Recent Work of Jürgen Habermas. Reason, Justice and Modernity*. Cambridge (1988) 1989, p 57 and pp 128 (White 1989).

33. L. von Bertalanffy, *General Systems of Theory. Foundations-Developments-Applications*. New York 1968, p 192 (Bertalanffy 1968).

34. T. M. Amabile, *The Social Psychology of Creativity*. New York 1983, pp 91 (Amabile 1983). Competition and positive feedback could, according to some research results, stimulate creativity: Amabile 1983, pp 100 and 114.

35. Amabile 1983, p 146 and Hodgson, in Marton et al 1986, p 142.

36. G. Dworkin, *The Theory and Practice of Autonomy*. Cambridge 1988, p 26 (Dworkin 1988) and Buchmann 1989, pp 177.

37. Eemeren et al 1984, p 209 and Baynes et al 1989, p 5.

38. For this particular interpretation of 'rhetoric', see Ch. Perelman, in Ch. Perelman and L. Olbrechts-Tyteca, *The New Rhetoric. A Treatise on Argumentation*. London 1971.

39. J. Derrida, *Margins of Philosophy*. Brighton (1982) 1986, pp XXVII.

40. H. S. Kariel, *The Feminist Subject Spinning in the Postmodern Project*, in *Political Theory*, Vol 18:2 1990, pp 257.

41. R. Rorty, *Contingency, Irony and Solidarity*. Cambridge 1989, pp 122 (Rorty 1989).

42. Rorty 1989, pp 26 and 51.

43. Rorty 1989, pp 141.

44. Furthermore, it is quite possible that the mathematical structure of chess is of a universal nature and is not a mere construction, see R. Penrose, *The Emperor's New Mind. Concerning Computers, Minds and the Laws of Physics.* Oxford 1989, p 96.

45. S. Lukes, *Some Problems about Rationality,* in *Archives Européennes de Sociologie 1967:VIII,* pp 247 and J. Margolis, *Texts without Referents (The Persistence of Reality). Reconciling Science and Narrative.* Oxford 1989, p 41.

46. C. R. Berger, *Social Power and Interpersonal Communication,* in M. L. Knapp and G. R. Miller (eds), *Handbook of Interpersonal Communication.* Beverly Hills 1985, pp 439.

47. The best-known champion of this view is probably Peter Winch, see White 1989, p 19. In the concept 'scientification', there is an intrinsic critique against the alledged disrespect in science towards practically all other kinds of knowledge.

48. cit B. Barry, *(A Treatise of Justice. Vol I) Theories of Justice.* London 1989, p 165 (Barry 1989).

49. A. Rescher, *Rationality. A Philosophical Inquiry into the Nature of Belief Systems and Personality Systems.* Oxford 1988, pp 141 (Rescher 1988).

50. J. Habermas, *Theorie des Kommunikativen Handelns. Bd. 1: Handlungsrationalität und gesellschaftliche Rationalisierung.* Frankfurt am Main 1981, pp 152 (Habermas 1981). In reality, Habermas' thinking could very easily include 'disputation', see for instance Habermas 1981, pp 25.

51 J. Elster, *The Market and the Forum: Three Varieties of Political Theories,* in J. Elster and Aa. Hylland (eds), *Foundations of Social Choice Theory.* Cambridge 1986, pp 112.

52. Dworkin 1988, p 45. Dworkin distinguishes between the reason to consider 'the *judgements* of authorities', and the *reason* to consider 'the *authorities'* judgements' to be valid. But one should observe that in both cases there must be *reasons* given. To accept an authority by referring to *reasons* means at least implicitly, that one has also evaluated his/her *arguments*.

53. H. Niser and E. S. Quade (eds), *Handbook of Systems Analysis. Overview of Users, Procedures, Applications and Practises.* Chichester 1985, where the concept 'system' refers to any cluster of causatively dependent phenomenons, and 'systems analysis' is undertaken in order to get a proper foundation for decisions. My concept is obviously more comprehensive. In Swedish political science 'systems analysis' became fashionable through the works of David Easton. His fundamental theoretical concepts can be found in *'Framework'*, but in his major work *'Systems Analysis'* (1965), he is trying to develop the theoretical concepts into tangible hypothesies. See also K. W. Deutsch, *The Nerves of Government. Models of Political Communication and Control.* New York (1963) 1967 (Deutsch 1967); E. Lazlo, *Introduction to Systems Philosophy.* New York 1972 and A. Etzioni, *The Active Society. A Theory of Societal and Political Processes.* London 1968.

54. R. E. Lane, *Political Man.* New York 1972, p 16 and P. E. Converse, *The Nature of Belief Systems in Mass Publics,* in D. E. Apter (ed), *Ideology and Discontent.* New York 1964, pp 207. For additional references, see also S. Björklund and O. Westin, *Politisk socialisation som effekt av utbildning. 1) Politisk åskådning som utbildningsmål. 2) Gruppen som arbetsform.* Uppsala universitet/PU-enheten 1974 and 1975.

55. Deutsch 1967, p 147 and W. Buckley, *Sociology and Modern Systems Theory.* Englewood Cliffs/NJ 1967, pp 48 (Buckley 1967), see also Bertalanffy 1968, pp 92, 97 and 191.

56. B. Collins, *Social Psychology. Social Influence, Attitude Change, Group Processes and Prejudice.* Reading/Mass. 1970, p 20.

57. Buckley 1967, p 83 and R. W. Cobb, 'Belief-System Perspectives: Assessment of a Framework', in *Journal of Politics* 1973, p 128.

58. On Quine's epistemology, see Dancy 1985, p 94 and Roth 1987, pp 6. On the connections between freedom, autonomy and a comprehensive 'belief systems', see S. A. Benn, *Theory of Freedom.* Cambridge 1986, p 179.

59. On 'reductio in absurdum', see Gearch 1976, pp 27.

60. White 1989, p 50.

61. D. King, *Toleration*. London 1976, pp 130.

62. *Ny vårdutbildning (VÅRD 77)/SOU 1978:50*, p 72 and H. Egidius and A. Norberg, *Teorier i omvårdnadsarbete*. Solna 1983, pp 117 and 125. Also *Lärare för skola i utveckling (LUT 74)/SOU 1978:80*), p 77 and I. Gabrielsson, *Riktlinjer, problemställningar, erfarenheter*, in *Lodet och spujtspetsen. En skrift om konstnärligt utvecklingsarbete*. Kungl. Musikaliska Akademiens skriftserie 50, Stockholm 1985, pp 222.

63. According to Coleman this represents an underdeveloped field in theory: '. . . most theory that is based on methodological individualism . . . disregards the existence of social norms . . . altogether. ', J. S. Coleman, 'Social Theory, Social Research and a Theory of Action', in *American Journal of Sociology* Vol 91 1985/86.

64. R. Hardin, *Morality within the Limits of Reason*. Chicago 1988, p 179.

65. cit Barry 1989, p 165.

66. Rescher 1988, p 101.

67. H. F. Pitkin, 'Slippery Bentham: Some Neglected Cracks in the Foundation of Utilitarianism', in *Political Theory*, Vol 18:1 1990, pp 104, and B. Williams, *Ethics and the Limits of Philosophy*. Cambridge/Mass. 1985, p 17A. Sen, *The Standard of Living*. Cambridge (1987) 1988, pp 7.

68. C. Taylor, *Human Agency and Language. Philosophical Papers I*. Cambridge 1985, pp 270 and Flathman 1987, pp 117 and 150.

69. Subjectivism is commonly seen as a necessary consequence of relativism. Herrnstein-Smith for instance, thinks both are consequences of the 'Münchhausen Trilemma', B. Herrnstein-Smith, *Contingencies of Value. Alternative Perspectives for Critical Theory*. Cambridge/ Mass. 1988, p 42, pp 63 and p 128.

70. Eemeren et al 1984, p 3.

71. E. H. Gombrich, *Art and Illusion. A Study in the Psychology of Pictorial Representation*. Oxford (1960) 1988, p 267 (Gombrich 1988).

72. Gombrich 1988, p 275.

73. Gombrich 1988, p 319.

74. On the role of tradition see also I. Stravinskij, *Poetics of Music: In the Form of Six Lessons*. Cambridge/Mass. (1942) 1982, p 67 (Stravinskij 1982).

75. J. Elster, 'Tolkning - kunst eller vitenskap?', in *Nytt Norsk Tidsskrift* 1987:2, pp 61.

76. B. Smith, in J. C. Nyiri and B. Smith (eds), *Practical Knowledge: Outlines of a Theory of Traditions and Skills*. London 1988, pp 192. Also Amabile 1983, pp 18 and 32, and A. Koestler, *The Three Domains of Creativity*, in D. Dutton and M. Kransy (eds), *The Concept of Creativity in Science and Art*. den Haag 1981, p 2. See also Stravinskij 1982, p 50: 'Step by step, link by link, it will be granted him to discover the work'. For a similar view, see also P. Hindemith, *Musik i vår tid*. Stockholm 1965, p 38.

Chapter 10, Birgitta Odén

1. E. Rudd, *The Highest Education: A Study of Graduate Education in Britain*. London 1975.

2. This article is a revised version of a lecture held at a Conference: '*Studies of Higher Education and Research Organisation*', at Rosenön/Dalarö, June 6-10 1983, initiated by Eskil Björklund.

3. For full documentation, see my forthcoming book *Forskarutbildningens miljö 1890-1975* (The Changing Milieu of Graduate Education in Sweden 1890-1975). Lund/Summer 1991. The present article includes only a few key references.

4. Odén, 'The Didactic of the Highest Education', in G. Behre & L-A. Norborg (eds), *Geschichtsdidaktik, Geschichtswissenschaft, Gesellschaft*. Stockholm 1985 (Odén 1985).

5. S. Gustavsson, *Debatten om forskningen och samhället*. Uppsala 1971. One example in Sweden, of this model, is the works on university history, by the former Vice-Chancellor at Uppsala, Professor Torgny Segerstedt. See also S. Lindroth, *The History of Uppsala University, 1477-1977*. Uppsala 1976.

6. G. Kahlson, *Minerva och bulldoggen*. Stockholm 1944, and G. Myrdal, *Universitetsreform*. Stockholm 1945.

7. The traditional historical introductions to the numerous official government investigations are often characterised by a purely administrative perspective. This could also be said of many of the existing historical works on different universities, see, for instance, J. Weibull, *Lunds universitets historia IV*. Lund 1968.

8. K. Fridjonsdottir, *Vetenskap och politik. En kunskapssociologisk studie*. Malmö 1983.

9. Recently, M. Riedel, 'Wilhelm von Humboldts Begründung der "Einheit von Forschung und Lehre" als Leitidée der Universität', in *Zeitschrift für Pädagogik 14, Beiheft Historische Pädagogik*. Basel 1977.

10. C. E. McClelland, *State, Society and University in Germany, 1700-1914*. Cambridge 1980.

11. T. N. Clark, *Prophets and Patrons: The French University and the Emergence of the Social Sciences*. Harvard 1973.

12. R. Gilpin, *France in the Age of the Scientific State*. Princeton 1968.

13. B. Gustafsson, Forskarutbildningens mål, in *Tiden* 1982:10, pp 609-20.

14. *Odén 1985*.

15. Odén, *Överföring av värderingar genom forskarutbildning*, in *'Vardag och evighet'. Festskrift till Hampus Lyttkens*. Lund 1981.

16. G. Bergendal, *Higher Education and Manpower Planning in Sweden*. Stockholm (UNESCO) 1977, also T. Husén, *Universiteten och forskningen*. Stockholm 1975.

17. P. Stevrin, *Den samhällsstyrda forskningen*. Stockholm 1978.

18. Odén 1985.

19. S. Gustavsson, *1985 års forskningsproposition*, in *Tiden* 1982:10, pp 605-8.

20. This applies in particular to the evaluation of Swedish history, commissioned by the Swedish Council for Research in the Humanities and the Social Sciences (HSFR), in 1988, see H. Landberg (ed), *Historia i belysning*. Stockholm/HSFR 1988. Concerning the goals and ambitions of the students, see esp *Bli lärd i Lund. Humanistiska synpunkter på forskarhandledningen*. Lund/PU-enheten 1983:125.

21. *Proposition 1986/87:80*, p 23. Government decision from the Ministry of Education, 10-11-1988.

22. See also T. Hägerstrand, in G. Ström (ed), *Erövra universiteten åter*. Stockholm 1984, pp 21.

23. *Report from PU-Enheten*/Lund 1982:113; 1982:118; 1983:124 and 1984:131.

24. Bli lärd i Lund, p 56.

Chapter 11, Martin Trow

Adapted from a paper presented to a conference on 'American Exceptionalism - A Return and Reassessment', Nuffield College, Oxford University, England, April 14-16, 1988.

1. F. Rudolph, *The American College and University: A History*. New York 1962, pp 47-48.

2. It is hard to estimate the proportion of the college age cohort who go on to some form of post-secondary education, since so much of higher education is also 'continuing education', available all through life. About 75 per cent of young Americans finish high school. In a follow-up of the high school graduation class of 1972, roughly two-thirds of those graduates report having had some exposure to higher education seven years later, which would mean about 47 per cent of the cohort, and about 35 per cent had earned a bachelors degree by 1984, see C. Adelman, *A Basic Statistical Portrait of American Higher Education*. Paper prepared for the Second Anglo-American Dialogue on Higher Education. Princeton/NJ, Sept. 1989.

3. R. Geiger, *The Limits of Higher Education: A Comparative Analysis of Factors Affecting Enrollment Levels in Belgium, France, Japan and the United States*, Working Paper of the Higher Education Research Group, Yale University New Haven/Conn. 1980, p 18, and R. Geiger, *Private Sectors in Higher Education*. Ann Arbor 1986 (*Geiger 1986*).

4. 'Facts in Brief', in *Higher Education and National Affairs*, Sept. 1988, p 3, and U. S. Department of Education. National Center for Education Statistics, *Digest of Education Statistics*. Washington DC. 1988, p 29, Table 23 (Digest 1988).

5. M. Trow, *American Higher Education: Past, Present, and Future*, in *Educational Research* Vol 17 1988, p 19(Trow 1988).

6. Digest 1988, p 140.

7. University of California: *The Last Five UC Budgets*, in *UC Focus* Vol 2 1987, p 21, and *Profile* 1990.

8. Th. W. Heyck, *The Idea of a University in Britain, 1870-1970*, in *History of European Ideas*, Vol 8 1987, pp 205-19, and P. G. Moore, 'University Financing 1979-1986', in *Higher Education Quarterly* Vol 41 1987, pp 25-41. Government policy is currently to reduce that proportion.

9. S. Rothblatt, *Modular Systems*. Paper prepared for the Anglo-American Conference on Higher Education. Princeton/NJ., Sept. 1987.

10. Also below, p 167, for discussion of faculty freedom.

11. M. Trow, *Comparative Reflections on Leadership in Higher Education*, in *European Journal of Education* Vol 20 1985, pp 143-59 (Trow 1985).

12. M. Trow, 'Comparative Perspectives on Higher Education in the UK and the US', in *Oxford Review of Education* Vol 14 1988, pp 81-96, and M. Trow, 'The Robbins Trap: British Attitudes and the Limits of Expansion', in *Higher Education Quarterly* Vol 43 1989:1, pp 55-75.

13. H. Wasser, 'Instrumental versus Disciplinary Curricula: A Comparative Perspective', in *European Journal of Education* Vol 20 1985, p 69.

14. M. Trow, *Problems in the Transition from Elite to Mass Higher Education*, in *Policies for Higher Education. General Report on the Conference on Future Structures of Post-Secondary Education*. Paris/OECD 1974, pp 55-101.

15. E. L. Boyer, *College: The Undergraduate Experience in America*. New York 1987, and A. Bloom, *The Closing of the American Mind*. New York 1987.

16. Trow 1988.

17. N. P. Eurich, *Corporate Classrooms: The Learning Business*. Princeton/Carnegie Foundation for the Advancement of Teaching 1985, and S. K. Bailey, *Academic Quality Control*. Washington DC/American Association for Higher Education 1979.

18. *Learning Opportunities for Adults*. General Report (Vol 1) Paris/OECD 1977.

19. Trow 1985.

20. Geiger 1986.

21. Though most 'private' universities on the Continent, eg, church-related universities in Belgium and the Netherlands, are fully funded by the state, and resemble the public institutions in their governance arrangements.

22. H. H. Hyman and C. R. Wright, *Education's Lasting Influence on Values*. Chicago 1979, K. A. Feldman and T. M. Newcomb, *The Impact of College on Students* (Vol 2). San Francisco 1969.

Chapter 12, Eskil Björklund

*Dr Eskil Björklund retired from his position as Director of *The Council for Studies of Higher Education* (formerly, *The Research on Higher Education Programme*), in May 1989. He has published a short historical account of the Programme's policy and activities: '*Two Decades of Swedish Research of Higher Education*', in *Studies of Higher Education and Research* 1989:2. His successor, Dr Thorsten Nybom, divides his time between the Directorship and an Associate Professorship of History at Uppsala University.

Chapter 13, Sverker Gustavsson

* A slightly revised essay originally published in L. Lewin (ed), *Festskrift till Carl-Arvid Hessler*, Uppsala 1987.

1. Key phrase in the speech made by Secretary of State George C. Marshall at Harvard University on the 5th June 1947, announcing the Plan. *The European Recovery Program. Basic Documents and Background Information*. Washington D. C/United States Government Printing Office, 1947, p 2.

2. *Science, Economic Growth and Government Policy*. Paris/OECD, 963, pp 15 et seq.

3. R. L. Geiger, 'The Home of Scientists' in B. Wittrock and A. Elzinga (eds), *The University Research System. The Public Policies of the Home of Scientists*. Stockholm 1985, pp 53-74 (Geiger 1985). His works include, for example, *To Advance Knowledge: the growth of American Research Universities, 1900-1940*. New York 1986 and *Private Sectors in Higher Education*. Ann Arbor/Mich. 1986.

4. *The Research System*, Vol 3. Paris/OECD, 1974, p 197.

5. Geiger 1985, p 71.

6. M. Walzer, *Spheres of Justice*. New York 1983 (Walzer 1983).

7. Walzer 1983, p 20.

8. Geiger 1985, p 71.

9. I have enlarged on the importance of this distinction in my essay *'Where Research Policy Erred'*, in P. R. Baehr and B. Wittrock (eds), *Policy Analysis and Policy Innovation*. London 1981, pp 45-58.

Chapter 14, Roger L. Geiger

1. David Madsen, *The National University: Enduring Dream of the USA*. Detroit 1966; Philip A. Bruce, *History of the University of Virginia, 1819-1919: The Lengthening Shadow of One Man*. New York 1920; Howard H. Peckham, *The Making of the University of Michigan, 1817-1967*. Ann Arbor/Mich. 1967.

2. Brooks Mather Kelley, *Yale: A History*. New Haven 1974; Edward D. Eddy, Jr, *Colleges for Our Land and Time: the Land-Grant Idea in American Education*. New York 1957; Morris Bishop, *A History of Cornell*. Ithica 1962.

3. Hugh Hawkins, *Pioneer: a History of the Johns Hopkins University, 1874-1889*. Ithica 1960; Charles W. Eliot, 'Liberty in Education', in R. Hofstadter and W. Smith (eds), *American Higher Education: a Documentary History*. Chicago 1961, p 712.

4. W. Carson Ryan, *Studies in Early Graduate Education: The Johns Hopkins, Clark University, and the University of Chicago*. New York/Carnegie Foundation for the Advancement of Teaching 1939; Orrin L. Elliott, *Stanford University: the First Twenty-Five Years*. Stanford 1937; Richard J. Storr, *Harper's University: the Beginnings - a History of the University of Chicago*. Chicago 1966; John W. Burgess, *Reminiscences of an American Scholar*. New York 1934, pp 191-244.

5. Samuel Eliot Morison, *Three Centuries of Harvard, 1636-1936*. Cambridge/Mass. 1936, pp 367 and 371-2; Henry James, *Charles W. Eliot: President of Harvard University, 1869-1909*. Boston 1930:II, pp 3-28; H. Hawkins, *Between Harvard and America: the Educational Leadership of Charles W. Eliot*. New York 1972, pp 45-79.

6. R. L. Geiger, 'Research, Graduate Education, and the Ecology of American Universities: An Interpretive History', in S. Rothblatt and B. Wittrock (eds), *The Three Missions* (forthcoming); R. L. Geiger, *To Advance Knowledge: the Growth of American Research Universities, 1900-1940*. New York 1986 (*Geiger 1986*); Edwin E. Slosson, *Great American Universities*. New York 1910.

7. The classic account remains, Laurence R. Veysey, *The Emergence of the American University*. Chicago 1965.

8. Geiger 1986, pp 67-93.

9. The material in this section draws chiefly upon Geiger 1986.

10. Joan Bulmer and Martin Bulmer, 'Philanthropy and Social Science in the 1920s: Beardsley Ruml and the Laura Spelman Rockefeller Memorial, 1922-1929', in *Minerva* 19:1981 pp 347-407; Robert E. Kohler, 'Science and Philanthropy: Wickliffe Rose and the International Education Board', in *Minerva* 23:1985, pp 75-95; R. E. Kohler, 'The Management of Science: the Experience of Warren Weaver and the Rockefeller Foundation Programme in Molecular Biology', in *Minerva* 14:1976, pp 279-306.

11. John W. Servos, 'The Industrial Relations of Science: Chemical Engineering at MIT, 1900-1939', in *Isis* 71:1980, pp 531-49; Arnold Thackray, 'University-Industry Connections and Chemical Research: an Historical Perspective', in *University-Industry Research Relationships: Selected Studies*. Washington, D. C. /National Science Board 1982; David Noble, *America by Design: Science, Technology, and the Rise of Corporate Capitalism*. New York 1977; John P. Swann, *Academic Scientists and the Pharmaceutical Industry: Cooperative Research in Twentieth-Century America*. Baltimore 1988.

12. The material which follows draws from R. L. Geiger, *Research and Relevant Knowledge: American Research Universities Since World War II*. New York (fc 1992).

13. A. Hunter Dupree, *Federal Support of Basic Research in Institutions of Higher Learning*. Washington, D. C. /National Academy of Sciences 1964; Harvey M. Sapolsky, 'Academic Science and the Military: the Years Since World War II', in Nathan Reingold (ed), *The Sciences in the American Contest: New Perspectives*. Washington, DC 1979, pp 379-99; Vannevar Bush, *Science - the Endless Frontier*. Washington, DC/National Science Foundation 1960 (reprint).

14. James B. Conant, *Forward*, in *National Science Foundation, Annual Report* 1950-51, p viii.

15. R. L. Geiger, 'Organized Research Units: Their Role in the Development of University Research', in *Journal of Higher Education* 61 1990:1, pp 7-79.

16. R. L. Geiger, 'What Happened after Sputnik: Reassessing the Federal Impact on University Research, 1958-1968', in N. Reingold and David van Keuren (eds), *Science and the Federal Patron: Post-World War II Government Support for American Science* (fc).

17. President's Science Advisory Council, *Scientific Progress, the Universities, and the Federal Government*. Washington, DC 1965.

18. Daniel S. Greenberg, *The Politics of Pure Science*. New York 1967; Kenneth Kofmehl, *'COSPUP', Congress and Scientific Advice*, in *Science* 1966:28, pp 100-20.

19. Bruce L. R. Smith and Joseph Karlesky, *The State of Academic Science* Vol 2 New York 1977-78.

20. Robert M. Rosenzweig with Barbara Turlington, *The Research Universities and Their Patrons*. Berkeley 1982.

21. *Research Universities and the National Interest: A Report of Fifteen University Presidents*. New York/The Ford Foundation 1978; American Society for Engineering Education, *The Quality of Engineering Education*. Washington, DC 1986; Don Fuqua, *American Science and Science Policy Issues*: Chairman's Report to the Committee on Science and Technology/Washington, DC 1986; Bruce L. R. Smith (ed), *The State of Graduate Education*. Washington, DC/Brookings Institution 1985.

The Contributors

Gunnar Bergendal

Professor and Rector of The Teacher's College in Malmö. A long standing member of the NBUC-Research Council. Secretary of the 'U68' - Royal Commission of Higher Education, that reshaped Swedish Higher Education in the 1970s. He has written extensively on problem related to didactics, the theory and praxis of knowledge, teaching and education: see for example *Knowledge Policies and the Traditions of Higher Education* (1984).

Eskil Björklund

Graduated in Practical Philosophy from the University of Stockholm in 1952. After co-directing a number of comparative research projects, he worked at the Institute for Military Psychology during the 1950s. In 1963 he and Nils-Eric Svensson created the Research Unit at the National Board of Education. In 1964 he also became Secretary of the Swedish Social Science Research Council. In 1970 he was appointed head of the new Research Programme at the NBUC. As director for 20 years he turned this Programme into what is now a well-established research council with intense international connections.

Stefan Björklund

Professor of Political Science at Uppsala University, where he graduated in 1964 in history. Docent and Lecturer at the Department of Political Science at Uppsala, 1965-1978. Vice-Chancellor of the University College in Örebro, 1978-1982. From 1983 to 1987 he served as Deputy University Chancellor at the NBUC. In 1987 he was appointed professor at the NBUC-Research Council. He has published several books and articles in the fields of research policy and political theory.

Burton R. Clark

Allan M. Cartter Professor of Higher Education and Sociology and Chairman of the Comparative Higher Education Research Group at UCLA. A graduate of UCLA (PhD 1954), he taught in departments of sociology and schools of education at Stanford, Harvard, Berkeley and Yale before assuming the Cartter Professorship at UCLA in 1980. He has published numerous books and articles in the field of Higher Education including for example: *The Open Door College* (1960); *The Distinctive College* (1970); *Academic Power in Italy* (1977); *The Higher Education System* (1983), *The Academic Life* (1987).

Roger L. Geiger

Professor of Higher Education at Pennsylvania State University. A historian who has written extensively on the history and current conditions of university research: *To Advance Knowledge: The Growth of American Research Universities, 1900 to 1940* (1986), and *Research and Relevant Knowledge: American Research Universities since World War II* (1992 fc). Until 1987 at Yale Institution for Social and Policy Studies where he worked on topics in comparative higher education, including *Private Sectors in Higher Education: Structure, Function and Change in Eight Countries* (1986).

Sverker Gustavsson

Docent of Political Science at Uppsala University, where he graduated in 1971 on a study of *The Debate on the Relations between Research and Society in the 20th Century*. Over the years he has published several works discussing research policy planning and research organisation. Between 1978 and 1986 he was a Research Fellow at The Swedish Council for Building Research. Since 1986 he is Under Secretary of State in the Ministry of Education and Cultural Affairs.

Thorsten Nybom

Docent of History at Uppsala University. Graduated in 1978 from the University of Stockholm. Several studies on the theory and ideology of history and in modern Swedish and German Historiography. Since 1989 he is Director of the Council for Studies of Higher Education at the NBUC. Presently, completing a study on Swedish research organisation after the Second World War.

Birgitta Odén

Prof. Emeritus of History at the University of Lund, where she graduated in 1955. Specialist in medieval and early modern Nordic history. She has also published several important studies on Swedish 20th Century historiography and research organisation. In the 1970s and 1980s she held a number of key positions in the national Swedish research organisation. Member of the original SCASSS-Board. Her study of the research training programs in some central disciplines since the 1890s will be published in 1991.

Rune Premfors

Docent and Lecturer of Political Science at the University of Stockholm, where he graduated in 1980. He has published several studies dealing with problems related to research policy planning, research organisation and research implementation, for example *The Politics of Higher Education in a Comparative Perspective*. An active member of The Group for the Study of Higher Education and Research at the University of Stockholm. Former Research fellow at the NBUC-Research Council. In 1989 he published a book on *Policy Analysis*.

Olof Ruin

Lars Hierta Professor of Political Science at the University of Stockholm. He graduated in 1960 from the University of Lund. He is a specialist in modern Swedish politics - especially the Social Democratic Party. During the 1970s he was Deputy Chancellor of the NBUC. He was among other things chairman of the TEMA-Council at the University of Linköping. In the 1970s he initiated The Group for the Study of Higher Education and Research at the University of Stockholm.

Nils Runeby

Professor of History of Ideas at the University of Stockholm. He graduated in 1962 in history from Uppsala University. From 1975 to 1979 he was professor at the University of Kiel, FRG. Among other things he has studied the rise and development of technical education in Sweden. He has also published several studies on the development of the research university, and on the role of the 'Intellectuals' in Sweden and Germany.

Rolf Torstendahl

Professor of History at Uppsala University where he graduated in 1964. From 1978 to 1981 he was professor at the University of Stockholm. Extensive writings on civil engineers, the processes of bureaucratisation and professionalisation, for example, *Bureaucratization in North-western Europe, 1870-1985* (1991), and on problems related to the theory and praxis of historical research. Director of The Swedish Collegium for the Advanced Study of the Social Sciences (SCASSS), 1985-89.

Martin Trow

Professor of Sociology at the Graduate School of Public Policy, at Berkeley. Director of the Center for Studies in Higher Education, 1976-1988. Started his career as an engineer. After the war he studied sociology at Columbia and graduated in 1957. In 1957 he joined the Sociology Department at Berkeley, and in 1969 the GSPP. Trow has written or edited numerous books and articles in the fields of political sociology and higher education. Member of the National Academy of Education, and Fellow of the American Association for the Advancement of Science. He is currently Chairman-Elect of the Academic Senate of the University of California, and representative of the faculty on its Board of Regents.

Björn Wittrock

Professor of Political Science at the University of Stockholm, where he graduated in 1974. Extensive research on research organisation and the development of the social sciences including, *The Three Missions: Universities and the Societal Transformations in the Western World* 1992 (fc) (with Sheldon Rothblatt); *The University Research System* (1985) (with Aant Elzinga) and *Discourses on Society* (1991) (with P. Wagner and R. H. Whitley). Director of SCASSS, and member of the NBUC-Research Council.

Index

Higher Education Policy Series

Edited by Maurice Kogan

Higher education is now the subject of far reaching and rapid policy change. This series will be of value to those who have to manage that change, as well as to consumers and evaluators of higher education. It offers information and analysis of new developments in a concise and usable form. It also provides reflective accounts of the impacts of higher education policy.

Maurice Kogan is Professor of Government at Brunel University and Director of the Centre for the Evaluation of Public Policy and Practice.

Graduate Education in Britain
Tony Becher, Mary Henkel and Maurice Kogan
ISBN 1 85302 531 3
Higher Education Policy Series 17
This book explores the nature of graduate education at two levels. It examines current national policies and the ways in which they are made. It provides a series of six case studies of individual disciplinary areas, highlighting the similarities and differences between them.

Higher Education in Europe
Edited by Claudius Gellert
ISBN 1 85302 529 1
Higher Education Policy Series 16
Higher Education in Europe is the first comprehensive analysis of institutional and functional changes in higher education throughout the European Community. Providing detailed descriptions of the relevant features of all EC higher education systems together with an account of overall trends and modifications, it also presents a number of challenges to accepted views.

National Systems for the Regulation of Quality in Higher Education
H R Kells
ISBN 1 85302 528 3
Higher Education Policy Series 15
The author describes the development and evolution of several major forms of regulatory systems for higher education on both sides of the Atlantic.

Jessica Kingsley Publishers, 118 Pentonville Road, London N1 9JN

Learning in Europe: The ERASMUS Experience
Friedhelm Maiworm, Wolfgang Steube and Ulrich Teichler
ISBN 1 85302 527 5
Higher Education Policy Series 14
The ERASMUS scheme provides grants for students spending some period of study in another country of the European Community. This study is based on a written questionnaire completed by about 3,200 ERASMUS students participating in 1988/89, and provides information on the participating students, their preparation for the sojourn, living and studying in the host country, supportive provisions by the home and host university, and financial resources and expenses. The academic, cultural and the foreign language impact of the study period abroad, as well as the degree of recognition granted and general assessments by the students, are covered.

Study Abroad Programmes
Edited by Barbara B. Burn, Ladislav Cerych and Alan Smith
ISBN 1 85302 522 4
Higher Education Policy Series 11, Volume I

The Impact of Study Abroad Programmes on Students and Graduates
Susan Opper, Ulrich Teichler and Jerry Carlson
Preface by Barbara B Burn, Ladislav Cerych and Alan Smith
ISBN 1 85302 523 2
Higher Education Policy Series 11, Volume II
These volumes analyse the structures and impacts of some of the main study abroad programmes offered by universities in four European countries (United Kingdom, France, Germany and Sweden) and in the United States.

Dimensions of Evaluation in Higher Education
Report of the I.H.M.E. Study Group on Evaluation in Higher Education
Urban Dahllöf, John Harris, Michael Shattock, André Starpoli
and Roeland in't Veld
ISBN 1 85302 526 7
Higher Education Policy series 13
This book addresses primary issues in evaluation in an international, a national and a long term perspective. Roeland int'Veld sets the policy frameworks within which the increased emphasis on evaluation must be considered. Michael Shattock analyses the contribution of universities to society through an historical and contemporary account of their goals and functions. André Staropoli assesses the evaluation of research. Urban Dahlöff reflects on the universally low priority given to the evaluation of teaching. John Harris reports a study of ways of comparing higher education in the USA with that of competitor nations.

Jessica Kingsley Publishers, 118 Pentonville Road, London N1 9JN

Major American Higher Education Issues and Challenges in the 1990s
Richard I Miller
ISBN 1 85302 514 3
Higher Education Policy Series 9
Professor Miller addresses a range of concerns for American higher education in the 1990s, discussing each first in terms of why the issue has come to prominence now, then looking at how American postsecondary education is currently reacting to it, and finally exploring the changes that should be made in the 1990s, focusing on implications for policy making.

Academics and Policy Systems
Edited by Thorsten Nybom and Ulf Lundgren
ISBN 1 85302 512 7
Higher Education Policy Series 8
This outstanding collection of essays examines the relationship between academics and policy making in different political systems and societies.

Governmental Strategies and Innovation in Higher Education
Edited by Frans van Vught
ISBN 1 85302 513 5
Higher Education Policy Series 7
'the professional job has been well undertaken, so that the resulting findings are soundly based and cast valuable light on some of what has been taking place.'
- Higher Education Quarterly

Evaluating Higher Education
Edited by Maurice Kogan
ISBN 1 85302 510 0
Higher Education Policy Series 6
'The introductory note by Professor Maurice Kogan is particularly valuable in providing a framework for and perspective on the range of evaluative approaches currently in progress.'
- Managerial Auditing Journal

Jessica Kingsley Publishers, 118 Pentonville Road, London N1 9JN

Changing Patterns of the Higher Education System:
The Experience of Three Decades
Ulrich Teichler
Foreword by Eskil Björklund
ISBN 1 85302 507 0
Higher Education Policy Series 5
'Ulrich Teichler is one of the leading practitioners in the field of comparative
higher education and in this brief volume he presents his readers with a distillation
of his encyclopedic knowledge. It is a book not to be skipped, for every word
counts.'

- Studies in Higher Education

Higher Education and the Preparation for Work
Chris J. Boys, John Brennan, Mary Henkel, John Kirkland, Maurice Kogan, Penny
Youll
ISBN 1 85302 505 4
Higher Education Policy Series 4
It is Government policy to make higher education more responsive to the
economic needs of society. But how responsive have higher education institutions
been in recent years? How much change has already taken place and what have
been the main forces driving it? Are some kinds of institution more responsive
than others? And how far does the pursuit of responsiveness threaten the
maintenance of traditional academic values? These are some of the questions
explored in this book.

Degrees of Success: Career Aspirations and Destinations of College,
University and Polytechnic Graduates
Chris J Boys with John Kirkland
ISBN 1 85302 502 X
Higher Education Policy Series 3
'Unique in comparing the aspirations of graduates of both higher education
sectors.'

-Higher Education News

Jessica Kingsley Publishers, 118 Pentonville Road, London N1 9JN

The Use of Performance Indicators in Higher Education:
A Critical Analysis of Developing Practice, 2nd edition
Martin Cave, Stephen Hanney and Maurice Kogan
ISBN 1 85302 518 6
Higher Education Policy Series 3

Reviews of the first edition

'. . . excellent . . . analytical and critical in the true sense of the word... we must all learn to make intelligent use of performance indicators and this little book is an invaluable critical introduction both to basic concepts and to practical applications.'

- Times Higher Education Supplement

'This book will be essential reading for anyone interested, as potential evaluator, or evaluatee, in the management of higher education . . .'

- Health Services Management Record

'The most comprehensive analysis of the subject to date.'

- Journal of Geography in Higher Education

'Should be read by anyone who is interested in the management of institutions of higher education, particularly universities.'

- Assessment and Evaluation in Higher Education

Graduates at Work: Degree Courses and the Labour Market
John Brennan and Philip McGeevor
ISBN 1 85302 500 3
Higher Education Policy Series 1

'. . . the authors do not shrink from commenting upon the policy implications of their findings . . . pertinent and perceptive . . . helps towards a clearer perception of the issues.'

- Higher Education News

Jessica Kingsley Publishers, 118 Pentonville Road, London N1 9JN